Responsible Leadership and Sustainable Management

This series aims to transform organizations into a more future-fit version by bringing forth latest perspectives from cross cultural and interdisciplinary learning, management and administrative paradigm. It will not only showcase systemic outlooks on how new institutions (public and private), organizations, and/or businesses look like, but also foray into specific key areas to comprehensively reveal their challenges and propose solutions.

The series intends to make varying concepts, research and practices of responsible leadership and sustainable management accessible, so as to promote their better understanding and implementation. The scope of this series will be interdisciplinary and lie in collaborating with global researchers, practitioners, policy makers and other stakeholders, so that responsible leadership and sustainable management becomes mainstream. The objectives of this series are:

(a) to foster collaboration between Europe and Asia in content creation and knowledge transfer on the topic
(b) to publish research that focuses on building strong, resilient international value chain and common market
(c) to advance a new sustainable, responsible thinking

The series publishes research monographs, both authored works and case studies, to highlight innovative and best practices on the topic; and edited volumes, putting together varied perspectives. The content covered should be international with fresh perspectives on topics that have the potential to bring about transformational leadership changes in organizations, for their seamless evolution into institutions of the future.

Mari Kooskora · Aleksandra Kekkonen
Editors

Performance Challenges in Organizational Sustainability

Practices from Public and Private Sector

 Springer

Editors
Mari Kooskora
Centre for Business Ethics
Estonian Business School
Tallinn, Estonia

Aleksandra Kekkonen
Estonian Business School
Tallinn, Estonia

ISSN 2730-9533   ISSN 2730-9541 (electronic)
Responsible Leadership and Sustainable Management
ISBN 978-981-97-5547-9   ISBN 978-981-97-5548-6 (eBook)
https://doi.org/10.1007/978-981-97-5548-6

This Springer imprint is published by the registered company Springer Nature Singapore Pte Ltd.
The registered company address is: 152 Beach Road, #21-01/04 Gateway East, Singapore 189721,
Singapore

If disposing of this product, please recycle the paper.

Dedicated to those diligently addressing challenges on the path to a more sustainable future

Foreword

It is my great pleasure to welcome a new research-based book on Organizational Sustainability helping to understand and cope with the major challenges related to sustainable performance, clarifying the meanings of green performance, addressing different sustainability metrics and regulation systems, as well as guiding organizations and their leaders towards more sustainable performance.

How timely work this is in our multipronged and urgent attempts to turn organizations into more sustainable ones. This work is edited by two leading business sustainability and responsibility scholars and written by an international team of experts from different countries, cultures, and practices. All the contributions to this topical work have gone through a rigorous scientific selection and reviewing process. They cover conceptual issues revolving around the notion of organizational sustainability, sustainability practices in public and private sectors of society, and practical case studies in organizational sustainability.

This book uncovers the multi-level nature of organizational sustainability as a phenomenon and how it needs to be addressed academically and practically from various perspectives aiming towards theoretical and practical integration. At the same time, this work offers an important reminder that the times of the hypocritical window dressing activities should be outdated in this setting and that organizational sustainability is a key challenge of real-life cooperation for different sectors of society. Instead of peripheral activity outsourced from the core of the organizations, it takes a central stage in current organizational life.

This book is a significant read for sustainability scholars, master and doctoral level students as well as practitioners, politicians, public officials, and organizational leaders and managers responsible to turn their organizational practices to be in line with the central requirements of sustainability. This work can be used as a course book, especially in the sustainability courses at master and doctoral levels and also for executive trainings. As a supplemental reading, it can be also used on bachelor level business ethics and sustainability courses.

Jukka Veikko Mäkinen
Professor of Business Ethics
Estonian Business School
Estonia and Docent of Corporate
Responsibility
Aalto University School of Business
Finland

Acknowledgements

We would like to acknowledge each author who has contributed to this book. We recognize the hard work you do to lead and support activities towards a more sustainable future in your roles at academia and public and private organizations, and we thank you for the time and effort spent on writing your respective chapters.

Next, we would like to express appreciation to all those who contributed to the refinement of the book and who reviewed and provided valuable feedback on the chapters. We sincerely thank all our colleagues and peers who offered insights, discussions, and moral support during this book's development and all collaborators who played a role in the creation of the book.

We extend our heartfelt gratitude to our partners and families, whose unwavering support has been the bedrock of this endeavour. To our life partners and children, thank you for your patience, understanding, and encouragement during the long hours spent in pursuit of this project. Your steadfast belief in our work has been our greatest motivator.

To our families, who have shared in the challenges and triumphs, your love and encouragement have been a source of strength. Your sacrifices and understanding during moments of intense focus on the book are deeply appreciated. This journey would not have been possible without your resilience, and we want to express our deepest thanks for being the pillars that upheld us throughout.

Finally, we would like to thank all our future readers for your interest in the book and your commitment to the topic of sustainability. Your engagement and interest in exploring the intricate facets of organizational sustainability performance contribute to the ongoing dialogue on sustainable practices. As you delve into the pages of this work, we appreciate your commitment to understanding and implementing principles that foster a more sustainable future. Your thoughtful consideration of these topics is integral to the collective journey towards organizational practices that align with the imperative requirements of sustainability. Thank you for being part of this meaningful exploration.

Mari Kooskora
Aleksandra Kekkonen

Contents

Editors and Contributors

About the Editors

Dr. Mari Kooskora Ph.D. is an Associate Professor, a Researcher, and a Trainer at Estonian Business School and has been recently engaged as ESG Senior Advisor at KPMG. She has expertise in Business Ethics, Responsible Leadership, and Sustainable Management for over 25 years in 12 countries. She is the author of research papers published in nationally and internationally recognized journals and has given numerous conference presentations. Her main research interests are ethics and responsibility in business and leadership, sustainability, and women in leadership. As a board member of ISBEE (International Society of Business and Economics Ethics); EUMMAS (European Marketing and Management Association) and previously also Responsible Business Forum Estonia (2017–2023) and Transparency International Estonia (2009–2014), member of Business and Professional Women and European Business Ethics Network, she is actively contributing to the development of more balanced and sustainable business and governance.

Dr. Aleksandra Kekkonen is a Head of the Green & CSR research team, Senior Researcher and Lecturer at Estonian Business School, Circular Economy and Sustainable Living enthusiast. EBS Green Ambassador 2022. She has a background in international relations and a Ph.D. in Economics in the field of regional human capital development, labour market, and education system development on the national and international levels from 2013. Currently, her specialisation and main areas of interest are green economy, sustainable development, and especially accelerating the transition to a circular economy on macro and local levels, as well as community involvement practices for green transition.

Contributors

Annika Arras Miltton New Nordics, Tallinn, Estonia

Rachel Azurel Calipha Academic College of Tel Aviv-Yaffo, Yaffo, Israel

Germán DelValle-Araluce University of Deusto, Bilbao, Spain

Regina Erlenheim Estonian Business School, Tallinn, Estonia

Emre Güven Estonian Business School, Tallinn, Estonia

Zsuzsanna Győri Department of Management and Entrepreneurship, Centre of Excellence for Sustainability Impacts in Business and Society (CESIBUS), Faculty of Finance and Accountancy, Budapest Business University, Budapest, Hungary

Shirit Katav Herz Academic College of Tel Aviv-Yaffo, Yaffo, Israel

Anushka Lydia Issac Westford University College, Sharjah, United Arab Emirates

Laima Jeseviciute-Ufartiene Vilnius Gediminas Technical University, Vilnius, Lithuania

Aleksandra Kekkonen Estonian Business School, Tallinn, Estonia

Katri Kerem Marketing and Communication Department, Estonian Business School, Tallinn, Estonia

Anita Kolnhofer-Derecskei Department of Business Economics, Centre of Excellence for Sustainability Impacts in Business and Society (CESIBUS), Faculty of Finance and Accountancy, Budapest Business University, Budapest, Hungary

Mari Kooskora Centre for Business Ethics, Estonian Business School, Tallinn, Estonia

Alena Labanava Tallinn University of Technology, Tallinn, Estonia

Meri Löyttyniemi Jyväskylä University School of Business and Economics, Jyväskylä, Finland

Renee Pesor Estonian Business School, Tallinn, Estonia

Regina Zsuzsánna Reicher Department of Management and Entrepreneurship, Centre of Excellence for Sustainability Impacts in Business and Society (CESIBUS), Faculty of Finance and Accountancy, Budapest Business University, Budapest, Hungary

Jose Luis Retolaza University of Deusto, Bilbao, Spain

Leire San-Jose University of the Basque Country UPV/EHU, Bilbao, Spain

Hava Yasin Vilnius Gediminas Technical University, Vilnius, Lithuania

Chapter 1
Introduction to Sustainable Performance Practices

Mari Kooskora⬤ **and Aleksandra Kekkonen**⬤

Abstract The introductory chapter highlights the growing importance of sustainability in organisational practices, emphasising the integration of environmental, social, and governance (ESG) objectives into core activities to maximise stakeholder value. It explores various challenges associated with transitioning to a sustainable economy, including the implications of major global and regional initiatives like the UN Sustainable Development Goals, the EU Green Deal, and the Paris Agreement. This chapter conceptualises sustainable performance from multiple perspectives, addressing the complexities and varied interpretations that different sectors have regarding sustainability. It aims to provide a holistic understanding of how policies and strategies can support organisations and societies in achieving sustainability. The chapter also introduces topics covered in subsequent chapters, including sustainable human capital management, responsible marketing, and sustainability metrics, and their impact on achieving sustainability goals at both macro and micro levels.

Keywords Sustainability · Sustainable performance · Environmental, Social and Governance (ESG) · Green economy transition · UN Sustainable Development Goals (SDGs) · Organisational sustainability

In recent years, the significance of sustainability has surged, compelling organizations to integrate it into their operations. Sustainable performance, in essence, involves harmonizing environmental, social, and governance objectives during core activities to maximize stakeholder value. This encompasses environmental, social, and economic impact, sustainable development, concerns for stakeholder groups, ethics, and volunteerism, each frequently defined in various ways. The shared

M. Kooskora (✉)
Centre for Business Ethics, Estonian Business School, Tallinn, Estonia
e-mail: mari.kooskora@ebs.ee

A. Kekkonen
Estonian Business School, Tallinn, Estonia
e-mail: alexandra.kekkonen@ebs.ee

1

M. Kooskora and A. Kekkonen (eds.), *Performance Challenges in Organizational Sustainability*, Responsible Leadership and Sustainable Management,
https://doi.org/10.1007/978-981-97-5548-6_1

commitment to sustainability propels leadership, investment, and operational expertise to create value, ensuring superior performance for societies and businesses. Consequently, the discipline and fundamentals required to balance capital needs, risk management, and growth remain paramount. Currently, "going green" and embracing sustainability are challenges faced by most countries and companies.

However, akin to similar concepts, sustainable performance holds different meanings for individuals, organizations, and societies. Thus, our book aims to holistically conceptualize and clarify the meaning of sustainable performance from various perspectives. We will delve into the challenges associated with vast movements aiming to transform the world economy into a more modern, resource-efficient, and competitive entity. These movements have spurred new initiatives, inviting people, communities, and organizations to participate in building a greener and more sustainable future for the next generations.

The initiatives under discussion include the UN Sustainable Development Goals (SDGs), EU Green Deal, Paris Agreement, and Environmental, Social, and Governance (ESG) metrics. Given that these movements have generated a growing need for societies and businesses to contribute to sustainable development through policies and strategies, integrating sustainable practices becomes crucial. To aid in this understanding, our book will provide a brief background overview of these policies and strategies, focusing on aspects relevant to societies and businesses to plan and implement their own activities.

Today, it is evident that climate change and environmental degradation pose an existential threat to the European Union and the world at large. In response, the United Nations has established 17 goals and 169 specific targets, indicators, and metrics of sustainability across various sectors, presenting a universally agreed-upon sustainable development vision for 2030. This framework, reflecting long-standing contestations over the meaning of sustainable development, includes goals translated into specific targets and indicators, guiding more concrete actions. The SDGs recognize the interrelated nature of issues such as poverty, inequality, decent work, gender equality, and ecosystem conservation. They highlight the necessity for all societal actors to jointly tackle these challenges, providing a comprehensive reference framework for essential sustainable development issues. The SDGs represent a common agenda for all stakeholders—both public and private—across diverse sectors and national contexts. Our book includes discussions and concrete examples of how these targets have been approached, the challenges that need to be overcome, and the specific actions societies and businesses have taken to meet these goals.

One of the flagship initiatives of the European Commission addressing climate change and environmental degradation aims to reduce greenhouse gas emissions to 55% by 2030 (from the current target of 40% of 1990 levels) by altering tax, trade, and regulatory systems—this initiative is known as the European Green Deal. The European Green Deal envisions transforming climate and environmental challenges into opportunities for sustainable development. Furthermore, the EU aspires to achieve climate neutrality by 2050, fostering the economy through green technology, establishing sustainable industry and transport, and reducing pollution. These objectives present both challenges and opportunities for societies and business organizations.

The environmental, social, and economic impacts of companies on their stake-holder groups determine the sustainability of society's development. The positive or negative trajectory of this development is shaped by the ethics of business activity, encompassing both voluntary (not regulated by law) and mandatory (regulated by law) aspects of a company's conduct. Within this book, we discuss these challenges across various sectors and present potential solutions to assist organizations and societies in better managing these issues.

A significant aspect of the main tasks related to the green transition involves newly developed policies and action plans for creating a sustainable economy and society. This aims to preserve nature and the environment, making them globally competitive and less vulnerable to climate threats and other foreseeable or unforeseen risks. More-over, an increasing number of studies support the notion that, considering all direct and indirect impacts, adopting green and sustainable practices can be less expensive than not doing so. However, these policies introduce new challenges and costs for societies and businesses, and investments in these activities may seem too expensive with a perceived lengthy payback time. Consequently, many organizational leaders remain hesitant to implement these practices in practice. Furthermore, the implemen-tation of the green and sustainability revolution is not uniformly distributed among countries and regions. In this context, we discuss and compare these aspects relevant to different regions and countries, focusing on macro and micro-level activities with concrete examples.

In the first part of the book, we present various conceptual approaches to under-standing sustainable performance and sustainable development from several angles, including public/private perspectives, human capital management, and responsible marketing mix. The second chapter, titled "Organizational Sustainable Performance: Definitions and Public/Private Perspectives", focuses on organizational sustainability performance (OSP). Authors Rachel Calipha and Shirit Katav-Herz conduct a liter-ature review and content analysis of 57 papers, commencing with a review of OSP definitions. The literature reveals several terms with vague definitions regarding how current (short-term) sustainability performance and its future impact (long-term) are measured. The chapter delves deeper into understanding the meaning of sustainability performance, particularly in the private and public sectors. In the public sector, conceptual frameworks are discussed, describing formal and informal sustain-ability performance assessment systems. In the private sector, three main aspects of sustainability performance evaluation were identified: accounting, assessment, and reporting. The chapter addresses the difficulty of implementation, challenges, and proposed solutions and concludes by providing recommendations to enhance future implementation.

In today's business world, striking a balance between a company's growth and the well-being and development of its employees is a critical challenge. Sustainable Human Capital Management (SHCM) has gained increasing importance as organiza-tions strive to achieve this equilibrium. However, what proves effective for SHCM in one context may not be applicable elsewhere due to varying organizational cultures, local norms, and workforce demographics. Moreover, an exclusive focus on SHCM might divert attention from systemic issues contributing to employee dissatisfaction and well-being disparities. It's crucial to note that an excessive emphasis on SHCM might detract from addressing broader systemic issues affecting employee satisfaction and well-being. The responsibility for well-being should extend beyond individual organizations, incorporating broader societal and governmental efforts to address factors such as income inequality, healthcare accessibility, and labour rights.

The third chapter, "Sustainable Human Capital Management: Fostering Employee Well-being and Growth", written by Anushka Lydia Issac, explores the intricate relationship between SHCM, employee well-being, and organizational growth. Specifically examining the United Arab Emirates (UAE), the chapter delves into the strategies, benefits, and challenges of implementing SHCM practices aligning human welfare with business progress. The study is anchored in a robust theoretical foundation, guiding the exploration of SHCM within a scholarly framework. It outlines effective SHCM implementation strategies derived from case studies, emphasizing leadership commitment, employee engagement, precise performance measurement, and a commitment to continuous improvement. The chapter also recognizes the challenges organizations may encounter on their SHCM journey and anticipates the future of SHCM, considering trends, technologies, and societal changes. Ultimately, the chapter envisions an environment where employee well-being thrives, propelling organizations towards holistic and enduring growth.

The chapter titled "The Responsible Marketing Mix: Aligning the 4 Ps with Sustainability Dimensions" explores the integration of environmental, social, and economic sustainability principles into the marketing mix, covering product, price, place, and promotion. Authored by Katri Kerem, the chapter underscores a holistic and incremental approach, offering practical insights for businesses seeking sustainable marketing strategies. Key findings include the need for life cycle sustainability assessments in product development, the delicate balance required in sustainable pricing, the impact of distribution channels on sustainability, and the role of transparent and responsible messaging in promotions. The proposed "responsible marketing mix" serves as both a decision-making tool and an educational resource. Addressing a research gap and emphasizing manageable steps towards sustainability, this approach contributes to a nuanced understanding of sustainable marketing practices, making it accessible for businesses and providing valuable insights for educators and researchers. The author advocates for a shift from unattainable goals to feasible and practical sustainable marketing, fostering positive impacts on the environment, society, and the economy.

There is a vast movement underway to transform the EU into a modern, resource-efficient, and competitive economy by 2050, with ambitious objectives already set at the EU level for 2030 and 2035. Initiatives such as the EU Climate Pact provide examples of EU-wide undertakings that invite people, communities, and organizations to participate in climate action and contribute to building a greener Europe. At the heart of this movement is the belief that top-down sustainability and climate approaches (e.g., UN, EU, or national level) need to be complemented with evidence-based and coherent bottom-up initiatives. These initiatives turn local authorities, various stakeholder/civil society groups, and individual citizens into key actors in achieving the green transition.

In recent years, significant strides have been taken to generate new data and information in both the public and private sectors related to sustainability performance and the green economy. However, maximizing the potential benefits from the smart reuse and combination of this data ("information asymmetry") remains an issue. The need for new and improved sustainability performance metrics is recognized, aiming to build on existing global and local best practices and methodologies, achieving better integration of different data sources to develop higher quality and more accurate indicators.

The second part of our book delves into sustainability performance challenges from the perspectives of public sector organizations and provides a brief background overview of sustainable development policies and strategies. Focusing on aspects relevant for societies and businesses to plan and implement their activities, the solutions to help public sector organizations overcome these challenges are presented.

The chapter titled "Operationalizing Doughnut Economics for Regional Green Transition: An Integrated Multi-Level Stakeholder Engagement Framework", authored by Aleksandra Kekkonen, aims to demonstrate that the development, implementation, and scaling of a country- and region-specific framework for integrated, multi-level stakeholder engagement to accelerate the green transition, using an adapted Doughnut Economics approach, can help local authorities become green and sustainable. Through analysis and practical examples from worldwide doughnut methodology implementation, a proposed framework can assist local authorities in planning, implementing, and monitoring the green transition in their regions, using an adapted Doughnut Economics approach as a starting point. Additionally, the framework helps local authorities develop and implement an integrated, interlinked set of measures, creating a direct connection with the EU's Green Deal objectives and associated policies at the national level to ensure that local authorities, stakeholder groups, and citizens can effectively contribute to achieving the green transition holistically.

The UN 2030 Agenda and the Sustainable Development Goals (SDGs) it proposes and seeks to attain have vast ramifications and potential in their implementation. However, a persistent challenge lies in monitoring and measuring their progress. Government Technology (GovTech) companies, in many ways, can assist governments in progressing towards some of the SDGs, yet the methods through which national governments manage and measure the SDGs differ from those of GovTech companies. Startups and entrepreneurs represent the new generation of businesses and leaders, serving as the nurturing ground for integrating evolving policies to ensure sustainable growth. The relevance of early integration of SDGs into the speed of business growth should be explored, and the short-term and long-term impact of these activities on all stakeholders should be elucidated.

The study presented in the chapter titled "GovTech Companies' Contributions to SDGs: exploring reporting and communication practices" by Alena Labanava and Regina Erlenheim aims to analyse how GovTech startups and small and medium enterprises communicate their contributions to the SDGs, comparing this with the ways governments measure similar contributions. The methodology employed involves qualitative methods, utilizing secondary data and document analysis. The authors provide an overview of various communication channels and tactics used by GovTech companies, comparing them with national reports. Additionally, recommendations are offered for companies seeking to improve profitability while making a societal impact through sustainability.

In the subsequent chapter, author Meri Löyttyniemi shifts focus to higher education institutions, emphasizing the need to address the global polycrisis. The organizational study discussed in the chapter titled "Organizational study on sustainability, hypocrisy, and Finnish universities" delves into Finnish universities' sustainability programs, management challenges, and the stifling factors for implementation despite accelerating sustainability and CSR commitments. The chapter explores the differences between universities' talk, decisions, and actions in the context of Finnish universities, discussing hypocrisy, greenwashing, and aspirational talk, and introducing managerial implications for transformative change in organizations. The empirical study is based on Finnish universities committed to national theses on advancing sustainable development. Utilizing mixed methods, grounded theory, and the Gioia method, the chapter examines how universities "walk the talk", mapping factors and impulses supporting or weakening SD-CSR implementation. Universities are categorized into three groups based on differences between sustainability talk and walk: beginners, question marks, and forerunners. The chapter concludes by providing potential solutions and managerial implications on how to prevent decoupling and turn hypocrisy into authenticity and transformative action.

The third part of our book addresses organizational sustainability performance challenges in private sector organizations. The chapter titled "Sustainability challenges of SMEs related to legal regulations – experiences from a survey of Hungarian entrepreneurs" written by Zsuzsanna Győri, Regina Zsuzsánna Reicher, and Anita Kolnhofer-Derecskei examines the impact of legal regulations on sustainability as perceived by SME leaders. This chapter explores the impact of laws and regulations within the entrepreneurial ecosystem at three levels: emotional or affective; cognitive motivational; and conative or behavioural. The authors aim to enrich the discourse on the importance and challenges of regulation in the context of sustainability by including this practical small business perspective. The study is part of a larger research on the role of Hungarian SMEs in achieving the Sustainable Development Goals. Results indicate that the legal system, i.e., policy, has a major—and at times controversial—impact on the sustainability of entrepreneurial activity. The policy implication is that sustainability issues should be addressed more comprehensively and holistically across all domains of the entrepreneurial ecosystem. Additionally, individual characteristics of the entrepreneur, such as gender, position, and decision-making power, as well as characteristics of the enterprise, such as size or ownership structure, influence the assessment of legislation and the perception and resolution of related challenges, which should be taken into consideration.

In the next chapter, authors Emre Güven and Renee Pesor seek to answer the following question: as climate change emerges as one of the most formidable material risks, can carbon emission metrics be the risk indicator investors need? Using a comprehensive dataset covering pillar and category level ESG scores along with CO2e emission data from global publicly listed companies across two decades (2002–2022), their research provides a comparative analysis of ESG scores and carbon emission metrics and their influence on abnormal stock returns. The methodological approach employs a two-step approach combining machine learning and fixed effects panel regressions. The results reveal that ESG scores, despite their significance in non-financial risk assessments, do not demonstrate a significant economic relationship with abnormal returns. In the examination of carbon emission metrics, the authors find that the effect size varied based on the specific measures employed. Notably, the emissions-to-size metric emerges as a potential indicator for predicting higher-than-expected returns for investors. The implications of the study extend beyond the financial markets, suggesting a broader impact within corporate sustainability initiatives and environmental policy.

The aim of the study conducted by Mari Kooskora and Annika Arras was to identify the attitudes of top-level executives in Estonia towards sustainability. The study also explored perspectives on corporate social responsibility and their adherence to the fundamental principles of sustainable development. Placed within a global context, this study emphasized sustainable development. The analysis in this study drew from academic literature and empirical research conducted by the authors. A web-based survey was administered to top-level executives from some of Estonia's most influential companies. The data reveals that the attitudes of Estonia's most influential top executives closely align with the sustainable development framework, with a primary focus on economic, social, and environmental concerns. However, it was observed that the social and economic dimensions are better balanced than the environmental dimensions, creating differences of opinion among top executives. The study did not confirm the perceived equilibrium between the three pillars of sustainable development in Estonia's most influential companies, as per the top executives' perspectives. Nevertheless, there is potential for achieving greater balance between the three pillars of sustainable development, as top executives express a significant commitment to sustainability issues in their companies' future business success, even at the expense of short-term profit margins.

The final part of the book chapters presents two case studies, practices from the fintech financial industry and discusses the role of socially responsible human resource management. After a period of fifteen years since Fintech birth, it has come a long way up to now in which almost every point of the financial value chain has been affected by their irruption. At present, what is less understood is which elements can definitively consolidate Fintech as a new, differentiated, and sustainable sector; these elements are connected to value creation. The research presented in the chapter "The Fintech Sustainability Model Proposal: A Reflection on the Economic and Social Values, a Double Materiality View" aims to identify those elements that contribute to their long-term sustainability. The authors Germán DelValle-Araluce, José Luis Retolaza, and Leire San-Jose analyse the economic and social view of the Fintech industry. They identified four key aspects: the relevance of business models, trust as a powerful mediator, the paradox around sustainability, the so-called Fintech Economic Unsustainability Paradox, and social value as a principal element in their social performance. The authors present the Fintech Sustainability Model, a new framework that aggregates the above four aspects, which could be the issues that underpin policies towards Fintech long-term sustainability, and allow understanding of the analysis of double materiality, what it entails for their competitiveness in comparison to the traditional financial industry.

Sustainability of the planet is an emerging and much-needed concept in the twenty-first century, and human capital is a major aspect of sustainability. Recent events, such as the emergence of the COVID-19 pandemic and Russia's invasion of Ukraine, have exacerbated global instability, transforming business operations worldwide. Now, economies face numerous challenges in adapting to these crises. In an organizational context, employees hold a prime position as the main source of competitive advantage. Therefore, organizations are grappling with how to adapt to the changes and challenges posed by these twin crises—global pandemic and climate change. The globe confronts issues of human capital deterioration, climate change, poverty, and inequality. Nevertheless, to protect the environment and human lives, natural assets, and civilization must operate sensibly and sustainably. The major vision of the United Nations (UN) is to transform the world through sustainable development.

Human capital is significantly affected and is a crucial component of the Sustainable Development Goals (SDGs) of the Organisation for Economic Co-operation and Development. Human capital management, concerning corporate social responsibility (CSR), covers the social aspects of sustainability. The focus of the study by Laima Jeseviciute-Ufartiene and Hava Yasin is to explore and review the role of socially responsible human resource management (SRHRM) for employee well-being, specifically in the context of employee voice enhancement strategies and addressing employee silence. The research discussed in the chapter "The Role of Socially Responsible Human Resource Management in Employee Voice Enhancement and Diminishing Silence: Bibliometric Analysis and Systematic Literature Review" determines trends regarding the focus on employee voice in the area of SRHRM through bibliometric analysis, applying R-Tool, and a systematic literature review using PRISMA methodology. The research results indicate how the emergence of sustainable human resource management (HRM) has enhanced the well-being of employees by encouraging the employee's voice, which is the most important internal stakeholder of organizations. It also involves providing productive employment opportunities and investing in the development of human capital. Findings fill research gaps, identifying where HRM practitioners, policymakers, and researchers need to focus in the future. Additionally, the study sheds light on the methodologies and theories used to explain the employee voice phenomenon in previous studies.

Bringing our chapter to conclusion, we note that this volume encompasses contributions from a cadre of distinguished scholars, university professors, researchers, and representatives from both public and private organizations. Their collective expertise spans various domains, providing invaluable insights into the intricacies of organizational sustainability performance. Beyond the editorial efforts of our editors and authors, the collaborative input from representatives of public and private entities enriches the scholarly discourse within this book. Each chapter adheres to a structured format, commencing with a introduction that clarifies the significance and relevance of its thematic focus for both scholars and practitioners alike. Subsequently, the chapters present and deliberate upon the principal findings derived from empirical studies. The synthesis of each chapter involves drawing conclusions coupled with practical insights, offering guidance to practitioners in the field.

This publication aspires to be a notable resource for sustainability scholars, as well as master and doctoral-level students. Furthermore, it aims to resonate with practitioners, policymakers, public officials, and organizational leaders and managers, who bear the responsibility of aligning organizational practices with the pivotal imperatives of sustainability. We trust that the content within this book will not only contribute novel insights but also serve as a source of inspiration and guidance for navigating the multifaceted challenges associated with organizational sustainability performance.

Mari Kooskora, PhD, is an Associate Professor, researcher, trainer, advisor and Head of Centre for Business Ethics at Estonian Business School who has expertise in business ethics, responsible leadership and organisational sustainability for over 20 years in 12 countries. She is the author of research papers published in nationally and internationally recognised journals and has given numerous conference presentations. Her main research interests are ethics and responsibility in business and leadership, sustainability and women in leadership. As a board member of ISBEE (International Society of Business and Economics Ethics) and EUMMAS (European Marketing and Management Association) and previously also Responsible Business Forum Estonia and Transparency International Estonia, member of Business and Professional Women, European Business Ethics Network and several other international and local networks she is actively contributing to the development of more balanced and sustainable business and governance.

Aleksandra Kekkonen is a Senior Research Fellow at RDI unit and lecturer at Estonian Business School and head of Green & CSR research team. She has a background in international relations and a Ph.D. in Economics in the field of regional human capital development from 2013. She worked as a researcher in human capital, labor market, and education system development on the national and international levels for more than 11 years. Currently her specialization and main areas of interest are green economy, sustainable development and especially accelerating the transition to a circular economy on macro and local level, as well as community involvement practices for green transition.

Part I
Conceptual Overviews

Chapter 2
Organizational Sustainability Performance in Public and Private Sectors: Review of Definitions, Main Aspects, and Challenges

Rachel Azurel Calipha and Shirit Katav Herz

Abstract In recent years, the importance of sustainability has grown significantly, compelling organizations to integrate it into their operations. This chapter reviews 57 papers from eight disciplines published between 1997 and 2023 on organizational sustainability performance (OSP) in the public and private sectors. The content analysis led us to identify five major themes: definitions of OSP and related terms, factors impacting OSP, the relationship between sustainability performance and financial performance, sustainability performance evaluation and challenges. In addition, a comparison between public and private sectors has been conducted. Finally, the chapter provides recommendations to improve future implementation.

Keywords Sustainable performance · Organizational sustainability performance · Corporate sustainability performance · Financial performance · Sustainability performance evaluation · Reporting · Public sector · Private sector

2.1 Introduction

Sustainability, researched in various disciplines and contexts, has multiple definitions. Since the 1980s, it has increasingly been linked with the notion of human sustainability on Earth, leading to the widely quoted definition of sustainable development by the UN's Brundtland Commission, "development that meets the needs of the present without compromising the ability of future generations to meet their own needs" (WCED, 1987).

Agenda 21, introduced by the United Nations in 1992, asked every nation to formulate its own strategies for sustainable development:

R. A. Calipha (✉) · S. K. Herz
Academic College of Tel Aviv-Yaffo, Rabenu Yeruham St., 6818211 Yaffo, Israel
e-mail: rachelca@mta.ac.il

© The Author(s), under exclusive license to Springer Nature Singapore Pte Ltd. 2024
M. Kooskora and A. Kekkonen (eds.), *Performance Challenges in Organizational Sustainability*, Responsible Leadership and Sustainable Management,
https://doi.org/10.1007/978-981-97-5548-6_2

> Governments will have to acknowledge their responsibility at all levels: international, national and local. The local authority plays a special role: it is at the local level that many sustainability problems are manifested. Global issues, like climate change and biodiversity loss, lead to problems at the local level, such as flooding and poor agricultural yields (Hoppe & Coenen, 2011, p. 229).

Consequently, public sector organizations (PSOs; organizations under government control)—as a significant employer providing services to citizens and influencing the national economy—should serve as a role model for sustainability (Ball & Grubnic, 2007). They should integrate social, economic, and environmental performance, as well as citizen satisfaction and participatory approaches in their sustainable development objectives. One approach to achieving these goals is the establishment of sustainability performance evaluation systems (Chai, 2009).

Sustainability performance is also vital for private organizations, as it enables them to gain deeper insights into their effects on shareholders, the environment, and communities, and to facilitate necessary steps to mitigate or improve these effects (Büyüközkan & Karabulut, 2018). Such assessment is essential for making well-informed, organizational goal-aligned operational decisions and meeting diverse stakeholder requirements (Donaldson & Preston, 1995).

The shift to sustainability has resulted in enhanced profitability and positive outcomes, prompting a transformation in business models (Grecu et al., 2020). Artiach et al. (2010) show that sustainable firms benefit from an increased size, enhanced growth, and greater returns on equity compared to conventional counterparts.

This chapter reviews studies on the sustainability performance of public and private organizations, highlighting the definitions and main topics addressed in Organizational Sustainability Performance (OSP), and offers recommendations for the future.

The study encompasses 57 papers addressing sustainability performance, dating to 1997–2023, 75% of them published in the last decade. These papers—from journals or working papers and excluding books—were selected from scientific databases including EBSCO, SCOPUS, and Google Scholar. The search utilized the keywords sustainability performance (SP), corporate sustainability performance (CSP), organizational sustainability performance (OSP), environmental performance (EP), social performance (SP), and sustainability performance in the public/private sector. Subsequently, three additional steps were taken: Definitions were gathered from the papers; then, based on titles, abstracts, or full texts when necessary, the papers were classified into two main categories—private sector and public sector; finally, content analysis was conducted.

The following sections present definitions and analyse the themes derived from content analysis, focusing on factors affecting OSP, the relationship between sustainability performance and financial performance, sustainability performance evaluation and challenges. They conclude with a discussion and future recommendations.

2.2   Definitions

Twenty-nine definitions were identified in this review (see Table 2.1). This section begins with definitions focusing on an organization's sustainability, subsequently adding the performance factor, the definitions of terms that are components of sustainability performance (SP), a definition combining SP with other terms, and finally, describes the newly developed definitions of SP.

2.2.1   Organizational Sustainability and Interchangeable Terms

The current search revealed that organizational sustainability (OS) is often used interchangeably with corporate sustainability (CP) and business sustainability (BS), although it is construed as universal, applying to all types of organizations and not to a particular business sector. The nine definitions of these terms identified emphasize the importance of considering stakeholders; incorporating social, environmental, and economic elements; and adopting sustainability as a strategy.

Organizational sustainability is defined as "the contribution of organizations in the process of achieving human development in an inclusive, equitable, and secure manner by delivering simultaneously economic, social, and environmental benefits" (Hart & Milstein, 2003, as cited in Nawaz & Koç, 2019, p. 3).

Corporate sustainability is defined as "meeting the needs of the firm's direct and indirect stakeholders (such as shareholders, employees, clients, pressure groups, communities, etc.), without compromising its ability to meet future stakeholder needs as well" (Dyllick & Hockerts, 2002, p. 131); or "demonstrating the inclusion of social and environmental concerns in business operations and in interactions with stakeholders" (Van Marrewijk, 2003, p. 8).

Business sustainability is defined as "Adopting business strategies and activities that meet the needs of the enterprise and its stakeholders today while protecting, sustaining and enhancing the human and natural resources that will be needed in the future" (Deloitte & Touche, ISSD, 1992, p.1).

2.2.2   Sustainability Performance

The achievement of sustainability or the ability to meet sustainability indicates an organization's "sustainability performance" (SP). This study found eight definitions for this term.

For example, sustainability performance is "the organization's ability to meet existing business and its stakeholders' needs while maintaining and enhancing the natural and human resources needed for the future" (Labuschagne et al., 2005 as

Table 2.1 List of definitions

Term	Definition	Source and year
Organizational sustainability (OS)	"The ability of a firm to nurture and support growth over time by effectively meeting the expectations of diverse stakeholders"	Neubaum and Zahra (2006), as cited in Nawaz and Koç (2019, p. 3)
	"The ones whose characteristics and activities are intended to bring a desirable future state for its stakeholders"	Funk (2003), as cited in Nawaz and Koç (2019, p. 3)
	"The ones which take a systems perspective to ensure that natural resources are not consumed faster than the rates of renewal, recycling, or regeneration of those resources"	Marshall and Brown (2003), as cited in Nawaz and Koç (2019, p. 3)
	"The contribution of organizations in the process of achieving human development in an inclusive, equitable, and secure manner by delivering simultaneously economic, social, and environmental benefits"	Hart and Milstein (2003), as cited in Nawaz and Koç (2019), p. 3
Corporate sustainability (CS)	"A business and investment strategy that seeks to use the best business practices to meet and balance the needs of current and future stakeholders"	WCED (1987) as cited in Artiach et al. (2010, p. 31)
	"Meeting the needs of the firm's direct and indirect stakeholders (such as shareholders, employees, clients, pressure groups, communities, etc.), without compromising its ability to meet future stakeholder needs as well"	Dyllick and Hockerts (2002), as cited in Searcy (2012, p. 239)
	"Demonstrating the inclusion of social and environmental concerns in business operations and in interactions with stakeholders"	Van Marrewijk (2003), as cited in Searcy (2012, p. 239)
	"The concept of sustainable development integrates the consideration of economic growth, environmental protection, and social equity, simultaneously and on a macrolevel. When incorporated by the firm, it is called corporate sustainability"	Lourenço et al. (2012, p. 417)
Business sustainability (BS)	"Adopting business strategies and activities that meet the needs of the enterprise and its stakeholders today while protecting, sustaining and enhancing the human and natural resources that will be needed in the future"	Deloitte and Touche, ISSD (1992) as cited in Labuschagne et al. (2005)

(continued)

Table 2.1 (continued)

Term	Definition	Source and year
Sustainability performance (SP)	"The organization's ability to meet existing business and its stakeholders' needs while maintaining and enhancing the natural and human resources needed for the future"	Labuschagne et al. (2005), as cited in Althnayan et al. (2022, p.1)
	"An outcome-related term measuring the intersection of economic, environmental and social dimensions"	Arora et al. (2020, p. 711)
	"It includes the social, environmental and economic impacts of an organization as it relates to the multiple and differing objectives of the complete set of stakeholders"	Epstein and Wisner (2006), as cited in Epstein and Widener (2010, p. 53)
	"A combination of both policy output and policy outcome"	Hoppe and Coenen (2011, p. 229)
	"It is indicating the companies' efforts and achievements regarding sustainability"	Mahoney (2013) as cited in Papoutsi and Sodhi (2020, p. 4)
	"It encompasses performance in connection with: natural resource conservation and emission levels; other environmental activities and initiatives; aspects of employment; occupational health and safety; community relations; stakeholder involvement; economic impacts of the organization other than those financial measures used in the financial accounts"	Adams et al. (2014) (HTML file)
	"A balanced integration among economic, social and environmental performance"	Shen et al. (2016, p. 4)
	"The aggregate negative or positive bottom line of economic, environmental and social impacts of an entity against a defined baseline"	Büyüközkan and Karabulut (2018, pp. 253–254)
Organizational sustainability performance (OSP)	"A dynamic process that necessitates achieving short-term performance (meeting current needs) without compromising long-term performance (meeting future needs) of the triple bottom lines—financial, social, and environmental"	Eccles et al. (2014), as cited in Lee and Ha-Brookshire (2017, p. 1)

(continued)

Table 2.1 (continued)

Term	Definition	Source and year
	"It deals with economic, environmental, and social aspects of corporate activity, within and outside a market or regulatory framework, and includes issues such as revenues, sustained profitability, competitive advantage, employee welfare, community programs, charitable donations, and environmental protection"	Carter and Rogers (2008), as cited in Arrora et al. (2020, pp. 709–710)
Corporate sustainability performance (CSP)	"Mainly focuses on the environmental, social, and economic performance of sustainable development"	Takala and Pallab (2000), as cited in Goyal et al. ((2013, p. 362)
	"Measures the extent to which a firm embraces economic, environmental, social, and governance factors into its operations, and ultimately the impact they exert on the firm and society"	Artiach et al. (2010), as cited in Lourenço et al. (2012, p. 417)
	"Commonly exhibits environment, social, and governance (ESG) scores, reflecting their motives and allegiance toward sustainable development in their annual sustainability reports as an outcome of corporate sustainability assessment (CSA)"	Jyoti and Khanna (2021, p. 2)
	"A construct that emphasizes a company's responsibilities to multiple stakeholders, such as employees and the community at large, in addition to its traditional responsibilities to economic shareholders"	Turban and Greening (1997, p. 658)
Environmental performance (EP)	"The degree to which an organization improves its performance in respect to its environmental responsibilities"	Kleindorfer et al. (2005) as cited in Yang et al. (2011, p. 252)
Environmental sustainability performance (ESP)	"On a company's level it is strongly related to environmental business targets, e.g. reduction of greenhouse gas emissions, resource efficiency as well as decrease of water consumption and waste output"	Zimek and Baumgartner (2017, p. 4)
Social performance	"A company's responsibilities to multiple stakeholders, such as employees and the community at large, in addition to its traditional responsibilities to economic shareholders"	Chen and Delmas (2011) as cited in Lee and Ha-Brookshire (2017, p. 3)
Sustainability performance evaluation (SPE)	"The quantification of an organization's total performance based on performance indicators, which can include its policies, decisions, and actions creating economic, social and environmental results"	Büyüközkan and Karabulut (2018, p. 254)

(continued)

Table 2.1 (continued)

Term	Definition	Source and year
First-order-sustainability performance–corporate level	"It refers to corporate sustainability performance. This means improvements and direct effects are given on a corporate level (of a focal firm)"	Zimek and Baumgartner (2017, p.13)
Second-order sustainability performance systemic sustainability performance	"Corporate sustainability activities by considering long-term impacts and improvements on the whole system, namely the company itself, the market (supply chains), the society and the nature by considering systemic effectiveness and the principles for sustainable development of the Framework for Strategic Sustainable Development rather than just relating to narrow issues of efficiency, which are defined as first-order sustainability performance"	Baumgartner and Rauter (2017), as cited in Zimek and Baumgartner (2017, p. 15)

cited in Althnayan et al., 2022, p.1); or "[T]he aggregate negative or positive bottom line of economic, environmental and social impacts of an entity against a defined baseline" (Büyüközkan & Karabulut, 2018, pp. 253–254).

In addition, the literature employs the term organizational sustainability performance (OSP) or corporate sustainability performance (CSP). This study found six definitions for these terms.

For example, organizational sustainability performance is defined as "a dynamic process that necessitates achieving short-term performance (meeting current needs) without compromising long-term performance (meeting future needs) of the triple bottom lines—financial, social, and environmental" (Eccles et al., 2014, as cited in Lee & Ha-Brookshire, 2017, p. 1).

Corporate sustainability performance is defined as "[M]easures the extent to which a firm embraces economic, environmental, social, and governance factors into its operations, and ultimately the impact they exert on the firm and society" (Artiach et al., 2010, cited in Lourenc et al., 2012, p. 417).

Some studies examine only part of SP, mentioning the terms "environmental sustainability performance" (ESP; Zimek & Baumgartner, 2017), "environmental performance" (e.g., Abidin et al., 2016; Kleindorfer et al., 2005), or "social performance" (Turban & Greening, 1997). These terms' definitions appear in Table 2.1.

Another type of definition identified was "sustainability performance evaluation" (Büyüközkan & Karabulut, 2018), which combines the definitions of four terms: sustainability performance (AccountAbility, 2005), performance evaluation (Hu & Gorton, 1997), performance measurement (Neely et al., 1995), and environmental performance assessment (Zhang, 2010) and defined as "the quantification of an organization's total performance based on performance indicators, which can include its policies, decisions, and actions creating economic, social and environmental results" (Büyüközkan & Karabulut, 2018, p. 254).

2.2.3 New Terms for Sustainability Performance

Recently emerging terminology differentiates between company-level and system-level perspectives. First-order sustainability performance refers to "corporate sustainability performance, i.e., encompassing improvements and direct effects at the corporate level of a focal firm" (Zimek & Baumgartner, 2017, p.13). Second-order sustainability performance refers to "corporate sustainability activities, by considering the long-term impacts and improvements on the entire system—consisting of the company itself, the market (supply chains), society, and nature—by considering systemic effectiveness and the sustainable development principles of the Framework for Strategic Sustainable Development (FSSD), rather than relating only to narrow efficiency issues defined as first-order sustainability performance" (Baumgartner & Rauter, 2017, as cited in Zimek & Baumgartner, 2017, p.15).

In summary, the term OSP (1) focuses on current (short-term) needs without damaging the future (long-term) ones; (2) considers stakeholders, including shareholders, employees, clients, pressure groups, communities, etc.; (3) refers to the measurement of the triple bottom lines—financial, social, and environmental—in addition to governance; and (4) includes the impact at the firm level and the whole system.

This definition presents significant challenges in terms of measuring organizational sustainability performance and examining its future impact on the entire system.

2.3 Factors Affecting Organizational Sustainability Performance

Several factors influence sustainability performance in private and public organizations. This section presents the common factor identified for both public and private sectors, "strategy" (see summary in Table 2.2) and describes additional factors examined in the private sector but not necessarily in the public sector, and vice versa (see summary in Table 2.3).

Table 2.2   Strategy and sustainability performance in private and public sectors

Strategy	Findings	References
Private sector		
Five activities: Resource efficiency, energy efficiency, bio-economy, product-service systems (PSS), and environmental management systems (EMS)	Examines the effect of the following five activities (based on Bocken et al., 2014 study): resource efficiency, energy efficiency, bio-economy, product-service-systems (PSS), and environmental management systems (EMS) on corporate and systematic sustainability performance	Zimek and Baumgartner (2017)
Strategic sustainable purchasing (SSP) = Strategic purchasing and environmental purchasing	Environmental collaboration is a mediator between Strategic sustainable purchasing (SSP) and organizational sustainable performance. The supply base size moderates the relationship between SSP and environmental collaboration, thus achieving OSP	Arora et al. (2020)
Coopetition strategy	Coopetition is significantly associated with increased dynamic capabilities and sustainability awareness, both of which are related to enhanced sustainability performance in firms	Mwesiumo et al. (2023)
Public sector		
Typology of management (Prospectors/defenders/reactors)	Prospectors are positively associated with sustainability performance	Enticott and Walker (2008)
Sustainable management	Sustainable management is positively related to sustainability performance	Enticott and Walker (2008)
Frontrunners/lagging behind	Local authorities considered as "frontrunners" have managed to embrace a wide range of sustainability policy measures. They have the local capacity and the ability to establish a local sustainability plan. Other authorities are considered as "lagging behind".	Hoppe and Coenen (2011)

2.3.1   Strategy and Sustainability Performance

To achieve sustainability performance, a corporation should adopt a strategic approach that recognizes its responsibility and significant role both in the context of the societies it operates in and on a global scale. According to Labuschagne et al. (2005), this approach involves evaluating the sustainability of internal initiatives in the context of three key dimensions: Environmental sustainability, social sustainability, and economic sustainability, which represent a comprehensive set of criteria

Table 2.3 Factor effect on OSP in private and public sectors

Factors	Findings	References
Private Sector		
Employees	An examination of the relationship between employees' attitudes and organizational sustainability performance through turnover intention revealed that high turnover intention has a negative effect on organizations' social and environmental performance, alongside their negative effect on financial performance. In addition, ethical climate lowered employee turnover intention, but also positively affected employees' job attitudes	Lee and Ha-Brookshire (2017)
	Green Human Resource (GHRM) and Corporate Social Responsibility (CSR) have a significant and positive influence on sustainable organizational performance (OP) Perceived Organizational Support (POS) mediates the relationship between GHRM/CSR and OP Affective Commitment (AC) mediates the relationship between GHRM/CSR and OP	Zhao et al. (2021)
Leadership	Environmental Transformational Leadership (ETL) indirectly impacts SP through Environmental Organizational Citizenship Behavior (EOCB) ETL positively affects employees' attitudes towards environment and leads them to engage in pro-environmental activities Employees' Work Passion (WP) moderates the relationship between ETL and EOCB	Althnayan et al. (2022), Liao and Zhang (2020)
Board gender composition	While the presence of women on boards has limited influence on financial performance, it has a significant correlation with corporate sustainability performance. In addition, there is an optimal level of gender quotas which maximizes sustainability performance	Provasi and Harasheh (2021)
Circular Economy (CE)	A literature review analysing the effect of CE practices on company sustainability performance	Prieto-Sandoval et al. (2018), Mora-Contreras et al. (2022)
Corporate Social Responsibility (CSR)	CSR positively has a positive impact on the adoption of sustainability performance measurement and organizational performance	Cochran and Wood (1984), Griffin and Mahon (1997), Harrison and Freeman (1999), McWilliams and Siegel (2000), Asiaei et al. (2021)

(continued)

Table 2.3 (continued)

Factors	Findings	References
Supply chain	Sustainable supply chain initiatives, particularly those involving collaboration with suppliers on environmental and social aspects, can lead to significant benefits across the "triple bottom line" of social, environmental, and economic dimensions	Bai and Sarkis (2010)
Public sector		
Municipality size	Municipality size is positively correlated with local sustainability performance	Kern et al. (2004), Hoppe and Coenen, (2011)
Network membership	Network membership is positively correlated with local sustainability performance	Hoppe and Coenen (2011)
Entrepreneurial orientation (EO)	EO indirectly affects perceptions of sustainability performance but serves as a mediator for the influence of capacities on such performance Additionally, strategic activities, such as performance management, venturing, and inter-organizational collaboration play a mediating role in the relationship between EO and perceived sustainability performance	Deslatte and Swan (2020)
Electronic human resource management (E-HRM)	A positive relationship between E-HRM and SP was found in Jordanian universities. Labour productivity (LP) was identified as a mediator and Organizational agility (OA) had a moderating effect	AlNawafleh et al. (2022), Bag et al. (2021), L'Écuyer et al., (2023)
Internal CSR	Health and safety, training and development, and workplace diversity have a positive and significant impact on social performance	Mory et al. (2016), Adu-Gyamfi et al. (2021)

that may be applied in the assessment of the sustainability of various elements, including projects and technologies, as well as the company's overall sustainability.

A corporate sustainability strategy may be implemented through sustainable activities. In the private sector, sustainable activities include resource efficiency, energy efficiency, bio-economy, product-service systems (PSS), and environmental management systems (EMS). The impact of these activities was analysed in both corporate and systemic contexts (Bocken et al., 2014; Zimek & Baumgartner, 2017). It was also found that "strategic sustainable purchasing" impacts organizational sustainable performance, through moderating and mediating factors (Arora et al., 2020). A significant association has been identified between the coopetition strategy and an increase in dynamic capabilities and sustainability awareness. Moreover, dynamic capabilities and sustainability awareness were found to be significantly related to firms' improved sustainability performance. Findings also indicate that open innovation partially mediates the relationship between coopetition strategy and sustainable performance (Bengtsson & Kock, 2014; Mwesiumo et al., 2023).

In the public sector, it was revealed that adopting a strategic approach, such as a prospector, is positively associated with sustainability performance. Additionally, sustainable management shows a positive correlation with sustainability performance (Enticott & Walker, 2008). Finally, "frontrunners" among local authorities have managed to embrace a wide range of sustainability policy measures (Hoppe & Coenen, 2011).

2.3.2 Additional Factors Effect on Sustainability Performance

Other factors identified as influential in the private sector are employees (Lee & Ha-Brookshire, 2017; Zhao et al., 2021), leadership (Althnayan et al., 2022; Liao & Zhang, 2020), board gender (Provasi & Harasheh, 2021), circular economy (CE) practices (Prieto-Sandoval et al., 2018; Mora-Contreras et al., 2022), corporate social responsibility (CSR) (Cochran & Wood, 1984; Griffin & Mahon, 1997; Harrison & Freeman, 1999; McWilliams & Siegel, 2000; Asiaei et al., 2021), and supply chain (Bai & Sarkis, 2010).

In the public sector, impacting factors identified are size (Kern et al., 2004; Hoppe & Coenen, 2011), network membership (Hoppe & Coenen, 2011), entrepreneurial orientation (EO) (Deslatte & Swan, 2020), electronic human resource management (E-HRM) (Bag et al., 2021; L'Écuyer et al., 2023; Al Nawafleh et al. 2022), and internal CSR (Adu-Gyamfi et al., 2021; Mory et al., 2016).

In summary, this review points to the fact that an organization's characteristics and its stakeholders impact its SP. Recent SP studies, in both the public and private sectors, have examined hot trends, including CE, EO, diversification, E-HRM, and CSR.

2.4 The Impact of the Firm's Sustainable Performance on Financial Performance

This section presents recent studies examining the impact of firms' sustainable performance on their financial performance.

Previous studies predominantly explored the relationship between financial performance and one of the three ESG components (environmental, social, or governance). Several comprehensive studies have considered all three (Waddock & Graves, 1997; Surroca et al., 2010; Goyal et al, 2013; Dou, 2015; Chelawat &

Trivedi, 2016; Zhao et al., 2018; Drempetic et al., 2020; Duque-Grisales & Aguilera-Caracuel, 2021). The findings were mixed, and limited research addressed developing countries.

Adding to this literature, the current study identifies a recent research that found a significant negative relationship between the environmental score and both the return on assets (ROA) and return on capital employed (ROCE) in the Indian market. The study also revealed a negative correlation between the social score and return on equity (ROE), while the overall ESG score was found to have a negative impact on both ROA and ROCE (Jyoti & Khanna, 2021).

In the context of the COVID-19 pandemic, recent research, as demonstrated by Ding et al. (2021), Lee et al. (2022), and others, revealed that firms with higher ESG scores exhibited superior performance during the pandemic. Additionally, the decision to go public through an initial public offering, positively impacted sustainability performance, signalling quality and compliance with emerging sustainability regulations (Harasheh, 2022).

2.5 Sustainability Performance Evaluation

Three main stages of the sustainability performance evaluation process emerge from the reviewed literature: (1) Planning, objectives, and key indicator determination; (2) Method determination for assessment analysis; (3) Reporting the information to both internal decision-makers and external stakeholders.

This section presents the findings in the private and public sector studies.

2.5.1 Sustainability Performance in the Private Sector

In the private sector research review, certain studies describe the entire evaluation process. For instance, Epstein and Widener (2010) present a structured process for managers to engage with stakeholders, assess sustainability performance, and utilize this knowledge to inform decision-making. Büyüközkan and Karabulut (2018) discuss three evaluation stages: Accounting, assessment, and reporting. Other studies focus on a specific part of the sustainability performance evaluation process. For instance, Searcy (2012) focuses on the measurement aspect, proposing the implementation of Sustainable Performance Measurement Systems (SPMS). Similarly, Batista and Francisco (2018) provide detailed insights into environmental, economic, and social practices. Merad et al. (2013) contribute by describing sustainability performance indicators (SPIs), shedding light on specific metrics for assessment. Some studies focus on the design process involved in determining indicators, as exemplified by the works of Keeble et al. (2003) and López-Arceiz et al. (2020). Roca and Searcy (2012) found a very wide range of disclosed indicators, which varied by theme and sector.

This diversity can be attributed to various factors. Firstly, discrepancies arise from varying interpretations of terms such as "sustainability" and "corporate social responsibility". Additionally, the absence of standardized frameworks in sustainability reporting allows for flexibility in the disclosure of indicators. Variations in sample size, sample composition, and national business systems further contribute to this diversity. The purposes and target audiences of the reports, as well as the resources available to corporations, also play a role in shaping indicator disclosure practices. Theoretical perspectives, such as stakeholder theory and legitimacy theory, offer insights into why different corporations may prefer certain indicators in their disclosures. This diversified explanation underscores the complexity and context-dependency of sustainability reporting practices.

Referring to the analytical methodologies of the collected data, several studies, such as Kore et al. (2017) and Büyüközkan and Karabulu (2018) refer to descriptive statistics, multicriteria decision-making (MCDM), composite indices (Arithmetic Weighting), data envelopment analysis (DEA, see Kao, 2014), and other methods. MCDM is the most prevalent method, examples including Analytical Hierarchy Processes (AHP) (Vaidya & Kumar, 2006) and the Technique for Order of Preference by Similarity to Ideal Solution (TOPSIS).

In sustainability performance evaluation's reporting stage, various tools are employed. Notable examples include the International Organization for Standardization (ISO), the Global Reporting Initiative (GRI) (Büyüközkan & Karabulut, 2018; Grecu et al., 2020), Carbon Disclosure Project (CDP) (Büyüközkan & Karabulut, 2018), and corporate sustainability indices (Büyüközkan & Karabulut, 2018). For a comparison of SPE Tools see Büyüközkan and Karabulut (2018).

2.5.2 Sustainability Performance in the Public Sector

The studies reviewed in the context of literature on the public sector suggest new methods for assessment, make adjustments to specific sectors, and, recently, provide a framework that includes formal and informal assessment systems. Chai proposes the use of Sustainability Performance Evaluation Systems (SPES) in order to apply the need for performance measurement system for the public sector. The objectives of SPES encompass both public accountability and performance improvement. SPES methods are based on ISO 14031 and, a balanced scorecard (BSC) and its implementation in the public sector, using New Public Management practices.

Adams et al. (2014) discuss output and outcome measures. Output measures refer to "the quantity of products and services completed or delivered", while outcome measures refer "the results or consequences of service delivery that are important for the public and customers" (Ho & Ni, 2005 as cited in Adams et al., 2014, p.50).

Miller et al. (2016) propose the Public Transit Sustainable Mobility Analysis Tool (PTSMAT), which categorizes sustainability into environmental, economic, social, and system effectiveness dimensions, utilizing multiple indicators within each category. Finally, a weighted sum of all category indices was calculated to create the Composite Sustainability Index (CSI).

Ramos et al. (2021) present a conceptual framework for the formal sustainability performance assessment system. The framework includes two assessment levels: Strategic and operational. The strategic assessment encompasses sustainability objectives and related practices to evaluate the sustainability performance associated with the existence of strategic instruments. The operational assessment consists of a set of indicators to assess the sustainability performance concerning organizational activities and operations. The system consists of 29 indicators divided into economic (EC), environmental (EN), and social aspects (SC).

Furthermore, Coutinho et al. (2018) argue that in addition to the formal assessment, which is managed by the technical staff, there should also be an informal stakeholder-driven performance assessment. They suggest an employee-driven sustainability performance assessment that includes three sustainability domains: Perceptions of organizational performance, individual practices potentially influencing the organization, and voluntary monitoring indicators encompassing the primary sustainability domains—economic, environmental, and social. These domains are examined through 85 questions.

Similarly, to private sector literature, the reporting aspect is also discussed in the literature. For example, Adams et al. (2014) argues that public organizations should convey the information about their direction and success to external users. External users encompass various stakeholders: resource providers (such as employees, lenders, creditors, and suppliers), recipients of goods and services (including ratepayers, taxpayers, and professional association members), and entities fulfilling oversight roles (such as parliaments, governments, regulatory agencies, analysts, labour unions, employer groups, the media, and special interest community groups). Reporting tools mentioned include ISO, GRI, and various indices (Chai, 2009; Miller et al., 2016; Ramos et al., 2021).

2.6 Challenges of Effective Sustainable Performance Evaluation

Effective sustainable performance evaluation faces several challenges, including various critical issues as identified in the literature of private and public sectors.

Private sector studies identify the following challenges:

1. Indicator Heterogeneity: The lack of standardized reporting frameworks and diverse indicators hinder a consistent approach to SPE (Adams et al., 2014; Grecu et al., 2020). Approximately 80% of the analytical publications analysed by Büyüközkan and Karabulut (2018) propose unique SPE criteria, indicating the need for well-defined, adaptable frameworks. While standardization benefits transparency and comparability, it raises concerns about erasing company distinctions and overlooking site-specific issues. Second-party verification with

ongoing engagement and constructive criticism can address these challenges (Warhurst, 2002).
2. Complex Organizational Structures: Many corporations' organizational structure is complex, with a multitude of business streams, functions, and projects, which compounds the measurement of sustainability performance (Keeble et al., 2003).
3. Cultural and Legal Contexts: External factors, such as cultural values and legal regulations, significantly influence the conceptualization of sustainability and the development of applicable indicators. Stakeholders often promote their own concepts of sustainability, making generic sustainability performance indicators less effective (Renneboog & Spaenjers, 2012).
4. The Lack of Sustainable Development Goal Evaluation: While the UN introduced 17 SDGs, evaluation of the progress towards achieving them is limited. This adds to the complexity of sustainability performance assessment and may confuse decision-makers (Grecu et al., 2020).

The public sector faces unique challenges stemming from its distinct nature:

1. A Low Level of Reporting: Unerman et al. (2007) observed a significant rise in sustainability reporting within the private sector but minimal progress within PSOs. Bellringer et al., (2011) suggest that the low level of reporting may be attributed to the fact that the information was primarily intended for internal stakeholders.
2. Partial Sustainability Performance Measurement: In a later study, A. Adams et al. (2014) examined the use of performance measures and specifically focusing on social and environmental measures and the adoption of a BSC approach in assessing the performance of public organizations in Australia. They found that the most commonly employed sustainability performance measures were employee diversity and economic activity, while ecological and social welfare concerns receiving little attention.
3. Niemann and Hoppe (2018) found that only the largest, most high-capacity cities typically participate in sustainability performance management. In contrast, the majority of medium-sized cities in the U.S. do not participate in performance measurement or management of sustainability activities (Alibašić, 2018).
4. Incorporation of Voluntary Standards as Sustainability Criteria to Achieve Goals: The review by Rainville (2022) discussed various challenges associated with integrating voluntary standards as sustainability criteria to achieve goals. These challenges encompassed the involvement of a large and diverse group of stakeholders throughout the project's duration, the numerous available standards for measuring and promoting sustainability within a given mission, uncertainties regarding the incorporation of standards into the project planning process, the relatively early stage of sustainability requirements, fragmentation across districts, and differences between individual projects.

2.7   Discussion and Future Recommendations

Private and public organizations make obvious contributions to the economy, including through the creation of products or services, as large employers, and functioning within supply chains. Simultaneously, they bear an obligation to protect the environment and maintain a safe society, a duty particularly pertinent to public organizations that control extensive geographical areas. Despite the seemingly straightforward nature of this obligation, its execution is a complicated mission.

In this context, understanding the definitions of sustainability performance, the factors affecting it, how it impacts financial performance, the process of measuring it, and how to overcome related challenges are essential for the success of the above-mentioned execution.

On the basis of the various definitions of SP and related terms identified in this study, it is recommended that researchers will refrain from using "organizational", "corporate", and "business" sustainability as synonymous. "Organizational" encompasses multiple types of organizations; thus, the definition cannot mark them as firms or corporates, which refer to private sectors only. The definitions are also vague in terms of how the current (short-term) sustainability performance and its future impact (long-term) are measured in practice.

In addition, this study discusses the factors affecting SP, starting with the importance of organizational strategy for achieving sustainability performance in both public and private organizations. The integration of sustainability into decision-making processes and the establishment of strategic plans to address long-term challenges are identified as essential steps. The development of dynamic capabilities by responding to the rapidly changing environment emerges as a need, in the context of which organizations can benefit from adopting sustainability practices established by experienced organizations. To enhance their sustainability performance, organizations should aim to become "prospectors" and "frontrunners", by actively seeking opportunities, responding to developing trends, fostering innovation, and being willing to take calculated risks.

Additional factors affecting SP span organization attributes (e.g., size) and stakeholders (e.g., employees). This underscores the importance of valuing employee efforts and ensuring their overall wellbeing, which involves safeguarding their health and safety and investing in their development and training. Developing environmental leadership is a key factor, as it can encourage employees to engage in pro-environmental activities. Other factors enhancing SP are connected to current trends, such as circular economy and electronic HRM. It is thus recommended to implement circular economy practices, such as green purchasing.

Consistently with past literature, the recent reviewed studies examining the relationship between financial performance and ESG cite mixed findings.

The literature reviewed here reveals the evaluation process presents numerous challenges for both public and private sector organizations. These challenges include the gap between strategy and its translation/implementation, which Chai (2009) suggests to bridge by combining methods, such as ISO and a Balanced Score Card.

Another challenge is the need to enhance the adoption of sustainability measures and reporting, particularly in the public sector, where implementation is currently at a low level, in addition to the absence of sustainability performance by medium–small size organizations requires specific guidance for this sector (Alibašić, 2018). Büyüközkan and Karabulut (2018) propose a sustainability performance evaluation framework comprised of accounting, assessment, and reporting, which has the potential to benefit both private and public organizations.

A third challenge is the lack of standardization, which can facilitate reporting: Voluntary standards may help in shaping and realizing missions for sustainable urban development at the municipal level. A fourth challenge lies in public institutions' accounting reports often lacking detailed information and references to impact. It is essential that their reports encompass both performance information and impacts in reporting. A fifth challenge is the multiplicity of indicators, a fact which highlights the necessity for standardization. Ramos et al. (2021) suggest a framework for public organizations, consisting of three dimensions: Economy, environment, and society, which is strongly recommended for implementation. Finally, in public organizations, such as local authorities, missions must be defined and linked to the parties responsible for implementing them (Rainville, 2022).

Overall, the transition to sustainability can expedite the achievement of citizen satisfaction in public organizations, increase profitability in private organizations, and lead to positive outcomes and additional benefits.

These conclusions and recommendation are subject to certain limitations. The study is based on only 57 papers. And while the recommendations apply to public and private organizations, there may be differences arising from the distinct characteristics of these sectors.

References

Adams, C. A, Muir, S., & Hoque, Z. (2014). Measurement of sustainability performance in the public sector. *Sustainability Accounting, Management and Policy Journal, 5*(1), 46–67.

Abidin, R., Abdullah, R., Hassan, M. G., & Sobry, S. C. (2016). Environmental sustainability performance: The influence of supplier and customer integration. *The Social Sciences, 11*, 2673–2678.

AccountAbility. (2005). Stakeholder Engagement Standard (Exposure Draft), Exposure Draft. https://www.accountability.org/standards/aa1000-stakeholder-engagement-standard/

Adu-Gyamfi, M., He, Z., Nyame, G., Boahen, S., & Frempong, M. F. (2021). Effects of internal CSR activities on social performance: The employee perspective. *Sustainability, 13*(11), 6235.

Alibašić, H. (2018). *Sustainability and resilience planning for local governments.* Springer International Publishing.

AlNawafleh, E. A. T., Addin al-sharari, F. E., Alsheikh, G. A. A., Al-Ghalabi, R. R., & Hamdan, K. B. (2022). Enhancing the sustainability performance through e-hrm and unveiling of the labour productivity and organizational agility in the Jordanian public universities. *International Journal of eBusiness and eGovernment Studies, 14*(2), 242–263.

Althnayan, S., Alarifi, A., Bajaba, S., & Alsabban, A. (2022). Linking environmental transformational leadership, environmental organizational citizenship behavior, and organizational sustainability performance: A moderated mediation model. *Sustainability, 14*(14), 8779.

Arora, A., Arora, A. S., Sivakumar, K., & Burke, G. (2020). Strategic sustainable purchasing, environmental collaboration, and organizational sustainability performance: the moderating role of supply base size. *Supply Chain Management: An International Journal, 25*(6), 709–728.

Artiach, T., Lee, D., Nelson, D., & Walker, J. (2010). The determinants of corporate sustainability performance. *Accounting & Finance, 50*(1), 31–51.

Asiaei, K., Bontis, N., Barani, O., & Jusoh, R. (2021). Corporate social responsibility and sustainability performance measurement systems: Implications for organizational performance. *Journal of Management Control, 32*(1), 85–126.

Bag, S., Gupta, S., & Kumar, S. (2021). Industry 4.0 adoption and 10R advance manufacturing capabilities for sustainable development. *International Journal of Production Economics, 231*, 107844.

Bai, C., & Sarkis, J. (2010). Integrating sustainability into supplier selection with grey system and rough set methodologies. *International Journal of Production Economics, 124*(1), 252–264.

Ball, A., & Grubnic, S. (2007). Sustainability accounting and accountability in the public sector. In J. Unerman, J. Bebbington, & B. O'Dwyer (Eds.), *Sustainability accounting and accountability* (pp. 243–265). Routledge.

Batista, A. A. D. S., & Francisco, A. C. D. (2018). Organizational sustainability practices: A study of the firms listed by the corporate sustainability index. *Sustainability, 10*(1), 226.

Baumgartner, R. J., & Rauter, R. (2017). Strategic perspectives of corporate sustainability management to develop a sustainable organization. *Journal of Cleaner Production, 140*, 81–92.

Bellringer, A., Ball, A., & Craig, R. (2011). Reasons for sustainability reporting by New Zealand local governments. *Sustainability Accounting, Management and Policy Journal, 2*(1), 126–138.

Bengtsson, M., & Kock, S. (2014). Coopetition—Quo vadis? Past accomplishments and future challenges. *Industrial Marketing Management, 43*(2), 180–188.

Bocken, N. M. P., Short, S. W., Rana, P., & Evans, S. (2014). A literature and practice review to develop sustainable business model archetypes. *Journal of Cleaner Production, 65*, 42–56.

Büyüközkan, G., & Karabulut, Y. (2018). Sustainability performance evaluation: Literature review and future directions. *Journal of Environmental Management, 217*, 253–267.

Carter, C. R., & Rogers, D. S. (2008). A framework of sustainable supply chain management: moving toward new theory. *International Journal of Physical Distribution & Logistics Management, 38*(5), 360–387.

Chai, N. (2009). *Sustainability performance evaluation system in government: A balanced scorecard approach towards sustainable development.* Springer Science & Business Media.

Chelawat, H., & Trivedi, I. V. (2016). The business value of ESG performance: The Indian context. *Asian Journal of Business Ethics, 5*(1–2), 195–210.

Cochran, P. L., & Wood, R. A. (1984). Corporate social responsibility and financial performance. *Academy of Management Journal, 27*(1), 42–56.

Chen, C. M., & Delmas, M. (2011). Measuring corporate social performance: An efficiency perspective. *Production and Operations Management, 20*(6), 789–804.

Coutinho, V., Domingues, A. R., Caeiro, S., Painho, M., Antunes, P., Santos, R., Ramos, T. B., et al. (2018). Employee-driven sustainability performance assessment in public organizations. *Corporate Social Responsibility and Environmental Management, 25*(1), 29–46.

Dou, X. (2015). The lagging effects of the influence of corporate social responsibility on corporate financial performance-empirical analysis based on the panel data of chinese listed companies. *Industrial Economics Research, 3*, 74–81.

Deloitte & Touche. (1992). *Business strategy for sustainable development: leadership and accountability for the 90s.* IISD.

Deslatte, A., & Swann, W. L. (2020). Elucidating the linkages between entrepreneurial orientation and local government sustainability performance. *The American Review of Public Administration, 50*(1), 92–109.

Ding, W., Levine, R., Lin, C., & Xie, W. (2021). Corporate immunity to the COVID-19 pandemic. *Journal of Financial Economics, 141*(2), 802–830. https://doi.org/10.1016/J.JFINECO.2021.03.005

Donaldson, T., & Preston, L. E. (1995). The stakeholder theory of the corporation: Concepts, evidence, and implications. *Academy of Management Review, 20*(1), 65–91.

Drempetic, S., Klein, C., & Zwergel, B. (2020). The influence of firm size on the ESG score: Corporate sustainability ratings under review. *Journal of Business Ethics, 167*, 333–360.

Duque-Grisales, E., & Aguilera-Caracuel, J. (2021). Environmental, social and governance (ESG) scores and financial performance of multilatinas: Moderating effects of geographic international diversification and financial slack. *Journal of Business Ethics, 168*(2), 315–334.

Dyllick, T., & Hockerts, K. (2002). Beyond the business case for corporate sustainability. *Business Strategy and the Environment, 11*, 130–141.

Eccles, R. G., Ioannou, I., & Serafeim, G. (2014). The impact of corporate sustainability on organizational processes and performance. *Management Science, 60*, 2835–2857.

Enticott, G., & Walker, R. M. (2008). Sustainability, performance and organizational strategy: An empirical analysis of public organizations. *Business Strategy and the Environment, 17*(2), 79–92.

Epstein, M. J., & Wisner, P. S. (2006). Actions and measures to improve sustainability. *The accountable corporation, 3*, 207-234.

Epstein, M. J., & Widener, S. K. (2010). Identification and use of sustainability performance measures in decision-making. *Journal of Corporate Citizenship, 40*, 43–73.

Funk, K. (2003). Sustainability and performance. *MIT Sloan Management Review, 44*(2), 65.

Goyal, P., Rahman, Z., & Kazmi, A. A. (2013). Corporate sustainability performance and firm performance research: Literature review and future research agenda. *Management Decision, 51*(2), 361–379.

Grecu, V., Ciobotea, R. I. G., & Florea, A. (2020). Software application for organizational sustainability performance assessment. *Sustainability, 12*(11), 4435.

Griffin, J. J., & Mahon, J. F. (1997). The corporate social performance and corporate financial performance debate: Twenty-five years of incomparable research. *Business & Society, 36*(1), 5–31.

Harasheh, M. (2022). Does it make you better off? Initial public offerings (IPOs) and corporate sustainability performance: Empirical evidence. *Global Business Review, 23*(6), 1375–1387.

Harrison, J. S., & Freeman, R. E. (1999). Stakeholders, social responsibility, and performance: Empirical evidence and theoretical perspectives. *Academy of Management Journal, 42*(5), 479–485.

Hart, S. L., & Milstein, M. B. (2003). Creating sustainable value. *Academy of Management Perspectives, 17*(2), 56–67.

Ho, A. T. K., & Ni, A. Y. (2005). Have cities shifted to outcome-oriented performance reporting?—A content analysis of city budgets. *Public Budgeting & Finance, 25*(2), 61–83.

Hoppe, T., & Coenen, F. (2011). Creating an analytical framework for local sustainability performance: A Dutch case study. *Local Environment, 16*(3), 229–250.

Hu, L., & Gorton, I. (1997). *Performance evaluation for parallel systems: A survey*. University of New South Wales.

ISO, ISO 14001:2015 (en), Environmental management systems—requirements with guidance for use. https://www.iso.org/obp/ui/en/#iso:std:iso:14001:ed-3:v1:en

Jyoti, G., & Khanna, A. (2021). Does sustainability performance impact financial performance? Evidence from Indian service sector firms. *Sustainable Development, 29*(6), 1086–1095.

Keeble, J. J., Topiol, S., & Berkeley, S. (2003). Using indicators to measure sustainability performance at a corporate and project level. *Journal of Business Ethics, 44*, 149–158.

Kern, K., Koll, C., & Schophaus, M. (2004). Local Agenda 21 in Germany: An inter-and intranational comparison.

Kleindorfer, P. R., Singhal, K., & Van Wassenhove, L. N. (2005). Sustainable operations management. *Production and Operations Management, 14*(4), 482–492.

Kao, C. (2014). Network data envelopment analysis: A review. *European Journal of Operational Research, 239*(1), 1–16.

Kore, N. B., Ravi, K., & Patil, S. B. (2017). A simplified description of fuzzy TOPSIS method for multi criteria decision making. *International Research Journal of Engineering and Technology (IRJET), 4*(5), 2047–2050.

Labuschagne, C., Brent, A. C., & Van Erck, R. P. (2005). Assessing the sustainability performances of industries. *Journal of Cleaner Production, 13*(4), 373–385.

L'Écuyer, F., & Raymond, L. (2023). Enabling the HR function of industrial SMEs through the strategic alignment of e-HRM: A configurational analysis. *Journal of Small Business & Entrepreneurship, 35*(3), 450–482.

Lee, S. H., & Ha-Brookshire, J. (2017). Ethical climate and job attitude in fashion retail employees' turnover intention, and perceived organizational sustainability performance: A cross-sectional study. *Sustainability, 9*(3), 465.

Lee, S., Lee, D., Hong, C., & Park, M. H. (2022). Performance of socially responsible firms during the COVID-19 crisis and trading behavior by investor type: Evidence from the Korean stock market. *Finance Research Letters*, https://doi.org/10.1016/J.FRL.2021.102660

Liao, Z., & Zhang, M. (2020). The influence of responsible leadership on environmental innovation and environmental performance: The moderating role of managerial discretion. *Corporate Social Responsibility and Environmental Management, 27*(5), 2016–2027.

López-Arceiz, F. J., Del Río, C., & Bellostas, A. J. (2020). Sustainability performance indicators: Definition, interaction, and influence of contextual characteristics. *Corporate Social Responsibility and Environmental Management, 27*(6), 2615–2630.

Lourenço, I. C., Branco, M. C., Curto, J. D., & Eugénio, T. (2012). How does the market value corporate sustainability performance? *Journal of Business Ethics, 108*, 417–428.

Marshall, R. S., & Brown, D. (2003). The strategy of sustainability: A systems perspective on environmental initiatives. *California Management Review, 46*(1), 101–126.

McWilliams, A., & Siegel, D. (2000). Corporate social responsibility and financial performance: Correlation or misspecification? *Strategic Management Journal, 21*(5), 603–609.

Merad, M., Dechy, N., Serir, L., Grabisch, M., & Marcel, F. (2013). Using a multi-criteria decision aid methodology to implement sustainable development principles within an organization. *European Journal of Operational Research, 224*(3), 603–613.

Miller, P., de Barros, A. G., Kattan, L., & Wirasinghe, S. C. (2016). Analyzing the sustainability performance of public transit. *Transportation Research Part d: Transport and Environment, 44*, 177–198.

Mahoney, L. S., Thorne, L., Cecil, L., & LaGore, W. (2013). A research note on standalone corporate social responsibility reports: Signaling or greenwashing?. *Critical Perspectives on Accounting, 24*(4–5), 350–359.

Mora-Contreras, R., Torres-Guevara, L. E., Mejia-Villa, A., Ormazabal, M., & Prieto-Sandoval, V. (2022). Unraveling the effect of circular economy practices on companies' sustainability performance: Evidence from a literature review. *Sustainable Production and Consumption.*

Mory, L., Wirtz, B. W., & Göttel, V. (2016). Factors of internal corporate social responsibility and the effect on organizational commitment. *The International Journal of Human Resource Management, 27*(13), 1393–1425.

Mwesiumo, D., Harun, M., & Hogset, H. (2023). Unravelling the black box between coopetition and firms' sustainability performance. *Industrial Marketing Management, 114*, 110–124.

Nawaz, W., & Koç, M. (2019). Exploring organizational sustainability: Themes, functional areas, and best practices. *Sustainability, 11*(16), 4307.

Neely, A., Gregory, M., & Platts, K. (1995). Performance measurement system design: A literature review and research agenda. *International Journal of Operations & Production Management, 15*(4), 80–116.

Neubaum, D. O., & Zahra, S. A. (2006). Institutional ownership and corporate social performance: The moderating effects of investment horizon, activism, and coordination. *Journal of Management, 32*, 108–131.

Niemann, L., & Hoppe, T. (2018). Sustainability reporting by local governments: A magic tool? Lessons on use and usefulness from European pioneers. *Public Management Review, 20*(1), 201–223.

Papoutsi, A., & Sodhi, M. S. (2020). Does disclosure in sustainability reports indicate actual sustainability performance?. *Journal of Cleaner Production, 260*, 121049.

Prieto-Sandoval, V., Jaca, C., & Ormazabal, M. (2018). Towards a consensus on the circular economy. *Journal of cleaner production, 179*, 605–615.

Provasi, R., & Harasheh, M. (2021). Gender diversity and corporate performance: Emphasis on sustainability performance. *Corporate Social Responsibility and Environmental Management, 28*(1), 127–137.

Rainville, A. (2022). Green public procurement in mission-orientated innovation systems: Leveraging voluntary standards to improve sustainability performance of municipalities. *Sustainability, 14*(14), 8591.

Ramos, T. B., Domingues, A. R., Caeiro, S., Cartaxo, J., Painho, M., Antunes, P., Huisingh, D., et al. (2021). Co-creating a sustainability performance assessment tool for public sector organisations. *Journal of Cleaner Production, 320*, 128738.

Renneboog, L., & Spaenjers, C. (2012). Religion, economic attitudes, and household finance. *Oxford Economic Papers, 64*(1), 103–127.

Roca, L. C., & Searcy, C. (2012). An analysis of indicators disclosed in corporate sustainability reports. *Journal of Cleaner Production, 20*(1), 103–118.

Searcy, C. (2012). Corporate sustainability performance measurement systems: A review and research agenda. *Journal of Business Ethics, 107*, 239–253.

Shen, L., Tam, V. W., Gan, L., Ye, K., & Zhao, Z. (2016). Improving sustainability performance for public-private-partnership (PPP) projects. *Sustainability, 8*(3), 289.

Surroca, J., Tribó, J. A., & Waddock, S. (2010). Corporate responsibility and financial performance: The role of intangible resources. *Strategic Management Journal, 31*(5), 463–490.

Takala, T., & Pallab, P. (2000). Individual, collective and social responsibility of the firm. *Business ethics: A european review, 9*(2), 109-118.

Turban, D. B., & Greening, D. W. (1997). Corporate social performance and organizational attractiveness to prospective employees. *Academy of Management Journal, 40*(3), 658–672.

Unerman, J., Bebbington, J., & O'Dwyer, B. (2007). *Sustainability accounting and accountability.* Routledge.

Vaidya, O. S., & Kumar, S. (2006). Analytic hierarchy process: An overview of applications. *European Journal of Operational Research, 169*(1), 1–29.

Van Marrewijk, M. (2003). Concepts and definitions of CSR and corporate sustainability: Between agency and communion. *Journal of Business Ethics, 44*(2), 95–105.

Waddock, S. A., & Graves, S. B. (1997). The corporate social performance–financial performance link. *Strategic Management Journal, 18*(4), 303–319.

Warhurst, A. (2002). *Sustainability indicators and sustainability performance management.* Mining, minerals and sustainable development [MMSD] project report, vol 43, 129.

World Commission on Environment and Development (WCED). (1987). *Our common future.* Oxford University Press.

Yang, M. G. M., Hong, P., & Modi, S. B. (2011). Impact of lean manufacturing and environmental management on business performance: An empirical study of manufacturing firms. *International Journal of Production Economics, 129*(2), 251–261.

Zhang, T. (2010). Environmental performance assessment of China's manufacturing. *Asian Economic Journal, 24*(1), 45–68.

Zhao, C., Guo, Y., Yuan, J., Wu, M., Li, D., Zhou, Y., & Kang, J. (2018). ESG and corporate financial performance: Empirical evidence from China's listed power generation companies. *Sustainability, 10*(8), 2607.

Zhao, F., Kusi, M., Chen, Y., Hu, W., Ahmed, F., & Sukamani, D. (2021). Influencing mechanism of green human resource management and corporate social responsibility on organizational sustainable performance. *Sustainability, 13*(16), 8875.

Zimek, M., & Baumgartner, R. (2017). Corporate sustainability activities and sustainability performance of first and second order. In *18th European roundtable on sustainable consumption and production conference (ERSCP 2017)* (vol. 10), Skiathos Island, Greece.

Rachel Calipha, PhD, is a senior lecturer of finance in the School of Management and Economics at Academic College of Tel Aviv-Yaffo, Israel, where she heads the Capital Market specialty track and the Research Institute of Society and Economics. Prior to this, she was a Visiting Professor at YU, New York, having earned her PhD from Ben-Gurion University of the Negev, Israel. Rachel's research fields are strategy and finance. She focuses mainly on Mergers and Acquisitions but she also expands her study to other hot topics in finance such as prediction markets and impact investing.

Shirit Katav-Herz, PhD, is a senior lecturer of Economics in the School of Management and Economics at Academic College of Tel Aviv-Yaffo, Israel, where she heads the Undergraduate Program of Economics and Management (B.A). She earned her PhD from Bar-Ilan University, Israel. Her current research focuses on impact investments, social effects of inequality on economic decision-making concerning risk aversion and also on the effect of social norms on household decision making concerning child labor. She is a member of the International Association for Research in Economics and Psychology (IAREP) and in the World Labour Organization (GLO).

Chapter 3
Sustainable Human Capital Management: Fostering Employee Well-Being and Growth

Anushka Lydia Issac⊙

Abstract In today's business world, balancing the growth of a company with the well-being and development of employees is a crucial challenge. Sustainable Human Capital Management (SHCM) has become increasingly important as organizations seek this balance (Ehnert in Sustainable human resource management. Physica-Verlag HD, Heidelberg, 2009). However, what works for SHCM in one place might not work in another due to different organizational cultures, local norms, and workforce demographics (Chams and García-Blandón in Resour Conserv Recycling 141:109–122, 2019; Ehnert in Sustainable human resource management. Physica-Verlag HD, Heidelberg, 2009). Additionally, the focus on SHCM may divert attention from systemic issues that contribute to employee dissatisfaction and well-being disparities (Banerjee in Cross Cult Manag Int J 20:216–234, 2013; Djuric and Filipovic in Sustain Dev 23(6), 343–354, 2015a). It's also noted that too much focus on SHCM might distract from systemic issues affecting employee satisfaction and well-being (Banerjee in Cross Cult Manag Int J 20:216–234, 2013; Djuric and Filipovic in Sustain Dev 23(6), 343–354, 2015a). The responsibility for well-being should extend beyond individual organizations to include broader societal and governmental efforts addressing factors like income inequality, healthcare accessibility, and labour rights. This chapter explores the complex relationship between SHCM, employee well-being, and organizational growth. Specifically focused on the United Arab Emirates (UAE), it looks into the strategies, benefits, and challenges of implementing SHCM practices that align human welfare with business progress. The study is built on a solid theoretical foundation, guiding the exploration of SHCM within a scholarly framework. The chapter outlines effective SHCM implementation strategies drawn from case studies, emphasizing leadership commitment, employee engagement, precise performance measurement, and a dedication to continuous improvement. It also acknowledges the challenges organizations may face on their SHCM journey and looks ahead to the future of SHCM considering

A. L. Issac (✉)
Westford University College, Sharjah, United Arab Emirates
e-mail: anu.lydia@gmail.com

© The Author(s), under exclusive license to Springer Nature Singapore Pte Ltd. 2024   37
M. Kooskora and A. Kekkonen (eds.), *Performance Challenges in Organizational Sustainability*, Responsible Leadership and Sustainable Management,
https://doi.org/10.1007/978-981-97-5548-6_3

trends, technologies, and societal changes. Ultimately, the chapter envisions an environment where employee well-being thrives, driving organizations towards holistic and enduring growth.

Keywords Sustainable human capital management · Employee well-being · Social exchange theory · Ethical leadership · Cultural nuances

3.1 Introduction

3.1.1 Sustainable Human Capital Management (SHCM)

Sustainable Human Capital Management (SHCM) represents a strategic approach to organizational management that seeks to balance the well-being and development of employees with long-term organizational growth, while also considering broader societal and environmental impacts. At its core, SHCM involves practices that ensure the holistic welfare of employees, recognizing that their well-being is intricately tied to the overall sustainability of an organization (Laskowska & Laskowski, 2022).

In essence, SHCM goes beyond traditional human resource management by integrating sustainability principles into the core of workforce strategies. Sustainability in human capital management is closely aligned with the three pillars of sustainability: economic, social, and environmental (Hitka et al., 2019b). Economically, SHCM aims to enhance organizational performance and competitiveness by fostering a skilled, motivated, and engaged workforce. Socially, it prioritizes the well-being, diversity, and inclusivity of employees, acknowledging that a thriving and satisfied workforce contributes to social stability and cohesion (Markaryan & Mezinova, 2023). Environmentally, SHCM considers the impact of organizational practices on the broader ecological context, promoting responsible resource use, minimizing waste, and aligning with environmentally conscious principles (Madero-Gómez et al., 2023).

By integrating these three pillars into its framework, SHCM not only addresses the immediate needs of employees and organizations but also recognizes the interconnectedness of human capital with larger societal and environmental concerns. This approach fosters a sustainable and resilient organizational culture, ensuring that growth is achieved without compromising the well-being of employees, the community, or the environment (Cheng et al., 2023; Shen et al., 2022). In essence, Sustainable Human Capital Management embodies a forward-thinking paradigm that reflects a commitment to creating lasting value for both individuals and the broader ecosystem in which organizations operate (Djuric & Filipovic, 2015b; Kimbu et al., 2019; Sukalova, 2020).

3.1.2 Unravelling the Tensions Between Employee Well-Being and Organizational Growth

The dynamic interplay between employee well-being and organizational growth encapsulates a perennial struggle within the modern workplace. On the surface, they appear as two complementary objectives, promising a harmonious coexistence. However, a critical examination reveals that beneath this facade lies a complex web of tensions that challenge the very foundations of sustainable human capital management. At the heart of this tension lies the fundamental question of priorities. Organizations, driven by the imperatives of competition and survival, are often compelled to prioritize short-term financial gains over the long-term well-being of their workforce. This inherent conflict of interest is exacerbated by the prevailing economic paradigm that places relentless pressure on businesses to maximize profits and shareholder value. In this milieu, the welfare of employees can become a secondary consideration, leading to decisions that compromise well-being for immediate financial gains (McGuire & McLaren, 2009). Moreover, the metrics used to quantify organizational success often perpetuate this tension. Traditional performance indicators tend to focus on quantifiable outputs, such as revenue, profit margins, and market share. These metrics, while essential for evaluating organizational performance, do not capture the intangible, yet crucial, aspects of employee well-being. Consequently, initiatives that promote employee welfare, such as flexible work arrangements, mental health support, and professional development opportunities, may not receive the attention or resources they deserve, further exacerbating the tension (Wattoo et al., 2018).

Cultural and societal norms also play a pivotal role in shaping this dynamic. In certain cultural contexts, the emphasis on hierarchies and rigid organizational structures may clash with the principles of employee empowerment and well-being. This clash is particularly evident in regions like the United Arab Emirates, where traditional values intersect with the demands of a rapidly evolving global business landscape (Jaiswal & Dyaram, 2020). The tensions between honouring cultural heritage and embracing progressive organizational practices underscore the complexities faced by organizations in navigating this delicate balance. Furthermore, the very nature of growth can be at odds with employee well-being. Rapid expansion, mergers, and acquisitions, while instrumental in achieving organizational objectives, can place immense strain on employees. Increased workloads, uncertainty, and changes in organizational culture can all contribute to heightened stress levels and decreased well-being (Singh & Jha, 2022). This tension between the imperative for growth and the toll it may take on employees is a critical consideration for organizations seeking to navigate this complex landscape. In confronting these tensions, organizations must resist the temptation to view employee well-being and organizational growth as mutually exclusive goals. Instead, they must recognize the potential for synergies (Oja et al., 2019). Studies have shown that a motivated, engaged, and healthy workforce is more productive and innovative, ultimately contributing to organizational success. Moreover, a positive workplace culture that prioritizes well-being can enhance employee retention, reducing recruitment and training costs in the long run (Teetzen, 2023). The tensions between employee well-being and organizational growth are not merely challenges to be overcome, but rather fundamental dynamics that shape the contemporary workplace. Recognizing and addressing these tensions requires a nuanced and holistic approach that places employee well-being at the core of organizational strategy (Djuric & Filipovic, 2015b; Jaiswal & Dyaram, 2020; McGuire & McLaren, 2009). Only through this approach can organizations hope to navigate this intricate landscape and truly reap the benefits of a thriving, sustainable workforce.

3.2 Interrogating Theoretical Foundations of SHCM

3.2.1 Human Capital Theory: Rethinking the Notion of "Valuable Assets"

Human Capital Theory, a cornerstone of Sustainable Human Capital Management (SHCM), stands as a seminal concept in understanding the role of employees within an organization. It posits that individuals, through their skills, knowledge, and experiences, constitute valuable assets that contribute to both personal and organizational development. However, a critical examination of this theory prompts a reevaluation of the notion of employees as mere assets, revealing both its strengths and limitations (Marginson, 2019).

At its core, Human Capital Theory offers a paradigm shift in viewing employees as more than just costs or liabilities on a balance sheet. It acknowledges the intrinsic value of their intellectual capital and the potential for this capital to be appreciated through investment in training, education, and skill development. This perspective, when integrated into SHCM, forms the bedrock for prioritizing employee development, thereby enhancing their well-being and, consequently, propelling organizational growth (Tan, 2014). However, the application of Human Capital Theory raises a series of critical questions. Firstly, it presupposes a level playing field, where all employees have equal access to opportunities for skill development and advancement. This assumption neglects the systemic barriers, such as discrimination, bias, and unequal access to resources, that often impede certain groups from fully realizing their potential (Ray et al., 2023). It is crucial, therefore, to recognize that not all employees start from the same baseline and to address these disparities in SHCM practices. Furthermore, the theory inherently commodifies labour, reducing the complex capabilities and contributions of individuals to quantifiable units of productivity. This reductionist perspective can lead to a dehumanizing effect, where employees are viewed primarily as instruments for achieving organizational objectives, rather than as autonomous individuals with their own aspirations and needs (Lepak & Snell, 1999). It is incumbent upon organizations to balance the utilization of human capital for productivity with a genuine respect for the dignity and autonomy of employees.

Moreover, Human Capital Theory tends to emphasize the instrumental value of employees in achieving organizational goals, often overlooking their intrinsic worth as individuals. This instrumentalization can lead to a transactional approach to employee development, where investments are made primarily for the purpose of extracting maximum productivity (Sweetland, 1996). This runs the risk of neglecting the broader holistic development of employees and their overall well-being. Additionally, Human Capital Theory assumes a linear and direct correlation between investments in employee development and organizational performance. While there is evidence to suggest a positive relationship, it is important to recognize that this relationship may be subject to diminishing returns. Overemphasis on human capital investments without a concurrent focus on other organizational factors, such as culture, leadership, and market dynamics, may not always yield commensurate returns (Gillies, 2015; Marginson, 2019; Ray et al., 2023; Tan, 2014; Teetzen, 2023). Human Capital Theory, while providing a valuable framework for understanding the contributions of employees to organizational success, necessitates a critical examination of its assumptions and potential limitations. To truly realize the potential of SHCM, organizations must go beyond viewing employees as mere assets and instead foster a culture that values their intrinsic worth, addresses systemic disparities, and balances instrumental goals with a genuine respect for individual well-being and autonomy (Gillies, 2015). Only through this nuanced approach can organizations harness the true potential of their human capital.

3.2.2 Social Exchange Theory: Trust, Power, and Exploitation in Organizational Relationships

Exploring the intricate dynamics of organizational relationships, the Social Exchange Theory provides a valuable lens. It suggests that individuals engage in social exchanges, expecting benefits in return for their contributions. Within this framework, crucial themes such as trust, power dynamics, and the potential for exploitation come to the forefront.

A critical examination of these elements reveals both the strengths and limitations of applying Social Exchange Theory in the context of modern workplaces (Lawler & Thye, 1999).

Trust forms the bedrock of any successful social exchange. In organizational relationships, trust is a multifaceted construct, encompassing beliefs about the reliability, integrity, and competence of others. When trust is established, individuals are more likely to engage in reciprocal exchanges, believing that their contributions will be met with fairness and mutual benefit. This trust serves as the foundation for collaborative efforts, open communication, and a positive work environment. However, the fragility of trust also exposes vulnerabilities within organizational relationships (Lambe et al., 2001). Breach of trust can have far-reaching consequences, eroding the willingness of individuals to engage in social exchanges. Instances of betrayal, dishonesty, or inconsistent behaviour can lead to a breakdown in relationships, resulting in reduced cooperation and a more transactional approach to interactions. This highlights the delicate nature of trust within the Social Exchange Theory framework and under-scores the need for organizations to prioritize transparency and ethical behaviour. Power dynamics are another critical dimension of organizational relationships within the context of Social Exchange Theory (Mitchell et al., 2012). Power disparities can significantly influence the nature of social exchanges, as individuals with greater power may have more control over resources and rewards. This can lead to a dynamic of dependency, where those with less power may feel compelled to comply with the demands or expectations of those in positions of authority. Such power imbalances can create an environment ripe for potential exploitation (Cropanzano & Mitchell, 2005a).

Exploitation within organizational relationships is a contentious issue that warrants careful consideration. While Social Exchange Theory assumes that exchanges are mutually beneficial, the reality is more complex. Instances of exploita-tion may arise when one party leverages its power to extract disproportionate benefits from the relationship, often at the expense of the other party. This can manifest in various forms, such as unequal distribution of resources, unfair work assignments, or even psychological manipulation. Organizations must be vigilant in identifying and addressing instances of potential exploitation to maintain a healthy and equitable work environment (Cook et al., 2013a). Moreover, the intersection of trust, power dynamics, and potential exploitation underscores the need for organizations to estab-lish clear norms, policies, and ethical guidelines. Creating a culture of transparency, fairness, and accountability can mitigate the risks associated with power imbalances and foster an environment where trust can thrive. The application of Social Exchange Theory in understanding organizational relationships provides valuable insights into the dynamics of trust, power, and the potential for exploitation. While trust forms the cornerstone of reciprocal exchanges, it is vulnerable to breaches that can have far-reaching consequences (Cropanzano & Mitchell, 2005a; Lambe et al., 2001; Mitchell et al., 2012). Power dynamics introduce complexities, potentially leading to imbalances that require careful management. The potential for exploitation under-scores the importance of ethical considerations within organizational relationships. By navigating these elements with sensitivity and vigilance, organizations can culti-vate healthy, mutually beneficial exchanges that contribute to a positive and produc-tive work environment (Cook et al., 2013a; Cropanzano & Mitchell, 2005a; Lambe et al., 2001).

3.2.3   Work-Life Balance: Liberation or Illusion in the UAE Work Landscape?

Exploring the intricacies of achieving a harmonious balance between professional commitments and personal well-being, "Navigating Work-Life Balance in the UAE

Work Landscape" delves into the unique context of the United Arab Emirates (UAE). This examination critically uncovers the complexities inherent in the pursuit of work-life balance, prompting questions about its feasibility and genuine attainability in the dynamic work environment of the UAE.

At first glance, the UAE's cosmopolitan cities and thriving economy may present an enticing environment for professionals seeking a balanced lifestyle (Oja et al., 2019; Singh & Jha, 2022; Teetzen, 2023). The presence of multinational corporations, a burgeoning entrepreneurial ecosystem, and a vibrant social scene contribute to an image of a work environment that is conducive to achieving work-life balance. The UAE's government has also taken steps to promote employee well-being, such as introducing flexible work arrangements and initiatives to improve the quality of life for residents. However, a closer examination reveals a more nuanced reality (McGuire & McLaren, 2009; Shen et al., 2021). The fast-paced nature of many industries in the UAE, particularly those related to finance, technology, and hospitality, can create an environment that demands long hours and high levels of dedication. The pressure to meet ambitious targets and maintain a competitive edge in a global market may inadvertently erode the boundaries between work and personal life (Cheng et al., 2023; Djuric and Filipovic, 2015b; Kimbu et al., 2019; Sukalova, 2020).

Moreover, cultural norms in the UAE place a strong emphasis on loyalty, commitment, and dedication to one's job. This cultural backdrop can create expectations of extended working hours and a willingness to prioritize professional responsibilities over personal pursuits. The pursuit of work-life balance may be perceived as a departure from these expectations, potentially leading to feelings of guilt or apprehension among employees (Hitka et al., 2019a; Markaryan & Mezinova, 2023). Additionally, the transient nature of the expatriate workforce in the UAE adds another layer of complexity to the work-life balance equation. Many professionals in the UAE are expatriates, and the inherent transience of expat life can lead to a desire to make the most of career opportunities during their tenure in the country. This can result in a willingness to invest substantial time and effort into their professional roles, potentially at the expense of personal pursuits (Guest, 2002; Khan & Fazili, 2016; Kutaula et al., 2020). Furthermore, the blurred boundaries between work and personal life in the digital age pose a significant challenge to achieving work-life balance. The ubiquity of technology means that professionals are often connected to their work around the clock, making it challenging to disconnect and allocate dedicated time to personal endeavours. While the dynamic work environment and vibrant lifestyle may initially appear conducive to achieving balance, the pressures of demanding industries, cultural expectations, the transient nature of the expat workforce, and the pervasive influence of technology all contribute to a more intricate reality. Organizations and individuals alike must engage in thoughtful reflection and proactive measures to navigate these complexities and strive for a work-life equilibrium that aligns with their values and priorities (Cook et al., 2013b; Cook & Rice, 2013; Cropanzano and Mitchell, 2005b; Ehnert & Harry, 2012; Seeck & Parzefall, 2008).

3.2.4   Flexibility or Exploitation? Rethinking Work-Life Balance Policies

"Flexibility or Exploitation? Rethinking Work-Life Balance Policies" scrutinizes the evolving landscape of work-life balance initiatives within organizations. While these policies are designed to offer greater flexibility and support to employees, a critical examination reveals the potential for unintended consequences and exploitative practices (Chams & García-Blandón, 2019; Djuric & Filipovic, 2015a; Ehnert, 2009).

On the surface, work-life balance policies are hailed as a progressive step towards creating a more inclusive and accommodating work environment. These policies encompass a range of initiatives, including flexible work hours, telecommuting options, and paid parental leave. They are designed to empower employees to better manage their professional and personal responsibilities, thereby enhancing their overall well-being. However, a closer look uncovers the potential pitfalls of these policies. The implementation of flexible work arrangements, for instance, can inadvertently blur the boundaries between work and personal life (Cropanzano and Mitchell, 2005b; Ehnert & Harry, 2012; Seeck & Parzefall, 2008; Taylor et al., 2006). The freedom to work remotely or set flexible hours may lead to an "always-on" mentality, where employees feel compelled to be constantly available, even during their designated personal time. This erodes the distinction between work and leisure, potentially resulting in heightened stress levels and decreased overall well-being. Furthermore, the expectation of constant availability in a flexible work environment may exacerbate feelings of job insecurity (Guest, 2002; Khan & Fazili, 2016; Kutaula et al., 2020). Employees may feel pressured to demonstrate their commitment and availability, fearing that failure to do so may jeopardize their standing within the organization. This dynamic can lead to a paradoxical situation where the very policies designed to enhance work-life balance inadvertently contribute to heightened stress and job insecurity.

Paid parental leave policies, while undoubtedly a step in the right direction towards supporting families, also warrant critical consideration. The implementation of such policies can inadvertently reinforce traditional gender roles, assuming that it is primarily mothers who require time off for childcare (Andersson & Formica, 2018; Delecta, 2011; Laskowska & Laskowski, 2022). This can inadvertently perpetuate gender disparities in the workplace and hinder progress towards true gender equality. Moreover, the availability of work-life balance policies can vary significantly depending on the industry, organizational size, and level of job security. In some industries or roles, particularly those with high levels of competition or demanding client expectations, the uptake of flexible work arrangements may be viewed as a sign of reduced commitment (Cropanzano & Mitchell, 2005b; Seeck & Parzefall, 2008; Taylor et al., 2006).

This creates a potential barrier for employees who may be hesitant to utilize these policies due to perceived professional consequences. Additionally, the potential for exploitation of flexible work arrangements cannot be ignored. In some cases, organizations may use these policies as cost-cutting measures, reducing overhead expenses associated with office space and utilities (Fleischhauer, 2007; Nafukho et al., 2004; Strober, 1990). This can inadvertently shift the burden of costs and responsibilities onto individual employees, who may be required to provide their own workspace, equipment, and resources. "Flexibility or Exploitation? Rethinking Work-Life Balance Policies" highlights the need for a critical and nuanced evaluation of work-life balance initiatives. While these policies hold the potential to enhance employee well-being and satisfaction, they also introduce complexities and potential risks. Organizations must approach the implementation of such policies with a keen awareness of the potential unintended consequences and work towards fostering a culture that supports true work-life balance without compromising employee well-being.

3.3 Case Studies in SHCM: Lessons from the UAE

3.3.1 Case Study 1: Etihad Airways—Elevating Innovation and Productivity Through Sustainable Human Capital Management (SHCM)

Introduction:

Etihad Airways, the national airline of the United Arab Emirates (UAE), has emerged as a prominent player in the global aviation industry. This case study critically examines how Etihad Airways has leveraged Sustainable Human Capital Management (SHCM) principles to foster innovation, enhance productivity, and drive organizational success in the unique context of the UAE (Bahman & Shaker, 2023).

SHCM Initiatives at Etihad Airways:

Continuous Learning and Development: Etihad Airways places a strong emphasis on employee skill development through comprehensive training programs. These initiatives aim to enhance employee competencies and align them with the dynamic demands of the aviation industry.

Diversity and Inclusion: Recognizing the multicultural nature of its workforce and the broader UAE context, Etihad Airways promotes diversity and inclusion. This approach not only fosters a culture of mutual respect but also brings diverse perspectives to problem-solving and innovation.

Employee Well-being Programs: Etihad Airways offers a range of well-being initiatives, including access to healthcare facilities, wellness programs, and mental health support. These programs are designed to prioritize employee health and work-life balance (Bahman & Shaker, 2023; Rakesh Jory et al., 2019; Tarihi and Sandybayev Asst., 2018).

Positive Outcomes:

Etihad Airways' Commitment to SHCM Has Yielded Positive Outcomes:

Innovation in Customer Experience: The airline has been recognized for its innovative approach to customer service and onboard experience. Initiatives like the "Etihad Innovation Academy" have empowered employees to propose and implement innovative solutions to enhance the passenger journey.

Employee Engagement: Etihad Airways has maintained high levels of employee engagement, with a motivated workforce contributing to improved customer service and operational efficiency.

Operational Excellence: By investing in employee development and well-being, Etihad Airways has achieved operational excellence, resulting in on-time performance and customer satisfaction metrics that consistently outperform industry benchmarks (Rakesh Jory et al., 2019; Sen et al., 2017; Tarihi and Sandybayev Asst, 2018).

Challenges and Considerations:

While Etihad Airways' approach to SHCM has been largely successful, it has faced some challenges: Industry Dynamics: The aviation industry is subject to various external factors, including economic fluctuations, geopolitical events, and global health crises. These factors can impact the feasibility of certain SHCM initiatives. Adaptability to Change: In a rapidly evolving industry, employees must be adaptable and receptive to change. Etihad Airways faces the challenge of ensuring that its workforce remains agile and capable of responding to industry shifts (Al-Qemaqchi, 2020; Koppalakrishnan & Muuka, 2022; Sen et al., 2017).

Conclusion:

Etihad Airways' case illustrates how SHCM can be effectively leveraged to drive innovation, enhance productivity, and achieve organizational success in the UAE context. By prioritizing employee development, well-being, and diversity, Etihad Airways has demonstrated that a strategic approach to human capital management can yield significant positive outcomes. However, it also highlights the need for organizations to navigate industry-specific challenges and maintain a balance between innovation, employee well-being, and adaptability in a rapidly changing landscape (Al-Qemaqchi, 2020; Rakesh Jory et al., 2019; Sen et al., 2017; Tarihi and Sandybayev Asst, 2018).

3.3.2   Case Study 2: Emirates Group—Sustainable Human Capital Management (SHCM) in a Large-Scale Organization

Introduction:

Emirates Group, a global aviation conglomerate headquartered in Dubai, UAE, is renowned for its expansive operations encompassing airlines, travel services, and aviation-related businesses. This case study critically examines how Emirates Group has implemented SHCM principles to enhance employee well-being, foster a culture of innovation, and sustain organizational growth in the context of the UAE (Katzman, 2017; Anwar & Sadiq Sohail, 2004).

3.4   SHCM Initiatives at Emirates Group:

Career Development and Training Programs: Emirates Group prioritizes employee development through comprehensive training and development programs. These initiatives are designed to enhance skills, promote career progression, and align employees' competencies with the evolving demands of the aviation industry. Diversity and Inclusion: Recognizing the diverse demographics of its workforce and the multicultural nature of the UAE, Emirates Group emphasizes diversity and inclusion. This approach creates an inclusive work environment and leverages a wide range of perspectives for creative problem-solving (Gallant & Pounder, 2008; Lusk & Mook, 2020).

Health and Wellness Initiatives: Emirates Group places a strong emphasis on employee well-being through various health and wellness programs, including access to healthcare facilities, fitness centres, and mental health support. These initiatives contribute to employee health and work-life balance (Katzman, 2017; Lusk & Mook, 2020; Anwar & Sadiq Sohail, 2004).

Positive Outcomes:

Emirates Group's Commitment to SHCM Has Led to Numerous Positive Outcomes:

Operational Excellence: The organization's emphasis on employee development and well-being has translated into operational excellence. The airline consistently maintains high on-time performance and safety standards, contributing to its reputation for reliability.

Innovation and Customer Experience: Emirates Group's culture of continuous learning and diversity has fostered innovation in customer service and operations.

Initiatives like the "Emirates Innovation Lab" have empowered employees to propose and implement creative solutions, enhancing the passenger experience.

High Employee Engagement: Emirates Group maintains a motivated workforce, resulting in high levels of employee engagement. Engaged employees contribute to improved customer service, operational efficiency, and a positive organizational culture (Gallant & Pounder, 2008; Hammad et al., 2017; Lambert, 2008; Reisinger et al., 2019).

Challenges and Considerations:

While Emirates Group's approach to SHCM has been successful, it has faced some challenges:

Global Industry Dynamics: The aviation industry is highly sensitive to global events, including economic fluctuations, geopolitical tensions, and public health crises. These external factors can impact the feasibility of certain SHCM initiatives.

Rapid Technological Advancements: The aviation industry is subject to rapid technological advancements, requiring employees to continually upskill. This can create pressure and a need for adaptability among the workforces (Hammad et al., 2017; Nadkarni & Haider, 2022; Seshadri et al., 2023; Yasin & Gilani, 2022).

Conclusion:

Emirates Group's case serves as a compelling example of how SHCM can be effectively implemented in a large-scale organization within the UAE. By prioritizing employee development, well-being, and diversity, Emirates Group has demonstrated that a strategic approach to human capital management can yield significant positive outcomes. However, it also underscores the importance of addressing industry-specific challenges and maintaining a balance between innovation, employee well-being, and adaptability in a dynamic and globally influenced industry (Awad et al., 2022; Hammad et al., 2019; Picton, 2010; United Arab Emirates, 2023; United Arab Emirates University, 2022).

3.4.1   Case Study 3: Hub71—Fostering Innovation and Community Through Sustainable Human Capital Management (SHCM)

Introduction:

Hub71, located in Abu Dhabi, UAE, is a prominent technology ecosystem that provides support and resources for startups and tech companies. This case study critically examines how Hub71 has implemented SHCM principles to cultivate a thriving community, drive innovation, and facilitate sustainable growth within the unique context of the UAE (McGuire & McLaren, 2009; Wattoo et al., 2018).

SHCM Initiatives at Hub71:

Entrepreneurial Support Programs: Hub71 offers a range of support programs tailored to the needs of startups, including mentorship, funding opportunities, and access to a global network of investors and partners. These initiatives aim to nurture innovation and provide the necessary resources for entrepreneurial success.

Community Building Events: Hub71 organizes regular events, workshops, and networking sessions to facilitate collaboration and knowledge-sharing among startups, investors, and industry experts. These events create a sense of community and foster an environment conducive to innovation (Djuric and Filipovic, 2015b; Hitka et al., 2019b).

Diversity and Inclusion: Recognizing the multicultural nature of the UAE and the global startup ecosystem, Hub71 promotes diversity and inclusion. This inclusive approach not only reflects the broader values of the UAE but also enriches the entrepreneurial community by incorporating diverse perspectives and experiences (Cheng et al., 2023; Madero-Gómez et al., 2023; Markaryan & Mezinova, 2023).

Positive Outcomes:

Hub71's Commitment to SHCM Has Resulted in Several Positive Outcomes:

Innovation and Collaboration: The ecosystem's emphasis on community building and support programs has led to increased innovation and collaboration among startups. This has resulted in the development of groundbreaking technologies and solutions (Laskowska and Laskowski, 2022; McGann et al., 2018).

Global Recognition and Attraction of Talent: Hub71 has gained international recognition as a hub for innovation and entrepreneurship. This has attracted startups, talent, and investors from around the world, further contributing to the ecosystem's growth and success.

Entrepreneurial Success Stories: Many startups within Hub71 have achieved significant milestones, including successful funding rounds, product launches, and international expansion. These success stories serve as testament to the effectiveness of Hub71's SHCM initiatives (Cucchiella et al., 2017; Obaideen et al., 2022; Tabasová et al., 2012).

Challenges and Considerations:

While Hub71's approach to SHCM has been successful, it has faced some challenges:

Scaling and Sustaining Growth: As Hub71 continues to grow, maintaining its sense of community and ensuring that support programs remain accessible and impactful for a larger number of startups presents a challenge.

Balancing Global and Local Needs: Catering to the diverse needs of startups from different regions and industries while maintaining a cohesive and supportive community requires careful planning and adaptation (Almohsen, 2023; Juchimiuk, 2022; Mo et al., 2022).

Conclusion:

Hub71's case exemplifies how SHCM can be effectively applied to cultivate community, drive innovation, and facilitate sustainable growth within the UAE's entrepreneurial ecosystem. By prioritizing community building, diversity, and tailored support programs, Hub71 has created an environment where startups can thrive. However, it also underscores the importance of addressing challenges associated with growth and ensuring that the ecosystem continues to adapt to the evolving needs of its diverse community of entrepreneurs (International Conference, 2022; Karthiga, 2022; Liu et al., 2023; Otivriyanti et al., 2023).

Through these cases, the chapter aims to establish a tangible link between the earlier-discussed theoretical underpinnings and real-world examples, demonstrating how organizations in the UAE navigate challenges and leverage opportunities to integrate employee well-being with organizational growth. These case studies serve as illustrative instances derived through a comprehensive literature review, providing valuable insights into the implementation of SHCM strategies by prominent organizations. The compilation of these cases is rooted in a comprehensive review of existing literature, organizational reports, and industry analyses, establishing a solid foundation for comprehending the nuanced dynamics of SHCM in practice.

3.5   Challenges in SHCM Implementation

3.5.1   Short-Term Financial Pressures vs. Long-Term Well-Being:

The tension between short-term financial pressures and long-term well-being objectives is a perennial challenge in the realm of Sustainable Human Capital Management (SHCM). Organizations often find themselves at a crossroads, torn between immediate financial imperatives and the more enduring goal of fostering employee well-being. This critical analysis delves into the complexities of this dichotomy, examining its implications for organizational ethics, employee satisfaction, and sustainable growth (Grimstad, 2011a).

The Primacy of Short-Term Financial Pressures:

In today's hyper-competitive business landscape, organizations often face intense pressure to deliver short-term financial results. Shareholders, investors, and market analysts scrutinize quarterly performance, demanding tangible returns on investments. This environment can create a myopic focus on immediate profitability, potentially leading to decisions that compromise long-term well-being objectives (Dao et al., 2011; Fathi et al., 2023).

The Aspiration for Long-Term Well-Being:

Conversely, the pursuit of sustainable growth hinges on the belief that prioritizing employee well-being is an investment in the organization's future success. By nurturing a motivated, skilled, and engaged workforce, organizations anticipate reaping long-term benefits in the form of increased productivity, innovation, and reduced turnover. This perspective sees well-being not as a cost, but as a strategic imperative (Dao et al., 2011; Dimmock & Musa, 2015; Ghosh et al., 2022).

Ethical Dilemmas and Organizational Integrity:

The tension between short-term financial pressures and long-term well-being objectives raises profound ethical dilemmas. Organizations must grapple with questions of integrity and responsibility. Does maximizing short-term profits at the potential expense of employee well-being align with the organization's values and ethical commitments? Striking a balance between immediate financial imperatives and a long-term well-being vision is a litmus test of an organization's commitment to its stakeholders (Czech, 2008; Grimstad, 2011b; Seraphin, 2022).

Impact on Employee Morale and Satisfaction:

The prioritization of short-term financial gains can have a direct impact on employee morale and satisfaction. When employees perceive that their well-being is compromised for the sake of short-term profits, it can lead to diminished trust, reduced job satisfaction, and a sense of disengagement. This, in turn, may have detrimental effects on productivity and organizational culture (Du et al., 2020; Thomas & Mishra, 2022; Tsujimoto, 2022).

Long-Term Implications for Organizational Growth:

While short-term financial gains may provide immediate gratification, the neglect of well-being objectives can have far-reaching consequences. A workforce that feels undervalued or disregarded is less likely to invest discretionary effort or remain committed to the organization in the long run. This can lead to higher turnover rates and reduced organizational resilience in the face of future challenges (Arabianbusiness, 2021; Singh, 2015).

Finding a Harmonious Balance:

Balancing short-term financial pressures with long-term well-being objectives is a formidable task, but not an insurmountable one. Organizations that cultivate a strategic vision emphasizing the symbiotic relationship between financial performance and employee well-being are better positioned to navigate this tension. This entails judicious decision-making that considers both immediate financial imperatives and the enduring value of a thriving workforce (Al-Shihabi et al., 2023; Haneef & Ansari, 2019; Olson, 2022).

The tension between short-term financial pressures and long-term well-being objectives is an inherent challenge in SHCM. Organizations must grapple with the ethical implications of their decisions and recognize that sustainable growth necessitates a holistic approach that values both financial performance and employee well-being. By navigating this tension with wisdom and foresight, organizations can forge a path towards enduring success and ethical leadership in the dynamic landscape of modern business (Andersson & Formica, 2018; Hitka et al., 2019a; Markaryan & Mezinova, 2023).

3.5.2   Cultural and Contextual Variances in SHCMs

The implementation of Sustainable Human Capital Management (SHCM) practices is not a one-size-fits-all endeavour. Cultural and contextual variances play a pivotal role in shaping how SHCM strategies are conceived, executed, and perceived across different organizational settings. This critical analysis delves into the intricate interplay between culture, context, and SHCM, highlighting the need for nuanced approaches that resonate with the specific values, norms, and circumstances of diverse work environments.

The Influence of Cultural Norms:

Culture serves as the bedrock upon which organizational practices are constructed. It encompasses deeply ingrained values, beliefs, and behaviours that shape how individuals perceive work, interact with colleagues, and interpret organizational objectives. SHCM initiatives must be attuned to these cultural nuances to be embraced and integrated effectively (Andersson & Formica, 2018; Delecta, 2011; Guest, 2002).

Adaptation to Local Contexts:

The contextual factors of a specific region or industry significantly impact the feasibility and reception of SHCM practices. For instance, the regulatory environment, labour laws, and prevailing industry norms can either facilitate or hinder the implementation of certain well-being initiatives. A SHCM strategy that thrives in one setting may encounter resistance or face logistical challenges in another (Kutaula et al., 2020; Seeck & Parzefall, 2008; Taylor et al., 2006).

Diversity and Inclusion in Practice:

A critical aspect of SHCM involves fostering diversity and inclusion within the workforce. However, the meaning and implications of diversity can vary drastically across cultures. Understanding how different cultures perceive and navigate issues related to diversity and inclusion is crucial for tailoring SHCM practices to resonate with the values and expectations of diverse workforces (Cook et al., 2013b; Cropanzano & Mitchell, 2005b; Fleischhauer, 2007).

Communication Styles and Feedback Mechanisms:

The way feedback is delivered and received can be heavily influenced by cultural norms. Some cultures may prioritize direct and candid communication, while others may value more nuanced and indirect forms of feedback. This variance necessitates thoughtful consideration of how performance evaluations and feedback mechanisms are structured within SHCM frameworks (Nafukho et al., 2004; Strober, 1990).

Ethical Considerations and Value Alignment:

SHCM initiatives must align with the ethical values and moral compass of the local culture. What is considered ethically responsible and socially acceptable can vary significantly from one context to another. Therefore, a SHCM strategy that is perceived as ethically sound in one cultural setting may face scepticism or even rejection in another (Djuric and Filipovic, 2015a; Ehnert & Harry, 2012; Nafukho et al., 2004).

Practical Implementation Challenges:

Case studies and best practices in SHCM provide valuable insights, but they should not be applied indiscriminately across all cultural and contextual settings. The practical implementation of SHCM initiatives requires a deep understanding of the unique challenges, opportunities, and sensitivities specific to each environment. The success of SHCM hinges on its ability to navigate and adapt to cultural and contextual variances. Organizations must recognize that there is no universal blueprint for SHCM that applies across all settings. Instead, they should approach SHCM with cultural sensitivity, a willingness to adapt to local contexts, and a commitment to aligning well-being practices with the values and expectations of diverse workforces. By doing so, organizations can create SHCM frameworks that are not only effective but also resonate deeply with the individuals they seek to serve. This nuanced approach holds the key to unlocking the true potential of SHCM in diverse and dynamic global work environments (Banerjee, 2013; Chams & García-Blandón, 2019; Ehnert, 2009).

3.6 Conclusion

The exploration of Sustainable Human Capital Management (SHCM) has yielded critical contributions and findings. Within the theoretical foundations, a reexamination of Human Capital Theory advocated for a holistic perspective, emphasizing the integral role of employee well-being in organizational success (Chams & García-Blandón, 2019; Ehnert, 2009). The exploration of the Social Exchange Theory underscored the pivotal role of trust and ethical considerations in organizational relationships, shedding light on potential challenges like power imbalances and exploitation (Cook & Rice, 2013; Seeck & Parzefall, 2008; Taylor et al., 2006). The scrutiny of work-life balance policies revealed the nuanced relationship between flexibility and potential exploitation, prompting a reevaluation of organizational approaches to safeguard the genuine well-being of the workforce (Cheng et al., 2023; Madero-Gómez et al., 2023). Through insightful case studies, including instances like Etihad Airways, Emirates Group, and Hub71, the tangible impact of SHCM in fostering innovation, productivity, and community building became apparent. Despite these successes, challenges persist, notably the tension between short-term financial pressures and long-term employee well-being, as well as the imperative for organizations to navigate cultural nuances for effective SHCM implementation (Hitka et al., 2019b; Laskowska and Laskowski, 2022). In navigating these complexities with discernment and unwavering commitment, organizations stand poised not only to survive but to thrive in an era marked by evolving expectations, emerging as beacons of ethical leadership shaping a future where employee well-being is inseparable from sustainable organizational success (Guest, 2002; Khan & Fazili, 2016; Kutaula et al., 2020).

References

Almohsen, R. A. (2023). *The Arab world: Scarce data in a water-scarce region.*

Al-Qemaqchi, N. (2020). The international and middle east conference on sustainability and human development (IMES). In *Proceedings of first international and middle east conference on sustainability and sustainable architecture view project design theory view project.*

Al-Shihabi, S., Aydin, R., Hadj-Alouane, A., & Alshanasi, A. (2023). Sustainable technologies, mega-events, and environmental awareness—lessons from expo 2020 dubai. *Frontiers in Sustainable Cities, 5*, Article 1192295. https://doi.org/10.3389/frsc.2023.1192295

Andersson, T., & Formica, P. (2018). Lessons from Abu Dhabi: The road towards an innovative entrepreneurial economy. In P. Formica (Ed.), *Smart tourism as a driver for culture and sustainability* (pp. 543–563). https://doi.org/10.1007/978-3-319-75913-5_20.

Anwar, S. A., & SadiqSohail, M. (2004). Festival tourism in the United Arab Emirates: First-time versus repeat visitor perceptions. *Journal of Vacation Marketing, 10*(2), 161–170.

Arabianbusiness. (2021). Official expo 2020 Dubai song released—'This is our time'.

Awad, J., Arar, M., Jung, C., & Boudiaf, B. (2022). The comparative analysis for the new approach to three tourism-oriented heritage districts in the United Arab Emirates. *Heritage, 5*(3), 2464–2487. https://doi.org/10.3390/heritage5030128

Banerjee, P. M. (2013). Sustainable human capital: Product innovation and employee partnerships in technology firms. *Cross Cultural Management: An International Journal, 20*(2), 216–234. https://doi.org/10.1108/13527601311313481

Bahman, N., & Shaker, M. (2023). Evaluating the effectiveness of sustainable aviation in the Middle East: A study of two UAE-based carriers. *Journal of Airline Operations and Aviation Management, 2*(1), 96–107. https://doi.org/10.56801/jaoam.v2i1.6

Chams, N., & García-Blandón, J. (2019). On the importance of sustainable human resource management for the adoption of sustainable development goals. *Resources, Conservation and Recycling, 141*, 109–122. https://doi.org/10.1016/j.resconrec.2018.10.006

Cheng, Y., Masukujjaman, M., Sobhani, F. A., Hamayun, M., & Alam, S. S. (2023). Green logistics, green human capital, and circular economy: The mediating role of sustainable production. *Sustainability, 15*(2), 1045. https://doi.org/10.3390/su15021045

Cook, K. S., Cheshire, C., Rice, E. R. W., & Nakagawa, S. (2013a). Social exchange theory. In K. Deaux & M. Snyder (Eds.), *The Oxford handbook of personality and social psychology* (pp. 61–88). https://doi.org/10.1007/978-94-007-6772-0_3

Cook, K. S., Cheshire, C., Rice, E. R. W., & Nakagawa, S. (2013b). Social Exchange Theory. In K. Deaux & M. Snyder (Eds.), *The Oxford handbook of personality and social psychology* (pp. 61–88). https://doi.org/10.1007/978-94-007-6772-0_3

Cook, K. S., & Rice, E. (2013c). Social exchange theory. In M. Mikulincer & P.R. Shaver (Eds.), *Handbook of social psychology* (pp. 53–76). https://doi.org/10.1007/0-387-36921-X_3

Cropanzano, R., & Mitchell, M. S. (2005a). Social exchange theory: An interdisciplinary review. *Journal of Management, 31*(6), 874–900. https://doi.org/10.1177/0149206305279602

Cropanzano, R., & Mitchell, M. S. (2005b). Social exchange theory: An interdisciplinary review. *Journal of Management, 31*(6), 874–900. https://doi.org/10.1177/0149206305279602

Cucchiella, F., D'Adamo, I., & Gastaldi, M. (2017). Sustainable waste management: Waste to energy plant as an alternative to landfill. *Energy Conversion and Management, 131*, 18–31. https://doi.org/10.1016/j.enconman.2016.11.012

Czech, B. (2008). Prospects for reconciling the conflict between economic growth and biodiversity conservation with technological progress. *Conservation Biology, 22*(6), 1389–1398. https://doi.org/10.1111/j.1523-1739.2008.01089.x

Dao, V., Langella, I., & Carbo, J. (2011). From green to sustainability: Information Technology and an integrated sustainability framework. *The Journal of Strategic Information Systems, 20*(1), 63–79. https://doi.org/10.1016/j.jsis.2011.01.002

Delecta, P. (2011). Work life balance. *International Journal of Current Research, 3*(4), 186–189.

Dimmock, K., & Musa, G. (2015). Scuba diving tourism system: A framework for collaborative management and sustainability. *Marine Policy, 54*, 52–58. https://doi.org/10.1016/j.marpol.2014.12.008

Djuric, M., & Filipovic, J. (2015a). Human and social capital management based on complexity paradigm: Implications for various stakeholders and sustainable development. *Sustainable Development, 23*(6), 343–354. https://doi.org/10.1002/sd.1595

Djuric, M., & Filipovic, J. (2015b). Human and Social capital management based on complexity paradigm: Implications for various stakeholders and sustainable development. *Sustainable Development, 23*(6), 343–354. https://doi.org/10.1002/sd.1595

Du, H. S., Ke, X., & Wagner, C. (2020). Inducing individuals to engage in a gamified platform for environmental conservation. *Industrial Management & Data Systems, 120*(4), 692–713. https://doi.org/10.1108/IMDS-09-2019-0517

Ehnert, I. (2009). *Sustainable human resource management*. Physica-Verlag HD. https://doi.org/10.1007/978-3-7908-2188-8

Ehnert, I., & Harry, W. (2012). Recent developments and future prospects on sustainable human resource management: introduction to the special issue. *Management Review, 23*(3), 221–238.

Fathi, L. I., Walker, J., Dix, C. F., Cartwright, J. R., Joubert, S., Carmichael, K. A., Huang, Y.-S., et al. (2023). Applying the Integrated Sustainability Framework to explore the long-term sustainability of nutrition education programmes in schools: A systematic review. *Public Health Nutrition*. https://doi.org/10.1017/S1368980023001647

Fleischhauer, K.-J. (2007). A review of human capital theory: Microeconomics. *SSRN Electronic Journal*. https://doi.org/10.2139/ssrn.957993

Gallant, M., & Pounder, J. S. (2008). The employment of female nationals in the United Arab Emirates (UAE). *Education, Business and Society: Contemporary Middle Eastern Issues, 1*(1), 26–33. https://doi.org/10.1108/17537980810861493

Ghosh, S., Balsalobre-Lorente, D., Doğan, B., Paiano, A., & Talbi, B. (2022). Modelling an empirical framework of the implications of tourism and economic complexity on environmental sustainability in G7 economies. *Journal of Cleaner Production, 376*, 134281. https://doi.org/10.1016/j.jclepro.2022.134281

Gillies, D. (2015). Human capital theory in education. *Encyclopedia of Educational Philosophy and Theory, 1–5*. https://doi.org/10.1007/978-981-287-532-7_254-1

Grimstad, S. (2011a). Developing a framework for examining business-driven sustainability initiatives with relevance to wine tourism clusters. *International Journal of Wine Business Research, 23*(1), 62–82. https://doi.org/10.1108/17511061111121416

Grimstad, S. (2011b). Developing a framework for examining business-driven sustainability initiatives with relevance to wine tourism clusters. *International Journal of Wine Business Research, 23*(1), 62–82. https://doi.org/10.1108/17511061111121416

Guest, D. E. (2002). Perspectives on the study of work-life balance. *Social Science Information, 41*(2), 255–279. https://doi.org/10.1177/0539018402041002005

Hammad, N., Ahmad, S. Z., & Papastathopoulos, A. (2017). Residents' perceptions of the impact of tourism in Abu Dhabi, United Arab Emirates. *International Journal of Culture, Tourism and Hospitality Research, 11*(4), 551–572. https://doi.org/10.1108/IJCTHR-04-2017-0048

Hammad, N. M., Ahmad, S. Z., & Papastathopoulos, A. (2019). The moderating role of nationality in residents' perceptions of the impacts of tourism development in the United Arab Emirates. *International Journal of Tourism Research, 21*(1), 61–75. https://doi.org/10.1002/jtr.2241

Haneef, S. K., & Ansari, Z. (2019). Marketing strategies of Expo 2020 Dubai: A comprehensive study. *Worldwide Hospitality and Tourism Themes, 11*(3), 287–297. https://doi.org/10.1108/WHATT-11-2018-0071

Hitka, M., Kucharčíková, A., Štarchoň, P., Balážová, Ž, Lukáč, M., & Stacho, Z. (2019a). Knowledge and human capital as sustainable competitive advantage in human resource management. *Sustainability, 11*(18), 4985. https://doi.org/10.3390/su11184985

Hitka, M., Kucharčíková, A., Štarchoň, P., Balážová, Ž, Lukáč, M., & Stacho, Z. (2019b). Knowledge and human capital as sustainable competitive advantage in human resource management. *Sustainability, 11*(18), 4985. https://doi.org/10.3390/su11184985

International Conference. (2022). Sustainable infrastructure and built environment (SIBE-2022)—challenges on sustainable and resilient infrastructure and built environment. *IOP Conference Series: Earth and Environmental Science, 1065*. https://doi.org/10.1088/1755-1315/1065/1/011001

Jaiswal, A., & Dyaram, L. (2020). Perceived diversity and employee well-being. Mediating role of inclusion. *Personnel Review, 49*(5), 1121–1139. https://doi.org/10.1108/PR-12-2018-0511

Juchimiuk, J. (2022). Renewable energy sources in architecture of the world expo *14*(54). https://doi.org/10.24427/aea-2022-vol14-no4-06

Karthiga, S. N. (2022). Sustainable infrastructure with smart technology for energy and environmental management. *IOP Conference Series: Earth and Environmental Science, 1125*(1), 011001. https://doi.org/10.1088/1755-1315/1125/1/011001

Katzman, K. (2017). *The United Arab Emirates (UAE): Issues for U.S. policy.*

Khan, O. F., & Fazili, A. I. (2016). Work life balance: A conceptual review. *Journal of Strategic Human Resource Management, 5*(2).

Kimbu, A. N., Ngoasong, M. Z., Adeola, O., & Afenyo-Agbe, E. (2019). Collaborative networks for sustainable human capital management in women's tourism entrepreneurship: The role of tourism policy. *Tourism Planning & Development, 16*(2), 161–178. https://doi.org/10.1080/21568316.2018.1556329

Koppalakrishnan, P., & Muuka, G. N. (2022). Strategies to combat the COVID-19 pandemic in the UAE, 68–92. https://doi.org/10.4018/978-1-7998-8451-4.ch004

Kutaula, S., Gillani, A., & Budhwar, P. S. (2020). An analysis of employment relationships in Asia using psychological contract theory: A review and research agenda. *Human Resource Management Review, 30*(4), 100707. https://doi.org/10.1016/j.hrmr.2019.100707

Lambe, C. J., Wittmann, C. M., & Spekman, R. E. (2001). Social Exchange theory and research on business-to-business relational exchange. *Journal of Business-to-Business Marketing, 8*(3), 1–36. https://doi.org/10.1300/J033v08n03_01

Lambert, L. (2008). A counselling model for young women in the united arab emirates: cultural considerations. *Canadian Journal of Counselling/Revue Canadienne de Counseling, 42.*

Laskowska, A., & Laskowski, J. F. (2022). 'Silver' generation at work—implications for sustainable human capital management in the industry 5.0 Era. *Sustainability, 15*(1), 194. https://doi.org/10.3390/su15010194

Lawler, E. J., & Thye, S. R. (1999). Bringing emotions into social exchange theory. *Annual Review of Sociology, 25*(1), 217–244. https://doi.org/10.1146/annurev.soc.25.1.217

Lepak, D. P., & Snell, S. A. (1999). The human resource architecture: Toward a theory of human capital allocation and development. *The Academy of Management Review, 24*(1), 31. https://doi.org/10.2307/259035

Liu, F., Mu, Y., & Chen, Z. (2023). Control strategy for improving the voltage regulation ability of low-carbon energy systems with high proportion of renewable energy integration. *Electronics, 12*(11), 2513. https://doi.org/10.3390/electronics12112513

Lusk, J., & Mook, A. (2020). Hyper-consumption to circular economy in the United Arab Emirates: Discarding the disposable and cherishing the valuable. *Socio Economic Challenges, 4*(3), 33–45. https://doi.org/10.21272/sec.4(3).33-45.2020

Madero-Gómez, S. M., Rubio Leal, Y. L., Olivas-Luján, M., & Yusliza, M. Y. (2023). Companies could benefit when they focus on employee wellbeing and the environment: A systematic review of sustainable human resource management. *Sustainability, 15*(6), 5435. https://doi.org/10.3390/su15065435

Marginson, S. (2019). Limitations of human capital theory. *Studies in Higher Education, 44*(2), 287–301. https://doi.org/10.1080/03075079.2017.1359823

Markaryan, J., & Mezinova, I. (2023). Human capital competitiveness management as a resource for sustainable development. *E3S Web of Conferences, 371*, 05028. https://doi.org/10.1051/e3sconf/202337105028

McGann, M., Blomkamp, E., & Lewis, J. M. (2018). The rise of public sector innovation labs: Experiments in design thinking for policy. *Policy Sciences, 51*(3), 249–267. https://doi.org/10.1007/s11077-018-9315-7

McGuire, D., & McLaren, L. (2009). The impact of physical environment on employee commitment in call centres. *Team Performance Management: An International Journal, 15*(1/2), 35–48. https://doi.org/10.1108/13527590910937702

Mitchell, M. S., Cropanzano, R. S., & Quisenberry, D. M. (2012). Social exchange theory. exchange resources, and interpersonal relationships: A modest resolution of theoretical difficulties.99–118. https://doi.org/10.1007/978-1-4614-4175-5_6

Mo, L., Lin, C., & Hu, H. (2022). *Sustainable design strategy of expo 2020 Dubai.*

Nadkarni, S., & Haider, I. (2022). Digital transformation, operational efficiency and sustainability: Innovation drivers for hospitality's rebound in the United Arab Emirates. *Worldwide Hospitality and Tourism Themes, 14*(6), 572–578. https://doi.org/10.1108/WHATT-05-2022-0054

Nafukho, F. M., Hairston, N., & Brooks, K. (2004). Human capital theory: Implications for human resource development. *Human Resource Development International, 7*(4), 545–551. https://doi.org/10.1080/1367886042000299843

Obaideen, K., Yousef, B. A. A., AlMallahi, M. N., Tan, Y. C., Mahmoud, M., Jaber, H., & Ramadan, M. (2022). An overview of smart irrigation systems using IoT. *Energy Nexus, 7*, 100124. https://doi.org/10.1016/j.nexus.2022.100124

Oja, B. D., Kim, M., Perrewé, P. L., & Anagnostopoulos, C. (2019). Conceptualizing a-hero for sport employees' well-being. *Sport, Business and Management: An International Journal, 9*(4), 363–380. https://doi.org/10.1108/SBM-10-2018-0084

Olson, E. D. (2022). Expo 2020 Dubai world expo (October 1, 2021—March 31, 2022) review. *Journal of Convention & Event Tourism, 23*(4), 362–364. https://doi.org/10.1080/15470148.2022.2068718

Otivriyanti, G., Fani, A. M., Yusuf, N. R., Haris, K. A., Alfatri, P., & Purwanta, W. (2023). A study on the implementation of a circular economy in municipal solid waste management in the new capital city of Indonesia. *IOP Conference Series: Earth and Environmental Science, 1201*(1), 012005. https://doi.org/10.1088/1755-1315/1201/1/012005

Picton, O. J. (2010). Usage of the concept of culture and heritage in the United Arab Emirates—an analysis of Sharjah heritage area. *Journal of Heritage Tourism, 5*(1), 69–84. https://doi.org/10.1080/17438730903469813

Rakesh Jory, S., Benamraoui, A., Tunahan, H., Üniversitesi, S., Sanem Çitçi, U., & Bakırçay Üniversitesi, İ. (2019). *A critical examination of Etihad airways equity alliance strategy using a case study approach.*

Ray, C., Nyberg, A. J., & Maltarich, M. A. (2023). Human capital resources emergence theory: The role of social capital. *Academy of Management Review, 48*(2), 313–335. https://doi.org/10.5465/amr.2020.0186

Reisinger, Y., Michael, N., & Hayes, J. P. (2019). Destination competitiveness from a tourist perspective: A case of the United Arab Emirates. *International Journal of Tourism Research, 21*(2), 259–279. https://doi.org/10.1002/jtr.2259

Seeck, H., & Parzefall, M. (2008). Employee agency: Challenges and opportunities for psychological contract theory. *Personnel Review, 37*(5), 473–489. https://doi.org/10.1108/00483480810891637

Sen, S., Chand, S., Roy, A., Hossain, J., Akhtar, S., & Mukherjee Saha, J. (2017). *Globsyn Management Journal* (GMJ) (Chief Academic Advisor Layout and Cover Design).

Seraphin, H. (2022). Understanding the traits of tourism sustainability activists through a life course framework. *Journal of Policy Research in Tourism, Leisure and Events*, 1–19. https://doi.org/10.1080/19407963.2022.2029873

Seshadri, U., Kumar, P., Vij, A., & Ndlovu, T. (2023). Marketing strategies for the tourism industry in the United Arab Emirates after the COVID-19 era. *Worldwide Hospitality and Tourism Themes, 15*(2), 169–177. https://doi.org/10.1108/WHATT-10-2022-0120

Shen, J., Iandoli, L., & Aguirre-Urreta, M. (2022). Human-centered design for individual and social well- being: Editorial preface. *AIS Transactions on Human-Computer Interaction, 14*(4), 446–460. https://doi.org/10.17705/1thci.00175

Shen, Y., Zheng, Q., Lei, X., & Hu, F. (2021). The influence of top management team human capital on sustainable business growth. *Frontiers in Psychology, 12*. https://doi.org/10.3389/fpsyg.2021.773689

Singh, A., & Jha, S. (2022). Relationship between employee well-being and organizational health: Symbiotic or independent? *Industrial and Commercial Training, 54*(2), 231–249. https://doi.org/10.1108/ICT-03-2021-0018

Singh, B. (2015). Smart city— smart life : Dubai expo 2020. *Middle East Journal of Business, 10*(4), 49–52. https://doi.org/10.5742/MEJB.2015.92720

Strober, M. H. (1990). Human capital theory: Implications for HR managers. *Industrial Relations, 29*(2), 214–239. https://doi.org/10.1111/j.1468-232X.1990.tb00752.x

Sukalova, V. (2020). Psychological aspects of contract in sustainable human capital management. In *Economic and social development: Book of proceedings*, Varazdin.

Sweetland, S. R. (1996). Human capital theory: Foundations of a field of inquiry. *Review of Educational Research, 66*(3), 341–359. https://doi.org/10.3102/00346543066003341

Tabasová, A., Kropáč, J., Kermes, V., Nemet, A., & Stehlík, P. (2012). Waste-to-energy technologies: Impact on environment. *Energy, 44*(1), 146–155. https://doi.org/10.1016/j.energy.2012.01.014

Tan, E. (2014). Human capital theory. *Review of Educational Research, 84*(3), 411–445. https://doi.org/10.3102/0034654314532696

Tarihi, G., & Sandybayev Asst, A. (2018). *Quality and supply chain management integration: A conceptual model at Etihad airways from Turkish.*

Taylor, T., Darcy, S., Hoye, R., & Cuskelly, G. (2006). Using psychological contract theory to explore issues in effective volunteer management. *European Sport Management Quarterly, 6*(2), 123–147. https://doi.org/10.1080/16184740600954122

Teetzen, F. (2023). *Preconditions and mechanisms of leadership: The impact on employee well-being.*

Thomas, A., & Mishra, U. (2022). A green energy circular system with carbon capturing and waste minimization in a smart grid power management. *Energy Reports, 8*, 14102–14123. https://doi.org/10.1016/j.egyr.2022.10.341

Tsujimoto, M. (2022). Achievement of both growth and environmental conservation by digital platform providers. *International Journal of Energy Economics and Policy, 12*(4), 78–86. https://doi.org/10.32479/ijeep.13152

United Arab Emirates, M. of E. (2023). The national entrepreneurship agenda.

United Arab Emirates University. (2022). UAEU keeps pace with the 'year of sustainability' with strategic research projects and high-quality outcomes. Retrieved July 2, 2023 from [https://www.uaeu.ac.ae/en/news/2023/january/uaeu-keeps-pace-with-the-year-of-sustainability-with-strategic-research-projects.shtml

Wattoo, M. A., Zhao, S., & Xi, M. (2018). Perceived organizational support and employee well-being. *Chinese Management Studies, 12*(2), 469–484. https://doi.org/10.1108/CMS-07-2017-0211

Yasin, N., & Gilani, S. A. M. (2022). 'Imitate or incubate?' Evaluating the current state of university-based business incubators in the United Arab Emirates. *FIIB Business Review, 231971452211127*. https://doi.org/10.1177/23197145221112744

Anushka Lydia Issac is a Professor and Program Manager—L3 Pearson Foundation Program at Westford University College, Sharjah, United Arab Emirates. With a background in Engineering [Hons.] and an MBA, she brings a unique perspective. Holding prestigious credentials such as an FHEA and a Lead IQA Certificate, she possesses the skills and knowledge to design, deliver, and assess high-quality learning experiences in higher education. Her passion for understanding people and their personalities has propelled her to excel in communications and public speaking at an international level. As an Professor and Program Manager at Westford University College, she actively contributes to the development of students. Her Ph.D. research from the University of Plymouth, UK focuses on flexible work arrangements.

Chapter 4
The Responsible Marketing Mix: Aligning the 4Ps with Sustainability Dimensions

Katri Kerem⊙

Abstract This chapter explores the integration of environmental, social, and economic sustainability principles into the marketing mix, encompassing product, price, place, and promotion. The author emphasizes a holistic and incremental approach, offering practical insights for businesses seeking sustainable marketing strategies. The chapter highlights key findings, including the need for life cycle sustainability assessments in product development, the delicate balance required in sustainable pricing, the impact of distribution channels on sustainability, and the role of transparent and responsible messaging in promotions. The proposed "responsible marketing mix" serves as both a decision-making tool and an educational resource. By addressing a research gap and emphasizing manageable steps towards sustainability, this approach contributes to a nuanced understanding of sustainable marketing practices, making it accessible for businesses, and providing valuable insights for educators and researchers. The author advocates for a shift from unattainable goals to feasible and practical sustainable marketing, fostering positive impacts on the environment, society, and the economy.

Keywords Sustainability · Marketing · Marketing mix · 4Ps · SMEs

4.1 Introduction

Sustainability has emerged as a prominent topic in various arenas, garnering significant attention from the media, becoming a focal point in business training, and finding its place high on the political agenda. As a result, businesses have been compelled to reassess their practices and align them with evolving sustainability thresholds and objectives. This transformative process, however, presents challenges for business owners and managers who often find themselves grappling with uncertainty and

K. Kerem (✉)
Marketing and Communication Department, Estonian Business School, Tallinn, Estonia
e-mail: Katri.kerem@ebs.ee

© The Author(s), under exclusive license to Springer Nature Singapore Pte Ltd. 2024   61
M. Kooskora and A. Kekkonen (eds.), *Performance Challenges in Organizational Sustainability*, Responsible Leadership and Sustainable Management,
https://doi.org/10.1007/978-981-97-5548-6_4

helplessness due to the substantial changes required. Meeting sustainability goals demands considerable investments in time, resources, and human motivation, which can lead to reluctance in embracing these changes, highlighting the performance challenges in organizational sustainability. Pursuing different sustainability goals is especially challenging for SMEs as they have limited resources and time to devote to multiple and often competing priorities (Khizar et al., 2023).

Moreover, businesses declaring themselves sustainable face heightened scrutiny from discerning consumers and watchdog organizations eager to expose any short-comings, controversies, or non-sustainable practices (Drury, 2021). Obtaining certifications, while crucial for credibility and authenticity, adds another layer of complexity, as the application process is often costly and entails significant changes and paperwork. Consequently, some business owners may be inclined to disregard sustainability issues altogether, viewing it as an all-or-nothing proposition.

Marketing, both as a field of study and a business practice, has frequently been identified as a primary contributor to the adverse sustainability effects of businesses. Martin and colleagues have argued that "Marketing has a well-earned reputation for driving overconsumption and consequentially environmental degradation, income inequity and humanitarian crises" (Martin et al, 2019, p. 72). Borland and Lindgreen (2013) have ironically called marketing and sustainability somewhat unusual bedfellows. The marketing process does indeed serve as a pivotal catalyst for a substantial portion of production-consumption activities. It functions by presenting and promoting consumption prospects that cater to human requirements and desires, effectively spurring economic exchanges and demand for goods and services (Sheth & Parvatiyar, 2021). Within the pursuit of organizational sustainability, challenges stemming from marketing are complex yet crucial. Therefore, it is highly beneficial to scrutinize the path to sustainability by dissecting a company's marketing activities and assessing them through the lens of enhancing sustainability.

Drawing on established theories of human behaviour, it is widely recognized that making incremental progress towards a goal is more effective than pursuing a significant goal all at once or, worse, remaining inactive. Cialdini's well-known statement from 1993 asserts: "Once we have made a choice or taken a stand, we will encounter personal and interpersonal pressures to behave consistently with that commitment. Those pressures will cause us to respond in ways that justify our earlier decision" (Cialdini, 1993). Lang and Goh (2020) contend that the pursuit of consistency is also evident in business contexts, with individuals tending to react and behave in ways that promote consistency, thereby fostering an organizational climate that upholds this principle. Even incremental measures towards sustainability can yield positive outcomes, proving more motivating and ultimately leading to tangible results. Thus, this paper proposes a framework for companies to enhance the sustainability of their marketing activities by incorporating sustainability factors into their strategic decision-making concerning the four key components of the marketing mix. This approach aims to facilitate a gradual and pragmatic path towards sustainability, recognizing that any positive step, no matter how modest, contributes to the overarching goal of building a more sustainable future.

As noted above, among the various business functions, marketing significantly influences the sustainability footprint of the company. Bouzige et al. (2023) attempted to classify the carbon drivers of the marketing mix, distinguishing among direct impact from marketing investments, incremental impact from marketing's role in sales, and long-term impact on social imagery, examining how marketing shapes consumption habits. This categorization aids marketers in outlining various origins and degrees of marketing's influence on sustainability. However, the model's limitation lies in its perspective of viewing marketing activities primarily as communication activities.

Marketing encompasses a comprehensive spectrum of functions that extend beyond mere communication. It includes critical aspects such as product development, pricing strategies, the selection of appropriate sales channels, and, finally, promotional or marketing communication activities. These components collectively constitute the core elements of marketing, known as the "4Ps" (Product, Price, Place, Promotion) (Constantinides, 2006). By focusing solely on communication, an organization overlooks the pivotal role marketing plays in shaping product attributes, setting competitive prices, and determining how and where products or services are made available to consumers. Acknowledging the holistic nature of marketing, which involves every facet of a product's lifecycle, enables a more comprehensive and effective approach to achieving organizational objectives, including sustainability goals.

This conceptual research paper will link the 4Ps of the classical marketing mix to the three dimensions of sustainability. The aim of the paper is to explain and demonstrate how to take into account environmental, social, and economic considerations while designing the actual product offering, crafting pricing strategy, designing promotion messages and channels, and taking decisions about the place of distribution. From the pragmatic point of view, this approach is helpful for small and medium-sized companies which make up 90% of businesses worldwide and over 50% of the global employment but have attracted comparatively limited attention in sustainability research (Khizar et al., 2023). Another key target group of this paper would be marketing and business students and educators who can use this simple framework to get a better understanding of how strategic marketing decisions can contribute to a better future. Catering for the needs of marketing education answers the call by Helm and Little (2022) who emphasized the need for marketing educators to embrace greater social responsibility. They pointed out that progress in this regard has been sluggish, partly due to universities adopting a neoliberal market-oriented approach and competing for tuition-paying students.

4.2   Conceptualizing the Marketing Mix and Sustainability

Both the marketing mix of 4Ps and the concept of sustainability seem to be almost like a common knowledge where specific definitions are not needed, yet an academic approach requires clarifying the meaning of the key constructs. The 4Ps were conceptualized as a marketing mix by McCarthy in 1960, who discussed the 4Ps as the marketing managers framework (McCarthy, 1960). He explained that the customer is the focal point of the marketing decisions, and the marketing manager has to manipulate product, price, place, and promotion variables to create a robust marketing strategy (Anderson & Taylor, 1995).

Booms and Bitner (1981) enhanced the marketing mix for the evolving service economy by introducing three additional elements: people, process, and physical evidence. "People" covers both personnel and customers, "process" outlines the service delivery steps, and "physical evidence" represents environmental factors influencing perceived service quality. While people, customer journey, and service environment are important components of marketing, they encompass several factors that are outside the direct control of the company. Different authors have expanded the mix with several new Ps or created alternative marketing mixes, but consensus regarding eligibility and practical implementation of the subsequent Ps or new marketing mixes has not been established (Goi, 2009).

The marketing mix has faced ongoing criticism since its inception, e.g., from the so-called Nordic school of services marketing (Grönroos, 1994; Gummesson, 1995). However, its enduring presence in academic textbooks and managerial toolkits signifies its lasting value, withstanding the test of time and societal and technological changes. The American Marketing Association, known for regularly updating the definition of marketing, has said in their latest 2017 revision: "Marketing is the activity, set of institutions, and processes for creating, communicating, delivering, and exchanging offerings that have value for customers, clients, partners, and society at large" (AMA, 2023). The definition covers the same set of activities that are part of the marketing mix: creating valuable offering (product/service), communicating the offers (promotion), delivering value (place), and exchanging offerings (price being the key variable in value exchange). The marketing mix of the 4Ps has been found useful in real business settings (Zineldin & Philipson, 2007) and the fiercest critics mostly don't bother to look up the original marketing mix visualization that has consumer placed in the centre of it (Anderson & Taylor, 1995), see Fig. 4.1. The feasibility of marketing mix has been empirically tested for social marketing (Lahtinen et al., 2020) with a conclusion that it is suitable not only for commercial purposes but also for promoting socially desirable behavioural outcomes. Thus for the purpose of discussing how to make marketing more sustainable, the marketing mix approach is robustly suitable as it encompasses factors mostly under the direct control of an organization, thus leaving it with a relative freedom to take sustainability considerations into account while strategically planning each of the Ps.

Sustainable development was defined in 1987 by the UN-sponsored World Commission on Environment and Development in Brundtland report (known as "Our

Fig. 4.1 Consumer-centric 4P approach based on the original conceptualization of McCarthy (McCarthy, 1960)

Common Future") as a development that meets the needs of the present without compromising the ability of future generations to meet their own needs (United Nations, 1987). It aims to harmonize economic growth with the protection of social and environmental equilibrium.

The ubiquitous three-dimensional conception of sustainability with social, economic, and environmental components (also known as three pillars, aspects, factors, etc., see Fig. 4.2) does not seem to have a clear origin (Purvis et al, 2019). The authors argue that the pillars do not often have uniform operationalization but rather just appear in the literature with an assumption that everyone takes these at face value (ibid). The three dimensions of sustainability are also intricately linked and mutually dependent. Human well-being relies on economic activity, which, in turn, is contingent on natural systems (Martin & Schouten, 2014).

A universally accepted definition for each of the three dimensions of sustainability is lacking, and comprehensive discussions on this diversity fall outside the scope of this paper. To maintain clarity, the dimensions are articulated in accordance with Khizar et al. (2023), recognizing that these concepts inherently allow room for differing interpretations.

Economic sustainability refers to the efficient utilization of assets and capabilities to achieve desired economic goals and secure livelihoods. Social sustainability centres on a company's influence on the communities where it functions. It covers factors like equitable labour practices, gender equality, and dedication to human rights. Evaluating a company's social performance involves assessing its reputation as a responsible corporate entity and its commitment to the greater good while meeting the needs of both internal groups (e.g., employees) and external stakeholders (e.g., society and communities). Environmental dimension addresses the sustainable use of natural resources such as energy, land, and water, with the aim of replenishing them and safeguarding the ecosystem in general (Khizar et al., 2023). Within the realm of

Fig. 4.2 The three
dimensions of sustainability
(Purvis et al., 2019)

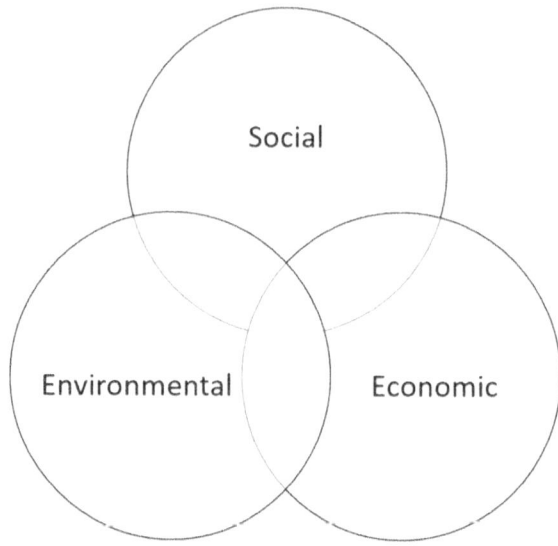

marketing, the concept of sustainability has often been reduced to a narrower interpretation. A significant portion of literature equates sustainable marketing with green
marketing (Dangelico & Vocalelli, 2017), primarily concentrating on environmental
concerns while often overlooking the social and economic dimensions (Jung & Kim,
2023). Therefore it is crucial to consciously address the connections of marketing to
sustainability across all the sustainability dimensions.

4.3 Aligning the 4Ps with Sustainability Dimensions

Martin and Schouten (2014, p. 6) have defined sustainable marketing as "The process
of creating, communicating, and delivering value to customers in such a way that
both natural and human capital are preserved or enhanced throughout. Marketing
must be done in a sustainable manner so that all the marketing processes are environmentally and socially benign while helping to bring about a society in which striving
for sustainability is the norm". This is one of the few comprehensive definitions that
links different facets of sustainability and strategic elements of marketing. Sheth
and Parvatiyar (2021) have argued that so far sustainable marketing has mostly
been market-driven, not market-driving, referring to the fact that marketers have
rather reacted to the consumer demands and not consciously and responsibly directed
markets towards greater sustainability. They proposed that one of the stepping stones
on the path towards sustainable development would be repurposing the marketing
mix to identify strategic opportunities for faster and more radical change (ibid).

The following subsection of the paper will look at aligning the components of the 4P marketing mix with the dimensions of sustainability with an aim to identify how to manage the marketing mix elements keeping sustainability goals in mind.

Disassembling the strategic marketing activities into smaller units serves two purposes. First, it makes it clearer for the stakeholders to understand the range of options available for making marketing more sustainable. Second, it creates a possibility for marketers to move towards sustainability step by step, having a clear understanding of the stepping stones alongside the path.

4.3.1 Product

The process of marketing mix planning starts with constructing an offering that delivers value to the intended customer base (Armstrong et al., 2023). Within discussions surrounding sustainability, this particular facet has received the lion's share of attention, creating an impression that achieving sustainability primarily revolves around making the product or service more environmentally friendly. It is imperative to recognize that other constituents of the marketing mix hold equal significance and provide viable avenues for adopting sustainability in a gradual manner, product decisions lay a foundation for more sustainable marketing. Product, in the context of marketing mix, refers to the actual offering, whether it is a tangible product or a service, encompassing various aspects such as features, design, quality, packaging, and branding (Singh, 2012). Products are a key element in the marketing mix and input to modifying the three other Ps.

The sustainability considerations of products should be kept in mind throughout their entire life cycle (Jørgensen, 2008), from sourcing and transportation of the resources, production, product or service use, recycling, and discarding of products. Life cycle sustainability assessment (LCSA) involves the comprehensive evaluation of both adverse and beneficial environmental, social, and economic impacts throughout the entire life cycle of products. This approach is instrumental in informing decision-making processes aimed at fostering sustainability in product development and consumption (United Nations Environment Program, 2011). Life cycle approach to product development helps businesses to recognize possibilities to increase the sustainability of their products beyond what is happening in their own production facilities and sales channels.

Another possible approach to look at the sustainability of the product is the approach of the closed-loop supply chain management (CLSCM) that also covers the full logistics cycle, from raw materials and production to distribution. It also includes reverse logistics for product collection, processing, reuse, repair, recycling, and disposal. Utilizing return policies is not only good for the environment but also boosts customer satisfaction, fosters loyalty, and bolsters product sales (Rajabzadeh et al., 2023).

The economic sustainability of product-related decisions is essential for business viability. While social and environmental concerns are prioritized for positive planetary impact, most businesses need to generate revenue. Reducing resource use, minimizing waste, and employing advanced technologies for efficient production can lower production costs. Regarding consumer-facing economic sustainability, the focus is on lifetime value, achieved through product durability and improved quality to extend product lifecycles.

Many of the negative social impacts of products occur in the manufacturing process (Martin & Schouten, 2014). Social sustainability can be reached via sourcing through local and fair-trade suppliers and making sure that the raw materials and supply chain follow the social and labour rights. Generating tax income and offering employment opportunities within a local community supports the survival and growth of smaller areas. Designing inclusive products or services has its roots in considering the needs of consumer groups with disabilities or specific requirements but often-times this approach makes products easier to use for the general population as well, thus minimizing clutter and unnecessary effort.

While products and services are subject to international and local health and safety regulations, these standards can sometimes be lenient, permitting the use of potentially harmful elements like preservatives or excess sugar. Going beyond regulatory requirements voluntarily can further enhance social sustainability efforts.

Improving the social aspect of sustainability involves also working with local communities and non-business stakeholders, either in alignment with the company's field of operation or through independent contributions to community well-being.

Environmental sustainability of the product component of the marketing mix is usually the top-of-mind connection for anyone devoting their thoughts to the connections between marketing and sustainability. This emphasis is rational because the product holds significant potential to exert adverse environmental impacts in numerous ways. Products and services need various inputs and prioritizing sustainable, renewable, and recyclable materials helps to considerably reduce the environmental impact of products.

The role of packaging in achieving environmental sustainability is multifaceted. Some of the changes and solutions are with clear impact and easy to execute while the influence of other changes is not so easy to estimate. We will look neither at the regulations governing package design and materials nor at specific requirements coming from logistics and retail since they're often beyond the control of SMEs. Instead, it's more productive to focus on aspects where producers have independent decision-making authority.

Packaging has a vital role in reducing product waste. However, contemporary overpackaging is a concern. While packaging should safeguard the contents, there's a noticeable tendency towards excessive layers, oversized packages, or the use of unsustainable materials, which may not be justified by the product's nature. Martin and Schouten (2014) have argued that of all aspects of a product, packaging often has the most immediate financial payback for sustainability efforts, because, for example, using smaller packages is also economically beneficial for the producer as it helps save space in storage and logistics and reduces fuel costs in transportation. Figure 4.3 presents an illustration of overpackaging. Prescription medicine is packaged in a box

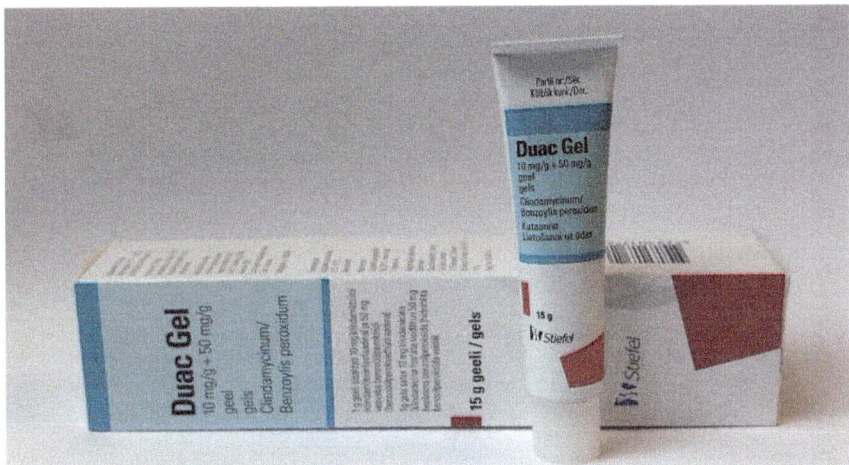

Fig. 4.3 A typical example of overpackaging (photo by the author)

that would fit several tubes of the cream. The consumer info is inside the package and the size of the packaging is absolutely not justified.

Sustainable packaging is usually related to choosing biodegradable or recyclable eco-friendly materials or even better, reusable packaging options. However, for an SME to make decisions on package materials is not so easy as there is no clear and finite info on the sustainability of materials. For example, the shift from plastic to paper bags in retail, touted as a more environmentally friendly choice, hasn't proven to be the perfect alternative as initially promised (Thompson, 2017).

Information about the components, features, and sustainability of a product is usually transferred to customers on the package of a product. Providing clear information to consumers about the product's environmental impact and sustainability enables them to make informed choices. If the company has decided to apply for using any sustainability-related labels it is vital to select a label that is officially recognized by the authorities and also preferably known to the consumers.

Branding is closely linked to product design and although there have been significant efforts to delineate the product and brand (Avis & Henderson, 2022), creating a brand needs, designing a product, and making it available in the market in the first place. Brand associations are a vital component of the brand and as such have a potential to signal consumers also the sustainability of the brand. Furthermore, brands are deeply rooted in culture and societal megatrends and designing brand values in line with that has a potential of having higher resonance with the consumers. Thus while taking decisions about brand value and brand promises it is worthwhile to consider if the actual properties of the product allow for including sustainability claims into the core of the brand.

Table 4.1 presents a brief summary of sustainability considerations and opportunities associated with products. It's important to recognize that this list isn't exhaustive

Table 4.1 Product decisions and sustainability concerns (composed by the author)

	Economic	Social	Environmental
Product design	Designing products that are efficient to produce, and use the optimum quantity of materials	Designing products with functionalities that are accessible to all. Creating new products based on real needs of the target group to solve their problems	Designing products with renewable, recycled, or organic materials
Production	Lean production	Fair labour practices	Saving natural resources, avoiding pollution
Product life cycle	Reusing materials helps to cut costs	Create easy and understandable solutions for the disposal of products	Designing products to be remanufactured or disassembled for material reuse and recycling
Branding	Strong brand brings economic value, and sustainable brands are demanded in the market	Developing brand values related to equality and inclusivity	Developing environment-related brand values
Quality	High-quality products allow to ask premium price	High-quality benefits users as the need for replacement diminishes	High-quality means longer time in use and less waste
Packaging	Cost advantage via sustainability, smaller/less packaging	Usability and ease of use of packaging	Packaging with sustainable materials, reducing material use
Product repair	Offering repairs creates extra revenue	Offering repairs solves customer problems and saves money for them	Offering repairs reduces waste and saves resources for producing new goods
Services	Offering renting (product as a service) instead of a final sale, thus taking care of the full life cycle—may provide higher returns, help consumers to split the cost across longer period of time and take care of the products after usage cycle		

and should be supplemented to align with specific industry, company requirements, and target consumer characteristics.

4.3.2 Price

Price component of the marketing mix refers to the amount of money charged for the product or service, but also a cost to the consumer that is not necessarily expressed only in monetary terms (Armstrong et al., 2023). Developing an effective pricing strategy entails achieving a delicate balance between attracting customers and ensuring profitability for the company. Integrating sustainability considerations into pricing strategy serves multiple purposes, including, for example, the assurance of fair pay for all participants in the value chain. Furthermore, price operates as a potent signal to consumers, influencing their perception of value and impacting purchasing decisions. Gruber et al. (2014) argued that perceived price is a particularly important proxy for assessing a product's performance on several other attributes. Their study found that expensive products were often automatically assumed to be sustainable even if no sustainability-related information was provided.

Fair pricing generates returns for the company but is also affordable to the consumers. Ochs (2022) has made a distinction between two aspects of price justice. The first is "upstream price justice", which concerns fair compensation for individuals involved in the value chain and addressing hidden ecological costs. The second is "downstream price justice", which pertains to how consumers perceive fairness in pricing. Both considerations have a bearing on the sustainability issues and should be taken into account by businesses developing their pricing strategies.

For upholding sustainability in pricing, the prices should reflect the true cost of production (including also environmental and social costs). Unfortunately, the real costs of products are often not reflected in the actual prices that consumers pay for them (Martin & Schouten, 2014) because companies either do not want to consider them or are not even aware of these costs. In the context of sustainability, researchers have also recommended dynamic pricing (see e.g., Scholz & Kulko, 2022). It is a specific revenue management strategy employed by businesses, involving setting prices for products based on real-time demand. Dynamic pricing means that the seller adjusts product prices in response to changes in the market, including shifts in demand or competition, perishability of the product or nearness of the event. If dynamic pricing is technically possible for a company, it enables maximizing the number of units sold and it increases sustainability via minimizing waste, especially in cases when a product would be otherwise discarded after the best before date, or the service would have been provided but just for fewer customers (like air travel or a concert). Dynamic price helps reaching more price-sensitive customers as well.

The social aspect of pricing for sustainability can sometimes clash with economic and environmental goals, where higher prices are necessary to offset environmental impact, reduce consumption, or generate profits. However, from a social standpoint, elevated prices might be inaccessible to various underprivileged consumer segments. Therefore, it's worth exploring options like producing more affordable product variants or offering instalment-based payment plans to address this challenge.

The environmental aspect of pricing is most directly linked to the principle of accounting for the carbon footprint and any possible hidden costs of the products. Higher prices, in general, have a propensity to decrease demand and thus minimize excessive consumption which is one of the easiest ways to contribute to the positive impacts to the environment. Depending on the nature of the product and specifics of the target group it may well be justified to set a higher value-based price for sustainable products without sacrificing the earnings of the company, as higher markups from fewer units sold are equal to the sum of lower markups from more units. An alternative line of thinking would be to encourage eco-friendly consumption by offering incentives such as discounts for eco-certified products if this is feasible from the economic point of view.

Regardless of the sustainability of a product itself, sustainability concerns can be addressed via pricing models that motivate customers to recycle, repair, or return products, promoting a circular economy. Research has shown that only a fraction of consumers has adequate social responsibility to return old products to collection facilities, but it is possible to motivate people with well-designed exchange programs where the consumer reward usually is in the form of a discount on a subsequent purchase (Rajabzadeh et al., 2023).

Table 4.2 presents a brief overview of the possibilities to address sustainability concerns via modifying the pricing decisions. As in the case of the product decisions, this list should be modified according to the real business situation.

4.3.3   Place

Place refers to the distribution channels used to get the product or service to the customer. It involves selecting the right channels such as retail stores, online platforms, or direct sales. Place decisions often include sustainability predicaments. Big international chains or online stores create economies of scale and enable resource efficiency. Moving the "place" physically closer to the consumer can yield positive local economic outcomes by stimulating regional economies, promoting local sourcing, and generating employment opportunities in smaller communities but is often costly. Nonetheless, it is imperative to underscore that, irrespective of the distribution channel, there exist possibilities to incorporate sustainability dimensions in the decision-making process (Adebayo et al., 2022).

Decisions made anywhere in the marketing channels have consequences for the overall sustainability, as well as the revenue of a business (Martin & Schouten, 2014, p. 171) but as several of the channel partners are outside the direct control of a single company, the orchestration of the channel system is close to mission impossible. If a company sells its products directly to consumers, life cycle management and closed-loop approach are easier to manage. However, in most of the categories, direct selling to consumers is not reasonable because this would require consumers to transact with too many businesses, which, in turn, is not sustainable.

Economic sustainability of the place component is reached via coordinating logistics and distribution processes to reduce costs and enhance resource efficiency. Working towards optimized distribution systems involves streamlining distribution networks to eliminate unnecessary intermediaries, ultimately reducing operational costs. Such efforts not only enhance economic sustainability but also improve overall efficiency. The second source for increased economic sustainability is efficient inventory management in order to minimize carrying costs, prevent overstocking, and maintain an economically sustainable approach to product distribution. Blockchain technology has emerged as a new tool for building resilient supply chain management. It enables real-time tracing of goods and services, fostering transparent connectivity.

Table 4.2 Pricing decisions and sustainability concerns (composed by the author)

	Economic	Social	Environmental
Pricing strategy	Pricing should guarantee the continuity of the business and generate revenue for the producer and delivery chain	Pricing should guarantee fair pay for everyone in the supply chain	Value-based pricing signals consumers the superiority of the product
Price discounts	May lead to price wars. Needs careful calculation to make sure profit from additional buyers covers loss from price reduction	Make product more affordable for less affluent consumers	Signal that the product may be less valuable requiring discounts for sales. Initiates unnecessary or excessive purchasing
Segmented pricing	Introducing differentiated prices for consumer categories may attract additional consumers	Lower price for less privileged segments allows them to buy products and services at lower cost	
Dynamic pricing	Helps to sell stock based on demand fluctuations, product due date or event date, thus maximizing profit	Dynamic pricing enables less affluent consumers to access services and products at a lower price when the demand in general is lower	Helps to minimize waste (e.g., by selling perishable goods at lower price close to the due date, selling transport tickets based on demand, etc.)
Payment methods	Offering different payment methods may attract additional customers	Consumer credits can appeal to financially inexperienced customers but at the same time extended payment options can assist less affluent consumers in affording essential items	Digital payment methods are generally more environmentally friendly, electronic receipts and billing reduce paper waste
Reuse and recycle-focused pricing	Active engagement in recycling creates positive brand capital and may be economically feasible if the company can reuse raw materials	Price-incentivized recycling gives consumers a clear and time saving way to solve the problem of out of use items	Creating price incentives for reuse and recycle helps proper recycling, decreases waste, and helps to reuse resources

Widely applied in various sectors, including finance, food distribution, and healthcare, blockchain contributes significantly to reliable and sustainable supply chain systems (Park & Li, 2021).

Carefully selecting suppliers for collaboration helps to negotiate mutually beneficial terms and have long-standing partnerships. These provide economic sustainability minimizing the need for constant re-negotiation while selecting new partners. Expanding into online marketing and distribution channels broadens the reach of the products and services while helping to save on overheads.

Partner and distribution channel selection has a potential to improve social sustainability of a business as well. A well-balanced channel mix grants equal access to products and services to various consumer groups regardless of their physical abilities, location, or other factors. Following the accessibility criteria and standards for online and offline stores beyond legal obligations can also bring financial revenues via attracting additional customers.

Fierce competition among retailers has led to questionable labour practices, thus making sure that both the employees of the company and employees of partners have an acceptable welfare level increases social sustainability and contributes to the socially responsible brand image.

Environmental sustainability of the place component is easier to grasp but not always so easy to implement. Nevertheless, when looking at all of the 4Ps and three sustainability components, then striving for increased environmental sustainability of the "place" has a potential of providing high economic savings as well. Building or partnering with energy-efficient physical stores reduces environmental impact and saves money. The same is true for using any other resources, from office supplies to water.

Table 4.3 gives an overview of the "place" decisions of the marketing mix and the possible sustainability gains associated with these decisions.

4.3.4 Promotion

Promotion, encompassing advertising, sales promotion, personal selling, public relations, and other activities a company uses to make its products or services known and appealing to its target market (Armstrong et al., 2023) plays a pivotal role in marketing products and services. This is the aspect of marketing that tends to receive the most fierce criticism because marketing communication is frequently believed to be a counterforce to sustainability goals.

Promotion in the context of the marketing mix is a broader term than marketing communications, which includes the specific set of tactics used to communicate with the target audience to promote products or services. Martin and Schouten have defined sustainable marketing communication as "messages and media directed to any of an organization's stakeholders for the purpose of achieving the organization's marketing and sustainability objectives" (2014, p. 205). Promotion and marketing communication-related terminology tend to suffer from a lack of universally agreed

Table 4.3 Place decisions and sustainability concerns (composed by the author)

	Economic	Social	Environmental
Distribution strategy	Inclusive distribution via big retailers creates economies of scale	Shorter distribution channels are often beneficial to the local communities (selling in smaller local shops)	Retailing via own channels enables it to take full control of the environmental sustainability of "place"
Channel selection: online sales	Helps to save on maintaining physical stores and floor staff	Enables access to goods and services for consumers in more remote communities and with e.g., reduced mobility. Saves time for consumers	Minimizes need for travel, saves resources from keeping up brick and mortar stores. Precise product descriptions help to decrease returns
Channel selection: offline sales	Products are returned less often	Provides jobs, keeps neighbourhoods livelier	Taking care of energy efficiency. Personal in-store selling can help the consumer make better decisions and select products that meet their need better
Channel partner selection	Channel partners should be credible and up for longer partnerships to create economic sustainability	Selling in local stores helps communities to strive and thus improves the perception of the brand locally	Selecting retailers that adhere to higher environmental standards and help to maintain closed-loop approach
Warehousing	Energy efficient buildings create savings	Taking into account the needs of local communities (e.g., reduce noise and traffic). Providing jobs locally	Energy efficient buildings and inventory management practices that minimize waste
Transportation	Using e.g., electric or gas vehicles where possible saves on fuel costs	Considering the interests of local communities when planning transport means, routes, and times	Local sourcing and distribution minimize environmental impact

definitions and interpretations and it is worthwhile to note that in practice the term "promotion" is used often as a synonym to "sales promotion" and marketing communication is considered equivalent to the promotion component of the marketing mix.

Discussions evolving around promotion and sustainability tend to focus on how to promote sustainable products more efficiently, but sustainability can be factored into promoting products that are not (fully) sustainable by design, minimizing the negative outcomes via careful managing of this component of the marketing mix. To enhance sustainability in promotional practices, several key opportunities can be harnessed. Firstly, ensuring transparent messaging builds consumer trust by aligning claims with actual realities. Secondly, backing up claims with evidence reinforces the credibility of promotional content. Additionally, thoughtfully managing promotional materials, opting for eco-friendly options, minimizes environmental impact. Respect for consumers' time and attention can be demonstrated through targeted and relevant messages. Sensitivity towards vulnerable groups ensures inclusive marketing. Encouraging responsible product use in marketing messages (e.g., reducing unnecessary consumption, using items longer, and recycling properly) promotes sustainable behaviours. Lastly, reevaluating promotional items to favour eco-friendly and reusable alternatives minimizes waste generation. Embracing these (and other) opportunities fosters sustainability in promotional activities, contributing to more sustainable marketing practices.

Before exploring methods to align marketing communication with sustainability objectives, it is vital to remember that, as emphasized by Whelan and Kronthal-Sacco (2023), ensuring that core category claims are effectively communicated and met is a prerequisite. Regrettably, consumers frequently experience disappointment when for example sustainable food products lack taste or shoes cause discomfort. Whelan and Kronthal-Sacco (2023) found that high-resonance sustainability claims focused on what is in it for the consumer have higher influence on the consumers. They suggested that communicating the following personal gains is most beneficial for the brands:

1. Personal and family health (without harmful ingredients)
2. Saving money (higher durability, lower energy consumption, access to repair)
3. Protecting children (this is one of the few future-oriented claims that works)
4. Helping local farmers and protecting animals
5. Sustainably sourced materials and ingredients.

Bouzige, Labarre, and Donnars (2023) have illustrated the impact marketing investments and activities have on different levels (see Fig. 4.4). This simple categorization is helpful for marketers to understand potentially negative sustainability influences also beyond carbon footprint in a clear way and indicate how their performance could be improved.

Businesses usually understand the direct environmental impact of marketing activities in terms of resource use and waste generation. Cutting back on printed materials and not using promotional gifts that are often of doubtful value and usefulness has become mainstream. The environmental cost of digital marketing is often neglected as it is difficult to quantify (Pärssinen et al., 2018) and impossible to observe. Avoiding excess digital advertising and content creation has besides environmental benefits also economic benefits (savings from content creation and advertising costs) and social benefits (not wasting consumers' attention on non-essential information). AI, as an emerging technology, facilitates detailed consumer profiling and enhances the targeting of content and communication. By providing consumer insights, it assists

Fig. 4.4 Carbon footprint of marketing activities (Bouzige et al., 2023)

in guiding customers through their journey. This approach ensures an optimal experience, enabling marketers to increase ROI by avoiding wasteful spending through a thorough analysis of consumer data and understanding genuine preferences (Haleem et al., 2022).

The very essence of marketing promotion is to drive sales, so it's almost paradoxical to consider reducing its impact on sales. Nonetheless, there is considerable flexibility to craft messages or develop sales promotions that incorporate sustainability while still aligning with sales goals. Several companies have successfully used a counter-messaging strategy calling consumers to cut down consumption instead of excessive buying and these campaigns have been very successful for brand building and linking the brand to sustainability values. Finnish online retailer of military and outdoor goods Varusteleka has been known to run anti-Black Friday ads with great success and the Patagonia Black Friday advertisement from 2011 is also a classic example of that approach (see Fig. 4.5).

Discussions about marketing's influence on long-term consumption trends and habits are common in popular media, but there is surprisingly limited in-depth research on this topic. While the complex effects of marketing messages on society and social processes are widely acknowledged, they remain insufficiently investigated (Zich, 2012). Hence it is complicated to provide businesses and other stakeholders with a comprehensive list of do's and don'ts that would enable them to systematically minimize unwanted long-term effects. It is clear that businesses should refrain from endorsing excessive consumption, promoting frequent product replacement due to obsolescence, and conveying values that contradict sustainability goals in their communication.

The economic sustainability of the promotion activities can be enhanced via careful consideration of the return on investment of promotional campaigns to allocate resources effectively and minimize waste. As mentioned before, resource efficient approach to producing advertising materials is beneficial both for the company, other stakeholders and the environment. Responsible messaging based on the value, durability, and long-term benefits of products can contribute to the improved brand perception as well as minimizing waste.

Fig. 4.5 Varusteleka.com and Patagonia Black Friday ads. Screenshots from the Varusteleka.com Facebook page and Patagonia website

Promotion is one of the marketing mix components that has close connections with social sustainability. Part of the social, ethical, and legal aspects of marketing communications are governed by different laws and regulations but that is often a minimal baseline. Merely avoiding deceptive and manipulative advertising is a hygiene factor but promoting products based on their genuine social value and benefits can generate extra goodwill from the target audience. Brands can contribute to social awareness via social marketing campaigns and supporting socially relevant causes. The promotion of diversity and inclusivity in marketing campaigns gained significant momentum and public attention through Dove's "Campaign for Real Beauty" in 2004 (Millard, 2009). Since then, it has become the norm to ensure representation and inclusion of various social demographics, body types, abilities, and orientations in marketing campaigns instead of marketing communication that creates a sense of inadequacy for the audience.

Environmental sustainability in promotional activities can be improved in all situations, whether the promoted products are inherently sustainable or regular. In both cases, encouraging responsible consumption and reducing the environmental impact of advertising are effective strategies. When promoting sustainable products, the focus is naturally on their sustainable features and values.

Table 4.4 Promotion decisions and sustainability concerns (composed by the author)

	Economic	Social	Environmental
Promotion strategy	Promoting products is inevitable to generate returns and economic sustainability	Socially responsible promotion strategy is built on ethical values, inclusivity, support for social causes, and consumer well-being	Promotion strategy should be developed keeping environmental concerns in mind-reducing direct waste, promoting circularity, etc
Advertising	Carefully crafted creative advertising attracts customers and generates returns	Creating advertising communication that does not promote sense of inadequacy and conspicuous consumption	Avoiding appeals that promote culture of disposability, focusing on responsible communication. Avoiding greenwashing
Sales promotion	Price-related sales promotions should be executed with care with an aim to keep brand value and not participate in price wars	Social responsibility concerns can be highlighted via linking promotion to social causes (e.g., donating to health-related nonprofits)	Avoiding promoting excessive consumption, overstocking, impulse buying, and waste generation with price discounts
Merchandising and in-store display	Purposefully planned in-store layouts and displays help to maximize profit and nudge consumers to buy specific items	Displaying socially responsible products more prominently in a clearly labelled manner	Displaying products with smaller environmental footprint more prominently in a clearly labelled manner

The discussions of promotion and sustainability are not complete without a reference to greenwashing, a practice of misleading consumers about corporate environmental practices or the environmental benefits of a product or service (Wang et al., 2023). Although greenwashing is mostly discussed as a purposeful activity, companies can also engage in this practice accidentally. It goes without saying that companies should avoid greenwashing and in order to do so they should meticulously check their supply chain partners, processes, and any other related details to make sure unbacked claims are presented to the consumers (Table 4.4).

4.4 Key Findings and Contributions

This chapter explored aligning the marketing mix elements with environmental, social, and economic sustainability principles. The key outcomes encompass valuable insights into sustainable marketing practices and theory. By integrating sustainability considerations into the product, pricing, place, and promotion strategies, businesses can foster positive environmental impacts, address social concerns, and support economic viability. The chapter underscores the importance of a comprehensive approach while also advocating for businesses to progressively embrace sustainability. This approach aims to enrich the existing knowledge on sustainable marketing practices by emphasizing both the broader perspective and the step-by-step progress companies can make. The main findings from the analysis of combining the 4Ps and sustainability dimensions are given below.

Marketing mix planning initiates with crafting an offering that delivers value to the target customers. The product component encompasses various aspects like features, design, quality, packaging, and branding. Sustainable products should be viewed through a life cycle sustainability assessment to consider environmental, social, and economic impacts throughout their entire lifecycle. Closed-loop supply chain management can enhance environmental sustainability by promoting product recycling and reuse. In terms of economic sustainability, businesses should strive to reduce production costs by minimizing resource use and enhancing product quality and durability.

Socially, businesses can enhance sustainability by sourcing from local and fair-trade suppliers, respecting social and labour rights, and contributing to local communities. They should also ensure their products meet or exceed health and safety regulations. Packaging plays a vital role in reducing product waste and should prioritize sustainable materials, such as biodegradable or recyclable options. Providing clear information to consumers about the product's environmental impact and sustainability enables informed choices. Branding, closely linked to product design, is rooted in culture and societal trends. Designing brand values in line with sustainability can resonate with consumers, reinforcing a product's sustainability claims.

Incorporating sustainability into pricing demands a delicate balance between attracting customers and ensuring profitability. Real costs, including hidden environmental and social expenses, are often omitted from consumer prices. Sustainable pricing aims to reflect the actual cost of production, promoting transparency.

Dynamic pricing, driven by real-time market demand, contributes to sustainability by reducing waste and reaching price-sensitive customers. However, sustainability-driven price increases may hinder accessibility for disadvantaged consumers. Alternatives, like offering affordable product variations or instalment-based payment options, help address this issue.

Environmental sustainability in pricing focuses on accounting for carbon footprints and hidden product expenses. Higher prices can reduce consumption, benefiting the environment. Setting higher prices for sustainable products is justifiable without compromising company earnings. Social aspects of pricing sustainability may conflict with economic and environmental goals. While higher prices can offset environmental impact, they might be unaffordable for underprivileged consumers. Exploring solutions, such as more affordable product variants and instalment-based payments, helps strike a balance.

Place in the marketing mix refers to the distribution channels employed to deliver products or services to customers. While international chains and online stores can drive resource efficiency, local proximity to consumers can stimulate regional economies and promote local sourcing. However, such closeness is often costly. Economic sustainability within the place component is achieved by optimizing logistics and distribution processes to reduce costs and enhance resource efficiency. This involves streamlining distribution networks, minimizing operational expenses, and efficiently managing inventory. Selecting and maintaining long-term supplier partnerships contribute to economic sustainability, reducing the need for constant re-negotiation. Expanding into online channels extends product reach and saves on overhead costs.

Enhancing social sustainability involves ensuring equal access to products and services for diverse consumer groups, and accommodating varying needs. Addressing labour practices and the welfare of employees, both within the company and among partners, contributes to a socially responsible brand image. Environmental sustainability in the place component entails building or partnering with energy-efficient physical stores and conserving resources, resulting in reduced environmental impact and cost savings.

Promotion, a fundamental element of the marketing mix, plays a vital role in making products or services appealing to target audiences. While discussions often centre on promoting sustainable products, it's equally important to incorporate sustainability into the marketing mix when dealing with products that are not inherently sustainable. Strategies to enhance sustainability in promotions include transparent messaging, substantiating claims with evidence, utilizing eco-friendly promotional materials, delivering targeted and relevant messages, and promoting responsible product use to encourage sustainable behaviours. Economic sustainability is achieved by optimizing resource efficiency and reducing costs, while the social dimension encompasses adhering to ethical and legal aspects, promoting diversity and inclusivity, and supporting socially relevant causes. Environmental sustainability is crucial, whether products are inherently sustainable or not, as responsible advertising and eco-friendly practices can reduce environmental impact. Avoiding greenwashing, or the misleading promotion of environmental practices, is a must.

This book chapter contributes to the current understanding of sustainable marketing by providing a comprehensive framework for aligning the elements of the marketing mix with environmental, social, and economic sustainability principles and presenting a visualization of the responsible marketing mix. It goes beyond the conventional focus on product sustainability and delves into how pricing, distribution channels, and promotional practices can contribute to sustainability goals. By exploring the interconnections between these elements and sustainability, the chapter offers new perspectives on how businesses can adopt a more holistic and integrated approach to sustainable marketing.

Moreover, it addresses a research gap by emphasizing the importance of small, manageable steps towards sustainability, making it accessible and feasible for businesses to embark on a sustainable marketing journey. By integrating various sustainability dimensions within the marketing mix, this chapter contributes to a more nuanced understanding of sustainable marketing practices and opens avenues for further research and exploration in the field.

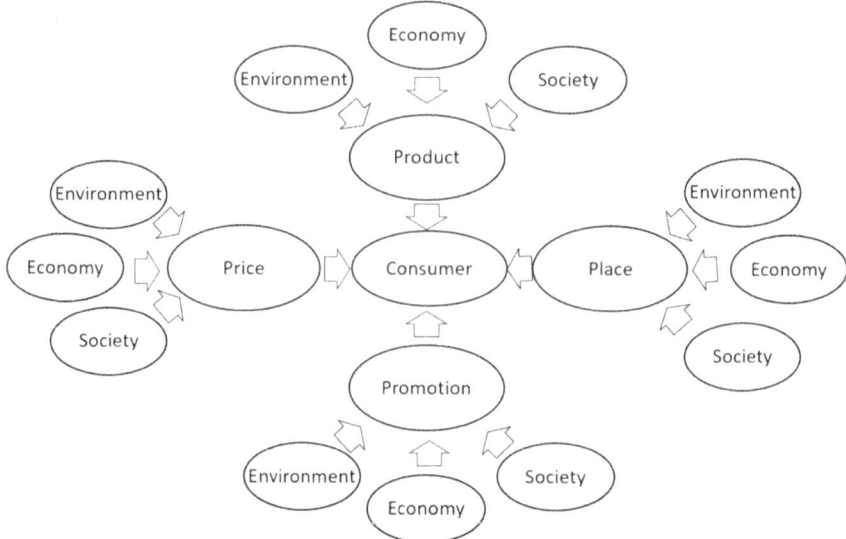

Fig. 4.6 Responsible marketing mix (composed by the author)

As a result of literature analysis and empirical observations, Fig. 4.6 describes a proposed new "responsible marketing mix" that could be both bases of practical decision-making and an educational tool.

4.5 Conclusion

This book chapter presents a new and comprehensive framework for sustainable marketing, covering product, price, place, and promotion aspects. By embracing incremental sustainability steps and interconnecting the marketing mix with sustainability principles, it contributes to a more nuanced understanding of holistic sustainable marketing practices, guiding businesses towards conscientious and responsible marketing strategies.

The key outcomes of the chapter are as follows:

- A comprehensive framework aligning the marketing mix with environmental, social, and economic sustainability.
- Suggesting how to incorporate sustainability considerations in product offerings, pricing, distribution channels, and promotional activities.
- Shifting emphasis from unattainable goals to incremental steps fosters feasible and practical sustainable marketing.
- Integration of sustainability across the marketing mix offers new perspectives on holistic approaches.

- Contributing valuable insights to sustainable marketing practices.
- An educational approach that can be utilized to incorporate sustainability topics into teaching the marketing mix and other marketing topics to the university students.

The primary limitation of this chapter and the proposed framework lies in its theoretical nature. Subsequent studies should explore diverse industries to evaluate its applicability and effectiveness in authentic business contexts. While the conceptualization intentionally maintains simplicity for seamless integration of marketing mix and sustainability, the complicated nature of real-world business scenarios demands continuous adaptation to specific contexts and evolving market trends.

The key ideas for future research involve conducting case studies across industries to empirically examine the effectiveness of the sustainable marketing framework. Investigating consumer responses to sustainability-aligned marketing strategies would provide insights into their impact on brand image and customer loyalty. Additionally, exploring the longitudinal effects of incremental sustainability measures on businesses will enhance comprehension of long-term implications and potential empirical challenges.

References

Adebayo, A. A., Greenhalgh, P., Muldoon-Smith, K., & Oyedokun, T. (2022). Towards attaining sustainable retail property locations: The relationships between supply, demand, and accessibility of retail spaces. *Sustainability, 14*(7), 3846.

American Marketing Association. (2023). *The definition of marketing: What is marketing?* https://www.ama.org/the-definition-of-marketing-what-is-marketing/

Anderson, L. M., & Taylor, R. L. (1995). McCarthy's 4Ps: Timeworn or time-tested? *Journal of Marketing Theory and Practice, 3*(3), 1–9.

Armstrong, G., Balasubramanian, S., & Kotler, P. (2023). *Principles of Marketing* (19th ed.). Pearson UK.

Avis, M., & Henderson, I. L. (2022). A solution to the problem of brand definition. *European Journal of Marketing, 56*(2), 351–374.

Booms, B. H., & Bitner, B. J. (1981). Marketing strategies and organisation structures for service firms. In J. Donnelly, & W. R. George (Eds.), *Marketing of services* (pp. 47–51). American Marketing Association.

Borland, H., & Lindgreen, A. (2013). Sustainability, epistemology, ecocentric business, and marketing strategy: Ideology, reality, and vision. *Journal of Business Ethics, 117*, 173–187.

Bouzige, J. B., Labarre, T., & Donnars, Q. (2023). *How marketing mix modeling can become a powerful tool for sustainable business performance*. Ekimetrics.

Cialdini, R. B. (1993). Influence. In *The psychology of persuasion* (Rev. ed.). Morrow

Constantinides, E. (2006). The marketing mix revisited: Towards the 21st-century marketing. *Journal of Marketing Management, 22*(3–4), 407–438.

Dangelico, R. M., & Vocalelli, D. (2017). "Green Marketing": An analysis of definitions, strategy steps, and tools through a systematic review of the literature. *Journal of Cleaner Production, 165*, 1263–1279.

Drury, R. K. (2021). *Communicating for sustainable consumption*. IIIEE Master Thesis.

Goi, C. L. (2009). A review of marketing mix: 4Ps or more. *International Journal of Marketing Studies, 1*(1), 2–15.

Grönroos, C. (1994). From marketing mix to relationship marketing: Towards a paradigm shift in marketing. *Asia-Australia Marketing Journal, 2*(1), 9–29.

Gruber, V., Schlegelmilch, B. B., & Houston, M. J. (2014). Inferential evaluations of sustainability attributes: Exploring how consumers imply product information. *Psychology & Marketing, 31*(6), 440–450.

Gummesson, E. (1995). Relationship marketing: Its role in the service economy. *Understanding Services Management, 244*, 68.

Haleem, A., Javaid, M., Qadri, M. A., Singh, R. P., & Suman, R. (2022). Artificial intelligence (AI) applications for marketing: A literature-based study. *International Journal of Intelligent Networks, 3*, 119–132.

Helm, S., & Little, V. (2022). Macromarketing our way to a zero-carbon future. *Journal of Macromarketing, 42*(2), 262–266.

Jørgensen, T. H. (2008). Towards more sustainable management systems: Through life cycle management and integration. *Journal of Cleaner Production, 16*(10), 1071–1080.

Jung, Y. J., & Kim, Y. (2023). Research trends of sustainability and marketing research, 2010–2020: Topic modeling analysis. *Heliyon, 9*(3).

Khizar, H. M. U., Iqbal, M. J., Murshed, F., & Ahsan, M. (2023). Sustainability Outcomes in SMEs: A Configurational View of the Interplay of Strategic Orientations and Environmental Conditions. *Journal of Macromarketing*, 1–20.

Lahtinen, V., Dietrich, T., & Rundle-Thiele, S. (2020). Long live the marketing mix. Testing the effectiveness of the commercial marketing mix in a social marketing context. *Journal of Social Marketing, 10*(3), 357–375.

Lang, J. W., & Goh, Z. (2020). Building an organizational science of behavioral consistency: Comment on Katz-Navon, Kark, and Delegach (2020). *Academy of Management Discoveries, 6*(1), 149–152.

Martin, D. M., Harju, A. A., Salminen, E., & Koroschetz, B. (2019). More than one way to float your boat: Product use and sustainability impacts. *Journal of Macromarketing, 39*(1), 71–87.

Martin, D. M., & Schouten, J. (2014). *Sustainable marketing* (p. 248). Pearson New International Edition.

McCarthy, E. J. (1960). *Basic marketing: A managerial approach.* McGraw-Hill Inc.

Millard, J. (2009). Performing beauty: Dove's "real beauty" campaign. *Symbolic Interaction, 32*(2), 146–168.

Ochs, A. (2022). How to create sustainable marketing: from strategy to marketing mix. *Executive Magazine*, Retrieved October 14, 2023, from https://www.executive-magazine.com/business-all/how-to-create-sustainable-marketing-from-strategy-to-marketing-mix

Park, A., & Li, H. (2021). The effect of blockchain technology on supply chain sustainability performances. *Sustainability, 13*(4), 1726.

Pärssinen, M., Kotila, M., Cuevas, R., Phansalkar, A., & Manner, J. (2018). Environmental impact assessment of online advertising. *Environmental Impact Assessment Review, 73*, 177–200.

Purvis, B., Mao, Y., & Robinson, D. (2019). Three pillars of sustainability: In search of conceptual origins. *Sustainability Science, 14*, 681–695.

Rajabzadeh, H., Altmann, J., & Rasti-Barzoki, M. (2023). A game-theoretic approach for pricing in a closed-loop supply chain considering product exchange program and a full-refund return policy: A case study of Iran. *Environmental Science and Pollution Research, 30*(4), 10390–10413.

Scholz, M., & Kulko, R.-D. (2022). Dynamic pricing of perishable food as a sustainable business model. *British Food Journal, 124*(5), 1609–1621.

Sheth, J. N., & Parvatiyar, A. (2021). Sustainable marketing: Market-driving, not market-driven. *Journal of Macromarketing, 41*(1), 150–165.

Singh, M. (2012). Marketing mix of 4P's for competitive advantage. *IOSR Journal of Business and Management, 3*(6), 40–45.

Thompson, C. (2017). Paper, plastic or reusable? *Stanford Magazine.* Retrieved October 15, 2023, from https://stanfordmag.org/contents/paper-plastic-or-reusable

United Nations. (1987). *Our common future*. United Nations. Retrieved October 4, 2023, from https://sustainabledevelopment.un.org/content/documents/5987our-common-future.pdf

United Nations Environment Program (UNEP). (2011). *Towards a life cycle sustainability assessment: Making informed choices on products*. Retrieved October 14, 2023, from https://www.unep.org/resources/report/towards-life-cycle-sustainability-assessment-making-informed-choices-products

Wang, W., Ma, D., Wu, F., Sun, M., Xu, S., Hua, Q., & Sun, Z. (2023). Exploring the knowledge structure and hotspot evolution of greenwashing: A visual analysis based on bibliometrics. *Sustainability, 15*(3), 2290.

Whelan, T., & Kronthal-Sacco, R. (2023). Research: How to effectively market green products. *Harvard Business Review Digital Articles*, 1–6. Retrieved October 14, 2023, from https://search.ebscohost.com/

Zich, F. (2012). On the theme of marketing communication side effects. *Communication Today*, 1.

Zineldin, M., & Philipson, S. (2007). Kotler and Borden are not dead: Myth of relationship marketing and truth of the 4Ps. *Journal of Consumer Marketing, 24*(4), 229–241.

Katri Kerem holds a Ph.D. in Economics from Tallinn Technical University since December 1, 2003. Presently, she serves as an Assistant Professor of Marketing at the Estonian Business School, where she was heading the Marketing and Communication Department 2010–2022 and is head of the bachelor programme in Entrepreneurship since 2023. With a rich background, Kerem's research focuses on various aspects of marketing mostly related to consumer behaviour. Her teaching expertise spans advertising, branding, consumer behaviour, and sustainable marketing. Additionally, she actively contributes to doctoral supervision and academic evaluation committees.

Part II
Practices in Public Sector

Chapter 5
Operationalizing Doughnut Economics for Regional Green Transition: An Integrated Multi-level Stakeholder Engagement Framework

Aleksandra Kekkonen🆔

Abstract There is a vast movement to transform the EU into a modern, resource-efficient, and competitive economy by 2050, with ambitious objectives already set at the EU level for 2030 and 2035. Initiatives such as the EU Climate Pact offer examples of EU-wide undertakings that invite people, communities, and organizations to participate in climate action and build a greener Europe. At the heart of such is the notion that top-down sustainability and climate approaches (e.g., UN, EU, or national level) need to be complemented with evidence-based and coherent bottom-up initiatives, which turn local authorities, different stakeholder/civil society groups, and individual citizens into key actors in achieving the green transition. In recent years, significant steps have been taken to generate new data and information in both the public and private sectors linked to sustainability performance and the green economy. However, maximizing the potential benefits from the smart reuse and combination of this data ("information asymmetry") remains an issue. The need for new and improved sustainability performance metrics, which build on existing global and local best practices and methodologies and achieve better integration of different data sources to develop higher quality and more accurate indicators, is recognized. The chapter aims to show that the development, implementation, and scaling of country- and region-specific framework for integrated, multi-level stakeholder engagement to accelerate the green transition in regions, using an adapted doughnut economics approach, will help local authorities to become green and sustainable. As a result of analysis and practical examples from worldwide on doughnut methodology implementation, framework is proposed that can help local authorities plan, implement, and monitor the green transition in their regions (using an adapted doughnut economics approach as a starting point), as well as help local authorities develop and implement an integrated, interlinked set of measures, which create a direct connection with the EU's Green Deal objectives and associated policies at the national

---

A. Kekkonen (✉)
Estonian Business School, Tallinn, Estonia
e-mail: alexandra.kekkonen@ebs.ee

© The Author(s), under exclusive license to Springer Nature Singapore Pte Ltd. 2024   89
M. Kooskora and A. Kekkonen (eds.), *Performance Challenges in Organizational Sustainability*, Responsible Leadership and Sustainable Management,
https://doi.org/10.1007/978-981-97-5548-6_5

level to ensure that local authorities, stakeholder groups, and citizens can effectively contribute to achieving the green transition holistically.

Keywords Doughnut economics · EU green transition · Multi-level stakeholder engagement · Stakeholder engagement framework

5.1 Introduction

There is a vast movement to transform the EU into a modern, resource-efficient, and competitive economy by 2050, with ambitious objectives already set at the EU level for 2030 and 2035. Initiatives such as the EU Climate Pact offer examples of EU-wide undertakings that invite people, communities, and organizations to participate in climate action and build a greener Europe. Many EU-wide initiatives and actions aimed at promoting climate action and building a greener Europe are developing. Alsamara et al. (2023) emphasize the importance of citizen participation in achieving the European Green Deal, suggesting policy options such as local climate measurements, sustainable food consumption, and urban gardening to increase engagement. Haupt (2018) discusses the Covenant of Mayors as a network that facilitates collaboration among European municipalities to enhance climate change mitigation and adaptation measures. Cohen (2014) highlights the significance of infrastructure projects in tackling climate change and suggests that investment in essential infrastructure can provide opportunities for individuals to engage in sustainable practices and foster a sense of European integration. The authors demonstrate the importance of involving people, communities, and organizations in EU-wide undertakings to address climate change and promote a greener Europe.

The chapter is conceptual one and it aims to show that the development, implementation, and scaling of country- and region-specific methodologies for integrated, multi-level stakeholder engagement to accelerate the green transition in regions, using an adapted doughnut economics approach will help local authorities to become green and sustainable. As a result of the analysis, the framework is proposed that can help local authorities plan, implement, and monitor the green transition in their regions, as well as help local authorities develop and implement an integrated, interlinked set of measures, which create a direct connection with the EU's Green Deal objectives and associated policies at the national level to ensure that local authorities, stakeholder groups, and citizens can effectively contribute to achieving the green transition holistically.

The European Green Deal is a tool to make Europe the first climate-neutral continent by 2050. To reach this goal, action is needed on all organizational levels. At the heart of this movement is the notion that top-down sustainability and climate approaches (e.g., UN, EU, or national level) need to be complemented with evidence-based and coherent bottom-up initiatives, which turn local authorities, different stakeholder/civil society groups, and individual citizens into key actors in achieving the green transition. The suggested framework aims to help local authorities and munici-palities build and carry out their green strategies in an integrated and inclusive manner, including transparent metrics and open innovation labs for citizens in different munic-ipalities. Therefore, it is a key tool in achieving the buy-in of all local stakeholders for the green transition. The chapter provides a theoretical foundation and the back-ground to the tool development and testing in the future, which, in turn, will lead to a number of positive results for communities.

The chapter is structured as follows. The theoretical perspectives and problem statement for green and sustainable local authorities will be presented, followed by the decomposition of the idea into several levels: top-down and bottom-up approaches for regional strategic development, community involvement practices and their impor-tance for green transition implementation, and governance aspects, including perfor-mance challenges, will be considered. Based on the analysis done, the framework will be presented, and, in conclusion, some recommendations for the further research will be developed.

5.2 Green and Sustainable Local Authorities: Theoretical Perspective and Problem Statement

5.2.1 Climate Change and Policymaking Approaches

Climate change and environmental awareness are the main topics of today's agenda. An IPCC assessment report says that "the scale of recent changes across the climate system as a whole… are unprecedented over many centuries to many thousands of years". "Global warming of 1.5 °C and 2 °C will be exceeded during the twenty-first century unless deep reductions in CO_2 and other greenhouse gas emissions occur in the coming decades" (IPCC, 2021).

Numerous countries have developed policies, strategies, action plans, and agendas to tackle these problems (e.g., IMD, 2021), but developed measures do not work out. At the same time, there is a rise of awareness among stakeholders, community repre-sentatives, and individuals of the practical implementation of strategies and measures developed on a local and regional level (e.g., the Smart Tampere Ecosystem Program). Another question is whether a climate change problem should be individual respon-sibility (Hiller, 2011; Kent, 2009; Rickard et al., 2014) or producer responsibility (Kibert, 2004).

Climate change is a complex problem, and the solution to it requires a systemic approach that enables the interaction of different actors at all levels. The currently proposed solutions do not work effectively because of the mix of factors. There are no significant results in policy measures implemented to stop climate change, slow it down, or change consumer culture. One assumption is that there is a lack of trust between actors on all levels, resulting in the indifference of individuals and slow policy measures implementation. Efficient solutions to this acute global problem must be found soon. The responsibility for change is sometimes placed on policymakers, local authorities, consumers, or energy producers. The question is, who has the final work to foster and achieve a change. What approach should be applied to solve a climate change issue: top-down or bottom-up? What are conversion points where community involvement, individual human responsibility, and policy intervention measures meet? What concrete intervention measures for social and environmental sustainability practical implementation on individual, local, and regional levels should be applied? What is a framework to put together a top-down and bottom-up approach to climate problem solutions on the local level?

There are plenty of studies on top-down policymaking approaches (Hare et al., 2010; Tuladhar, 2009). The brightest example here is the solution to the ozone depletion problem in the 1980s by the Montreal Protocol (Velders et al., 2007). Another stream of academic literature discusses the bottom-up approach through leadership (Deisenrieder et al., 2020), role models, and how new change models can tackle climate problems (Sun & Yang, 2016), as well as nudge people towards an environmentally friendly lifestyle (Khare, 2015; Mataracı & Kurtuluş, 2020; Alamsyah, & Othman, 2021). Two more research directions discuss customer or producer responsibility for environmental problems (Kibert, 2004; Zulfiqar & Shafaat, 2015; Leal Filho et al., 2019).

A solution to those problems could be finding conversion points so that bottom-up and top-down approaches meet and practical measures develop together with an integrated framework. A new scientific solution is doughnut economics approach testing (Raworth, 2017a, b) through the creation of digital tools, as its implementation has no practical results. Doughnut economics allows combining two approaches because there are both policies from above and an active position of the population, communities, and civil society.

Doughnut economics is a visual framework for sustainable development[1] combining the concept of planetary boundaries with the complementary concept of social boundaries (Raworth, 2012, 2017a, b; Rockström et al., 2009) (Fig. 5.1). The centre hole of the model depicts the proportion of people who lack access to life's essentials (healthcare, education, equity, and so on). At the same time, the crust represents the ecological ceilings (planetary boundaries) that life depends on and must not be overshot. The doughnut economy approach is already used for different country, regional, and city regions to create doughnut city portraits and represent how cities are meeting the challenges of staying within ecological limits while ensuring social foundations for their inhabitants.

The framework of the doughnut economic model applied for a local level would consider actors on individual, local, and regional levels together. The search for a conversion point of translating individuals' attempts (bottom-up approach) and policy initiatives (top-down approach) into practical results could be applied through doughnut economics framework adaptation to local authorities' needs.

The local level for framework development is chosen as this is a level where communities' interests, individual initiatives, and local authorities' measures and

---

[1] https://doughnuteconomics.org/about-doughnut-economics.

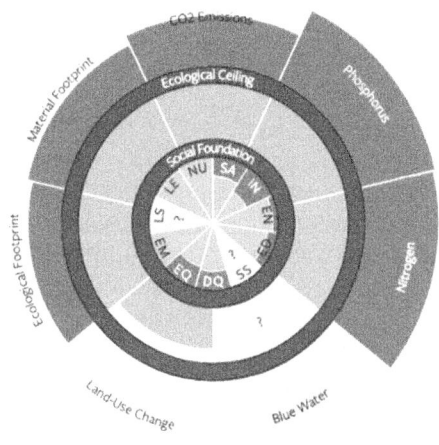

LS - Life Satisfaction	LE - Life Expectancy	NU - Nutrition	SA - Sanitation
IN - Income Poverty	EN - Access to Energy	ED - Education	SS - Social Support
DQ - Democratic Quality	EQ - Equality	EM - Employment	

Fig. 5.1 Doughnut economics concept visualization and world state of planetary boundaries and social foundations in 2015. By Kate Raworth and Christian Guthier, CC-BY-SA 4.0.

policies meet. As an example of local implementation, smart and circular city ideas are developing rapidly (Prendeville et al., 2018; Williams, 2019; Viglioglia et al., 2021), and the topic is highly researched. Recently, there has been a shift of paradigm in regional and city development strategies towards a circular and sustainable-oriented mentality (Bertassini et al., 2021; Brown et al., 2019, 2020, 2021), where human plays a central role as a customer, business leader, and worker. Questions of quality of life, trust, human rights, and safety are discussed at all levels with rising frequency (Weingaertner & Moberg, 2014; Khatoun & Zeadally, 2017; Flak & Hofmann, 2020; Kempin, 2019).

Researchers collectively suggest (Leal-Arcas, 2018; Stewart et al., 2013) that top-down sustainability and climate approaches must be complemented with evidence-based and coherent bottom-up initiatives involving local authorities, stakeholders, civil society groups, and individual citizens to achieve the green transition. Leal-Arcas (2018) emphasize the importance of a symbiotic relationship between government/businesses and individual prosumers in transitioning to clean energy and highlight the role of cities and local governments in developing and implementing climate action plans. Stewart et al. (2013) propose a bottom-up strategy involving smaller-scale transnational cooperative arrangements to achieve greenhouse gas reductions and contribute to global climate action.

5.2.2 Stakeholders' Involvement

Communities are levels where individuals can implement ideas and motivate and inspire others for change. Community building on the local level and considering environmental awareness is a developing topic (Reith & Orova, 2014; Holden, 2016), which raises questions about the well-being of individuals and social sustainability (Rogers et al., 2012; Magee et al., 2012; Helne & Hirvilammi, 2015). Social sustainability is a measure of human welfare. Social sustainability occurs through formal and informal processes, systems, and structures. Social sustainability includes community development, well-being, product responsibility, resilience, and cultural competence. At the same time, it is strongly connected to environmental sustainability. The doughnut economics framework can be used for joining together top-down and bottom-up approaches, as this is a systemic way unites planetary boundaries (which are environmental sustainability, e.g., Li et al., 2021) and social foundation (social sustainability, e.g., Eizenberg & Jabareen, 2017).

The significance of involving diverse stakeholders at different governance levels in decision-making processes is fundamental. The shift from traditional government-centric approaches to more participatory governance models is discussed in several papers. Matsuura and Shiroyama (2018) discusses how stakeholders, instead of the government, take on public sector functions and actively participate in policymaking processes. Tyagi (2019) explores the prospects, significance, and challenges of stakeholder engagement in public policy in India, emphasizing the need for continuous engagement across multiple stakeholders with varying levels of influence. Helbig et al. (2015) examines international cases of stakeholder engagement in policy development and identifies various tools and processes that can support effective stakeholder participation. Bayley and French (2008) focuses on designing participatory processes for stakeholder involvement in societal decisions, highlighting the benefits of greater public involvement in decision-making and the need for a comprehensive framework to assemble different participatory instruments.

In contemporary public policy discourse, the notion of "stakeholders" occupies a central position, especially as there is a notable transition from a traditional "government" paradigm to one of "governance" (Matsuura & Shiroyama, 2018). Traditionally, bureaucratic governmental structures operated under a "command and control" mechanism. However, such models are increasingly viewed as incompatible within democratic and globalized contexts. Instead, networked entities are taking over roles previously designated to government bodies. Within this governance-oriented framework, stakeholders, including individuals and organizations, actively formulate policy and assume responsibilities for executing mutually agreed policies. Stakeholder involvement signifies a departure from governance structures dominated by elite decision-makers. Participatory policymaking involves stakeholders in various stages of the policy process. It can focus on both the substance of the policy problem and on improving the tools and processes of policy development (Helbig et al., 2015).

In public policy research, the term "stakeholder" is inclusive, capturing a spectrum of organizations and individuals directly or indirectly interfacing with a policy of interest to the analyst. While formal entities possessing legal participatory rights are pivotal, the distinction between stakeholders and non-stakeholders in the political sphere is often ambiguous. Thus, comprehensive stakeholder-focused policy analyses should encapsulate entities impacting the policy, irrespective of their formal rights. Stakeholder analysis is especially salient at localized levels, where decisions about specific development projects often involve distinct organizations, corporations, or individuals (Matsuura & Shiroyama, 2018).

One more aspect of the problem is individual environmental responsibility. The success of strategies to tackle climate change, resource scarcity, and negative environmental impacts increasingly depends on whether individual behaviour changes can complement the technical solutions currently available. A relatively new way of influencing behaviour in a sustainable direction is with the help of changing values and nudging people. Nudge can be used to help people make choices that are best for the environment or their health (Mont et al., 2014; Ranchordás, 2020). Systems leadership could affect individual choices (Dreier et al., 2019). This approach includes individuals' skills of collaborative leadership to enable learning, trust-building, and empowered action among stakeholders who share a common goal, and communities' coalition-building and advocacy tactics to develop alignment and mobilize action among stakeholders in the system, both within and between organizations. Information about individual CO_2 emissions might mostly enhance individual environmental friendliness regarding values, beliefs, concerns, attitudes, intentions, and behaviour (Yamashita et al., 2021). The research would consider all these factors and aspects as a bottom-up approach to environmental changes.

5.2.3   Governance Approach

Various participatory governance approaches, conflict resolution mechanisms, and power dynamics are inherent in multi-stakeholder decision-making processes. Maccallum (2009) examines tensions between interactive processes and traditional forms of rationalist legitimacy in participatory planning, highlighting the negotiation of power relations in multi-scalar governance. Brouwer et al. (2012) emphasizes the imbalanced distribution of power, capacity, and resources in multi-stakeholder processes, which can hinder joint learning and innovative solutions. Ali et al. (2011) explores the impact of collaborative decision-making systems on building social capital through access to justice in local communities. Ahuja et al. (2008) discusses the challenges and potential pitfalls of participatory policy processes, including the potential for influential partners to hijack the agenda. These papers underscore the importance of recognizing power dynamics, promoting inclusive participation, and addressing conflicts in multi-stakeholder decision-making processes.

The much-vaunted shift from "government" to "governance" in recent years involves (among other things) increased attention to the participation of "stakeholders" in policymaking, a trend affecting not only politicians' actions but also public servants' day-to-day practice. In the field of urban/regional planning, this attention has led to a "communicative turn" in the academy; planning practice is increasingly seen as discursive rather than technical. This reframing leads to some significant tensions between interactive processes and traditional forms of rationalist legitimacy and between local aspirations and strategic concerns at other geo-political scales (Maccalum, 2009).

Advocates of multi-stakeholder processes (MSPs) contend that stakeholder interdependence fosters trust and encourages inclusive participation. However, inherent power disparities, societal imbalances, and varying access to resources and information can impede genuine dialogue and joint problem-solving. The authors delve into how local researchers assist communities in deconstructing power dynamics within MSPs to navigate interactions with dominant entities effectively (Brouwer et al., 2012).

Creating dispute resolution forums where community members can actively generate shared objectives, collect and access information, and take action on issues of collective concern represents an important foundation for developing social capital (Ali et al., 2011).

5.2.4   Performance Measurements for Local Authorities

A systematic approach that unites top-down and bottom-up approaches would allow looking in a new way to find patterns and indicators for measures implementation. Few studies describe the role of the individual as a part of the whole in decision-making and practical implementation in tackling climate change problems (Hiller, 2011; Kenis & Mathijs, 2012; Kwon et al., 2019).

In recent years, significant steps have been taken to generate new data and information in both the public and private sectors linked to ESG performance and the green economy. However, maximizing the potential benefits of smart reuse and combining this data ("information asymmetry") remains an issue. Therefore, the need for new and improved ESG metrics is recognized, which build on existing global and local best practices and methodologies and better integrate different data sources to develop higher quality and more accurate indicators.

Different authors highlight the need for new and improved ESG metrics to maximize the potential benefits of data and information in the public and private sectors, particularly in relation to the green economy. Arvidsson (2021) emphasizes the importance of focusing on creating better ESG outcomes rather than solely improving reporting regulations. Kamp-Roelands (2013) emphasizes the necessity of high-quality information to support decisions driving green growth. Also, the paper states that high-quality information is necessary to support decisions that drive green growth. Fisher (2011) discusses incorporating information on the quality of human, social, and environmental conditions in economic indicators to achieve more authentic and comprehensive measures of progress. Saxena et al. (2022) suggests that Industry 4.0 technologies, such as IoT, AI, blockchain, and big data, can be crucial in obtaining accurate ESG data and reports. These findings collectively support the need for improved ESG metrics that integrate different data sources and achieve higher quality and more accurate indicators. Mitigating problems such as the impacts of climate change and COVID-19 calls for improved ESG performance, not improved ESG reporting quantity or quality. Thus, rather than focusing on improving ESG reporting regulations, there is a need to redirect focus towards creating better ESG outcomes (Arvidsson & Dumay, 2022).

ESG reporting is necessary in the context of the European Green Deal. Although the practice of ESG reporting has grown in importance in recent years, there is still a considerable gap between the information contained in ESG reporting and the supply of information. This gap is caused by factors such as different ESG reporting standards and frameworks, different reporting regimes (each country has its own reporting regulations), and high data collection and reporting costs (Dănilă et al., 2022).

5.3 Framework Development

Developing, implementing, and scaling country- and region-specific methodologies for integrated, multi-level stakeholder engagement will accelerate the green transition in regions and help local authorities become green and sustainable.

Several researchers collectively emphasize the importance of developing and implementing country- and region-specific methodologies for integrated, multi-level stakeholder engagement to accelerate the green transition in regions. Adeniran and Onyekwena (2020) highlights the need for aligning domestic policy frameworks with regional requirements and compensating possible losers to ensure broader support for renewable energy transition and says that the development and implementation of the country- and region-specific methodologies for integrated multi-level stake-holder engagement is crucial to accelerate the green transition in regions. Li and Lange (2023) emphasizes the significance of community empowerment and early planning participation in achieving net-zero carbon emissions, proposing a six-step cycle principle that includes collective action commitments and flexible strategic energy system plans. Wilker et al. (2015) focus on stakeholder participation in green infrastructure planning, highlighting the relevance of planning-cultural context and integrating stakeholders' preferences and values in decision-making processes. Overall, the authors underscore the crucial role of tailored stakeholder engagement methodologies in driving the green transition at regional levels.

Engagement and governance methodologies are becoming increasingly perti-nent to enhance the quality, acceptance, and legitimacy of planning and execution processes. An imperative exists for strategies that coalesce public, private, scientific, and community stakeholders to collaboratively devise innovative and sustainable solutions. This urgency is underscored by local authorities' mounting fiscal and personnel constraints. Consequently, the integration of stakeholder perspectives is not only becoming challenging. However, it is also progressively vital to ensure that societal segments have equitable representation in planning processes, guaranteeing alignment with their needs and optimized effectiveness (Wilker et al., 2015).

Local governmental bodies are progressively turning to green infrastructure as a strategic response to climatic perturbations, particularly in addressing flooding and water quality concerns, and as an economical alternative to augmenting dated "grey" stormwater frameworks (Gallagher et al., 2018). Concurrently, a burgeoning interest is in amplifying citizen engagement in expanding urban green infrastructure. However, notwithstanding this recognition of the significance of participatory engagement, numerous green infrastructure endeavours persist in adhering to a hierarchical, expertise-centred approach to site allocation and conceptualization. This incongruence between procedural execution and engagement aspirations may result in the non-optimal long-term sustainability of projects, hinder the realization of multifunctional inclusive environments, and overlook potential enhancements in civic capacity for urban planning. Moreover, the pivot towards green infrastructure has faced scrutiny for its insufficient inclusivity in its planning and implementation phases, leading to instances of green gentrification.

Fostering collective endeavours by forging connections among private entities, public institutions, and the broader community has been a recurrent theme in community practice initiatives (Natarajan, 2017). For instance, delineating a sustainable community elucidates the diverse external actors synergizing with community-led actions for renewable energy advancement. This definition encompasses "governors, politicians, project developers, technology market protagonists, professionals, and general citizens collaborating to amplify intelligent energy provisions, thereby advocating for sustainable energy alternatives" (IEE Sustainable Energy Communities, 2006). Championing cross-sectoral participation in community-wide collective actions to bolster community empowerment offers multifarious advantages (Cunha et al., 2021). Primarily, it addresses the practical impediment of mobilizing individuals towards innovative technological adoption—a significant hurdle in sustainability. This shift can be facilitated by sustained engagement, knowledge dissemination, and reciprocal trust-building (Gallagher et al., 2018).

An adapted doughnut economics approach can help local authorities become green and sustainable (Kekkonen & Beliatskaya, 2023; Luukkanen et al., 2021). There is a need for cities to tackle the sustainability crisis through a blend of top-down and bottom-up processes, incorporating the principles of doughnut economics and digital collective intelligence (Kekkonen & Beliatskaya, 2023). Luukkanen et al. (2021) propose the Sustainability Window method as a means to quantify and operationalize the doughnut economy, providing a framework for analysing the minimum and maximum economic development necessary for sustainable social and environmental outcomes. Dillman et al. (2021) extend the application of the doughnut economy to the urban mobility sector, presenting a framework for evaluating and designing sustainable consumption corridors in the context of safe and just urban mobility. These findings offer insights and tools for local authorities to adopt a green and sustainable approach to governance and development.

Local authorities often struggle to have a holistic vision and prioritize long-term goals. White (1982) highlights the challenges councillors face in setting priorities and goals, often consumed by responding to specific demands. Huggins (2012) discusses the paradigm shift in democratic governance that has led to limited public roles for citizens and diminished local communities' capacity to act on challenging issues. Khan and Johnson (2021) explore the potential for coproduction of spatial information between local governments and citizens, highlighting different approaches and motivations. Local authorities may benefit from adopting tools like doughnut economics to foster a more holistic and inclusive approach to decision-making and goal-setting.

Municipalities can implement cross-sectoral and multi-level stakeholder engagement using the doughnut economics framework, resulting in swift responses to challenges, building trust, network development, and bringing the Interreg program closer to citizens.

The doughnut economics tool proposes the development and practical implementation of measures through several means. The initial task is to ask stakeholders and citizens to analyse the current state of the region or city through four lenses: social and ecological, local and global. The results of this analysis give insights and initiatives from a bottom-up perspective. The authority-level methodology has the following steps to implement regional development 9-M strategies (Raworth, 2017a, b):

- Mirror—reflecting the current state of your city/region.
- Mission—vision.
- Mobilize—transformation.
- Map existing policies.
- Mindset (holistic) by values and ways of working.
- Methods (connect) that you are using.
- Momentum of an iterative process of action and reflection.
- Monitor the progress of doughnuts.

The proposed methodology would help to understand what local economic development and action are needed to promote local living conditions within our planetary boundaries for the majority of citizens and how one makes the best use of the available material and knowledge resources for a decent development path. Using the proposed framework will allow experimentation, "thinking outside the box", and working across different sectors to find suitable solutions (Fig. 5.2).

The proposed doughnut economics framework for implementation is overarching. The flowchart (Fig. 5.3) represents a framework that revolves around regional and local strategies for implementing environmental and social initiatives, especially within the context of the EU Green Deal package.

The description of the proposed framework is as follows:

1. **The EU Green Deal package** is the overarching initiative and guideline from which the subsequent processes stem. The package is directly linked to the "Formal requirements" box, suggesting that reports on its implementation or outcomes are required from local authorities.

Fig. 5.2 Target groups perspective. Developed by the author

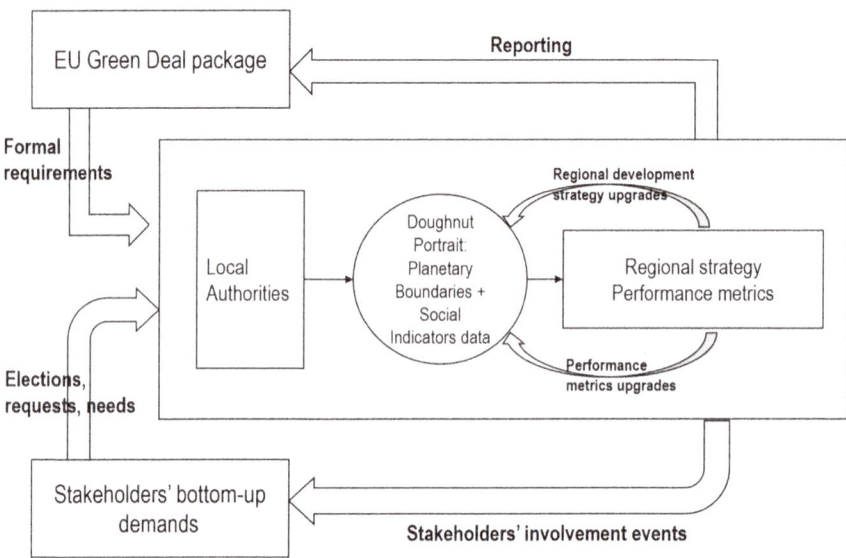

Fig. 5.3 An integrated multi-level stakeholder engagement framework. Developed by the author

2. **Formal requirements** serve as a basis for local authorities to act upon. The flow indicates that the EU Green Deal package influences these requirements.
3. **Local authorities** or local governing bodies or organizations play a central role in this framework. They receive directives from formal requirements and, in turn, contribute data to the "Doughnut Portrait" tool, which is used to collect and analyse input data from different sources.

4. **Doughnut Portrait: Planetary Boundaries + Social Indicators Data** is a central repository and methodology that gathers data about environmental (planetary) and social metrics. This data is crucial for updating regional development strategies and their performance metrics. The result of the Doughnut Portrait analysis influences stakeholder involvement events and is the central element or conversion point for stakeholder and community involvement. "Doughnut Portrait" is related to city portraits, but focuses on sustainability aspects more. It could represent how cities are meeting the challenges of staying within ecological limits while ensuring social foundations for their inhabitants.

5. **Regional strategy and performance metrics** are directly influenced by the Doughnut Portrait. This is the result of the tool, and it provides a set of metrics or standards to evaluate the performance of regional strategies. Additionally, it is subject to "Performance metrics upgrades". Here, paying attention to information dissemination.

6. **Regional development strategy upgrades** and refining can be done based on the development of performance metrics. This process is cyclical, as strategy upgrades can further influence the Doughnut Portrait data.

7. **Stakeholders' involvement events**. At this stage, feedback and concerns or inputs from various stakeholders are gathered. This feedback process impacts the bottom-up demands from stakeholders' input during further iterations.

8. **Stakeholders' bottom-up demands** are aggregations of the needs and requests of various parties. They should be considered equally by local authorities and together with formal requirements and possibly provide the connection for the EU Green Deal package. Infrastructure and authorities' input should support local, community, and group initiatives. Furthermore, people should feel safe proposing ideas and implementing them. Information dissemination and better practices should be scaled to other regions or municipalities if they work out well. Finally, local contests of ideas from citizens could stimulate new visions and creative proposals.

The overall framework suggests a cyclical and iterative process where strategies are continually refined based on performance metrics, stakeholder inputs, and changing requirements from the EU Green Deal package. It emphasizes collaboration between local authorities, stakeholders, and overarching guidelines to achieve desired environmental and social outcomes. The framework of doughnut economics (Raworth, 2012, 2017a, b) was chosen for its complexity and simplicity at the same time. The dynamic balance is the most attractive idea. Imbalance causes excesses and loss of resilience, and it is also far from the idea of systems thinking. We cannot reframe the narrative landscape without collaborating with innovators and influencing the policy regime. All those aspects are interlinked and should be developed in systems.

Development of the doughnut portrait and policy intervention measures or regional strategies for local authorities can be implemented using AI tools and should be strongly connected with the information collected. The framework's final objective is the development of an analytical toolbox that automatically calculates data on planetary boundaries and social dimensions according to the doughnut economics framework using Machine Learning methods of AI. The AI would be used to collect and aggregate data according to the developed methodology using data mining and focusing on exploratory data analysis through unsupervised learning.

The further development of the framework requires additional research from a theoretical perspective as well as practical testing in the field:

– metanalysis of operational language: smart/sustainable local authority/city, the well-being of individual, social sustainability, individual environmental responsibility, and community should be done to reveal and put together common parameters that can be used for the automatized Doughnut Portrait analysis;
– decomposing indicators in doughnut economics and revealing key indicators for AI deployment from policy measures, planetary boundaries, social foundations, and individual measurements;
– research on mechanisms of community involvement practices, collected policies systematization and revealing of culture and country-specific traits, classification;
– research on human-centric approach towards climate change problem solution through environmental sustainability as an individual human responsibility problem, CO_2 footprint calculations, and it's influencing the issue; and
– concrete intervention measures for social and environmental sustainability practical implementation on individual, local, and regional levels should be developed.

5.4 Conclusion

This chapter presents perspective and analysis of the intersecting domains of Green Transition strategies, Doughnut Economics applications, and multi-level stakeholder engagement within sustainable development. Building upon existing research in these areas, the study synthesizes insights from various scholarly works. Drawing from the principles of doughnut economics, the chapter explores how this innovative framework can be utilized across various sectors, such as urban planning, policymaking, and business strategies, to achieve balanced well-being within planetary boundaries.

Also, this chapter presents the realm of multi-level stakeholder engagement, shedding light on the significance of involving diverse actors at different governance levels. It investigates the participatory governance approaches and power dynamics inherent in multi-stakeholder decision-making processes.

Through the lens of governance metrics, the paper examines the development of measurable indicators that evaluate governance practices' effectiveness, inclusiveness, and transparency using an integrated multi-level stakeholder engagement framework. Furthermore, it identifies gaps in the current literature by highlighting the need for more comprehensive studies that bridge the connections between different domains. It offers a holistic understanding of how Green Transition strategies and Doughnut Economics applications can be integrated into multi-level stakeholder engagement frameworks to drive sustainable development.

References

Adeniran, A. P., & Onyekwena, C. (2020). Accelerating green energy transition in Africa through regional integration. SAIIA Policy Briefing 21. https://cseaafrica.org/wp-content/uploads/2020/10/Policy-Brief-216-adeniran-onyekwena.pdf

Ahuja, V., Gustafson, D. J., & Otte, J. M. (2008). Process, people, power and conflict: Some lessons from a participatory policy process in Andhra Pradesh, India.

Alamsyah, D. P., & Othman, N. A. (2021). Consumer awareness towards eco-friendly product through green advertising: Environmentally friendly strategy. In *IOP conference series: Earth and environmental science* (Vol. 824, No. 1, p. 012043). IOP Publishing.

Ali, S., Davis, W. E., & Lee, J. (2011). Multi-stakeholder dispute resolution: Building social capital through access to justice at the community level. *Pepperdine Dispute Resolution Law Journal, 11*(2). https://ssrn.com/abstract=1673952

Alsamara, I. M., Beinert, S. F., de Jong, J. C., Klapp, M. J. B., Marewsk, V. S., & Orhan, R. (2023). IMPACT: Ideal measures for participation and awareness of climate change: stronger together citizen participation in achieving the European green deal in the Meuse-Rhine Euroregion. *South Eastern European Journal of Public Health.* https://doi.org/10.56801/seejph.vi.282

Arvidsson, S., & Dumay, J. (2022). Corporate ESG reporting quantity, quality and performance: Where to now for environmental policy and practice? *Business Strategy and the Environment, 31*(3). 1091–1110. https://doi.org/10.1002/bse.2937

Bertassini, A. C., Ometto, A. R., Severengiz, S., & Gerolamo, M. C. (2021). Circular economy and sustainability: The role of organizational behavior in the transition journey. *Business Strategy and the Environment.*

Brouwer, J. H., Hiemstra, W., & Martin, P. (2012). Using stakeholder and power analysis and BCPs in multi-stakeholder processes.

Brown, P., Bocken, N., & Balkenende, R. (2019). Why do companies pursue collaborative circular oriented innovation? *Sustainability, 11*(3), 635.

Brown, P., Bocken, N., & Balkenende, R. (2020). How do companies collaborate for circular oriented innovation? *Sustainability, 12*(4), 1648.

Brown, P., Von Daniels, C., Bocken, N. M. P., & Balkenende, A. R. (2021). A process model for collaboration in circular oriented innovation. *Journal of Cleaner Production, 286*, 125499.

Bayley, C., & French, S. (2008). Designing a participatory process for stakeholder involvement in a societal decision. *Group Decision and Negotiation, 17*(3), 195–210. https://doi.org/10.1007/s10726-007-9076-8

Cohen, C. (2014). EU governments should place greater emphasis on infrastructure projects in their efforts to tackle climate change. http://eprints.lse.ac.uk/72074/1/blogs.lse.ac.uk-EU%20governments%20should%20place%20greater%20emphasis%20on%20infrastructure%20projects%20in%20their%20efforts%20to%20tackle%20cl.pdf

Cunha, F. B. F., Carani, C., Nucci, C. A., Castro, C., Silva, M. S., & Torres, E. A. (2021). Transitioning to a low carbon society through energy communities: Lessons learned from Brazil and Italy. *Energy Research & Social Science, 75*, 101994. https://doi.org/10.1016/j.erss.2021.101994

Dănilă, A., Horga, M. G., Oprișan, O., & Stamule, T. (2022). Good practices on ESG reporting in the context of the European green deal. *Amfiteatru Economic, 24*(61), 847–860. https://doi.org/10.24818/EA/2022/61/847

Deisenrieder, V., Kubisch, S., Keller, L., & Stötter, J. (2020). Bridging the action gap by democratizing climate change education—the case of k.i.d.Z.21 in the context of fridays for future. *Sustainability, 12*(5), 1–19. https://doi.org/10.3390/su12051748

Dillman, K., Czepkiewicz, M., Heinonen, J., & Davíðsdóttir, B. (2021). A safe and just space for urban mobility: A framework for sector-based sustainable consumption corridor development. *Global Sustainability, 4*, E28. https://doi.org/10.1017/sus.2021.28

Dreier, L., Nabarro, D., & Nelson, J. (2019). Systems leadership for sustainable development: strategies for achieving systemic change. *CR Initiative at the Harvard Kennedy School*. https://www.hks.harvard.edu/sites/default/files/centers/mrcbg/files/Systems%20Leadership.pdf

Eizenberg, E., & Jabareen, Y. (2017). Social sustainability: A new conceptual framework. *Sustainability, 9*(1), 68.

Flak, L. S., & Hofmann, S. (2020). The impact of smart city initiatives on human rights.

Fisher, W. P. (2011). Measuring genuine progress by scaling economic indicators to think global & act local: An example from the UN Millennium development goals project. https://doi.org/10.2139/ssrn.1739386

Hare, W., Stockwell, C., Flachsland, C., & Oberthür, S. (2010). The architecture of the global climate regime: A top-down perspective. *Climate Policy, 10*(6), 600–614.

Haupt, W. (2018). European municipalities engaging in climate change mitigation and adaptation networks: Examining the case of the covenant of mayors. In Y. Yamagata, & A. Sharifi (Eds.), *Resilience-oriented urban planning*. Lecture Notes in Energy, vol 65. Springer, Cham. https://doi.org/10.1007/978-3-319-75798-8_5

Helbig, N., Dawes, S., Dzhusupova, Z., Klievink, B., & Mkude, C. (2015). Stakeholder engagement in policy development: Observations and lessons from international experience. In M. Janssen, M. Wimmer, & A. Deljoo (Eds.), *Policy practice and digital science*. Public Administration and Information Technology, vol 10. Springer, Cham. https://doi.org/10.1007/978-3-319-12784-2_9

Helne, T., & Hirvilammi, T. (2015). Wellbeing and sustainability: A relational approach. *Sustainable Development, 23*(3), 167–175. https://doi.org/10.1002/sd.1581

Hiller, A. (2011). Climate change and individual responsibility. *The Monist, 94*(3), 349–368.

Holden, A. (2016). *Environment and tourism*. Routledge.

Huggins, M. (2012). Community visioning and engagement: Refreshing and sustaining implementation. *Nat'l Civic Rev, 101*, 3–11. https://doi.org/10.1002/ncr.21084

Gallagher, J., Coughlan, P., Williams, A. P., & McNabola, A. (2018). Innovating for low-carbon energy through hydropower: Enabling a conservation charity's transition to a low-carbon community. *Creativity and Innovation Management, 27*, 375–386.

IEE. (2006). Sustainable energy communities—8 innovative projects for an energy intelligent Europe. In *Intelligent energy Europe*. Brussels, Belgium.

IMD (2021). Data shows effects of COVID-19 and climate change on citizens' perceptions of how smart their cities are. *Imd*. https://www.imd.org/news/updates/data-shows-effects-of-covid-and-climate-change-on-citizens-perceptions-of-how-smart-their-cities-are/

IPCC. (2021). *Climate change 2021: The physical science basis*. Contribution of Working Group I to the Sixth Assessment Report of the Intergovernmental Panel on Climate Change [V. Masson-Delmotte, P. Zhai, A. Pirani, S. L., Connors, C. Péan, S. Berger, N. Caud, Y. Chen, L. Goldfarb, M. I. Gomis, M. Huang, K. Leitzell, E. Lonnoy, J. B. R., Matthews, T. K. Maycock, T. Waterfield, O. Yelekçi, R. Yu, & B. Zhou (Eds.)]. Cambridge University Press (In Press).

Kamp-Roelands, N. (2013). *Private sector initiatives on measuring and reporting on green growth*. OECD Green Growth Papers, No. 2013/06. OECD Publishing. https://doi.org/10.1787/5k483jn5j1lv-en

Kekkonen, A., & Beliatskaya, I. (2023). Tackling the sustainability crisis through digital collective intelligence: the principles of doughnut economics in smart cities. In *Proceedings of the 24th annual international conference on digital government research (DGO '23)* (pp. 261–269). https://doi.org/10.1145/3598469.3598498

Kenis, A., & Mathijs, E. (2012). Beyond individual behavior change: The role of power, knowledge, and strategy in tackling climate change. *Environmental Education Research, 18*(1), 45–65.

Kent, J. (2009). Individualized responsibility and climate change: 'If climate protection becomes everyone's responsibility, does it end up being no-one's?' *Cosmopolitan Civil Societies: An Interdisciplinary Journal, 1*(3), 132–149.

Kempin Reuter, T. (2019). Human rights and the city: Including marginalized communities in urban development and smart cities. *Journal of Human Rights, 18*(4), 382–402.

Khan, Z. T., & Johnson, P. A. (2021). Coproducing spatial information: Exploring government approaches and motivations at the local level.

Khare, A. (2015). Influence of green self-identity, past environmental behaviour and income on Indian consumers' environmentally friendly behaviour. *Journal of Global Scholars of Marketing Science, 25*(4), 379–395. https://doi.org/10.1080/21639159.2015.1073423

Khatoun, R., & Zeadally, S. (2017). Cybersecurity and privacy solutions in smart cities. *IEEE Communications Magazine, 55*(3), 51–59.

Kibert, N. C. (2004). Extended producer responsibility: A tool for achieving sustainable development. *Journal of Land Use & Environmental Law, 19*(2), 503–523.

Kwon, S. A., Kim, S., & Lee, J. E. (2019). Analyzing the determinants of individual action on climate change by specifying the roles of six values in South Korea. *Sustainability, 11*(7), 1834.

Leal-Arcas, R. (2018). Re-thinking global climate change: A local, bottom-up perspective. *Seton Hall Journal of Diplomacy and International Relations, 20*(1), 4–20.

Leal Filho, W., Saari, U., Fedoruk, M., Iital, A., Moora, H., Klöga, M., & Voronova, V. (2019). An overview of the problems posed by plastic products and the role of extended producer responsibility in Europe. *Journal of Cleaner Production, 214*, 550–558.

Li, L., & Lange, K. W. (2023). Planning principles for integrating community empowerment into zero-net carbon transformation. *Smart Cities, 6*(1), 100–122. https://doi.org/10.3390/smartciti es6010006

Li, M., Wiedmann, T., Fang, K., & Hadjikakou, M. (2021). The role of planetary boundaries in assessing absolute environmental sustainability across scales. *Environment International, 152*, 106475.

Luukkanen, J., Vehmas, J., & Kaivo-oja, J. (2021). Quantification of doughnut economy with the sustainability window method: Analysis of development in Thailand. *Sustainability, 13*(2), 847. https://doi.org/10.3390/su13020847

Maccallum, D. (2009). Practising governance: Multi-party decision making in a multi-scalar context. *Critical Approaches to Discourse Analysis Across Disciplines, 3*, 92–117. https://www.lancas ter.ac.uk/fass/journals/cadaad/wp-content/uploads/2015/01/Volume-3_MacCallum.pdf

Magee, L., Scerri, A., & James, P. (2012). Measuring social sustainability: A community-centered approach. *Applied Research in Quality of Life, 7*(3), 239–261.

Mataracı, P., & Kurtuluş, S. (2020). Sustainable marketing: The effects of environmental consciousness, lifestyle, and involvement degree on environmentally friendly purchasing behavior. *Journal of Global Scholars of Marketing Science, 30*(3), 304–318.

Matsuura, M., & Shiroyama, H. (2018). Stakeholder perspective and multilevel governance. In K. Takeuchi, H. Shiroyama, O. Saito, & M. Matsuura (Eds.), *Biofuels and sustainability.* Science for Sustainable Societies. Springer, Tokyo. https://doi.org/10.1007/978-4-431-54895-9_3

Mont, O., Lehner, M., & Heiskanen, E. (2014). *Nudging: A tool for sustainable behaviour?* Swedish EPA Report 6643. https://www.researchgate.net/publication/271211332_Nudging_A_tool_for_sustainable_behaviour

Natarajan, L. (2017). Socio-spatial learning: A case study of community knowledge in participatory spatial planning. *Progress in Planning, 111*, 1–23. https://doi.org/10.1016/j.progress.2015. 06.002

Prendeville, S., Cherim, E., & Bocken, N. (2018). Circular cities: Mapping six cities in transition. *Environmental Innovation and Societal Transitions, 26*, 171–194.

Ranchordás, S. (2020). Nudging citizens through technology in smart cities. *International Review of Law, Computers & Technology, 34*(3), 254–276.

Raworth, K. (2012). *A safe and just space for humanity.* Oxfam Discussion Paper. https://www. oxfam.org/sites/www.oxfam.org/files/dp-a-safe-and-just-space-for-humanity-130212-en.pdf

Raworth, K. (2017a). *Doughnut economics: Seven ways to think like a 21st-century economist.* Penguin Random House.

Raworth, K. (2017b). Why it's time for doughnut economics. *IPPR Progressive Review, 24*(3), 216–222.

Reith, A., & Orova, M. (2014). Do green neighborhood ratings cover sustainability? *Ecological Indicators, 48*, 660–672.

Rickard, L. N., Yang, Z. J., Seo, M., & Harrison, T. M. (2014). The "I" in climate: The role of individual responsibility in systematic processing of climate change information. *Global Environmental Change, 26*, 39–52. https://doi.org/10.1016/j.gloenvcha.2014.03.010

Rockström, J., Steffen, W., Noone, K., Persson, Å., Chapin III, F. S., Lambin, E., Lenton, T. M., Scheffer, M., Folke, C., Schellnhuber, H., Nykvist, B., De Wit, C. A., Hughes, T., van der Leeuw, S., Rodhe, H., Sörlin, S., Snyder, P. K., Costanza, R., Svedin, U., Falkenmark, M., Karlberg, L., Corell, R. W., Fabry, V. J., Hansen, J., Walker, B., Liverman, D., Richardson, K., Crutzen, P., & Foley, J. (2009). Planetary boundaries: Exploring the safe operating space for humanity. *Ecology and Society, 14*(2), 32. http://www.ecologyandsociety.org/vol14/iss2/art32/

Rogers, D. S., Duraiappah, A. K., Antons, D. C., Munoz, P., Bai, X., Fragkias, M., & Gutscher, H. (2012). A vision for human well-being: Transition to social sustainability. *Current Opinion in Environmental Sustainability, 4*(1), 61–73.

Saxena, A., Singh, R., Gehlot, A., Akram, S. V., Twala, B., Singh, A., Montero, E. C., & Priyadarshi, N. (2022). Technologies empowered environmental, social, and governance (ESG): An industry 4.0 landscape. *Sustainability, 15*, 309. https://doi.org/10.3390/su15010309

Smart Tampere Ecosystem Program Ecosystem program—Smarttampere. https://smarttampere.fi/en/about-smart-tampere/ecosystem-program/

Stewart, R., Oppenheimer, M., & Rudyk, B. (2013). Building a more effective global climate regime through a bottom-up approach. *Theoretical Inquiries in Law, 14*(1), 273–306. https://doi.org/10.1515/til-2013-014

Sun, J., & Yang, K. (2016). The wicked problem of climate change: A new approach based on social mess and fragmentation. *Sustainability, 8*, 1312. https://doi.org/10.3390/su8121312

Tuladhar, S. D., Yuan, M., Bernstein, P., Montgomery, W.D., & Smith, A. (2009). A top–down bottom–up modeling approach to climate change policy analysis. *Energy Economics, 31*, S223–S234.

Tyagi, A. (2019). Prospects of stakeholder engagement in public policy: A case of India. *IJASOS—International E-journal of Advances in Social Sciences, 4*(12), 813–822. https://doi.org/10.18769/ijasos.478238

Velders, G. J., Andersen, S. O., Daniel, J. S., Fahey, D. W., & McFarland, M. (2007). The importance of the Montreal protocol in protecting climate. *Proceedings of the National Academy of Sciences, 104*(12), 4814–4819.

Viglioglia, M., Giovanardi, M., Pollo, R., & Peruccio, P. P. (2021). Smart district and circular economy: The role of ICT solutions in promoting circular cities. *Sustainability, 13*(21), 11732.

Weingaertner, C., & Moberg, Å. (2014). Exploring social sustainability: Learning from perspectives on urban development and companies and products. *Sustainable Development, 22*(2), 122–133.

White, L. G. (1982). Improving the goal-setting process in local government. *Public Administration Review, 42*(1), 77–83. https://doi.org/10.2307/976095

Wilker, J., Rusche, K., & Rymsa-Fitschen, C. (2015). Stakeholder participation in North-West Europe: Lessons learnt from green infrastructure case studies. *Proceedings REAL CORP 2015 Tagungsband*, 5–7 May 2015, Ghent, Belgium. https://repository.corp.at/16/1/CORP2015_23.pdf

Williams, J. (2019). Circular cities. *Urban Studies, 56*(13), 2746–2762.

Yamashita, H., Kyoi, S., & Mori, K. (2021). Does information about personal emissions of carbon dioxide improve individual environmental friendliness? A survey experiment. *Sustainability, 13*, 2284. https://doi.org/10.3390/su13042284

Zulfiqar, Z., & Shafaat, M. (2015). Green marketing: Environmental concern and customer satisfaction. *European Journal of Business and Management, 7*(1), 2222–2839.

Aleksandra Kekkonen is a Senior Research Fellow at RDI unit and lecturer at Estonian Business School and head of Green & CSR research team. She has a background in international relations and a Ph.D. in Economics in the field of regional human capital development from 2013. She worked as a researcher in human capital, labor market, and education system development on the national and international levels for more than 11 years. Currently her specialization and main areas of interest are green economy, sustainable development and especially accelerating the transition to a circular economy on macro and local level, as well as community involvement practices for green transition.

Chapter 6
GovTech Companies' Contribution to SDGs: Exploring Reporting and Communication Practices

Alena Labanava and Regina Erlenheim ⓘ

Abstract The UN 2030 Agenda and the Sustainable Development Goals which it proposes and seeks to attain have vast ramifications and potential in their implementation but a continuing problem is the progress and measurement of them. Government Technology (GovTech) companies in many ways can help governments make steps towards some of the SDGs but the ways through which the national governments manage and measure the SDGs are not the same way that the GovTech companies do the same thing. This study seeks to analyse the ways that GovTech startups and small and medium enterprises communicate their contributions to the SDGs and compare it to the ways the governments measure the same thing. The methodology employed is qualitative methods with the use of secondary data and document analysis. The authors provided an overview of a number of communication channels and tactics of GovTech companies and how they compare with national reports as well as recommendations for companies seeking to improve profitability and have an impact upon their society through sustainability.

Keywords GovTech · SDGs · Sustainable development goals · Sustainability

6.1 Introduction

Businesses possess the potential to exert substantial influence in the realization of Sustainable Development Goals (SDGs) (UN General Assembly, 2015; Dauliyeva et al., 2020). This is especially true for Government Technology (GovTech) enterprises as their business activities are tightly connected with creating the common good

A. Labanava (✉)
Tallinn University of Technology, Tallinn, Estonia
e-mail: alena.labanava@taltech.ee

R. Erlenheim
Estonian Business School, Tallinn, Estonia
e-mail: regina.erlenheim@ebs.ee

© The Author(s), under exclusive license to Springer Nature Singapore Pte Ltd. 2024   109
M. Kooskora and A. Kekkonen (eds.), *Performance Challenges in Organizational Sustainability*, Responsible Leadership and Sustainable Management,
https://doi.org/10.1007/978-981-97-5548-6_6

(Labanava et al., 2023). The domain of GovTech has been experiencing escalating attention as of late (Govtech market size with emerging trends 2022: Top key players updates, business growing strategies, competitive dynamics, industry segmentation and forecast to 2027, 2022; Allen, 2022). Nonetheless, the specific influence of startups and small and medium-sized enterprises (SMEs) in the attainment of SDGs remains inadequately explored. Although a company's role in achieving SDGs often depends on its mission and how it operates, there's a strong need to create ways to show how a company is making a difference in reaching SDGs. The formulation and dissemination of SDG reports on a company level could additionally furnish valuable support to the voluntary national progress SDG reports that governments compile to document advancements made in the realm of SDG accomplishment.

The primary aims of this book chapter encompass the comprehension of the methodologies employed by GovTech enterprises in the execution of Sustainable Development Goals (SDG) reporting and communication. It seeks to ascertain the integration of such reporting practices within national SDG reports and discern the potential modalities for enhancing the efficacy of SDG reporting.

The study utilizes a case study approach to investigate a cohort of startups chosen for participation in the GovTech Connect Bootcamp, which is focused on tackling sustainability issues. GovTech Bootcamp is a pilot project funded by the European Commission to foster the digitization of the public sector through the use of an innovative European GovTech Platform. It is delivered by a Consortium led by Intellera Consulting, along with partners PUBLIC Deutschland, Lisbon Council, and Politecnico di Milano (GovTech Connect Boot Camps, n.d.).

The following research questions are proposed in the current book chapter to understand:

– How do GovTech companies communicate their commitment to and alignment with SDGs in their corporate communications, such as annual reports, websites, and social media platforms?
– How do GovTech companies' communications regarding their contributions to the SDGs align with the priorities of their respective countries?
– How can GovTech companies enhance their reporting and communication practices to provide more meaningful and transparent insights into their contributions to SDGs and meet the evolving expectations of stakeholders?

To answer the research questions, the authors used desk research, which is "the process of gathering information available in published form, rather than obtaining data directly" (Woolley, 1992). The information for answering the first research question was obtained through careful examination of the companies' websites and social media channels. The answer to the second research question was made through the comparison of the company's data with the data from Voluntary National Reviews on SDG progress in the companies of incorporation and with the data from Sustainable Development indexes. Based on the flaws in communication of sustainable development activities, the recommendations were made on improving communication practices, which comprises the answer to the third research question.

6.2 Theoretical Framework of SDG Communication in GovTech Companies

6.2.1 Definition of GovTech and Communication Framework

There is no unanimous opinion on the definition of GovTech. Among the dominating opinions are those from the World Bank (Dener et al., 2021) and the one by Bharosa (2022). While the first sees GovTech as the next step of "digital government", the latter understands GovTech as "socio-technical solutions – that are developed and operated by private organisations – intertwined with public sector components for facilitating processes in the public sector". For the purposes of this research, the authors are using the definition offered by Bharosa (2022).

The other definitions tend to come from grey literature, which includes reports coming from government, academia, businesses, and industry. This type of document may not undergo peer review, but still can contain valuable and up-to-date information (Pavlovska, 2018). The coexistence of multiple definitions of GovTech is a phenomenon that can be observed. However, it also gives rise to a notable inconvenience. This inconvenience becomes particularly pronounced when we consider that the definition of GovTech offered by the World Bank, an immensely influential organization, diverges significantly from definitions originating from other sources.

The absence of a unified definition can create difficulties in policy-making when it comes to targeting a particular set of challenges related to GovTech. It also complicates the evaluation of impact of GovTech initiatives and creates a risk of miscommunication between different stakeholders.

The primary communication analysed in this paper is the communication mediated by Information and Communication Technology (ICT). Part of the reason for this is that ICT-mediated technologies allow for a richness of media for the researchers' analysis. Although researchers have been investigating the use of ICTs in communication since the turn of the twenty-first century (Jones et al., 2004), the theories related to interorganizational ICT-mediated communication are still somewhat new (Schumate et al., 2016) and the theoretical contribution to this paper primarily deals with the reasons for sample selection, described in the methodology.

6.2.2 Setting the GovTech Scene

In an increasingly technologically complex and fast-moving world, GovTech companies can fill the role of providing agility to government entities. These contributions to the public good are functions that the government may have at one time fulfilled. However, due to many reasons, such as the lack of competence in an area or skill set, governments may choose to procure solutions from private entities, like GovTech startups and SMEs to bring the capability to fruition.

On a company level, it is oftentimes difficult to define if a company belongs to the GovTech scope. At the same time, there are companies that offer technology solutions tailored for the public sector. Taking into account that the Sustainable Development Agenda encompasses a wide range of public values, some of which are traditionally ensured by the government. A few examples include companies like Balancing Act (n.d.) (citizen participation), MySideWalk (n.d.), StormsSensor (n.d.), Citibeats (n.d.) (local needs), Signatura (n.d.), Tyler Technologies (n.d.) (legal and regulatory affairs), Acivilate (n.d.), RightHear (n.d.) (social care), ResourceX (n.d.) (budgeting) (Nebula, 2023).

In recent times there have emerged multiple organizations that in one way or another promote GovTech. They include GovTech Lab Lithuania (n.d.), Accelerate Estonia (Estonia's Governmental Innovation Lab, 2023), GovTech Sweden (n.d.), Digicampus (Digicampus, Samen Innoveren over Grenzen Heen, 2023), Fastfwd Belgium (FASTFWD Belgium: Digitisation of Belgian companies, n.d.), GovTech Lab Luxembourg (n.d.), Publictech Lab (PublicTech lab: Ie university, 2021). The emergence of these organizations, which serve as an intermediary between the public and the private sector, can be viewed as evidence of the growing interest of public–private sector collaboration.

6.2.3   SDG vs ESG Reporting

Various terms, such as CSR communication, green communication, global responsibility communication together with corporate sustainability communication, and social responsibility communication, have been used to refer to different aspects of sustainability communication (Signitzer & Prexl, 2008).

ESG reporting and SDG reporting are both essential tools for measuring and communicating a company's sustainability efforts. ESG reporting focuses on a company's performance in areas such as environmental impact, social responsibility, and corporate governance disclosure, while SDG reporting focuses on the company's alignment with the SDGs set by the United Nations.

ESG reporting is compulsory for many companies, especially those that are listed on stock exchanges or regulated by government bodies. However, small enterprises may not be required to report on ESG factors. What concerns SDG reporting, it is not obligatory for companies, but it is seen as a voluntary commitment to contribute to the achievement of the 17 Sustainable Development Goals and address global challenges.

There are several guidelines on incorporation of SDGs into business strategies, like "SDG Compass, the Guide for business action on SDGs", which has been developed by UN Global Compact, GRI, and wbcsd (2018), or "Integrating the SDGs into Corporate Reporting: a Practical Guide ESG reporting" (UN Global Compact and GRI, 2018). ESG reporting tends to be subject to national or regional regulations.

An example here can be a set of regulations in the EU like Corporate Sustainability Reporting Directive, European Sustainability Reporting Standards, and other legislative acts that set the rules for disclosing business sustainability efforts.

According to SDG Compass (UN Global Compact, GRI and wbcsd, 2018), communication on SDG performance is the last step of business sustainability action after understanding SDGs, defining priorities, setting goals, and integrating sustainability into business. However, all these steps can serve as a good starting point for sustainability communication. For example, disclosing why and how sustainability priorities have been set and describing business processes that have been changed in pursuit of sustainability.

ESG reporting and SDG communication exhibit a closely intertwined relationship, whereby the data derived from ESG reports can be effectively leveraged to convey the extent of an organization's contribution to the SDGs to diverse stakeholder groups. This symbiotic connection between ESG reporting and SDG communication underscores the intrinsic alignment between corporate sustainability practices, as reflected in ESG disclosures, and the broader global sustainability agenda encapsulated in the SDGs. Consequently, ESG data serves as a valuable reservoir of pertinent information that can be strategically employed to elucidate an entity's multifaceted impacts and progress in advancing the SDGs, catering to the distinct informational needs of various target audiences, be they investors, consumers, regulators, or the broader society. This integrative approach not only enhances transparency and accountability but also reinforces the linkages between corporate activities and the global pursuit of sustainable development.

6.2.4 SDG Communication on a Company Level

Companies and organizations are increasingly embracing the opportunity to incorporate sustainability into their core business functions and activities (Ott, Wang and Bortree, 2019). Bortree argues that a prominent trend in corporate communication is to also include sustainability into its key business strategy (Bortree, 2014). Enhancing sustainability strategy increases the satisfaction among stakeholders, higher purchase intention among potential customers, stronger brand and market position of the organization together with company reputation, and higher levels of trust (Ott, Wang and Bortree, 2019).

The use of microblogs and social networks can operate as valuable channels through which organizations can communicate their sustainable development contributions with a variety of diverse stakeholders (Lee, 2017), (Araujo & Kollat, 2018). Communication seems to be very important for promotion and further implementation of the SDGs with Losa-Jonczyk suggesting that companies who provide this impact on society should also have a role in this effort (2020).

In addition to marketing via these other channels Yang et al. (2018) recommend engaging with multiple stakeholders bilaterally, rather than just broadcasting marketing information. However, when most corporations in Etter's study (2014) use these strategies applying Corporate Skill strategy, they focus on marketing products and services. When these same groups communicate SDG information they tend to use one-way tools (Losa-Jonczyk, 2020).

6.2.5   SDG Communication on a Country Level

Countries report on their progress towards the Sustainable Development Agenda through Voluntary National Reviews (VNRs). The UN has proposed guidelines on the reporting for these VNRs. The initial recommendations were presented in 2015 and updated in 2017 and 2019 (Updated Voluntary guidelines). The guidelines are relatively general, allowing for countries to insert their own particular information and style as they see fit to reflect their country's efforts towards achieving the 2030 Agenda. They do include in the 2019 iteration of the guidelines the recommendation by Kroll and team to highlight the trade-offs, interlinkages, and synergies between individual SDGs (Kroll et al., 2019). This structure gives a lot of latitude in the format and content. This latitude given to national governments in voluntary reporting is somewhat informative and a full analysis of the entire VNRs of these countries would be beyond the scope of this chapter.

According to Losa-Jonczyk, there is a challenge in being able to compare VNRs in an apples to apples fashion (2020). Because of this, the desk research for this chapter consists primarily of a discussion of trends among four countries which are the nations of incorporation for the GovTech Startups and SMEs that were in the study.

One consistent theme among the countries and reporting of Sustainable development goals is that in their literature these countries do not phrase their initiatives in the explicit framing of the SDGs. Instead, each country has their own language and terminology which they embed in their national strategies. However, upon further analysis, many of the initiatives do have an impact upon individual SDGs. The policy documents of Norway, Finland, and Portugal similarly state goals that align with individual SDGs in terms other than those directly written in the UN labels of SDGs. For example, Sweden has a goal in their voluntary national review that states, "Being a strong voice for democracy, the rule of law and gender equality" (Government Offices of Sweden, 2021). Although this is not the direct language, it obviously would contribute to Peace Justice and strong institutions and likely SDG 5—Achieve gender equality and empower all women and girls. As recommended by the UN VNR guidelines, the countries do detail progress and lessons learned about each of the SDGs even though their expressed strategies at a national level may not be expressed in the exact same language.

Sweden, for example, has initiatives that build upon reporting on their 2030 agenda sent to the Riksdag every second year. Many of the initiatives deal with overall implementation and strategy meant to help enable the attainment of the SDGs. These include modifying business processes for reporting, integrating the 2030 agenda into those processes, and bringing these values and initiatives into decision-making processes (Government Offices of Sweden, 2021). There seems to be a tendency for the countries who are higher on the SDG achievement rating measure to have more defined processes around their approach as well as a focus on communication. And in some cases, they have a strategic focus on the application of processes and integration across organization levels (Government Offices of Sweden, 2021), (Norwegian Ministry of Local Government and Modernisation, Norwegian Ministry of Foreign Affairs, 2021), (Finland Prime Minister's Office, 2020). Sweden organized voluntary local reviews in four municipalities that occurred at the same time as the Swedish VNR (Government Offices of Sweden, 2021). Finland has initiatives to integrate sustainability assessments into the government reporting planning and budgeting. As a part of their practices, Finland is also conducting voluntary local reviews in several cities with one region that has "integrated the SDGs into its core strategies" (Finland Prime Minister's Office, 2020). In comparison, Portugal seeks to standardize practices at the local and regional levels but does not have practices that they report being already in place and processes to continue into the future (The Portuguese Republic, 2023).

The seeming maturity difference in processes manifests in a further way. In the surveyed VNRs all of the countries had feedback from private sector and civil society organizations. However, there were varying levels with which the countries reported this collaboration. Norway and Sweden involve the business sector and state their engagement and importance (Government Offices of Sweden, 2021), (Norwegian Ministry of Local Government and Modernisation, Norwegian Ministry of Foreign Affairs, 2021). In Portugal, several companies and civil society organizations participated in focus groups (The Portuguese Republic, 2023). In Finland, they report in a longitudinal manner the engagement of companies in bringing SDGs into their business priorities with the number going from 32% in 2015 to 52% by 2019 (Finland Prime Minister's Office, 2020). In addition, the Finnish government has chosen to also include the other stakeholders in the evaluation process, giving for each individual SDG both a governmental score and a score from civil society. Portugal and Norway specifically discuss the importance of small and medium enterprises (SMEs) to achieving the SDGs in their countries (The Portuguese Republic, 2023) (Norwegian Ministry of Local Government and Modernisation, Norwegian Ministry of Foreign Affairs, 2021). The variance between these could itself be an interesting research topic.

6.3   Methodology

The study utilizes an exploratory case study approach. The exploratory case study methodology is appropriate because the primary area of investigation is still not well researched (Yin, 2014). The choice of the case study method is appropriate when attempting to investigate a phenomenon in its environment. The group under investigation is a cohort of startups chosen for participation in the GovTech Connect Bootcamp (Govtech Connect Boot Camps, n.d.), an integral facet of the GovTech

Connect initiative. This initiative, supported by funding from the European Commission, is dedicated to advancing the digital transformation of public sector entities. The data acquisition strategy encompasses an examination of the digital resources of the selected GovTech startups, encompassing websites, reports, blog posts, and social media content.

The data acquisition strategy and data collection methods are tied in this research inherently in the sample selection. The method of sampling is convenience sampling. The reason for this choice is that the group in question created a sample that ideally fit the purpose of the case study research in a way that no other observed group could. In addition, the groups from the selected sample had, upon investigation, the requisite amount of publicly available data to be informative regarding the research questions. Due to the findings of the interorganizational hyperlink relationships defined in Shumate et al. (2016) in which it was observed that many organizations have links, but few have the majority of the links or "highly skewed indegree distributions" (pp. 17) it was decided to focus on one of the organizations which fit the research focus and also had a highly skewed communicational relationship to other entities. The reason for selecting this particular cohort of startups lies in the fact that the selection criteria for participating in the GovTech Connect Bootcamp was addressing sustainability issues, such as the use of technologies to promote transparency about sustainability outcomes in government projects, the use of technology to improve energy efficiency in public buildings and the use of technology to enhance sustainable tourism and reduce its environmental impact. The selection of the boot camp then suited both the sampling criteria and the communicational criterion.

Considering the inherent variations in the delineation of the GovTech concept, the inclusion of companies in a GovTech Bootcamp program can, to a certain extent, mitigate the responsibility of authors in definitively categorizing a company as belonging to the GovTech sector.

The unit of analysis is the websites and social media communication channels that communicate the B2G and B2B information on sustainability in a B2C accessible format.

Table 6.1 gives the overview of cases (research objects).

6.4   Results

6.4.1   Trends in Communicating Sustainability Activities by GovTech Startups

Aiming to understand how companies communicate their commitments to sustainability, researchers investigate the companies' websites to see if the enterprises explicitly mention the SDGs they contribute to, how they explain their sustainability commitments, what audiences they target, and what channels they choose to transfer their activities.

Table 6.1 Startups that participate in the first cohort of GovTech Bootcamp. *Source* authors

Company name	Country	Website	Nature of business
Klimato	Sweden	Klimato.co	Carbon footprint calculations (Klimato, n.d.)
Storvix	Sweden	Storvix.eu	Software for integrated data protection and cyber resilience hardware to extend the lifecycle and reduce the energy impact (Storvix, n.d.)
OpenHydro	Sweden	Openhydro.net	Calculations of carbon emissions from water reservoirs (OpenHydro, n.d.)
Measure and change	Sweden	Measureandchange.se	Climate impact analysis and calculation software (CO_2 calculations) Consulting services (Measure and Change, n.d.)
ChromaWay	Sweden	Chromaway.com	Blockchain solutions for land administration, commercial real estate, and finance (Chromaway, n.d.)
Skenario labs	Finland	Skenariolabs.com	Real estate energy and carbon footprint measurement through heating and cooling calculation method (based on ISO 52016–1:2017 monthly method) (Skenario Labs, n.d.)
Combine DAO	Finland	Combinedao.com	Smart legal contracts, forming business contracts quickly, safely, and confidentially Sustainable way of forming cross-party contracts (Combine DAO, n.d.)
Clean sea solutions	Norway	Cleanseasolutions.no	Waste collection from water (Clean Sea Solutions, n.d.)
Builtrix	Portugal	Builtrix.tech	Energy data platform that simplifies energy data collection from offices and properties to drive significant time and cost savings for energy and sustainability experts (Builtrix, n.d.)

Table 6.2 illustrates how the companies describe their sustainability efforts and contributions and specifies the SDGs they contribute to.

Although Klimato didn't issue a sustainability report, it has published Klimato's climate impact report in 2021, which to some extent serves as a sustainability report.

The solutions of Chromaway and Combine Dao are blockchain-based. There are multiple ways to apply this technology, therefore, the contribution to one particular SDG is hardly possible. In the case of companies like Builtrix and Skenario Labs, attribution of their efforts to a single SDG is also difficult, taking into account the interrelatedness of SDG 9 (Industry, Innovation, and Infrastructure) and SDG 11 (Sustainable cities).

Although the researchers allocated the SDGs, which are primarily influenced by the companies under research, it is worth stating that the influence of a company's

Table 6.2 General sustainability policy and evaluation of SDGs the companies primarily contribute to. *Source* authors

Company name	General policy on SDGs	Explicitly mentions the SDG contributes to	Separate SDG report	SDG contributes to (researchers' analysis)
Klimato	Mission—to cut food-related emissions	Yes (13)	Yes	13
Storvix	A dedicated page on the website, which claims the company's efforts in sustainable packaging, Reduced power consumption in use, longer useful life, disposal at end of life	No	No	9/7/13
OpenHydro	The company's vision is "a climate resilient, zero carbon planet where water and energy are accessible to all"	No	No	13
Measure and change	The "about us" webpage begins with "for the sake of the climate", which highlights the primary value of the company	No	No	13
Chromaway	N/a, there is a post on Linkedin describing the company's contribution to sustainable future (RBN eco, 2023)	No	No	16
SkenarioLabs	A brief sustainability policy statement in the Culture section of the website	No	No	9/11
Combine DAO	A brief sustainability overview section on the website	No	No	16
Clean sea solutions	Preservation of oceans is mentioned in the mission statement	No	No	14
Builtrix	A vision statement on the company's website	No	No	9/11

business on sustainable development can be multi-layered. Making an impact on one primary SDG may create "a chain reaction". Clearly mapping by the company's stakeholders their main focus, direct and indirect contribution of business activities on SDGs could be beneficial.

Thus, in absence of formal reports, companies tend to find ways to communicate their contribution to sustainable development in the form of mission or vision statements as well as dedicated webpages on websites or posts on social media.

Table 6.3 shows the target audience and various communication channels that the companies considered using. It should be noted that all of them use LinkedIn.

However, a smaller percentage uses Blogs, YouTube, or non-business-related social media platforms.

An analysis of communication preferences reveals a prevalent utilization of LinkedIn, while a notably lower proportion of startups engage with platforms such as Twitter, Instagram, and Facebook.

This predilection for LinkedIn can be attributed to its professional-oriented environment, which aligns with the typical B2B (business-to-business) and networking-focused strategies commonly adopted by startups. LinkedIn provides a platform conducive to showcasing expertise, networking with industry professionals, and seeking potential partners or investors, making it a natural choice for many startups.

However, it is worth acknowledging that startups with a strong emphasis on sustainability face a unique set of challenges and opportunities. Sustainability-oriented startups often operate in industries where raising awareness and gaining mass support for eco-friendly practices and products are paramount. In this context, there exists a compelling rationale for these startups to expand their social media presence to platforms like Twitter, Instagram, and Facebook.

These platforms possess broader user bases, including a substantial number of environmentally conscious consumers. By diversifying their social media presence, sustainability-focused startups can effectively reach a wider audience, disseminate information about their eco-friendly initiatives, and engage with individuals passionate about sustainability issues. This approach not only bolsters their visibility but also fosters community-building and fosters greater awareness of sustainable practices among the masses.

Since the startups under the current research are a part of the GovTech Bootcamp, which implies that they already collaborate or wish to collaborate with the government, researchers aim to identify the ways of these collaborations presented in Table 6.4.

The collaboration with governments can be done in several ways:

- joint research with government institutions,
- financial support,
- municipalities and other public sector institutions as clients,
- methodology/solution can be approved by government,
- participation in accelerators and bootcamps.

The collaboration is often done on the level of municipality, not a whole country. From the website content, it is often not entirely clear if having a public sector organization as a client is a result of procuring a solution or if the solution has been to some extent tailored for the needs of the concrete public sector organization.

Table 6.3 Target audience and communication channels. Source: authors

Company	Target audience	LinkedIn	Twitter	Facebook	Instagram	YouTube	Blog/news on the website
Klimato	General public, scientists, and potential clients	Yes		Yes	Yes		Yes
Storvix	Enterprises who need data storage	Yes	Yes	Yes	Yes		Yes
OpenHydro	Hydropower asset owners and utility companies Financial institutions that consider greenhouse gas emissions Private sector investors	Yes					
Measure and Change	Businesses and public sector	Yes					Yes
ChromaWay	Businesses	Yes	Yes	Yes	Yes	Yes	
Skenario Labs	Real estate developers and maintenance, Investors	Yes	Yes	Yes			
Combine DAO	Businesses and public sector	Yes					
Clean Sea Solutions	Businesses and municipalities	Yes		Yes	Yes		
Builtrix	Facility and property managers, energy services providers, and ESG consultants	Yes	Yes	Yes			

Table 6.4 Ways of collaboration with the government. *Source* authors

Company	Examples of collaborations with government
Klimato	Methodologies are approved by Swedish Environmental Research Institute Grant from Swedish Innovation Agency Participation In EIT Food Accelerator
Storvix	N/a
OpenHydro	HydroPower reporting guideline was compiled in collaboration with EDP Produção, Empresas Públicas de Medellín (EPM), Hydro Québec, Instituto Costarricense de Electricidad (ICE), and Statkraft (See acknowledgements sector in the guideline) Supported by Carbon13, UK Research and Innovation, the Lab
Measure and change	Financially backed by Vinnova and Almi Invest and Visive Framework agreement with Sinfra, a trade organization, which has a lot of municipalities as members Framework agreement with Karlstad municipality Collaboration with Lessebo municipality as a testbed Collaboration with Kronoberg County (investigation and a workshop)
ChromaWay	Partnership with the government of Andhra Pradesh to build a blockchain-powered system for land registration Research by Lantmäteriet (The Swedish Mapping, Cadastre and Land Registration Authority), Landshypotek Bank, SBAB, Telia, ChromaWay, and Kairos Future to study and test the possibilities of using blockchains as a technical solution for real estate transactions and the mortgage deed processes Being a partner at a platform for validating green investment claims and reporting on the impact of green projects. The project is funded and co-developed by the Emerging Markets Dialogue on Finance (EMDF) which is a project of Deutsche Gesellschaft für Internationale Zusammenarbeit (GIZ) GmbH, commissioned by the German Federal Ministry for Economic Cooperation and Development (BMZ) Partnership with a Taiwanese fintech Snowbridge (eID, notary, land registry)
Skenario Labs	N/a
Combine DAO	N/a
Clean Sea Solutions	Collaboration with Oslo Harbour, Kristiansand municipality, Rotterdam municipality Financially backed by the Research Council of Europe, The EEA and Norway Grants, The Directorate for Administration and Financial Management (DFØ), Innovasjon Norge Claims to have industrial and academic partners
Builtrix	N/A

6.4.2   Alignment of Companies' Activities with Their Countries' SDG Performance

Sustainable Development Report evaluates countries' performance related to SDGs. The performance is split into the categories "SDG achieved", "Challenges remain", "Significant challenges remain", "Major challenges remain", and "Information

Table 6.5 Alignment of companies' activities with their countries' SDG performance. Source: authors

Country	Company	SDG	Country's progress on the SDG (SDG index)	Trend
Sweden	Klimato	13	"Major challenges remain"	Stagnating trend
Sweden	Storvix	9/7/13	9 "Challenges remain" 7 "SDG achieved" 13 "Major challenges remain"	Moderately improving Moderately improving Stagnating trend
Sweden	OpenHydro	13	"Major challenges remain"	Stagnating trend
Sweden	Measure and change	13	"Major challenges remain"	Stagnating trend
Sweden	ChromaWay	16	"Challenges remain"	Moderately improving
Finland	Skenario labs	9/11	"Challenges remain" (both)	Moderately improving (both)
Finland	Combine DAO	16	"Challenges remain"	Moderately improving
Norway	Clean sea solutions	14	"Significant challenges remain"	Stagnating trend
Portugal	Builtrix	9/11	"Significant challenges remain" "challenges remain"	Moderately improving Moderately improving

unavailable". It also analyses the trends in countries' performance, which can be "On track or maintaining SDG achievement", "Moderately improving", "Stagnating", and "Increasing".

As shown in Table 6.5, the SDGs that are primarily influenced by startups under research tend to have a moderately improving trend with a few exceptions (SDG 13 "Climate action" in Sweden and SDG 14 "Life below water" in Norway have a stagnating trend). This illustrates that it is possible to gain progress on some of these items but then lose progress. If stagnating trends continue, countries will not succeed in reaching their goals for the already ambitious 2030 agenda. Thus, communication and progress should work in a feedback cycle to improve attainment.

6.4.3 Ways of Improving Sustainability Communication Practices

One continual problem as identified in the above research is that the SDG reporting at the national level has varying degrees of integration with the startup and SME SDG communication activities. Although there are many structural and organizational activities that the national governments can implement this paper primarily provides recommendations to the ecosystem of government and business cooperation activities as they intersect with the evaluation of progress towards achievement of the SDGs. One of the integral items in this cooperation is the communication activities from the SMEs and Startups, because without communication, the governments involved have no ability to see what is going on in their respective areas of influence.

Some guidelines for the startup and SME communities to better communicate the contributions to SDG attainment or even progress towards related initiatives can help make it easier for the government entities to find the relevant data for their own calculations and tracking. This is especially important when the companies and communities in question are not part of the working coalition that the government has assembled in task forces and other activities to participate in the VNRs at a national or local level.

6.4.3.1   Unlocking Visibility: Presenting Sustainability Clearly

One way to ensure that the governments are able to better discover these communications is to have a separate webpage that the company uses to explain all sustainability-related matters. This would be helpful to have a clear message embedded in a place where it is easily discoverable. This can aid in being found in web searches, but also to have the information more readily available to the potential measuring entities. In a constantly changing electronic ecosystem like the World Wide Web, it can be difficult to find what Nate Silver would call "the signal in the noise" (Silver, 2012). If the sustainability efforts of a GovTech startup are buried deep in the copywriting of informational pages this is much harder for anyone to find—be it interested community members and citizens or government authorities seeking to measure impact towards sustainable efforts. In addition to this, although it may sound like common sense it would help the entities involved if the linguistic conventions used when explaining the contribution of the SME or startup is similar to those that the government or UN would use when describing sustainability efforts. Simply put, this would make the material more discoverable and able to be considered for the VNR, or other purposes of report.

6.4.3.2   Strategic Collaborations: Prioritize, Co-Create, and Communicate

The organization should consider partnerships with local organizations, research institutions, or NGOs to help in the co-creation process or attest to the ability of the organization in their sustainability sphere. The organization should foster a participatory approach in SDG prioritization by engaging a diverse array of stakeholders, recognizing that the selection of priority SDGs should involve collaborative decision-making processes that incorporate multiple strategic methodologies. Using the collaborative methods to create strategies while keeping in mind the key competencies of the company can aid in the formulation of SDG-related objectives encompassing not only the SDGs directly linked to the core business activities of the organization but also extending to embrace additional SDGs that align with the organizational values and broader society impact objectives.

6.4.3.3 Articulating Impact: Direct and Indirect Contributions Unveiled

Indirect contributions to the SDGs are better understood when clearly explained. Some contributions of startups and SMEs are very closely tied and related to the SDGs in an obvious way. However, if the connection to an SDG is a small part of or not explicitly a part of an SDG it would help anyone observing the progress of the SDGs if the company explained what the sustainability connection is in a clear and direct way. Once again, adhering to the best practices of using keywords that are easily discoverable through web searching platforms would help this. However, sometimes there can be a seemingly small thing that does not immediately indicate the connection to an SDG. An example might be an eID company who states that they are broadly helping SDG 16. If that company were to state that this use of their ID system increases the ability for governments to provide "accountable and inclusive institutions" using the exact wording of the SDGs the connection is more immediate for anyone reading.

6.4.3.4 Showcasing Collaboration: Highlighting Government Partnerships

Sometimes the startup or SME might be part of specific government efforts in which they play an integral role in an initiative which the government might want to tout as aiding in the sustainability effort. In this case, it is recommended that the company also communicate their contribution as a stakeholder in the government efforts. Similarly, when there are public sector clients who have projects which may aid in the attainment of the SDGs it is important to underline the cooperation with those organizations and explain how the solution was made to help the entity and sustainability efforts. Ideally, this could be in the form of a joint webpage or statement on a dedicated electronic location.

Communication of initiatives within GovTech startups and SMEs can have additional benefits for the companies in question. This is because even though the government may not specifically procure projects with expressly stated purpose of achieving SDG targets, it can be considered additional favourable criteria in the procurement process. Some GovTech companies are considered B2B in addition to their B2G offerings. However, having more government projects can help to bring more business, having more impact than profit. Therefore, it is recommended that GovTech startups and SMEs follow certain practices when communicating the contributions made for sustainability and SDG attainment—especially when those contributions align with the country's goals.

6.4.3.5 Strategic Alignment: Connect Company Activities with Government Priorities

The desk research revealed that many times the SMEs and startups who may already be engaged in activities related to the SDGs do not always communicate that activity or relate it directly to the priorities of the governments. What follows is a series of suggestions to integrate data from national SDG reports to potentially help companies achieve a competitive advantage through a mutually beneficial process of prioritizing the achievement of the SDGs. This follows the recommendations by the Nordic countries as stated in the VNRs about how to integrate the processes and collaborate better across helix actor silos.

GovTech companies considering entering or expanding to new markets or regions are advised to meticulously review and draw insights from the latest voluntary national reports on the SDG progress of the country in which they intend to operate. This allows them to leverage the identified counter-specific and regional SDG priorities as a foundational framework for effectively articulating their innovative solutions to government entities or participating in the above-mentioned co-creation and stakeholder engagement processes.

6.4.3.6 Effective Communication: Tailor Messages for Impact and Understanding

Once the co-creation process is ongoing the company can start to mould the vision and strategy to appeal to the decision-makers and stakeholders to develop further their value proposition to the stakeholders including sustainability as a key objective. This is possible using the information gathered during sessions with stakeholders to quantify the impact of the GovTech solution. By providing concrete data and evidence of the social, economic, and environmental impact the solution offers, it is possible to use the metrics of the stakeholders to showcase case studies, metrics, and real-world examples to state the impact in the stakeholders' and seven customers' own language, measurable, and terminology. If applicable, emphasizing the local or regional impact of the solution can highlight for decision-makers the support of local job creation, economic development, or environmental conservation efforts in an area that matters to the decision-makers. Companies are recommended to demonstrate how their GovTech solutions can lead to cost savings and operational efficiency for the government agency. This showcases how sustainability efforts can be economically advantageous to the government and other stakeholders. By focusing on the benefits known and in the language of potential customers, the communication materials and presentations are clear, concise, and free of jargon. If the organization follows the above processes the communication materials will use language that resonates with the government's sustainability objectives from the inception of the project.

6.4.3.7   Pilot Programs for Progress: Showcase Practical Benefits

One strategy to gain implementation of a technology and showcase its value is to offer to initiate a pilot program to demonstrate the practical benefits and value of the solution within the government. The results of this pilot can serve as a showcase for broader adoption. When put together with the co-creation methods discussed earlier, applying agile methods and establishing a feedback mechanism to gather input from the government stakeholders and incorporate their suggestions and concerns into future proposals and solutions will allow for further co-creation improving the solution and continually showing more value.

6.4.3.8   Continuous Engagement: Post-Implementation Educational Initiatives

The implementation process of technologies is usually not complete once the development and initial installation take place. By ensuring the adoption and use of the technologies within the organization, additional value is realized. By offering to conduct educational workshops or seminars to educate employees and leaders about the solution, how to use it, the sustainability benefits and potential of the solution, and even giving hands-on demonstrations companies can help in ensuring the value is seen and felt in the customer organizations.

6.4.3.9   Strategic Compliance: Stay Ahead of Sustainability and Regulation

By staying ahead of sustainability and compliance companies can achieve a competitive advantage because companies that adopt sustainable processes may have less legal and regulatory challenges. In addition, this can attach socially responsible investors and impactive investors who seek companies with a strong track record of ESG performance. The access to capital can aid in the ability of the organization to weather the storms of the economic cycle or to grow and scale. This process begins with understanding the government priorities by researching thoroughly and understating the specific sustainability priorities, policies, and goals of the government bodies engaged in the SDG-related processes and projects.

Understanding these priorities will allow the company to engage stakeholders within the government agencies. This by nature must include the decision-makers, procurement officers, and sustainability experts. This will further inform the goals of the company. By taking a collaborative approach and emphasizing the willingness and ability of the company to work jointly with the government and other stakeholders to co-create solutions that address sustainability issues. It helps if the company can point to past success in joint development with public sector organizations.

6.4.3.10   Formal Accountability: Regular Sustainability Reporting

It is recommended that the companies communicate their commitment to transparency and accountability by offering to regularly report on the sustainability performance of the olution. Discuss how the company will measure and track relevant metrics. Uphold the principles of transparency and disclosure in instances where GovTech startups have achieved notable successes in the implementation of their solutions within the public sector. These achievements should be communicated extensively through a diverse array of communication channels, unless contractual obligations, such as Non-Disclosure Agreements (NDAs) impose restrictions on these disclosures.

By effectively communicating the sustainability contributions and alignment of the GovTech solution with the government's goals and aiding the customer in achieving that value, the likelihood that the company with gain government contracts and partnerships that support both environmental and societal objectives will be increased. Additionally, it may be possible for GovTech companies to streamline communication by adopting established SDG reporting frameworks and methodologies such as the comprehensive guide "integrating the SDGs into Corporate Reporting: a Practical Guide", which has been jointly developed by respected organizations including the Global Reporting Initiative (GRI), the Principles for Responsible Investment (PRI), and the United Nations Global Compact, as a means to structure and enhance their reporting on SDG progress.

6.4.3.11   Diversify Communication: Explore Varied Outreach Modalities

Deliberately contemplate the prospect of expanding the scope of target audiences of solutions, while taking into the account the inherent characteristics of the product or solution, recognizing that diversifying the audience can amplify the reach and impact of sustainability endeavours. By embracing an inclusive approach to communicating by diversifying the modalities through which the progress on SDGs is disseminated, encompassing a wide spectrum of formats, ranging from online and offline platforms to textual auditory, and visual mediums, companies can ensure accessibility and comprehensibility across a broad audience.

6.4.3.12   Active Participation: Contribute to Voluntary National Reviews

Actively engaging in the discourse surrounding the SDG progress within the private sector can also help communication efforts, as these discussions are commonly reflected in voluntary national reports even in countries in which the private sector is not directly included in the assembling process of the VNRs. GovTech startups and

SMEs should strive to make meaningful contributions to the private sector engagement with government bodies regarding the SDG 2030 Agenda, with the potential inclusion of their sustainability efforts as noteworthy use cases in Voluntary National Reviews.

6.5 Discussion

The existence of an organization pertaining to environmental protection and other activities with a sustainability focus does not necessarily mean that organizational communication is a priority for that organization, or that any communication which does take place describes the company's efforts and contributions to the SDGs. The challenges related to the many facets of interorganizational communication in B2B, B2G, and B2C contexts in ICT mediums are well documented (Shumate et al., 2016).

The visibility of sustainability efforts is a critical consideration. Separate webpages dedicated to the sustainability efforts which include not only statements of support of sustainability but also presenting action steps and measurable impacts would be a starting place for companies can help facilitate this communication. This would help the customers ascertain the "signal in the noise" in the digital world. If this information is presented in a clear manner in an easily discoverable presentation, it can help facilitate community engagement as well as give government entities with accessible data that is very important for the evaluation of progress towards the SDGs.

Strong collaboration among organizations in different sectors is a key to success. A participatory approach in decision-making processes and partnerships with local entities is essential for successful sustainability efforts. Alignment of core business activities to specific SDGs as well as extending efforts to embrace additional SDGs which resonate with the values of the specific organization can be a way to increase the impact of these efforts. The emphasis on collaboration extends to highlighting existing cases of cooperation with government authorities and underlining the interconnectedness between private and public sector efforts towards attaining the SDGs.

Creating effective communication efforts is key for companies to articulate both their direct and indirect contributions to the SDGs. The significance of language alignment cannot be understated in that it is beneficial for the narratives of the companies to mirror the government and UN conventions. If the communication can explicitly connect activities to specific SDGs with language that resonates with stakeholders it becomes possible for governments to use the communication as a tool to measure and acknowledge the impact of SMEs and startups more directly.

Companies have different goals than governments, on a fundamental level the companies are attempting to make a profit in addition to their sustainability efforts, but here strategic alignment could be an important difference maker. By emphasizing the sustainability efforts in ways that understand the importance of government priorities and integrating with them, companies can better communicate the difference they are already making or trying to make. By researching in a thorough way, the national SDG reports, legislation, and sustainability requirements, the company can communicate what it is doing in a way that makes it clear the impact they are having. The collaborative approach is key to the sustainable focus in any country, and alignment can aid this effort. Regular sustainability reports can help align with the global push towards transparency and accountability.

The strategic foresight to stay ahead of sustainability and compliance requirements can be a source of competitive advantage, attracting investors who are or want to be perceived as socially responsible. Pilot programs and educational workshops demonstrate a commitment to sustainability and its solutions and can provide grounds for further collaboration. It is also crucial to go beyond the ideation, development, and initial installation phases. By having continuous engagement strategies post-implementation, it is possible for the sustainable efforts and associated technologies to diffuse further and have more impact.

Broadening impact and outreach is very important to the achievement of the SDGs. By diversifying communication modalities, companies can appeal to a broader audience. By increasing and expanding outreach including contributing to a co-creation process of contributing to Voluntary National Reviews, it may be possible to increase the opportunities for GovTech startups and SMEs to play a more prominent role in the SDG discourse.

Fostering effective collaborations between governments, SMEs and startups in the GovTech field can help in measuring and achieving the SDGs. Through clear communication, strategic alignment and continuous engagement in realizing sustainable development objectives improvement in the processes and measurement may improve. As the discourse on sustainable practices evolves, adhering to these practices can provide a roadmap to navigating the complex evolving landscape of SDG collaborations between GovTech firms and governments.

This study used data collection and analysis methods that relied upon desk research and secondary documentary data. If the researchers had access to stakeholders and were able to conduct interviews with them, more insight could have been gleaned into the reasons why these communication choices were made. Because of this, there is a limit to the amount of triangulation that can be expected.

Future work may include researching a bigger sample of GovTech enterprises, including those who operate outside the EU. Also, understanding the drivers and barriers to communicating sustainability information can be further explored. Understanding the ways, in which governments can effectively collect data and measure the contribution of private enterprises, including GovTech companies, could, on the one hand, help the private sector to promote their products and services, and on the other hand, ensure that the public sector utilizes available technology solutions to achieve SDGs.

6.6 Conclusion

GovTech enterprises do not communicate their sustainability efforts in the best possible way. They tend to limit themselves to making short sustainability statements. Formal sustainability reports are not usually prepared, SDGs that these companies influence are not explicitly mentioned, and communication channels are underused. These omissions in communication can be explained by the startup status of the companies under research and the need to focus on generating revenue first. At the same time, GovTech companies, especially those whose nature of business is tightly connected to the environmental block of SDGs, could use some guidance as to the ways they communicate their sustainability efforts. The recommendations suggested by authors for GovTech include clearly explaining the direct and indirect impact of the company's activities on different SDGs on the websites and through communication channels, aligning business efforts with the government's priorities on the markets they operate, making formal sustainability reports, showcasing existing collaborations with public authorities.

References

Acivilate. (no date). *Acivilate*. Retrieved October 15, 2023, from https://acivilate.com/
Allen, P. (2022). *The rise of GovTech: Why startups should work with governments (sponsored): EU-Startups, EU*. Retrieved January 30, 2023, from https://www.eu-startups.com/2022/08/the-rise-of-govtech-why-startups-should-work-with-governments-sponsored/
Araujo, T., & Kollat, J. (2018). Communicating effectively about CSR on Twitter: The power of engaging strategies and storytelling elements. *Internet Research, 28*(2), 419–431. https://doi.org/10.1108/IntR-04-2017-0172
Bharosa, N. (2022). 'The rise of GovTech: Trojan horse or blessing in disguise? A research agenda. *Government Information Quarterly*. https://doi.org/10.1016/j.giq.2022.101692
Bortree, D. (2014). The state of CSR communication research: A summary and future direction. *Public Relations Journal*. Retrieved October 15, 2023, from https://prjournal.instituteforpr.org/wp-content/uploads/2014BORTREE.pdf
Builtrix. (no date). *Builtrix*. Retrieved September 15, 2023 from https://www.builtrix.tech/
ChromaWay. (no date). *ChromaWay*. Retrieved September 15, 2023, from https://chromaway.com/
Citibeats. (no date). *CitiBeats*. Retrieved October 15, 2023, from https://www.citibeats.com/
Clean Sea Solutions. (no date). *Clean sea solutions*. Retrieved September 15, 2023, from https://www.cleanseasolutions.no/
Combine DAO. (no date). *Combine DAO*. Retrieved September 15, 2023, from https://combinedao.com/
Dauliyeva, G., Yeraliyeva, A., Sadykhanova, G., & Bimendiyeva, L. (2020). The partnership of governments for sustainable development. In *Proceedings of the 1 st international conference on business technology for a sustainable environmental system (BTSES-2020)* viewed January 30, 2023
Dener, C., et al. (2021) *GovTech maturity index, open knowledge repository*. World Bank. Retrieved January 15, 2023, from https://openknowledge.worldbank.org/handle/10986/36233
Digicampus, *Samen Innoveren over Grenzen Heen*. (2023). *Digicampus*. Retrieved October 15, 2023, from https://digicampus.tech/

Estonia's Governmental Innovation Lab. (2023). *Accelerate Estonia*. Retrieved October 15, 2023, from https://accelerateestonia.ee/

Etter, M. (2014). Broadcasting, reacting, engaging—three strategies for CSR communication in twitter. *Journal of Communication Management, 18*(4), 322–342. https://doi.org/10.1108/JCOM-01-2013-0007

FASTFWD Belgium: Digitisation of Belgian companies. (no date). *Fastfwd Belgium|Digitisation of Belgian companies*. Retrieved October 15, 2023, from https://en.fastfwd-belgium.be/

Finland Prime Minister's Office. (2020). *Voluntary national review 2020*. Report on the implementation of the 2030 Agenda for Sustainable Development. Retrieved October 15, 2023, from https://sustainabledevelopment.un.org/content/documents/26261VNR_Report_Finland_2020.pdf

Government Offices of Sweden. (2021). *Voluntary national review 2021*. Report on the implementation of the 2030 Agenda for Sustainable Development. Retrieved October 15, 2023, from https://www.government.se/reports/2021/06/voluntary-national-review-2021---sweden/

Govtech Connect Boot Camps. (no date). *EU GovTech Boot Camp*. Retrieved October 15, 2023, from https://www.govtechbootcamps.com/

Govtech in the Nordic-Baltic region. (no date). *Nordic cooperation*. Retrieved January 30, 2023, from https://www.norden.org/en/publication/govtech-nordic-baltic-region-part-1

GovTech Lab Lithuania. (No date). *GovTech Lab Lithuania*. Retrieved October 15, 2023, from https://govtechlab.lt/

GovTech Lab Luxembourg. (no date). *The lab—govtech lab—Luxembourg*. Retrieved October 15, 2023, from https://govtechlab.public.lu/en/lab.html

Govtech market size with emerging trends 2022: Top key players updates, business growing strategies, competitive dynamics, industry segmentation and forecast to 2027. (2022). *Digital Journal*. Retrieved January 30, 2023 from https://www.digitaljournal.com/pr/govtech-market-size-with-emerging-trends-2022-top-key-players-updates-business-growing-strategies-competitive-dynamics-industry-segmentation-and-forecast-to-2027

Govtech Sweden. (no date). *GovTech Sweden*. Retrieved October 15, 2023 fromhttps://govtechsweden.se/

GRI, United Nations Global Compact, wbcsd. (2018). SDG Compass. The guide for business a actions on the SDGs. Retrieved October 15, 2023 from https://www.undp.org/ukraine/publications/sdg-compass-guide-business-action-sdgs

GRI, United Nations Global Compact. (2018). Integrating the SDGs into corporate reporting: a practical guide. Retrieved October 15, 2023 from https://sdghelpdesk.unescap.org/sites/default/files/2020-04/GRI_UNGC_Reporting-on-SDGs_Practical_Guide.pdf

Jones, E., Watson, B., Gardner, J., & Gallois, C. (2004). Organizational communication: Challenges for the new century. *Journal of Communication, 54*(4), 722–750. https://doi.org/10.1111/j.1460-2466.2004.tb02652.x

Klimato. (no date). *Klimato*. Retrieved September 15, 2023 from https://www.klimato.co/

Klimato's Climate Impact Report. (2021). Retrieved October 15, 2023 from https://www.klimato.co/blog/klimato-climate-impact-report-2021#:~:text=Reducing%20the%20climate%20impact%20from,of%20455%25%20compared%20to%202020

Kroll, C., Warchold, A., & Pradhan, P. (2019). Sustainable development goals (SDGs): Are we successful in turning trade-offs into synergies? *Palgrave Communications, 5*, 140. https://doi.org/10.1057/s41599-019-0335-5

Labanava, A., Liiv, I., & Pappel, I. (2023). Capacity building in GovTech for measuring and achievement of sustainable development goals. https://doi.org/10.54941/ahfe1003888

Lee, T. (2017). The status of corporate social responsibility research in public relations: A content analysis of published articles in eleven scholarly journals from 1980 to 2015. *Public Relations Review, 43*(1), 211–218.

Losa-Jonczyk, A. (2020). Communication strategies in social media in the example of ICT companies. *Information (Switzerland), 11*(5), 1–15. https://doi.org/10.3390/INFO11050254

Measure and Change. (no date). *Measure and change*. Retrieved September 15, 2023 from Measureandchange.se

Ministerie van Algemene Zaken. (2021). GovTech in the Netherlands: Building a leading Govtech Nation, Report|Government.nl. Ministerie van Algemene Zaken. Retrieved January 30, 2023 from https://www.government.nl/documents/reports/2021/06/30/govtech-in-the-netherlands

MySidewalk. (no date). *mySidewalk*. Retrieved October 15, 2023 from https://www.mysidewalk.com/

Nebula, A StateUp database. (2023). Retrieved October 15, 2023 from https://stateup.co/nebula/

Norwegian Ministry of Local Government and Modernisation, Norwegian Ministry of Foreign Affairs. (2021). *Voluntary National Review 2021*. Report on the implementation of the 2030 Agenda for Sustainable Development. Retrieved October 15, 2023 from https://sustainabledevelopment.un.org/content/documents/28233Voluntary_National_Review_2021_Norway.pdf

OpenHydro. (no date). *OpenHydro*. Retrieved September 15, 2023 from https://openhydro.net/

Ott, H., Wang, R., & Bortree, D. (2016). Communicating sustainability online: An examination of corporate, nonprofit, and university websites. *Mass Communication and Society, 19*(5), 671–687. https://doi.org/10.1080/15205436.2016.1204554

Pavlovska, E. (2018). "Grey literature" in electronic archives. *Digital Presentation and Preservation of Cultural and Scientific Heritage, 8*, 105–108. https://doi.org/10.55630/dipp.2018.8.8

PublicTech lab: Ie university. (2021). *IE PublicTech Lab*. Retrieved October 15, 2023 from https://publictechlab.ie.edu/

RBN eco. (2023). *Chromaway: Revolutionizing blockchain technology for a sustainable future*. Retrieved October 15, 2023 from https://www.linkedin.com/pulse/chromaway-revolutionizing-blockchain-technology-sustainable-future%3FtrackingId=gGIcqX2cInHM1d2It7f2RA%253D%253D/?trackingId=gGIcqX2cInHM1d2It7f2RA%3D%3D

ResourceX. The Future of Budgeting. (no date). *ResourceX*. Retrieved October 15, 2023 from https://www.resourcex.net/

RightHear. (no date). *RightHear*. Retrieved October 15, 2023 from https://www.right-hear.com/

Shumate, M. D., Atouba, Y., Cooper, K. R., & Pilny, A. (2016). Interorganizational communication. In C. R. Scott, & L. Lewis (Eds.), *The international encyclopedia of organizational communication*. Wiley-Blackwell Publishing.

Signatura. (no date). *La Plataforma de Firma digital más segura Y resiliente del mundo, Signatura*. Retrieved October 15, 2023 from https://signatura.co/

Signitzer, B., & Prexl, A. (2008). Corporate sustainability communications: Aspects of theory and professionalization. *Journal of Public Relations Research, 20*, 1–19. https://doi.org/10.1080/10627260701726996

Silver, N. (2012). *The signal and the noise: Why so many predictions fail–but some don't*. Penguin Press.

Simulation-based public engagement tools for government. (no date). *Balancing Act*. Retrieved October 15, 2023 from https://abalancingact.com/

Skenario Labs. (no date). *Skenario Labs*. Retrieved September 15, 2023 from https://www.skenariolabs.com/

StormSensor. A Climate Technology Company. (no date). *StormSensor*. Retrieved October 15, 2023 from https://stormsensor.io/

Storvix. (no date). *Storvix*. Retrieved September 15, 2023 from https://storvix.eu/

Technologien für die zukunft von staat und verwaltung. (no date). *GovTech Campus Deutschland*. Retrieved October 15, 2023 from https://govtechcampus.de/

The Portuguese Republic. (2023). *Voluntary national review*. Retrieved October 15, 2023 from https://hlpf.un.org/countries/portugal/voluntary-national-review-2023#:~:text=AN%20INCLUSIVE%20VOLUNTARY%20NATIONAL%20REVIEW&text=In%202022%2C%20significant%20steps%20were,the%20Portuguese%20Cooperation%20Strategy%202030

Tyler Technologies. (no date). *tylertech*. Retrieved October 15, 2023 from https://www.tylertech.com/

UN General Assembly. (2015). *Transforming our world: the 2030 Agenda for Sustainable Development*, 21 October 2015, A/RES/70/1. Retrieved January 30, 2023, from https://www.refworld.org/docid/57b6e3e44.html.

Woolley, M. (1992). Using statistics for desk research. *Aslib Proceedings, 44*(5), 227–233. https://doi.org/10.1108/eb051276

Yang, J., Basile, K., & Letourneau, O. (2018). The impact of social media platform selection on effectively communicating about corporate social responsibility. *Journal of Marketing Communications., 26*, 1–23. https://doi.org/10.1080/13527266.2018.1500932

Alena Labanava, an e-governance specialist, seamlessly blends a robust legal foundation with a keen interest in the convergence of digital government transformation and sustainability. Her expertise spans public-private partnerships, public procurement, and capacity building for civil servants. Beyond academia, Alena volunteered for UN DESA and actively contributes to various initiatives at the e-Governance Academy, showcasing her commitment to shaping innovative solutions at the nexus of governance and technology.

Regina Erlenheim is vice rector of research at Estonian Business School and e-governance lecturer at the Tallinn University of Technology on an international Master's programme E-Governance Technologies and Services where she focuses on public service development, service design, and entrepreneurship. She earned her PhD from a joint programme between the Tallinn University of Technology and Swinburne University of Technology in Melbourne, Australia. By combining her academic work and teaching activities she focuses on different facets of designing proactive services from customers', service providers' and design process's point of view.

Chapter 7
Organizational Sustainability, Hypocrisy, and Finnish Universities

Meri Löyttyniemi

Abstract Higher education institutions need to address the global polycrisis. This organizational study delves into Finnish universities´ sustainability programs, management challenges and what are the stifling factors for implementation despite the accelerating sustainability and CSR commitments. This chapter introduces how differences between universities´ talk, decisions, and actions appear in the context of Finnish universities. Hypocrisy, greenwashing, and aspirational talk will be discussed, and managerial implications for transformational change in the organizations will be introduced. Empirical study is based on Finnish universities, 14 in total, all committed to national theses on advancing sustainable development. By using mixed methods, grounded theory, and Gioia method, walking the talk is examined. Strong stakeholder expectations and moderate priority of sustainability implementation seem to lead to hypocritical activities. Factors and impulses supporting and weakening the SD-CSR implementation are mapped, and universities are categorized into four groups in terms of differences between the sustainability talk and walk: beginners, followers, question marks, and forerunners. The typical challenges are strong but ambiguous commitment combined with low implementation, minimal human and other resources, unclear organizational status, ambiguous responsibilities, and temporary positions. The chapter will provide possible solutions and managerial implications on how to prevent decoupling and turn the hypocrisy into authenticity and transformative action.

Keywords Hypocrisy · Greenwash · Aspirational talk · Universities · Higher education

Abbreviations:

SD   Sustainable Development

M. Löyttyniemi (✉)
Jyväskylä University School of Business and Economics, Jyväskylä, Finland
e-mail: meri.loyttyniemi@uef.fi; meri.loyttyniemi@aalto.fi; meri.lm.loyttyniemi@student.jyu.fi

© The Author(s), under exclusive license to Springer Nature Singapore Pte Ltd. 2024   135
M. Kooskora and A. Kekkonen (eds.), *Performance Challenges in Organizational Sustainability*, Responsible Leadership and Sustainable Management,
https://doi.org/10.1007/978-981-97-5548-6_7

ESD   Education for Sustainable Development, DESD as Decade of ESD
SD-CSR   Sustainable Development and Corporate Social Responsibility, referring
              to universities´ sustainability and responsibility work
HEI   Higher Education Institution

7.1   Introduction

7.1.1   Overview

The global polycrisis requires urgent transformation. This chapter explores the sustainability implementation of Finnish universities, finding reasons for the modest progress and recommendations for improved performance. It is essential to understand the contradictions between the walk and the talk: *How do differences between universities´ talk, decisions, and actions appear in the context of Finnish universities?* The decoupling between universities´ sustainability targets and implementation will be analyzed through hypocrisy and other concepts of organizational theory. Hypocrisy is a rational response to contradictory stakeholder demands but there are also similar pitfalls for organizational performance like greenwash and aspirational talk. All fourteen universities in Finland and their research, teaching, campus, and societal impact are analyzed and e.g., The Impact ranking is used for comparing the performance. By investigating the methods and challenges of leadership, logic, and appearances of hypocrisy can be found. Despite positive attitudes, there are recurring topics like lack of designated human resources and strategic focus of activities. The study suggests managerial implications on how to turn the hypocrisy into better sustainability performance.

7.1.2   How Universities' Sustainability Management is Progressing

During the 1990s, management studies understood the significance of environmental management and corporate responsibility (Seeck, 2008, Whiteman et al., 2012, Tienari & Meriläinen, 2021, Sandberg et al., 2022). A strong paradox was apparent between the ecological concerns despite increasing eco-efficiency and other measures. Academy of Management Review and other journals published pioneering sustainability issues and research started to bloom (Gladwin et al., 1995). Studying organizational sustainability within higher education expanded as well.

Organizational theory is an important framework if we are to develop universities to make transformational changes. Finnish universities provide a lucrative environment to study the sustainability implementation, due to the time, where sustainable development grew from a minor topic to a major phenomenon. Relevant research especially within the Finnish universities of applied sciences has been conducted on education, quality systems, and sustainable development (Asikainen & Kangastie, 2023; Holm, 2014; Rohweder, 2001; Salminen & Friman, 2022). However, research on managing universities' sustainability in Finland has been scarce. Finnish universities´ joint commitment, sustainability thesis (Unifi, 2020; Böhling et al., 2022), sparked even further the interest.

Despite the global and national SD-CSR (Sustainable Development and Corporate Social Responsibility) commitments, there is a significant gap between the talk and the walk. Through abductive reasoning (Mantere & Ketokivi, 2013) hypocrisy was chosen as an approach due to the observations and findings along the journey. The general feeling of research participants can be summarized in the quote: *"Our organization should be more of a pioneer in these matters than we are, to be honest"*.

7.2 Theoretical Background

7.2.1 Organizational Management, Sustainability, and Higher Education

A substantial amount of research has been conducted by European and global research institutions and private and governmental stakeholders on universities' and sustainability management (Bekessy et al., 2007; Leal Filho et al., 2017; Lozano, 2011). International Journal of Sustainability in Higher Education and other management journals has published relevant studies (Disterheft et al., 2012; Wals & Jickling, 2002), and sustainability movements within universities and sustainability cover all continents (Molthan-Hill et al., 2019; Mulà et al., 2017).

Universities are typically committed to sustainability issues, but the action is restrained. Why sustainability is not addressed properly in universities despite commitments (Lozano et al., 2013)? Thierry et al. (2023) are challenging HEIs and asking why even universities are not capable of preserving the socio-ecological conditions for academia and insisting that there is no research on a dead planet. Researchers ask for radical interventions within HEIs (Lotz-Sisitka et al., 2015, Elo et al., 2023). How to address universities as organizations with transformative ideas?

7.2.2 Contested Approaches to Sustainability Demands

Decreasing the negative impact on Earth is taken severely also by management sciences in increasing pace at least by the sheer number of articles (Williams et al., 2017). Here organizational phenomena stifling the change will be introduced.

7.2.2.1   Hypocrisy

The gap between the organizational talk and managerial walk is explained by organizational hypocrisy. What is hypocrisy? It is defined as a morally discrediting interpretation of perceived word-deed misalignment (Effron et al., 2018). Discourse, decisions, and actions of an organization operate seemingly independent of one another, and decoupling takes place by different patterns for external and internal use, even in organizations like schools (Kiliçoğlu, 2017). Hypocrisy is a rational and strategic response to contradictory stakeholder demands, e.g., environmental pressures. Hypocrisy is relevant in the context of understanding how talk, decisions, and action differ from each other and why sustainability is often not put into practice (Allam et al., 2020; Cho et al., 2015). Thus, hypocrisy is one useful way for understanding better, and explaining the complicated nature of organizational behaviour.

The father of organizational hypocrisy is Swedish organizational theorist and professor Nils Brunsson. He argues that organizations frequently engage in hypocrisy, where there is a discrepancy between their stated goals, policies, or values and their actual behaviour or decision-making processes (Brunsson, 1989). Hypocrisy can be seen in areas such as ethics, corporate social responsibility, or organizational values. Organizations engage often in impression management, strategic communication, and symbolic acts to create an appearance of consistency and adherence to their stated values, even when their behaviour may not align with those values (Brunsson, 2003, 2006).

How about hypocrisy and universities? A commendable investigation of hypocrisy within universities was conducted by Yang et al. (2020) in organizational and employee pro-environmental behaviours. In that study, motivational incentives were the national funding (in UK), cost reduction, positive PR, and student recruitment were the focal points of managerial efforts and the concealed reasons for organizational-level hypocritical pro-environmental behaviour. How about in the context of business schools? Snelson-Powell et al. (2020) have found clear talk-action inconsistencies with sustainability commitments and MBA programs of UK business schools. One of their insights is that the local context is relevant in explaining organizational hypocrisy. Universities should recruit specialists with the knowledge to deliver the action to meet the talk. Parallel findings by Gioia and Corley (2017) are shown about American business schools. In their study it is showcased how educational programs are under the pressure of external forces and internal willingness. Besides, similar findings on the responsibility of the Finnish business schools´ management education are found by Pesonen (2003), Aaltonen and Siltaoja (2022), and Wegelius (2022).

7.2.2.2   Greenwashing

Greenwashing is the process of providing misleading information about how company's products are more environmentally sound (Avlonas & Nassos, 2020;

Parguel et al., 2011). According to Seele and Gatti (2017), to be considered greenwashing, a green message must combine falsity with an accusation of being misleading. According to a literature review on greenwashing within universities states that greenwashing appears to be present in higher education and educational proposals or experiences should tackle greenwashing (Álvarez-García & Sureda-Negre, 2023).

Universities may engage in greenwashing for various reasons, including enhancing their reputation, attracting environmentally conscious students and faculty, and aligning with trends. There have been critical voices like Jones (2012) on UK universities and their greenwashing. Lyon and Montgomery (2015) call for multilevel work in order to understand the broad variety of misleading communication and very heterogenic attitudes towards greenwashing.

7.2.2.3 Aspirational Talk

Aspirational talk refers to communication that is intended to inspire and motivate individuals towards achieving a specific goal. Christensen et al. (2020, 2021) argue that aspirational talk is a form of strategic communication employed by organizations to create a positive image of corporate sustainability, even if there is limited evidence of concrete actions.

Most of the literature concentrates on the positive aspects of CSR, although a growing number of studies are pointing opposite. When organizations engage in misleading aspirational talk without substantive actions, it can lead to accusations of greenwashing or deceptive practices (Lauriano et al., 2022). This can erode trust among stakeholders and undermine the credibility of sustainability efforts (Koep, 2017). On the other hand, Penttilä (2020) presents valuable views on aspirational CSR talk and how it can reinforce communications about responsibility within regular organizational communication processes. Talk is not "only talk", but as an act itself.

Overall, research provides valuable insights into the dynamics of corporate sustainability communication and the potential challenges associated with aspirational language and rhetoric (Koep, 2017), also within universities (Álvarez-García & Sureda-Negre, 2023). Their research encourages organizations to move beyond mere talk and focus on genuine sustainability efforts to create a meaningful impact.

7.2.3 Decoupling—Understanding the Reverse Sides of Sustainability Efforts

Hypocrisy, greenwashing, and aspirational talk can be claimed to be persistent in organizational culture. Understanding organizations and their (in)capabilities of attaining SD-CSR requires genuine observations of organizational and human behaviour. Aim of this research is to understand the complexities of organizational decoupling—why universities are negligent to their own SD-CSR commitments although it would mean better performance.

By comparing these phenomena, several similarities, but also differences can be observed. I would refer also these as the reverse side of sustainability efforts. Typically, the positive impact is emphasized in the formal and informal communications by the universities (Lozano & Barreiro-Gen, 2019, Leal Filho et al., 2017; Gatti et al., 2019). It is relevant to study the conceptions why are we stuck to the status quo. One study was conducted by Gioia and Chittipeddi (1991) on how to initiate strategic change within a large public, multiple-campus university. Universities are characterized by multiplicity of goals and are frequently politicized in their work.

Firstly, an ample amount of stakeholder expectations seems to lead to hypocritical activities. Prevailing theories assume that the coordination and control of activity are the critical dimensions on which formal organizations have succeeded in today's modern world, but much of the empirical research on organizations casts doubt on this assumption (Demers, 2007). Decoupling is a function of inconsistent stakeholder expectations, and an inevitable management reality (Brunsson & Olsen, 2018; Higgins et al., 2020; Yang et al., 2020). Hence, we should adapt to recognize hypocritical activities better, rather than cling to the modernist thinking of rational organizations.

Secondly, recognizing the intentionality and different ways of decoupling is relevant. Whereas some employees rationalize word-deed misalignments and might believe that aspirational talk will turn into actions, others might interpret the same situations as hypocrisy (Lauriano et al., 2022). There is a wide array of behaviour, from deliberate deception to unintentional "muddling through". In this (un)intentionality, hypocrisy is an obvious explanation to organizational behaviour (Crilly et al., 2012). Greenwashing and aspirational talk can be seen sometimes as more intentional than hypocrisy at least in marketing (Alonso-Calero et al., 2022). As Higgins et al. (2020) describe, hypocrisy is more of an inevitable phenomenon and a management reality.

Thirdly, how universities are walking the talk? When organizations are competent to recognize their organizational hindering factors more precisely, they are capable of proceeding with strategic sustainability implementation better. This research will analyze the manifestations of organizational behaviour of universities in their SD-CSR implementation and explain the reasons characterizing the features and differences—and why limited, incremental, and even superficial change is more comfortable than transformative change. This study will suggest solutions on how to prevent decoupling and improve sustainability performance.

7.3   Methodology

In this research, *mixed methods* with qualitative and quantitative methods and data triangulation are a legitimate choice. As a research approach, grounded theory and more specifically Gioia method were chosen. To enable comprehensive data collection, data triangulation was used, and various datasets were collected in a versatile manner.

Grounded theory is a qualitative research method that aims to develop theories or explanations based on data collected from the field. It involves a systematic process of coding and analyzing data to uncover patterns and concepts, ultimately leading to the generation of new theories or insights grounded in the data itself (Puusa & Juuti, 2020). Grounded theory is one of the most insightful methods of researching organizational concepts, and especially organizational change (Corley, 2015).

The Gioia method is a qualitative approach with its roots in grounded theory. It focuses on deriving theories from data rather than testing pre-existing hypotheses. The key steps include data collection, data coding with first-order analysis, theoretical sampling and second-order analysis, constant comparison, and theory development. It emphasizes iterative data analysis to develop contextually grounded theories for understanding complex organizational phenomena (Gioia & Corley, 2017, Gioia, 2021).

7.4   Results

The collected data and results derived from the material will be presented. Research findings are based on these datasets.

(a) **Workshop at Tampere University 3–4 Nov 2022 with all 14 Finnish universities**:

Aalto University, Hanken School of Economics, LUT University, National Defence University, Tampere University, University of Eastern Finland, University of Helsinki, University of Jyväskylä, University of Lapland, University of Oulu, University of the Arts Helsinki, University of Turku, University of Vaasa and Åbo Akademi University.

These universities were invited to a workshop in a joint sustainability conference of Finnish universities (Tampere University, 2022). The invitation to participate in the workshop was sent to the rector and sustainability responsible and the universities appointed the most suitable participants. Pre-assignments contained sustainability by basic figures and reports, strategic focus areas (research, education, societal impact, and campus), and management means and challenges of sustainability (max 5 priorities under each).

(b) **Semi-structured interviews in spring 2023**:

25 university representatives responsible for sustainability ranging from advisors to professors and vice-presidents (1–3 from each university). In these interviews, the concept of organizational hypocrisy was tested by asking the sustainability talks, decisions, and actions of these organizations, and how it displays in the management and sustainability activities.

(c) **Questionnaire on Personnel figures Feb´23**:

During the process, it became evident that personnel resources are the key for SD-CSR implementation. Thus, an additional survey was sent to universities´ registries and HR directors. This questionnaire asked the personnel figures divided to academic and administrative service personnel, and how many are targeted towards SD-CSR. 12 out of 14 universities replied, and figures were collected also from university property companies.

7.4.1 Key Figures on the SD Activities of Finnish Universities

In all Finnish universities, SD-CSR is mentioned in the strategy, most in many ways and cross-cuttingly, covering all functions. Additionally, all universities´ rectors are committed to SD-CSR theses (Unifi, 2020). The SD-CSR activities are reasonably established and clearly visible in the public documents. However, in most cases the statements are broad and abstract. Approximately one-third of the universities can be categorized proactive within sustainability and there is support by the leadership. About half of the universities are eager to advance but the activities are either only started or executed by a very small team, or a single individual, with challenging organizational status without organizational support. Rest of the universities are only starting the journey, and most of them are eager to go forward with SD-CSR. In most cases, the SD-CSR responsibility within the management team is not clearly stated. In terms of HR and budget, the programs are minimal, the human resources typically temporary and with low organizational status. Most often, the duties are covered by integrative and cross-cutting principles.

The scope of universities' activities was measured by key figures which can be accessed also in detail (JYU Converis, 2023). SD-CSR budgets are small. Most universities do not have a separate budget, stating that operations are integrated. The highest SD-CSR budget is €150,000 (not including personnel costs). The number of SD staff at universities is very limited. It is challenging to determine the number of SD-CSR faculty; the answers ranged from zero to 710 people. Many universities also stated that the entire faculty can be said to implement SD-CSR as part of their jobs.

The administrative staff of SD is considerably more limited than the academic SD staff. In most universities it was one or two persons, and possibly a few people with part-time duties. There was also one university where there was no appointed, even part-time, person in charge to promote SD-CSR. The average for SD-CSR service personnel was 1.8 person-years, which is a very low figure in comparison with any other service function. When asked how many actual persons had been responsible for the matter part-time, the figure was, on average, 2.9 persons part-time, at a single university. These low figures also reflect the strong competence and productivity of the few staff members.

It is clear from the data and discussion that, low number of staff emphasizes universities´ low priority of sustainability. However, sustainability is actively highlighted in the public branding. The statement from the workshop was blatant: *"The biggest slowdown is the lack of concretization and working reactively only by a few people, on top of your work. It's greenwashing in a sense"*.

7.4.2 Ways for Managing Finnish Universities to Achieve Sustainability Goals

Regarding the university's management methods to promote SD-CSR, the responses highlighted especially strategy, policies, and structures as well as responsibilities, processes, systems, and communications (see Table 7.1). Regarding challenges of SD-CSR work, the clearest issue in almost all responses was the lack of either human or financial resources (see Table 7.2).

The slowness of decision-making was a recurrent theme. In the workshop it was well-recognized: *"These kinds of bureaucratic issues and bottlenecks like this, and when it comes from down there, it's insanely slow"*. Another quote is quite descriptive on the everyday of sustainability advisors in almost any university: *"Perhaps the biggest problem, is that quite a lot of sustainability issues are dealt with* ad hoc, *so there is no such thing, for example, a certain meeting practice where sustainable development issues would always be involved"*.

Table 7.1 Management methods to promote SD-CSR

Strategy, guidelines	10
Structures, clearing responsibilities	9
Processes, systems, reporting	7
Communications, communities	7
Culture, attitude influencing	4
Management support, intent, commitment	4
Human resources	4
Education, competences	3
Organization	3
Participation, connection to everyday activities	2
Annual planning cycle, continuous improvement	2
Money, resources of the economy	2

(n = 14 universities)

Table 7.2 Challenges to the promotion of SD		
	Lack of human resource or time, rush	10
	Lack of financial resources	8
	Organizational hierarchy/location challenges	6
	Ownership, opportunities to influence	5
	Contradictory objectives	5
	Cultural challenges (attitude, atmosphere)	4
	Multidisciplinary, global challenges	3
	Prioritisation (and development overload)	3
	Lack of strategy, alignment	3
	Know-how	3
	Technical challenges	2

7.4.3 Interviews of University Representatives

The interviews with the university representatives were conducted in spring 2023. The interview started with the sustainability team and responsibilities, and key working areas within university´s SD-CSR-issues. Typically, most of the respondents had responsibilities within all areas (research, teaching, societal impact, campus).

The interview questions were about the sustainability perspectives of inter-viewee´s own university:

(1) Means and challenges of leadership
(2) Sustainability talk, decisions and actions
(3) HR and financial resources to SD-CSR
(4) Commitment and performance.

All were having at least a partial sustainability responsibility. The experience of the interviewees on SD-CSR and higher education ranged from 1 year to more than 20 years, and average being 5, 8 years of experience (Table 7.3).

Table 7.3 Positions of the interviewees		
	Dean/provost/vice-rector/vice-president	6
	Director position, incl. SD responsibility	5
	Manager position, incl. SD responsibility	4
	Sust. advisor position: senior or junior level	7
	Academic: professor/lecturer/researcher	3
	Total amount of interviews	25

7.4.3.1 Interview Findings

Weight of sustainability is growing within universities, especially the visibility and understanding of these issues. The organizational models and methods are somewhat varied in each university, but the topics are very similar, also within stakeholder collaboration. Awareness of sustainability challenges is growing, and need for impact as well, even pressure. Capabilities of identifying the needs for change, and ways to change, are growing. Willingness to change is omni-present, however, necessary skills to make transformative changes are there but not applied. Possible greenwashing is a challenge because the talk is there, but the walk is less evident. There is plenty of positive development, but disbelief in making true and impactful changes and permanent strategic moves is prevalent, also due to temporary positions and project-thinking. Lack of mandate and resources is a dominant obstacle for transformative changes, although a few forerunner universities and their leadership are somewhat engaged. Incapability for significant and revolutionary changes in priorities and focus is a major hindrance—the transformational pace of higher education could and should be hastened radically.

As some quotes show, the reality is somewhat bleak: *"When reporting to the university board, one will tell a bit of a smoothed picture"* and *"On top level, everyone is unanimous that this is what our university is all about. But then, when it comes to start deciding where to put money and resources..."*. The selected quotes throughout the chapter are individual, but they are being selected as a typical example of similar opinions. Thus, they are descriptive for a more general overview.

7.4.3.2 Is SD-CSR in the Speech of University Rectors and Management Team? Appearance of Talks, Decisions, and Actions

Finnish universities´ rectors and management team members do speak about sustainability on different occasions, but most often only mentioned and on an abstract level. The mentions when rectorate is the initiator and capable of speaking freely on the subject are very rare. These occasions do correlate strongly with the forerunner universities. A typical notion by the interviewees: *"Well, I'd say if I'm being honest now, sometimes you see, but somewhat glued on top of it"*. As one faculty member puts it: *"Frankly, the lack of a critical view of sustainability is obvious to me in most of the Finnish higher education institutions, including our institution"*.

It's a continuous competition about the attention of the leadership, and about meeting agendas. A constructive and basic SD report aiming for advancement, an internal blog on suggesting improvements, or an editorial about climate crisis couldn't be published; neither a report on SDGs was not handled. A faculty member stated: *"Even now in the 2020´s, it is not easy to call a spade a spade in Finnish universities (*on sustainability challenges and needed actions)"*. These examples are first and foremost in the "beginner", "follower", or "question mark" organizations in the following chapter.

7.4.3.3   Decisions and Factors Supporting SD-CSR Implementation

While discussing with the interviewees and the talk leading for decisions improving the sustainability activities, the answers were most often ambiguous. Like in this:'*I wonder what I would say when there is no such thing between the speech and the decision, because there is not much of that speech either.*'

However, these findings were repeatedly found, coded, and emerging from the materials:

– Resources, especially human resources, were mentioned by each interviewee. Only one institution was content with their current human resourcing for SD-CSR (but only fixed-term positions)
– A working group and people with a clear mandate
– Strong commitment by the responsible management team member
– Commitments like PRME or Fairtrade University etc. support successful implementation and especially the continuity of the work
– Longterm implementation, and persistent work. *"There is no magic wand and we shouldn't wait for it"*.

7.4.3.4   Factors Weakening SD-CSR Implementation

Weakening factors are grouped thematically here:

– Willingness and capabilities of decision-making. *"The difficulty of decision-making is the biggest bottleneck"*
– No structure or project approach of temporary staff members, even in the more advanced universities
– No separate budget, all finances applied separately.
– Knowledge varies a lot, e.g., SDGs are not comprehended
– Priorities are elsewhere, e,g, digitalization, international relations, or RDI
– National metrics or incentives are not focused in SD-CSR
– No visibility: *"I would say that SD-CSR actions are nowhere near visible enough to staff or students"*.

What are the possible reasons for the inertia of SD-CSR implementation? It is uncomplicated to find several reasons like no-one in the management board is giving or taking formal leadership, not to talk about genuine and inspirational leadership. Other challenges are minimal resources with maximal plurality of issues and availability of (too) many subjective opinions. Complexity grows without standard procedures for management systems, and there are too many options. Additionally, universities are following each other rather than taking the lead. In general, the peer group(s) is not incentivizing powerful sustainability changes without the initiative from the major funding source nationally. Only the Finnish ministry of education and culture, and major research funders, are powerful enough stakeholders to demand and pose impactful steering mechanisms and possible reporting procedures. How about the drivers for such work? Are the drivers weak or somewhat inaccurate? It is essential to investigate the current standing of Finnish universities.

The decisions and actions are lacking, although the "speech" is there. In some universities, the chief financial officer was hindering the improvements. Budgetary issues were put in front in a few "question mark" universities÷"*Our management looks at SD-CSR from an economic point of view, which means that ecological and social sustainability are secondary to that economic sustainability. So, it's a question of will that SD becomes top priority*".

The recurrent theme is the rectorate´s lack of focus for SD-CSR (except in three institutions with genuine top-level commitment), the priorities in resourcing, and how to steer the implementation towards positive outcomes. Only in a few universities, there is a designated top-level member with a SD-CSR responsibility. Interviewees´ quotes:

 – "*We have a sustainability action plan - but there are no strict guidelines*".
 – "*We had other organizational changes that were more important, and this was left a bit on the sidelines*".
 – "*Today, e.g. climate denialism is no longer about outright denial, but about making it somehow, you know, a bit more veiled, but in practice the function is the same*".

Summa summarum, factors weakening the SD implementation were not arduous to list.

7.4.3.5   Impulses for SD-CSR Work—Where Do They Come From?

The impulses for the sustainability actions materialized from varied sources, most often staff or students were mentioned. Also, external stakeholders´ demands and price of energy seemed to incentivize. In only a few cases the leadership team or board had been active, so this leaves room for action for the future leaders of universities. "*The focus is not on SD issues, they are caught up in bureaucracy, because SD is not a priority*".

7.4.4   Aggregating the Findings

The interview transcriptions were analyzed first by listing the appearing concepts. The second-order analysis consisted of finding emerging concepts (14 in total). Aggregating these findings resulted in 4 different dimensions. The original interview questions were created to understand the positioning of the organizations and its sustainability work, the interdependency and relations between talk, decisions, and actions. Hypocrisy as such was not directly questioned, because the innate answers would not produce insightful answers. Firstly, the recurring topics were chosen, and second-order themes built upon the first round. Aggregating the dimensions resulted in the dimensions of talk, decisions, action, and sustainability performance and how to improve it (Table 7.4).

7.4.5 Resources on Sustainability Staff

During the research process, it became evident that insufficient resources and focus, especially personnel dedicated or steered towards sustainability, are the key for implementation. Thus, an additional survey was sent to registries and HR directors. This questionnaire asked the personnel figures divided to academic and administrative service personnel, and how many of these are targeted towards SD-CSR.

With the figures (JYU Converis, 2023) it became evident, that there is also a clear difference between the conceptions of the HR functions and sustainability responsables on the number of sustainability-related personnel. This showed how vaguely established the sustainability functions are within universities. Only two universities have persons responsible (one in each) by the conception of HR functions. Estimates around academic personnel varied clearly, and definitions are unclear. Despite the challenges of definitions, this shows what is hypocrisy in practice. The reality of a typical university is how blurry the sustainability positions are even within the HR of these organizations. This resource scarcity becomes evident in the interviews: "*For CO2 calculations, we can´t find anyone, even though it's important, and then it just doesn't progress*".

7.5 Discussion

The aim of this paper is to analyze how do differences between universities´ talk, decisions, and actions appear in the context of Finnish universities. Is hypocrisy a relevant concept for explaining Finnish universities´ sustainability activities? There are seemingly contradictions between the walk and the talk, strategies, and implementation. How to narrow the gap?

The emerging themes and patterns have been summarized. Due to the sensitivity of the issue, the following figure is summarizing the university efforts, and in an anonymous manner.

7.5.1 Sustainability Efforts and Sustainability Talk in Finnish Uni´s

This figure represents Finnish universities based on their sustainability actions and estimation of hypocrisy in relation to sustainability demands. How the metrics have

Table 7.4 Aggregation of findings

First-order categories	Second-order themes	Aggregating the dimensions
Commitment to Unifi theses (or SDSCR)	About differenct SD-CSR commitments	*Appearances of talk*
Focus areas of the university organisational culture *Management system for SD-CSR*	Strategic dimensions, text as a talk	
Is SD-CSR present in leadership talks communications on SD-CSR reporting on SD-CSR	How is sustainability communicated	
Action versus talk	Examples of hypocritical action	
Sustainability responsibilities	Organisational positioning of sustainability	*Appearances of decisions*
Decision-making impulses—where do they come from Roles of the organisational actors like board and top mngt	Decisions supporting SD-CSR in the organisation	
Implementation of decisions Decisions by leadership	Means of leadership in reaching towards SDCSR targets	
Roles of the organisational actors like board and top mngt	Decisions supporting SD-CSR in the organisation	
About HR resources About other than HR resources	Importance of management decisions	
Team members, colleagues, key working groups personal responsibility division in SDCSR (research, teaching, societal impact, campus)	Human and financial resources to SD-CSR work, about the balancing act	*Appearances of action*
About personnel capabilities How to engage personnel	Managing human resources	
Examples of SD-CSR gaps, between walk and talk Barriers for change competition about leadership attention	Challenges in reaching towards sustainability targets	
What is impactful	Impactful implementation	
How to succeed Good examples of SD-CSR work	How do SD-CSR realize	

(continued)

Table 7.4 (continued)

First-order categories	Second-order themes	Aggregating the dimensions
Role and sufficiency of unifikeketeesit commitment	SD-CSR performance on national, regional + global level	*Sustainability performance, how to improve it*
Organizational structures and positions	How to manage and improve sustainability	
Unawareness of SD and CSR ideas and wishes for the future		

been evaluated? The horizontal axis, **sustainability actions** are based on Times Higher Education Impact Rankings results from 2023. Nine Finnish universities participated in 2023, and one university had earlier participated. "THE Impact Ranking" is a global ranking assessing universities against UN's Sustainable Development Goals (SDGs). Other universities in the figure are placed comparing their efforts relatively with other institutions (strategy and stated goals and actions, track record of years put on sustainability management, responsibilities, and positions´ permanency, how clearly the responsibilities are defined). It is essential to understand the limitations of rankings. Nevertheless, based on the empirical study, also the tailor-made ranking of universities based on this research effort would have been very similar with THE Impact 2023.

The vertical axis, *estimation of* **talk** is based on universities public documents like strategies and sustainability reports, and especially on the information provided by the interviewees and the workshop. The figure is relative but giving an estimation on the sustainability performance and degree of hypocrisy. A few notions:

– The forerunners are less likely to have a greater amount of hypocrisy.
– The more explicit the organization and responsibilities, the less there is hypocrisy.
– The less hypocrisy, the more trustworthy the efforts are considered by staff and stakeholders.
– The beginners are less likely to have hypocrisy, due to low or non-existent level of ambition. Like one respondent put it: *"Action and talk do not quarrel with each other, because they are both quite modest".*
– The weakest correlation of hypocrisy and sustainability efforts is within the category of followers. It varies on the organizational culture, past and present efforts, leadership talk, resources and confidence on the prospects and actions.
– The more hypocrisy, the more there are critical attitudes and doubts towards leadership´s capability and willingness to support SD-CSR.
– Hypocrisy is most likely to appear where the SD-CSR efforts have been decreased.

One respondent gave clear evidence on a typical hypocritical action: *"We have a strong SD commitment, but also our own rector is lobbying for direct flights between the capital and our campuses. Although there are train connections too.'* Another respondent stated in the joint workshop: *Not in a way that it is viewed with outright rejection, no one dares to say [laughs] that sustainability is a bad thing"*.

There are several cynical views concerning reporting and rankings, like: *"It's nice to look at some categories, answer something and pat each other on the back, and then once again, not to do much"*. Also Bautista-Puig et al. (2022) take a critical view on the rankings asking if they are to promote universities, than actually enhance the SDGs. However, ranking as such is far from the optimal way for measuring, but it is the best available way of measuring SD-CSR performance. Recently QS (2023) also launched a new sustainability ranking, but in the first round it might be premature to rely on its evaluations. That is why THE Impact Ranking and its 5th evaluation year was chosen.

7.5.2   How to Avoid Decoupling, and Refine the Discussion on Universities and Hypocrisy

In general, there seems to be some amount of hypocrisy in each organization, and it can be also mixed with aspirational talk and even greenwashing. There is no simple shortcut to avoid these, but rather a broad set of various organizational aspects. Gardner et al. (2021) recommend transferring urgently *"from publications to public actions"*, but in this research, interviewees and organizational representatives were somewhat submissive. They recognized the need for action, but couldn´t imagine transformative actions to be materialized. Brunsson and Olsen (2018) are asking how to bring administrative change? The answer probably exists in between the cultural layers like temporalities, dynamics of an organization (Christensen et al., 2020, 2021), and looking into the incorporation of factors to the management systems (Lozano et al., 2019). Also using the current management systems like quality assurance or other systems seems a fruitful starting point for coupling the talk, decisions, and actions (Holm, 2014; Janssens et al., 2022). Internal and external stakeholder pressures lead universities to respond with ambitious strategies and oversized targets although the activities and resource planning are not following the path that quickly.

In the case of Finnish universities, it seems that "muddling through", not typically that intentionally, seems like an existent strategy (Crilly et al., 2012). Like Seele and Gatti (2017) also found, existing definitions of greenwashing overemphasize the strategic intention to mislead. This seems also to be the case with Finnish universities, although conscious and even misleading aspirational talk for attaining positive sustainability branding, and questionable leadership practices are regularly put in place.

Context of societal and political concerns need to be addressed and avoid the pitfalls of higher education surrendering to become an instrument for political regimes like neocapitalism (Ruuska, 2017). The glass cage of greenwashing (Jones, 2012) can be avoided by systematically implementing the basics of good university performance. The ratio between voluntary and mandatory actions within an organization (Gatti et al., 2019) needs to be decided, but from the Finnish empirical evidence it stems that only voluntary actions are far from effective. As Disterheft et al. (2012) recommend, a top-down approach prioritizes efficiency, concentrating on enhancing operational environmental performance and ensuring compliance with regulations. In contrast, a participatory approach adopts a holistic perspective, fostering the development of innovative teaching and learning environments, albeit with a potentially longer time commitment. Whichever, the management system needs to be conducted diligently and patiently.

7.6   Conclusion

7.6.1   *Theoretical Contribution*

Stakeholder expectations on SD-CSR are abundantly provided in the society and especially the burden is on organizations like universities. It seems that universities in Finland are not immune to this pressure. Consequently, to incorporate sustainability into a university, the hypocritical tendencies should be addressed, but also accepted. It can be stated that in all Finnish universities there is hypocrisy of some degree. This leads to the suggestion that hypocrisy should be recognized better. An open approach towards organizational behaviour should be an ordinary task. Nonetheless, it needs self-examination, heightened awareness, and mindful demeanour to tackle the challenge.

How to recognize the different ways of decoupling? How to reverse the SD-CSR efforts? It seems that there are both unintentional and intentional hypocritical activities, even greenwashing. In several universities, organizational culture and leadership seemed very negative towards regular sustainability efforts with some impact. In these cases, recruitments were postponed, cancelled, or awkwardly conducted, and decisions were not based on merit. In these organizations, neither did the leadership give resources to key sustainability functions, and instead blocked or ceased the activities. On the other hand, there are plenty of excellent examples of determined and impactful activities. As a conclusion, it would be critical to differentiate between hypocrisy, greenwashing, and aspirational talk. By understanding the motivational factors and incentives of universities, the organizational behaviour can be steered. A final remark is, that universities aim to become sustainable and support the society in the transition, but only a few of them are starting to take it seriously (Fig. 7.1).

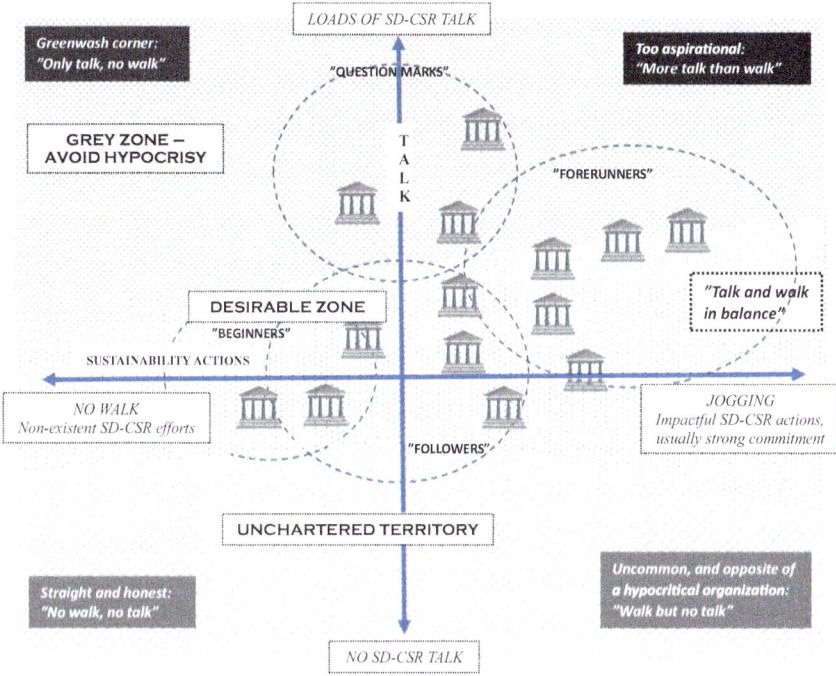

Fig. 7.1 Talk versus walk—comparison of Finnish universities

7.6.2 *Managerial Implications*

This summary will introduce a recipe for transformative action. It is based on the research and especially interviewees´ notions.

Number one rule: Avoid committing to SD-CSR goals if there´s no intention to pursue them. Hereby you avoid the danger of greenwashing.

Self-assessment: Compare the talk, decisions, and actions—are they in line? Don´t be afraid of critical voices, turn them to the organization´s benefit.

Definition of key goals: Do the materiality analysis
to define focus. Use your institutional expertise when appropriate.
- *Research:* Key areas and scientific knowledge.
- *Education:* Programs and proper courses for students and staff.
- *Societal impact:* Excellent opportunities for outreach.
- *Campus:* Opportunity for action, platform for research and education.

Goals, action plan, and communications: Define and publicize strategic goals, but also implementation. Use external commitments if needed.

Responsibilities: the importance of designated academic and administrative officer(s) cannot be over-emphasized.

– SD-CSR responsibilities (faculty and services) stated clearly, as part of the management team, and not as an add-on
– Roles and contact points defined (steering groups, stakeholders)
– Appoint permanent positions, different levels and units
– Integration is powerful—but avoid the pitfall *"when it's everywhere– it is nowhere".*

Resources: Steer the university´s budget and human resources towards strategic goals, not only a separate sustainability budget. A shared view in each Finnish university (except one): *"The situation with human resources is absolutely not good".* About temporary positions, similar feelings were shared with many: *"The short-term and temporary employment contract (of the SD advisor) is a bit of a worry for me".*

Management system: Integrate SD goals. Use plan-do-check-act and proper accreditations, rankings, or labels if needed.

Continuous improvement: Adopt the principle– no organization is ever ready with this.

The low-hanging fruits are already picked: Be ready to work relentlessly.

Funding: Change incentives of the organization, internally and externally.

Point on funding is pointed towards the funders of universities. This issue was raised in repetitively. A commendable example is from 2006 when the Swedish Parliament amended the Swedish Higher Education Act: "Universities shall, in their activities, work for sustainable development, which means that present and future generations are assured of having a healthy and good environment, economy, and social welfare and justice" (Swedish Code of Statues 1992: 1434, translation by Sammalisto and Lindhqvist 2008). Same message is pronounced in Finnish universities´ SD-CSR commitment (Unifi, 2020).

7.6.3   Assessment of the Reliability of the Study

There is strong evidence that participants provide answers that they think the researcher wants (Roxas & Lindsay, 2012). In this assessment, both the researcher and the response bias should be considered. These influence the way data is collected, analyzed, or interpreted. Also, the interviewees might describe their universities in the best possible way and overstate them as "best in the class".

The reliability of findings could improve with more interviewees. However, the gathered sample seemed to pinpoint towards the same issues. The used methods have potential drawbacks, including limited generalizability, theoretical ambiguity, and bias through subjectivity. In short, the methods and theory have strengths but should be applied with awareness of the potential pitfalls. And as Gioia puts it (2021), there is no "right answer".

7.6.4   Recommendations for Future Research

Often the delicate topics like hypocrisy or greenwashing are avoided in the research, due to the sensitivity and difficulties in obtaining empirical evidence. However, we should delve more profoundly into these issues within organizations to support transformative action. Similar research should be conducted in other continents and countries, with different languages, understanding local conditions, gender issues, and minorities. Thus similarities, differences, and measures for hypocrisy could be pointed out in a more descriptive way.

References

Aaltonen, V., & Siltaoja, M. (2022). How they walk the talk: Responsible management education in Finnish business schools. *Business Ethics, the Environment and Responsibility, 31,* 1117–1135.

Allam, I., Scagnelli, S., & Corazza, L. (2020). Sustainability reporting, a new type of companies' hypocrisy: Zara and Volkswagen cases. In *Chapter in the CSR, sustainability, ethics & governance book series* (CSEG).

Alonso-Calero, J. M., Cano, J., & Guerrero-Pérez, M. O. (2022). Is the "green washing" effect stronger than real scientific knowledge? Are we able to transmit formal knowledge in the face of marketing campaigns? *Sustainability, 14*(1), 285.

Álvarez-García, O., & Sureda-Negre, J. (2023). Greenwashing and education: An evidence-based approach. *The Journal of Environmental Education, 54*(4), 265–277.

Asikainen, E., & Kangastie, H. (2023) *Handbook for sustainable universities of applied sciences. [Kestävän ammattikorkeakoulutuksen käsikirja].* Lapland University of Applied Sciences Publications [*Lapin ammattikorkeakoulun julkaisuja*] 17/2023, ISSN 2954-1654 (online publication).

Avlonas, N., & Nassos, G. P. (2020). *Green marketing and communication and how to avoid green and blue washing.* Wiley.

Bautista-Puig, N., Orduna-Malea, E., & Perez-Esparrells, C. (2022). Enhancing sustainable development goals or promoting universities? An analysis of the times higher education impact rankings. *International Journal of Sustainability in Higher Education, 23*(8), 211–231.

Bekessy, S. A., Samson, K., & Clarkson, R. E. (2007). The failure of non-binding declarations to achieve university sustainability: A need for accountability. *International Journal of Sustainability in Higher Education, 8*(3), 301–316.

Brunsson, N. (1989). *The Organization of hypocrisy—talk, decisions and actions in organizations.* John Wiley & Sons Ltd.

Brunsson, N. (2003). Organized hypocrisy. In B. Czarniawska, & G. Sevón (Eds.), *The Northern lights—organization theory in Scandinavia* (pp. 201–222). Copenhagen Business School Press.

Brunsson, N. (2006). *Mechanisms of hope: Maintaining the dream of the rational organization.* Liber.

Brunsson, N., & Olsen, J. P. (2018). *The reforming organization: Making sense of administrative change.* Routledge Library Editions: Management.

Böhling, T., Koivuranta, R., & Löyttyniemi, M. (2022) *The theses of Finnish universities as leaders of the sustainability transition [Suomen yliopistojen teesit kestävyysmurroksen suunnannäyttäjänä],* Book Keys to Sustainability [Kestävyyden avaimet]. In T. Halonen et al. *Gaudeamus* (pp. 239–240).

Cho, C., Laine, M., Roberts, R., & Rodrigue, M. (2015). Organized hypocrisy, organizational façades, and sustainability reporting. *Accounting, Organizations and Society, 40,* 78–94.

Christensen, L. T., Morsing, M., & Thyssen, O. (2020). Timely hypocrisy? Hypocrisy temporalities in CSR communication. *Journal of Business Research, 114*, 327–335.

Christensen, L. T., Morsing, M., & Thyssen, O. (2021). Talk–action dynamics: Modalities of aspirational talk. *Organization Studies, 42*(3), 407–427.

Corley, K. G. (2015). A commentary on 'What grounded theory is…' Engaging a phenomenon from the perspective of those living it. *Organizational Research Methods, 18*(4), 600–605.

Crilly, D., Zollo, M., & Hansen, M. T. (2012). Faking it or muddling through? Understanding decoupling in response to stakeholder pressures. *The Academy of Management Journal, 55*(6), 1429–1448.

Demers, C. (2007). *Organizational change theories*. Sage Publications.

Disterheft, A., da Silva Caeiro, S. S. F., Ramos, M. R., & de Miranda Azeiteiro, U. M. (2012). Environmental Management Systems (EMS) implementation processes and practices in European higher education institutions—top-down versus participatory approaches. *Journal of Cleaner Production, 31*, 80–90.

Effron, D. A., Connor, K. O., Leroy, H., & Lucas, B. J. (2018). From inconsistency to hypocrisy: When does "saying one thing but doing another" invite condemnation? *Research in Organizational Behaviour, 38*, 61–75.

Elo, M., Hytönen, J., Karkulehto, S., Kortetmäki, T., Kotiaho, J.S., Puurtinen, M., & Salo, M. (2023). *Interdisciplinary perspectives on planetary well-being*. Routledge Studies in Sustainable Development.

Gardner, C. J., Thierry, A., Rowlandson, W., & Steinberger, J. K. (2021) From publications to public actions: The role of universities in facilitating academic advocacy and activism in the climate and ecological emergency. *Frontiers in Sustainability, 2*, 679019.

Gatti, L., Seele, P., & Rademacher, L. (2019). Grey zone in – greenwash out. A review of greenwashing research and implications for the voluntary-mandatory transition of CSR. *International Journal of Corporate Social Responsibility, 4*(6), 1–15.

Gioia, D. (2021). A systematic methodology for doing qualitative research. *The Journal of Applied Behavioral Science, 57*(1), 20–29.

Gioia, D., & Chittipeddi, K. (1991). Sensemaking and sensegiving in strategic change initiation. *Strategic Management Journal, 12*(6), 433–448.

Gioia, D., & Corley, K. (2017). Being good versus looking good: Business school rankings and the circean transformation from substance to . *Academy of Management Learning & Education, 1*(1).

Gladwin, T. N., Kennelly, J. J., & Krause, T. S. (1995). Shifting paradigms for sustainable development: Implication for management theory and research. *Academy of Management Review, 20*, 874–907.

Higgins, C., Tang, S., & Stubbs, W. (2020). On managing hypocrisy: The transparency of sustainability reports. *Journal of Business Research, 114*, 395–407.

Holm, T. (2014). *Enhancing education for sustainable development with tools for quality assurance* [Doctoral dissertation]. University of Turku, series 289.

Janssens, L., Kuppens, T., Mulà, I., Staniskiene, E., & Zimmermann, A. B. (2022). Do European quality assurance frameworks support integration of transformative learning for sustainable development in higher education? *International Journal of Sustainability in Higher Education, 23*(8), 148–173.

Jones, D. R. (2012). Looking through the "greenwashing glass cage" of the green league table towards the sustainability challenge for UK universities. *Journal of Organizational Change Management, 25*(4), 630–647.

JYU Converis. (2023). Survey and interview data on sustainable development management in Finnish Universities 2022–2023 [Kysely- ja haastatteluaineisto kestävän kehityksen johtamisesta suomalaisissa yliopistoissa 2022–2023]; Löyttyniemi, M. Retrieved November 26, 2023, from https://converis.jyu.fi/converis/portal/detail/ResearchDataset/182774505?lang=fi_FI

Kiliçoğlu, G. (2017). Consistency or discrepancy? Rethinking schools from organizational hypocrisy to integrity. *Management in Education, 31*(3), 118–124.

Koep, L. (2017). Investigating industry expert discourses on aspirational CSR communication. *Corporate Communications: An International Journal, 22*(2), 220–238.

Lauriano, L., Reinecke, J., & Etter, M. (2022). When Aspirational talk backfires: The Role of moral judgements in employees hypocrisy interpretation. *Journal of Business Ethics, 181*, 827–845.

Leal Filho, W, Azeiteiro, U., Alves, F., & Molthan-Hill, P. (2017). *Handbook of theory and practice of sustainable development in higher education.* World Sustainability Series, vol. 4.

Lotz-Sisitka, H., Wals, A. E. J., Kronlid, D., & McGarry, D. (2015). Transformative, transgressive social learning: Rethinking higher-education pedagogy in times of systemic global dysfunction. *Current Opinion in Environmental Sustainability., 16*, 73–80.

Lozano, R. (2011). The state of sustainability reporting in universities. *International Journal of Sustainability in Higher Education, 12*(1), 67–78.

Lozano, R., & Barreiro-Gen, M. (2019). Analysing the factors affecting the incorporation of sustainable development into European higher education institutions' curricula. *Sustainable Development, 27*, 965–975.

Lozano, R., Barreiro-Gen, M., Lozano, F. J., & Sammalisto, K. (2019). Teaching sustainability in European higher education institutions: Assessing the connections between competences and pedagogical approaches. *Sustainability, 11*(6), 1602. https://doi.org/10.3390/su11061602

Lozano, R., Lukman, R., Lozano, F. J., Huisingh, D., & Lambrechts, W. (2013). Declarations for sustainability in higher education: Becoming better leaders, through addressing the university system. *Journal of Cleaner Production, 48*, 10–19.

Lyon, T. P., & Montgomery, A. W. (2015). The means and end of greenwash. *Organization & Environment, 28*(2), 223–249.

Mantere, S., & Ketokivi, M. (2013). Reasoning in organization science. *Academy of Management Review, 38*, 70–89.

Molthan-Hill, P., Erlandsson, L., Ndlovu, T., Patton, I., & Goodwin, F. (2019) Global alliance of tertiary education and sustainable development. In W. Leal Filho (ed.) *Encyclopedia of sustainability in higher education* (pp. 1–13). Springer Nature Switzerland

Mulà, I., Tilbury, D., Ryan, A., Mader, M., Dlouhá, J., Mader, C., Benayas, J., Dlouhý, J., & Alba, D. (2017). Catalysing change in higher education for sustainable development: A review of professional development initiatives for university educators. *International Journal of Sustainability in Higher Education, 18*(5), 798–820.

Parguel, B., Benoît-Moreau, F., & Larceneux, F. (2011). How sustainability ratings might deter "greenwashing": A closer look at ethical corporate communication. *Journal of Business Ethics, 102*(1), 15–28.

Penttilä, V. (2020). Aspirational talk in strategy texts: A longitudinal case study of strategic episodes in corporate social responsibility communication. *Business & Society, 59*(1), 67–97.

Pesonen, H.-L. (2003). Challenges of integrating environmental sustainability issues into business school curriculum: A case study from the University of Jyväskylä, Finland. *Journal of Management Education, 27*(2), 158–171.

Puusa, A., & Juuti, P. (2020) Qualitative research approaches and methods [Laadullisen tutkimuksen näkökulmat ja menetelmät], *Gaudeamus.*

QS Sustainability University Rankings. (2023). Retrieved August 20, 2023, from https://www.top universities.com/university-rankings/sustainability-rankings/2023

Rohweder, L. (2001). *Environmental education in polytechnics: Developing a curriculum theory model for business education [Ympäristökasvatus ammattikorkeakoulussa: Opetussuunnitelmateoreettisen mallin kehittäminen liiketalouden koulutukseen].* Doctoral dissertation, Acta Universitatis oeconomicae Helsingiensis, Aalto University School of Business, Finland.

Roxas, B., & Lindsay, V. (2012). Social desirability bias in survey research on sustainable development in small firms: An exploratory analysis of survey mode effect. *Business Strategy and the Environment, 21*, 223–235.

Ruuska, T. (2017). *Reproduction of capitalism in the 21st century: Higher education and ecological crisis.* Aalto University, Department of Management Studies, doctoral dissertation 97/2017.

Salminen, J., & Friman, M. (2022). Sustainable development in Finnish universities of applied sciences [Kestävä kehitys suomalaisissa ammattikorkeakouluissa]. *Tiedepolitiikka, 4*, 23–38.

Sammalisto, K., & Lindhqvist, T. (2008). Integration of sustainability in higher education: A study with international perspectives. *Innovative Higher Education, 32*, 221–233.

Sandberg, M., & Tienari, J. (eds.) (2022). *Transformative action for sustainable outcomes—responsible organising.* Routledge.

Seeck, H. (2008). Leadership in Finland [Johtamisopit Suomessa], *Gaudeamus.*

Seele, P., & Gatti, L. (2017). Greenwashing revisited: In search of a typology and accusation-based definition incorporating legitimacy strategies. *Business Strategy and the Environment, 26*(2), 239–252.

Snelson-Powell, A. C., Grosvold, J., & Millington, A. I. (2020). Organizational hypocrisy in business schools with sustainability commitments: The drivers of talk-action inconsistency. *Journal of Business Research, 114*, 408–420.

Tampere University. (2022) *Conference UNIFI & Arene Seminar for sustainability and responsibility.* Retrieved September 27, 2022, from https://events.tuni.fi/sustainabilityseminar2022/

The Impact rankings. (2023). Results and methodology. *Times Higher Education.* Retrieved July 27, 2023, from https://www.timeshighereducation.com/impactrankings#!/length/25/locations/FIN/name/A/sort_by/rank/sort_order/asc/cols/undefined

Thierry, A., Horn, L., von Hellermann, P., & Gardner, C. J. (2023). "No research on a dead planet": Preserving the socio-ecological conditions for academia. *Frontiers of Education, 8*, 1237076. https://doi.org/10.3389/feduc.2023.1237076

Tienari, J., & Meriläinen, S. (2021) Johtaminen ja globaali talous. *Alma Talent.*

Unifi. (2020). *Theses on sustainability and responsibility.* Rectors´ Council of Finnish Universities. Retrieved June 4, 2023, from https://unifi.fi/en/universities-publish-12-ambitious-theses-and-intend-to-become-leaders-in-sustainable-development/

Wals, A., & Jickling, B. (2002). "Sustainability" in higher education: From doublethink and newspeak to critical thinking and meaningful learning. *International Journal of Sustainability in Higher Education, 3*(3), 221–232.

Wegelius, E. (2022). *Universities for a sustainable future: Employee perceptions shaping institutional sustainability change* [Master's thesis]. Aalto University.

Whiteman, G., Walker, B., & Perego, P. (2012). Planetary boundaries: Ecological foundations for corporate sustainability. *Journal of Management Studies, 50*(2).

Williams, A., Kennedy, S., Philipp, F., & Whiteman, G. (2017). Systems thinking: A review of sustainability management research. *Journal of Cleaner Production, 148*, 866–881.

Yang, L., Manikab, D., & Athanasopouloua, A. (2020). Are they sinners or saints? A multi-level investigation of hypocrisy in organisational and employee pro-environmental behaviours. *Journal of Business Research, 114*, 336–347.

Meri Löyttyniemi is a pioneer in advancing the sustainability of higher education institutions since the 1990's. She is the founder and longtime chair of the Nordic NSCN network of universities, former vice-chair of the national sustainability working group for Finnish universities and an engaged and renowned actor within universities' global sustainability movement. Löyttyniemi works as research manager at University of Eastern Finland and is affiliated as senior sustainability advisor at Aalto University and doctoral researcher at Jyväskylä University School of Business and Economics.

Part III
Practices in Private Sector

Chapter 8
Sustainability Challenges of SMEs Related to Legal Regulations—Experiences from a Survey of Hungarian Entrepreneurs

Zsuzsanna Győri⬤, Regina Zsuzsánna Reicher⬤, and Anita Kolnhofer-Derecskei⬤

Abstract This book chapter examines the impact of legal regulations on sustainability as perceived by SME leaders. The impact of laws and regulations is explored within the framework of the entrepreneurial ecosystem at three levels: emotional or affective; cognitive motivational; and conative or behavioural. Through the inclusion of this practical small business perspective, we aim to enrich the discourse on the importance and challenges of regulation in the context of sustainability. This study is part of a larger research on the role of Hungarian SMEs in achieving the Sustainable Development Goals. In our mixed-method research we first used focus group interviews to identify the terms and phrases used by SMEs in relation to sustainability. Based on the qualitative results, a questionnaire was designed and administered to a representative sample of Hungarian SMEs. The results show that the legal system, i.e., policy, has a major—and at times controversial—impact on the sustainability of entrepreneurial activity. The policy implication is that sustainability issues should be addressed more comprehensively and in a more holistic, integral way across all domains of the entrepreneurial ecosystem. At the same time, individual characteristics of the entrepreneur, such as gender, position, and decision-making power, as well as characteristics of the enterprise, such as size or ownership structure, influence the

Z. Győri (✉) · R. Z. Reicher
Department of Management and Entrepreneurship, Centre of Excellence for Sustainability Impacts in Business and Society (CESIBUS), Faculty of Finance and Accountancy, Budapest Business University, Budapest, Hungary
e-mail: gyori.zsuzsanna@uni-bge.hu

R. Z. Reicher
e-mail: reicher.regina@uni-bge.hu

A. Kolnhofer-Derecskei
Department of Business Economics, Centre of Excellence for Sustainability Impacts in Business and Society (CESIBUS), Faculty of Finance and Accountancy, Budapest Business University, Budapest, Hungary
e-mail: kolnhofer-derecskei.anita@uni-bge.hu

assessment of the legislation and the perception and resolution of related challenges which should be taken into consideration.

Keywords SME · Sustainability · Entrepreneurial ecosystem · Policy · Legal regulation

8.1 Introduction

The introduction of the Sustainable Development Goals (SDGs) in 2015 has raised the sustainability discourse and related expectations for economic actors to a new level. The UN sustainability policy, the document entitled "Transforming our world: the 2030 Agenda for Sustainable Development" (UN, 2015) is a top-down action plan for people, planet, and prosperity. This is the first document to explicitly link solidarity, the reduction of inequality at all levels, and sustainable development. Previously, the Millennium Development Goals (UN, 2000) had already mentioned all three pillars of sustainability. However, there the main message was still one of global solidarity, and most of the goals and targets as well as the expectation of partnership were primarily directed at Member States. The framework provided a roadmap for the most important challenge of our time, the transition to a sustainable development path and can be interpreted at the individual, corporate, public, and global levels. Given that the majority of companies belong to this sector, that they play a major role in employment and that their value added is growing, the role of small and medium-sized enterprises (SMEs) in achieving SDGs is prominent.

From a bottom-up perspective, the state is an important stakeholder in the entrepreneurial ecosystem. National and international regulation related to sustainability have a significant impact on enterprises and the ecosystem in which they operate. In the long run legislation helps enterprises to perform better and more sustainably, but in the day-to-day operation and planning it poses challenges or even burdens for companies, especially for SMEs with fewer organizational, human, and financial resources.

This book chapter examines the impact of the legal system and regulations on sustainability as perceived by SME leaders. The impact of laws and regulations is studied within the framework of the entrepreneurial ecosystem at three levels: (1) the emotional or affective level (2) the cognitive motivational level, and (3) the conative or behavioural level. Through the inclusion of this practical small business perspective, we aim to enrich the discourse on the importance and challenges of regulation in the context of sustainability and the SDGs.

The main research questions are the following:

1. What is the role of the state in achieving sustainability in the opinion of SME leaders?
2. What are the challenges that Hungarian SMEs face in their day-to-day operations, longer-term planning, and strategizing in the face of general and sustainability-related legislation?
3. What is the impact of personal and business characteristics on the attitudes, motivations, and behaviour of companies towards sustainability?

8.2 Theoretical Background

8.2.1 Entreprenurial Ecosystem as a Theoretical Lens

To illustrate the role of regulation in general and in sustainability issues in particular, we use the ecosystem model as a theoretical lens. In the case of corporate social responsibility (CSR) and sustainability, stakeholders as the parties representing the social and natural environment—the non-economic dimensions of sustainability—are prominent actors and feature prominently in both theory and practice. Although it is rare for the two theoretical frameworks to be treated together, stakeholders are also relevant in the entrepreneurial ecosystem. Admittedly, while the basic premise of stakeholder theory is that the company is responsible for its stakeholders, the ecosystem theory is more concerned with the other direction of the interrelationship, namely how different actors can help the company. An entrepreneurial ecosystem includes numerous stakeholders, such as policy makers, government agencies, industry associations, and many others and the various models and theories describe these components in different ways (Simatupang et al., 2015, Malecki, 2018). Based on this, the entrepreneurial ecosystem as a complex, multi-level construct makes it possible to create an environment that ensures the implementation of the principles of sustainable development. Some models emphasize the effective use of economic, social, and environmental components (Tolstykh et al., 2021), while Isenberg organizes the different actors into six main domains: Culture, Markets, Human Capital, Finance, Support, and Policy (Isenberg, 2010, 2014). The diversity of actors makes it difficult to capture the complexity of the ecosystem (Stam, 2017, Csákné Filep & Radácsi, 2019). Moreover, it is embedded in the national cultural, legal, and institutional environment (Maroufkhani et al., 2018). Culture includes societal norms related to business (social status of entrepreneurs, risk tolerance, innovation, creativity, well-being), as well as social norms related to sustainability, and the acceptance of the SDGs. Market means the customers and consumers of a company's products and services, as well as the entrepreneurial relationships and networks from which orders can be placed. Human Capital includes the situation of the labour market and education, the system of general education, and entrepreneurship training which is the source of future human capital. Finance means microcredits, private capital, business angels, venture capital, and the general financing environment, i.e. banking, and other available financial resources and the process of accessing them. Isenberg identifies three sub-areas of Support: NGOs supporting enterprises, professional support services, and infrastructure (Isenberg, 2010). All of the domains effect, foster, or hinder the realization of sustainability and related issues (Csillag et al., 2022; Ray & Sharma, 2022; Bihari, 2023).

The focus of our research is Policy that can be divided into two parts: leadership, which is the clear support given to enterprises, the social legitimacy of entrepreneurship provided by prominent political and economic leaders emphasizing the importance of the issue. The other component of the domain is business-friendly government regulation, legislation, related (including research) institutions, and the availability of governmental financial support (Isenberg, 2010). From a sustainability perspective it is important to mention not only general, but sustainability-related legislation and support as well.

8.2.2 Sustainability-Related Attitudes, Motivations, and Behaviours—Affective, Conative, and Cognitive Interpretations

All of the ecosystem domains influence attitudes, motivations, and behaviour of the entrepreneurs (Győri et al., 2022a). Examining the domains separately and analyzing their interaction can provide advice on how to improve regulation (Daniel et al. 2017, Fuentelsaz et al., 2017). It may be important to look at the extent to which sustainability considerations are reflected in general legislation, as well as in the specific sustainability legislation itself when considering the impact of policy on the contribution of SMEs to sustainability.

In the European Union, the legislative process towards a more sustainable EU has been almost continuous since the 1970s, and has a huge impact on Hungarian legislation since the EU accession in 2004 aligns with the activity of multinational companies (Győri et al., 2021). The Europe 2020 Strategy (EC, 2010), its related regulations, and more recently the EU Taxonomy (EP and EC, 2020), the Sustainable Finance Disclosure Regulation (SFDR, EP and EC, 2019), and the Corporate Sustainability Reporting Directive (CSRD, EP and EC, 2022) represent important milestones also from an SME perspective, which can be interpreted at different levels. SMEs have a particular desire to take responsibility for the environment and society, at the same time, their possibilities are different from those of larger companies. These characteristics lead to a special mindset, vocabulary, motivational patterns, and activities within the sustainability framework.

If we look at sustainability as a moral issue, each person has a different set of values and morals regarding sustainability, and the awareness-raising, social education, the practice of shaping attitudes to be more sustainable implies changes at the individual, mezzo, and macro levels. Attitudes, skills, knowledge, and competences regarding sustainability are influenced by different ecosystem factors including the changes in regulations. The attitudes are of course interrelated (Csizmadia et al., 2022), but the attitude of a leader shapes sustainability on the enterprise level (Sharma & Ray, 2022; Talat & Bhaduri, 2022), in the case of SMEs, the entrepreneur's attitude is of paramount importance (Chandler, 2022; Gosztonyi, 2022; Németh et al., 2022; Uvarova et al., 2021; Vajdovich et al., 2022).

The next level of analysis interprets legal regulation as an external motivation (Győri et al., 2019). The two main sets of motivations for taking responsibility and addressing sustainability issues in business are moral considerations and the business case. Moral obligation stems from the recognition and acknowledgement of the impact on stakeholders, society, and the natural environment as an essentially intrinsic and based on previous research (Győri et al., 2022b), strongmotivation. In contrast, the business case suggests that the company can achieve economic benefits, even in the short term, by meeting the sustainability needs and expectations of the ecosystem actors, and its stakeholders (Economist, 2008; Fenwick et al., 2022; Kotler & Lee, 2004; Martins et al., 2022; Porter & Kramer, 2002; Vogel, 2006), e.g. the enterprise can comply with the relevant regulations (Salvetti & Jeurissen, 2022, Shalhoob & Hussainey, 2022). On the other hand, legislation can be a disincentive as well. Bakos et al., (2020) had an existing literature review on SMEs' sustainability and identified the main barriers to sustainability adoption. The barriers were categorized into six clusters, of which government and legislation were identified as the major challenges for SMEs. Namely, a lack of government support or limited financial incentives to encourage sustainable projects hindered firms from engaging in sustainability. Another barrier can be that many SMEs are not aware of the environmental legislation affecting their business or feel that it does not apply to them.

At the third, behavioural level, the sustainability performance of the enterprise, we can observe that SMEs tend to worse perform (MPRSZ, 2017, BCSDH, 2017, Bikefe et al., 2020, Metzker & Štreimikis, 2020, Mahmood et al., 2021). They usually start to use explicit CSR tools, typically quality or environmental standards, when they are forced to do so, usually because they want to supply a large company that requires them, or because of legal regulation, in order to act as a reliable part of the entrepreneurial ecosystem. Cornejo-Cañamares and his colleagues (2021) found that environmental compliance is a key driver of better innovation outcomes. The results of Hoogendoorn et al. (2015) suggest that firm size, activity, and regulatory environment influence sustainability practices. Szennay and his colleagues (2021) claim that size, organizational culture, and the leader's attitude are the determining factors of sustainability performance. More than 20 years ago the EU had expectations as follows: "In the future, the most significant pressure on SMEs to adopt CSR practices is likely to come from their large business customers, which in return could help SMEs cope with these challenges through the provision of training, mentoring schemes and other initiatives" (EP and EC, 2022:12). Most standards and guidelines now extend to the supply chain, with the aim of providing measurable and accurate information on the majority of the value created, and the social and environmental impacts associated with that value creation to improve performance. SMEs have far fewer resources to comply with regulations and to meet supply chain expectations and therefore they often choose the simplest, least burdensome solutions to tick the relevant boxes. The activity is often outsourced, for example through hiring lawyers or accountants. Simple tools and calculators at affordable prices are available to many SMEs, but these tend to have validity and reliability issues (Harangozó & Szigeti, 2017). While this is cost-effective, it also prevents employees or managers from really integrating sustainability thinking and activities into day-to-day operations which presents a major barrier to truly embedding sustainability into their entrepreneurial activities. According to Generali and SDA Bocconi's White Paper 2021 and 2022, the national and international legal requirements are the third most important drivers that are needed to achieve environmental and/or social practices among Hungarian SMEs. In this sense, these are negative drivers, even more barriers. Those include lack of institutional support, excessive regulations and bureaucratic governmental support (or hinder access to public tenders), regulatory uniformity, administrative complexity, and excessive costs (Generali and SDA Bocconi, 2021, 2022).

At the same time, implicit CSR activities can be more easily identified (Matten & Moon, 2008). In our previous study (Győri et al., 2023), based on our focus group results, we also claimed that the lower visibility of sustainability does not necessarily mean less sustainable and less responsible operations than in the case of large companies, as SMEs operate along different logic resulting in different stakeholder relationships, responsibility performance, and communication.

In sum, we can say that legislation has a huge—and at times controversial—impact on the sustainability of entrepreneurial activity. Regulation is an important attitude shaper and motivator and has a strong influence on business behaviour. However, it sometimes fails to make a real impact, as it is sometimes easier and more cost-effective to use sham solutions than to introduce a real change. At the same time, in the case of SMEs, it is sometimes difficult to detect real activity because of implicit solutions.

8.3 Methods

This study is part of a larger research on the role of Hungarian SMEs in achieving the Sustainable Development Goals. In our mix-method research we first used focus group interviews in order to identify the terms and phrases used by SMEs in relation to their responsibility and sustainability. Based on the qualitative results, a questionnaire was designed and administered to a representative sample of Hungarian SMEs.

8.3.1 Qualitative Method

Three focus group studies were conducted. To make the focus groups comparable, the same moderator interviewed the three groups and asked the same questions every time (so-called structured guide was used). Each session was video and audio recorded, and transcribed. Finally, NVivo12 software was used to conduct a broader content analysis of the transcripts. As for the sample frame, those managers of both small and medium-sized companies were invited whose companies run either sustainably or contrary, those who did not place a particular emphasis on this. This selection satisfied the group heterogeneity.

Two researchers carried out the coding and content analysis independently. The reliability of the coding was assessed using the Kappa index and the percentage of linking, and there was robust agreement between the two codings. The elements of the used code table used based on the literature (grounded theory) and the interviews' content analysis (open coding). This process involved the assumption of classical content analysis where each text was read and placed into the corresponding codes.

8.3.2 Quantitative Methods

The wording and the topic of the instrument were determined based on the content analysis of the focus group conversations and the existing literature. In addition, a so-called modified-adapted questionnaire was created in which the items were adapted and partly modified from Benedek et al. (2016), Málovics (2009), and the ISO 26000 (ISO, 2010). These procedures improve the conceptual and policy coverage while they preserve the cultural characteristics of this sub-population (i.e. SME entrepreneurs). A pilot testing phase (involving 8 sample members and 2 experts) allowed us to assess the questionnaire under real survey conditions. The final version was executed using a split-halves design for the two statement sections. Meanwhile, Cronbach's alpha was used to measure reliability and internal consistency. Its value for the whole survey was 0.629 (n = 32 items). This value indicates an acceptable or good reliability.

The questionnaire was divided into five main parts. The first part consisted of a free word association about responsibility in relation to sustainability. The second and fourth parts were an adaptation and modification of the questions from the above-mentioned research. These two sections included several statements on CSR and sustainability activities, motivations, organizational characteristics, and management factors in the SME sector. In the third part of the questionnaire, we were interested in business practices. The questions were based on modified ISO 26000 standards. Finally, the last section aimed to assess basic demographic features of the respondents such as age, gender education, etc.

The present study first examines and evaluates the free association section and the three statements related to law, legislation, and regulation according to main parameters (like the position of the respondent in the company). Each statement measured the respondents' beliefs, attitudes, and understanding on a 7-point ordinal scale, two of the statements on a bipolar scale. In addition, two further questions were added to identify business practices in relation to the legal approach.

Laws and regulations were studied on three levels:

(1) emotional or affective

Two statements were addressed here, both measured on a bipolar 7-item Likert scale (-3—Strongly disagree.... 0—Neither agree nor disagree ..... 3—Strongly agree). In total, all respondents (n = 300) provided reliable answers.

Economic legislation is a major constraint on what we can do to address social and environmental issues.
Compliance with Hungarian sustainability legislation is not difficult.

(2) cognitive motivational level

In this section, one statement was addressed (1—Definitely not ... 4—Possibly ... 7—Definitely). One respondent refused to answer (n = 299).

Our company meets environmental and social expectations by complying with the relevant legislation.

(3) conative or behavioural level

Here, two true or false statements (Yes, we have; No, we have not; I don't know/I don't want to answer) were provided, both were related to the ISO 26000 standards. In the first case, altogether 22 respondents (n = 278) and in the second case, 6 respondents (n = 294) refused to answer.

Our company uses international standards (especially sustainability standards).
Our company has, in addition to the legal requirements, equipment and facilities that reduce negative environmental impact associated with the company's activities.

The split-halves tests for each selected statement (i.e. selected for this study; n = 3 items) showed a strong similarity, which means that the reliability of the instrument can be considered satisfactory.

8.3.3 Sample Description and Methodology

The validated questionnaire was queried by the IPSOS market researcher company via telephone calls on a representative sample of Hungarian SME leaders in May 2023.

Stratified random sampling was used, which means that a random sample was taken from identifiable groups (strata) that are homogeneous with respect to three desired characteristics, namely (1) company size based on the number of employees; (2) region; and (3) economic activity classification as detailed in Table 8.1.

So-called strata weights were calculated and applied for economic activities where a subsample was over- or under-represented. As far as the demographic background of the respondents is concerned: 121 females and 178 males participated (one refused

Table 8.1 Sample characteristics. *Source* Own elaboration and HCSO[1]

Strata		National/domestic (%)	Research sample (%)
		Distribution	
Company size	Small (10–49)	86.70	86
	Medium (50–249)	13.40	14
Region	Budapest	36.70	36.71
	West-Dunántúl	8.30	8.29
	Middle-Dunántúl	7.80	7.81
	South-Dunántúl	5.50	5.50
	Middle-Hungary	15.20	15.19
	North-Hungary	5.50	5.54
	North-Alföld	10.10	10.11
	South-Alföld	10.90	10.85
Economic activities*	A	4.58	4.80
	B, D, E, F	13.82	14.40
	C	18.82	19.60
	G	21.72	22.60
	M	6.86	7.10
	I	7.50	7.80
	H	6.26	6.50
	N, J, L, O, P, Q, R, S, K	20.45	17.20

* A = Agriculture, forestry and fishing; B = Mining and quarrying; C = Manufacturing; D = Electricity, gas, steam and air conditioning supply; E = Water supply; sewerage, waste management and remediation activities; F = Construction; G = Wholesale and retail trade; repair of motor vehicles and motorcycles; H = Transportation and storage; I = Accommodation and food service activities; J = Information and communication; K = Financial and insurance activities; L = Real estate activities; M = Professional, scientific and technical activities; N = Administrative and support service activities; O = Public administration and defence; compulsory social security; P = Education; Q = Human health and social work activities; R = Arts, entertainment and recreation; S = Other service activities

to answer), with an average age of 49.67 years. Representativeness was normally distributed, but items measured on ordinal scales required non-parametric tests to compare measures of central tendency across subsamples. We worked mainly with NVivo12 and SPSS29 software.

For inferential statistics, we used non-parametric techniques because the variables were measured on ordinal and nominal scales, and the methods were organized according to the statements as in Table 8.2.

---

[1] Hungarian Central Statistical Office; website: www.ksh.hu.

Table 8.2 Methods used for the calculation of inferential statistics. *Source* Own elaboration

Characteristics	Outcomes	Emotional or affective		Cognitive motivational	Conative or behavioural	
Name		*Economic legislation significantly limits what we can do for social and natural issues*	*Compliance with Hungarian legislation on sustainability is not difficult*	*Our company meets environmental and social expectations by complying with the relevant legislation*	*Our company uses international standards (especially sustainability standards)*	*Our company has, in addition to the legal requirements, equipments, and facilities that reduce negative environmental impact associated with the company's activities*
Gender	Male/female/refuse to answer	Non parametric, independent-samples Mann–Whitney U test			Proportion testing (Z test) (where it is needed to be paired) independent samples	
Position	Owner but not manager/owner and manager/manager but not owner/Something else					
Involvement in decision-making	Yes, as owner/yes, as manager/yes, from a different area					
Ownership	Domestically owned/foreign-owned/jointly owned					
Company size	Small 10–49 employees/medium 50–249 employees					

8.4 Results

8.4.1 Qualitative Results

We analyzed the full transcripts of the three focus groups and then highlighted the sections that dealt with a topic with any legal connection. If we examine the frequency of the terms and plot them (Fig. 8.1) we see that the terms "law", "politics", "policy", and "state" often occur together and with a similar frequency. The terms "litigation", and "decision" appear with very high frequency. The terms "tax" and "difficulties related to legislation" appear often, but not with any outstanding frequency. Respondents claimed that legislation is sometimes controversial, focused on large companies' needs and bureaucratic which means disincentive for complying the regulation.

Only one of the three focus groups had female participants. Examining the terms 'law' or law-related synonyms we found that in the group where women were in the majority, terms related to 'law' did not appear at all. In the first group, in which there were only men, terms containing only 'law' or a form of the word occurred 19 times. While in the third group, which was also composed of only men, terms including 'law' or a form of the word occurred 18 times. The number of references to 'law' in the survey, or the fact that the topic was ignored, may indicate that law for women is not a central issue and that compliance with sustainability legislation is seen as an obvious matter. Our quantitative analysis later confirmed this assumption.

Fig. 8.1 Word cloud—frequency of legislation related words in focus groups. *Source* Own elaboration

In our focus group study, we examined the textual content of the codes from several perspectives. In the present research, we investigated legal issues in the framework of the entrepreneurial ecosystem, so we also looked at the weight of external stakeholders in the discussions. These include the state, the government, the legal environment, legal regulation as a source of motivation, and corporate life and its elements as a part of the forms "sustainability" appears in. The hierarchical structure of the codes included in the study is shown in Fig. 8.2.

Our hierarchy diagram (Fig. 8.3) shows that legal factors are explicitly emphasized in the text as a source of motivation or an external environmental element. However, there is no overlap with the third area of investigation, "corporate life".

Fig. 8.2 Hierarchical structure of the codes included in the study. *Source* Own elaboration

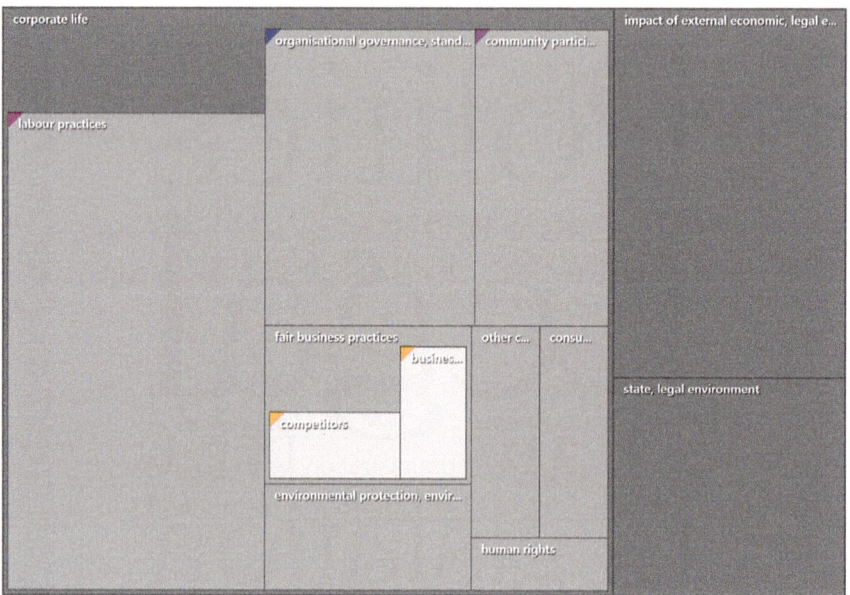

Fig. 8.3 Hierarchy diagram. *Source* Own elaboration

Fig. 8.4 Items clustered based on word similarity. *Source* Own elaboration

With regard to corporate life, three areas of emphasis can be identified. One of these areas is "organizational governance, standardization", the other is "labour practices", while the third is "community participation and development".

It is also apparent that respondents approached fair market practices from two perspectives both of which can be linked to the Culture domain of the ecosystem. One is the appropriate business behaviour, or lack thereof, with co-operating partners that they need to address. The other perspective they considered important was competitive relationships.

Since the codes included in the analysis dealt with legislators, state actors, and their involvement in business as external stakeholders, the results show that the legislator as the shaper of the entrepreneurial ecosystem should address the conditions of competition, ethical market conduct, and labour practices.

In a further examination of the same codes, we analyzed the text passages included under the codes. We identified three distinct clusters based on the similarity of textual content covered by each code (Fig. 8.4). Here we also can see how the legislation is interconnected with other ecosystem domains.

The sources of motivation to act sustainably within the ecosystem were found in the first and largest cluster, with roughly similar weights. This cluster also contains the manifestations of sustainability which are closely linked to the company's day-to-day activities.

In the second cluster, we find codes of fair market conduct, with the main emphasis on words related to competitors.

Market, consumer issues, and environmental protection and awareness formed the third cluster. This constellation of codes also shows that business managers are aware of their communication responsibility and that consumers are putting pressure on their companies to ensure sustainability.

Thus, our cluster analysis showed that the role of the state and legislative tasks are most often associated by company managers with the day-to-day life of the company. This means that the legal framework can be an important motivating factor for corporate sustainability measures.

Table 8.3 Word frequencies (with synonyms) for the question "Who is responsible for sustainability?". *Source* Own elaboration

Category	Count	Weighted percentage (%)
Everyone, public, individuals, people	190	31.09
Government, state, citizen	78	11.87
Companies, manager, leader	75	12.27

8.4.2 Quantitative Results

As it was expected based on the ecosystem model as the theoretical framework, SME owners and managers attach a considerable importance to legislation, particularly in relation to sustainability requirements. This was already a compelling finding from the qualitative part of the research, which is why we included several questions related to this topic in our questionnaire.

In the first section of the questionnaire, we asked respondents who were responsible for sustainability, world cloud shows the most frequently used terms, see Fig. 8.4. Most agreed that there is a shared responsibility, with everyone being mentioned by more than half of the respondents ("everyone" was mentioned 132 times). The state or government (the "state" was mentioned 22 times and the "government" was mentioned 52 times) was the second most frequently mentioned terms and the "companies" came third. Manager and management came fourth (with synonyms mentioned 29 times). If synonyms are also taken into account, the order is as follows (see Table 8.3).

While all citizens need to be made aware of how to achieve a sustainable future, the role of the state and the tools of legislation are undoubtedly important. The next chapter can be divided into two main methodological sections based on the literature: first, descriptive statistics have been approved in order to identify any patterns or trends. Then, the appropriate inference statistics have been implemented in order to uncover significant differences and investigate the main research questions.

8.4.2.1 Descriptive Statistics

In Hungary, the attention of many SMEs is still focused on regulatory compliance, even though personal interest is also emphasized. Our representative sample allows us to, we can provide a national overview of the Hungarian SME sector, see Table 8.4.

According to the three aspects of attitudes (as described in the previous section), perceptions and emotions appear to be neutral. The respondents do not consider the legal system as hindering. Meanwhile, they do not find Hungarian regulations difficult to follow or implement in their daily business. They are rather neutral or unconcerned. At the same time, the managers behave and act in accordance with regulations. Several companies apply requirements, equipment, and facilities to reduce

Table 8.4 Descriptive statistics (n = 300). *Source* Own elaboration

Statements	Economic legislation significantly limits what we can do for social and natural issues	Compliance with Hungarian legislation on sustainability is not difficult	Our company meets environmental and social expectations by complying with the relevant legislation
Mean	0.82	0.09	6.36
Median	1.00	0.00	7.00
Mode	0	0	7
Std. Deviation	1.729	1.658	1.120

Our company has, in addition to the legal requirements, equipments, and facilities that reduce negative environmental impact associated with the company's activities

	N	%
Yes, we have	195	65,0%
No, we have not	99	33,0%
Missing	6	2,0%

Our company uses international standards (especially sustainability standards)

	N	%
Yes, we have	152	50,6%
No, we have not	126	42,1%
Missing	22	7,3%

their negative impact on the environment. In addition, approximately half of them have implemented international standards.

8.4.2.2 Inferential Statistics

The preliminary research of the survey based on a representative sample showed that (1) the gender (2) the position and decision-making level of the managers, (3) the proportion of domestic or foreign ownership, and finally, (4) the size of the company have a major influence on the assessment of the legal systems regarding the legislations on sustainability. Our final results are structured in Table 8.5, while in this section, only the significant differences are highlighted, and the consequences are organized based on the four main characteristics.

1. Personal characteristics, gender differences

From a gender perspective, the motivational aspect showed significant differences (see Table 8.5), with female leaders and managers (n = 121, Mean 6.55, Std. Dev. 0.94) more likely than men (n = 177, Mean 6.24, Std. Dev. 1.217) to deal in an

Table 8.5 Results and statistical probability levels (p-values) structured according to the characteristics and levels of investigation. *Source* Own elaboration

Characteristics	Outcomes	Emotional or affective		Cognitive motivational	Conative or behavioural	
Name		*Economic legislation significantly limits what we can do for social and natural issues*	*Compliance with Hungarian legislation on sustainability is not difficult*	*Our company meets environmental and social expectations by complying with the relevant legislation*	*Our company uses international standards (especially sustainability standards)*	*Our company has, in addition to the legal requirements, equipments, and facilities that reduce the negative environmental impact associated with the company's activities*
Gender	Male/female/ refuse to answer	p = 0.355	p = 0.272	p = 0.010 **	p = 0.913	p = 0.264
Position	Owner but not manager/owner and manager/ manager but not the owner/ something else	p = 0.129	p = 0.036**	p = 0.178	Owner not manager/owner manager p = 0.610; owner but not manager/manager not owner p = 0.981; owner and manager/manager not owner p = 0.402	Owner not manager/owner manager p = 0.407;owner but not manager/manager not owner p = 0.348; owner and manager/manager not owner p = 0.746
Decision-making involvement	Yes, as owner/ yes, as manager/ yes, from a different area	p = 0.071*	p = 0.552	p = 0.580	p = 0.595	p = 0.444
Ownership	Domestically owned/ foreign-owned/ jointly owned	p = 0.003**	p = 0.664	p = 0.362	Domestic/foreign p = 0.336; Foreign/shared p = 0.825; Domestic/joint p = 0.394	Domestic/foreign p = 0.294; Foreign/shared p = 0.015**; Domestic/joint p = 0.030**
Company size	Small 10–49 person/medium 50–249 person	p = 0.769	p = 0.975	p = 0.081*	p = 0.337	p = 0.118

** Significant on 0.05 alpha level * Significant on 0.1 alpha level

obvious way with the fact that the company must meet sustainable expectations by complying with registrations. This result mirrors the qualitative results explained earlier.

2. Position and decision-making level of the respondents

The level of difficulty in complying with the Hungarian sustainability legislation shows significant differences (see Table 8.5) between "owners and managers" (n = 145, Mean −0,1, Std. Dev. 1,681) and "managers" (n = 41, Mean 0.69, Std. Dev. 1.696). "Managers" who are not owners struggled more with Hungarian legislation than "owners". In line with this, "managers" (n = 41, Mean 6.26, Std. Dev. 1.044) were more likely than "owners but not managers" (n = 16, Mean 6.11, Std. Dev. 1.188) to consider that the company meets sustainable expectations by complying with legislation. Regarding the level of decision-making, we found that "owners" experienced significantly (see Table 8.5) greater legal restrictions (n = 106, Mean 1.07, Std. Dev. 1.706) on what the company can do for sustainability than "managers" (n = 94, Mean 0.60, Std. Dev. 1.908). As far as the aspects of sustainability are concerned, we did not find any significant differences.

3. Ownership (share of domestic or foreign investments)

After scanning the opinions of the respondents as to how the economic legislation limits the impact of the companies on sustainability, the results showed a significant difference (see Table 8.5) between the foreign and the domestic companies. Domestically owned companies received a higher average score (n = 261, Mean 0.92, Std. Dev. 1.719) than foreign-owned ones (n = 26, Mean -0.23, Std. Dev. 1.588). Domestically owned companies seem to have more difficulties (n = 261, Mean 0.06, Std. Dev. 1.669) with Hungarian legislation than foreign-owned companies (n = 42, Mean 0.42, Std. Dev. 1.595). There were significant differences in standards and equipment/facilities (see Table 8.5) as well. However, these differences can be explained by the small number of jointly owned companies. Therefore, so-called paired comparisons were examined, where jointly owned companies appeared to make less effort in terms of a sustainable approach.

4. The size of the company (i.e., number of employees)

As emphasized in the current state of the art (Málovics, 2009, Benedek et al., 2016, Bikefe et al., 2020, Metzker & Štreimikis, 2020, Mahmood et al., 2021), smaller companies perceive a lower environmental impact and consequently put less effort into sustainability. Small companies tend to have lower expectations (n = 258, Mean 6.31, Std. Dev. 1.166) than medium-sized ones (n = 41, Mean 6.71, Std. Dev. 0.686) regarding whether the company meets sustainable expectations by complying with the legislation. This difference was significant at the 10% level (see Table 8.5).

Finally, some differences were found in behavioural routines and business practices. Although 34.375% of medium-sized company leaders said that they do not use international standards this number was 46.94% in case of the small enterprises. More medium-sized companies (79.49%) seem to use additional equipment and facilities in order to reduce negative environmental impacts than small companies (64.31%).

8.5   Discussion

This book chapter examined how the legal system and regulations affect sustainability from the perspective of SME leaders. Laws and regulations—as a part of the Policy domain of the entrepreneurial ecosystem—were studied on three levels (1) emotional or affective (2) cognitive motivational, and (3) conative or behavioural. The main research questions were the following:

1. What is the role of the state in achieving sustainability in the opinion of SME leaders?

The results of the focus groups showed that the legal system and policy (i.e., regulative framework, incentives) have a significant impact on the sustainability of entrepreneurial activity, therefore it can be treated as a crucial part of the ecosystem. Our quantitative results also reaffirm this opinion. SME leaders attribute great importance to legislation, especially focusing on sustainability requirements, it means real motivation for companies to be more responsible and sustainable, regulations shape the attitudes of SME leaders and have direct impacts on related behaviour as well. That is why SMEs have great expectations regarding sustainability towards the state as regulator, attitude shaper, and market actor. Other ecosystem actors are less mentioned except for the general responsibility of everyone (Fig. 8.5) which can be linked to the strong moral commitment of SME leaders in our research. This result confirms Generali and SDA Bocconi's White Paper 2021 and 2022 and other previous research work (Csillag et al., 2022; Ray & Sharma, 2022; Bihari, 2023), namely the national and international legal requirements are highly important drivers that need to be achieved.

2. What are the challenges that Hungarian SMEs face in their day-to-day operations, longer-term planning, and strategising in the face of general and sustainability-related legislation?

SME leaders are motivated by both moral and business case and within the second one, state regulation is considered to be an important factor even if they do not think

Fig. 8.5   Word cloud answering the question Who is responsible for sustainability? *Source* Own elaboration

that complying with sustainability regulations is difficult. This is partly in parallel with previous research pieces (Málovics, 2009, Benedek et al., 2016).

While recognizing the positive effects of legislation, SME managers pointed out that regulation is often inconsistent and sometimes even works against greener, more sustainable operations, for example in terms of energy mix, taxation or bureaucratic paperwork requirements. This result is in line with the previous research (Harangozó & Szigeti, 2017; Bakos et al., 2020, Generali and SDA Bocconi, 2021, 2022). There is also the problem that regulation often focuses on the interests and operational logic of large companies and does not take into account the difficulties and scarce resources of SMEs. Integrative thinking in ecosystem dimensions does not really characterize either entrepreneurs or the state.

3. What is the impact of personal and company characteristics on the attitudes, motivations, and behaviour of companies towards sustainability?

Personal and company characteristics can be linked to more ecosystem domains, most notably Human Capital and Culture. By understanding the characteristics of SME leaders who are more committed to sustainability, we can better target them and give them more focus and space in the development of the entrepreneurial ecosystem.

Regarding the gender both qualitative and quantitative results showed that women tend to better comply with regulations. For them compliance with legislation related to sustainability is seen as an evidential issue. Considering the position and decision-making power of the respondents we found that managers are more likely to think that it is easy to comply with regulations than owners. We suppose that it means less responsibility from the side of managers. Owners are more committed, which is very similar to the principal-agent problem, usually mentioned related to large organizations. The effect of company size can be seen in the significantly higher use of environmentally friendly equipment and facilities and international standards by medium-sized companies than by smaller ones. We found similarities with the studies dealing with large companies (MPRSZ, 2017, BCSDH, 2017, Bikefe et al., 2020, Metzker & Štreimikis, 2020, Mahmood et al., 2021), which means that handling sustainability issues in a company can be interpreted as a scale where companies have special characteristics, but there are also many similarities (Bikefe et al., 2020, Metzker & Štreimikis, 2020, Mahmood et al., 2021). The impact of international connections is further reflected in the fact that companies with a higher share of foreign ownership are also more likely to use these explicit sustainability tools. The Hungarian CSR and sustainability practice has been characterized by the example of multinational companies since the change of regime (Málovics, 2009, Benedek et al., 2016, Győri et al., 2021), so this research result is also consistent with the literature. In this sense, it seems even more important to adopt and enforce international, specifically EU sustainability regulations and ensure that they truly permeate the whole entrepreneurial ecosystem.

8.6   Conclusion

As mentioned above, this study is the part of a broader research on the sustainability-related attitudes, motivations, and behaviours of Hungarian SMEs. In Hungary, there has not been any comprehensive research carried out on the sustainability activities of SMEs in recent years, and the few studies that have been conducted have only and generally examined some specific examples, good practices (BCSDH, 2017; Győri et al., 2021; MPRSZ, 2017). In our previous study (Győri et al., 2023), based on our focus group results, we argued that lower visibility of sustainability does not necessarily mean less sustainable and less responsible operations than in the case of large companies, because SMEs operate along a different logic resulting in different stakeholder relationships, responsibilities and communication. Our findings are in support of the literature that claims that SMEs may have stronger implicit than explicit responsibility (Matten & Moon, 2008) for sustainability. This is also confirmed by our quantitative results.

Taking this a step further and to the present study, only a few studies discuss SME sustainability in the context of the entrepreneurial ecosystem, and even fewer focuses specifically on the impact and challenges of legislation on SMEs. In this chapter we seek to reinforce the crucial role of policy, legislation, in the entrepreneurial ecosystem as it relates to sustainability and to present its practical implications in SME operation on emotional, motivational, and behavioural level.

The ecosystem perspective places the study of how SMEs contribute to sustainability in a new, more integrated context. The research shows that, within this framework, the legal and policy system has a major—and at times controversial—impact on the sustainability of entrepreneurial activity.

Policy is the leading domain in the sense that business leaders look to regulation and the state to provide the systemic changes and foundations that will make the economy truly more sustainable. This expectation and attribution of responsibility is also the reason why they are very critical of the state, and have a very poor view of the status quo in terms of the reduction of red tape, the greening of the economy, and/or the consideration needs and interests of SMEs. The policy implication is that sustainability issues should be more addressed and in a more holistic and integral way across the different domains of the entrepreneurial ecosystem. At the same time, individual characteristics of the entrepreneur, such as gender, position, and decision-making power, as well as characteristics of the enterprise, such as size or ownership structure, also influence the assessment of the legislation and the perception and resolution of related challenges which should be taken into consideration. Personal and company characteristics can be linked to more ecosystem domains, mostly to Human Capital and Culture. By understanding the characteristics of SME leaders who are more committed to sustainability, we can better target them and give them more focus and space through legislation in the development of the entrepreneurial ecosystem.

One of the limitations of our research is that at this stage we have only asked Hungarian entrepreneurs at this stage, but a possible further research direction is going to be to ask the same questions in other EU countries (beginning with the V4). In addition, the present study has examined the emergence of policy, legislation largely independently of the other ecosystem domains, and it is worth analyzing the results in a more integrated way in the future. Moreover, as is usually the case in quantitative research, the causes for the results can only be inferred from the qualitative phase of the preliminary work. In a further phase of our research, it will be worthwhile to test our presumptions on causes in a further qualitative round.

Funding This research was supported by the Ministry of Innovation and Technology of Hungary from the National Research, Development and Innovation Fund, financed under the Tématerületi Kiválósági Program 2021 (TKP2021-NKTA) funding scheme (Project no. TKP2021-NKTA-44).

References

Bakos, J., Siu, M., Orengo, A., & Kasiri, N. (2020). An analysis of environmental sustainability in small & medium-sized enterprises: Patterns and trends. *Business Strategy and the Environment, 29*(3), 1285–1296. https://doi.org/10.1002/bse.2433

BCSDH, Business Council for Sustainable Development Hungary. (2017). *Environmental responsibility in focus, BCSDH survey 2017.* Budapest, https://bcsdh.hu/wp-content/uploads/2017/10/Felmeres_2017_ENG.pdf

Benedek, A., & Takácsné, György, K. T. (2016). The personal factors of responsible corporate leadership: A study on the attitudes of CSR managers in small and medium-sized enterprises. [A felelős vállalatirányítás személyi tényezői: A CSR-központ felelős vállalatvezetők attitüdjének vizsgálata a kis- és középvállalatok körében.] *Budapest Management Review, [Vezetéstudomány], 58*–67. https://doi.org/10.14267/veztud.2016.01.05

Bihari, A. (2023). Corporate social responsibility, social Start-Ups, and a case of diversity and inclusion in India. In *Responsible leadership and sustainable management* (pp. 59–74). https://doi.org/10.1007/978-981-99-5366-0_5

Bikefe, G., Zubairu, U. M., Araga, S., Maitala, F., Ediuku, E., & Anyebe, D. I. (2020). Corporate Social Responsibility (CSR) by small and medium enterprises (SMEs): A systematic review. *Small Business International Review, 4*(1), 16–33. https://doi.org/10.26784/sbir.v4i1.243

Chandler, N. (2022). Entrepreneurial personality and motive: A study of Hungarian early-stage entrepreneurs using GEM data. *Prosperitas, 9*(4), 1–10. https://doi.org/10.31570/prosp_2022_0007

Cornejo-Cañamares, M., Medrano, N., & Pascual, C. O. (2021). Environmental objectives and non-technological innovation in Spanish manufacturing SMEs. *Journal of Cleaner Production, 296,* 126445. https://doi.org/10.1016/j.jclepro.2021.126445

Csákné Filep, J., & Radácsi, L. (2019). Hungarian start-up community compass. [Magyar start-up közösség iránytű] In Kőszegi, Irén Rita (szerk.) *3rd Scientific conference on economics and management: Competitiveness and innovation* [III. Gazdálkodás és Menedzsment Tudományos Konferencia: Versenyképesség és innováció.] John von Neumann University [Neumann János Egyetem] (pp. 945–950).

Csillag, S., Király, G., Rakovics, M., & Géring, Z. (2022). Agents for sustainable futures? The (unfulfilled) promise of sustainability at leading business schools. *Futures, 144,* 103044. https://doi.org/10.1016/j.futures.2022.103044

Csizmadia, P., Csillag, S., Szászvári, K., & Bácsi, K. (2022). To learn and let learn? Characteristics of the learning environment in knowledge-intensive medium-sized enterprises. *Journal of Workplace Learning, 34*(7), 661–674. https://doi.org/10.1108/jwl-09-2021-0120

Daniel, L., Medlin, C. J., O'Connor, A., Statsenko, L., Vnuk, R., & Hancock, G. (2017). Deconstructing the entrepreneurial ecosystem concept. In *International studies in entrepreneurship* (pp. 23–44). https://doi.org/10.1007/978-3-319-63531-6_2

Economist. (2008). *Special CSR report*. (ed. Daniel Franklin), 17 January.

European Council, EC. (2010). *EUROPE 2020 A strategy for smart, sustainable and inclusive growth*.

European Parliament and Council. (2019). *Regulation (EU) 2019/2088 of the European Parliament and of the Council of 27 November 2019 on sustainability-related disclosures in the financial services sector (SFDR)*.

European Parliament and Council. (2020). *Regulation (EU) 2020/852 of the European Parliament and of the Council of 18 June 2020 on the establishment of a framework to facilitate sustainable investment, and amending Regulation (EU) 2019/2088 (EU Taxonomy)*.

European Parliament and Council. (2022). *Directive (EU) 2022/2464 of the European Parliament and of the Council of 14 December 2022 amending Regulation (EU) No 537/2014, Directive 2004/109/EC, Directive 2006/43/EC and Directive 2013/34/EU, as regards corporate sustainability reporting (CSRD)*.

Fenwick, M., Joubert, T., Van Wyk, S., & Vermeulen, E. (2022). ESG as a business model for SMEs. *Social Science Research Network*. https://doi.org/10.2139/ssrn.4098644

Fuentelsaz, L., Maícas, J. P., & Mata, P. (2017). Institutional dynamism in entrepreneurial ecosystems. In *International studies in entrepreneurship* (pp. 45–65). https://doi.org/10.1007/978-3-319-63531-6_3

Generali and SDA Bocconi Research. (2021). *Generali SME EnterPRIZE fostering sustainability in small and medium-sized enterprises*. White Paper. 1st Edition https://www.sme-enterprize.com/

Generali and SDA Bocconi Research (2022). *Generali SME EnterPRIZE fostering sustainability in small and medium-sized enterprises. white paper* (2nd Edition) https://www.sme-enterprize.com/; Generali and SDA Bocconi's White Paper, a guide to the sustainable transition of SMEs—SME EnterPRIZE. (2022). SME EnterPRIZE. https://www.sme-enterprize.com/white-paper/

Gosztonyi, M. (2022). COVID-19 positivism: Has COVID-19 changed Hungarian entrepreneurs' perception of business opportunities? *Prosperitas, 9*. https://doi.org/10.31570/prosp_2021_0006

Győri, Z., Svastics, C., & Csillag, S. (2019). Push and pull motivations of entrepreneurs with disabilities in Hungary. In: *7th International OFEL conference on governance, management and entrepreneurship: Embracing diversity in organisations*, 5–6 April 2019, Dubrovnik, Croatia. https://www.econstor.eu/bitstream/10419/196093/1/ofel-2019-p351-366.pdf

Győri, Z., Szirmai, A. M., Csillag, S., & Bánhegyi, M. (2021). Corporate social responsibility in Hungary. In *CSR, sustainability, ethics & governance* (pp. 193–211). https://doi.org/10.1007/978-3-030-68386-3_9

Győri, Z., Csillag, S., Svastics, C., & Hidegh, A. L. (2022a). Examining the entrepreneurial ecosystem and the entrepreneurial life cycle in enterprises of people with disabilities. In: Leko-Šimić Mirna (Ed.) *11 International scientific symposium region, entrepreneurship, development* (pp. 252–270)

Győri, Z., Kása, R., & Szegedi, K. (2022). Hungarian entrepreneurs' sustainability motivations based on GEM 2021 results. *Prosperitas, 9*(4), 1–16. https://doi.org/10.31570/prosp_2022_0012

Győri, Z., Kolnhofer-Derecskei, A., Reicher R., & Szigeti, C. (2023). Implementation of sustainability issues at Hungarian SMEs. In: Šimić Mirna Leko (szerk.) *12th international scientific symposium: Region, entrepreneurship, development*, Osijek.

Harangozó, G., & Szigeti, C. (2017). Corporate carbon footprint analysis in practice—with a special focus on validity and reliability issues. *Journal of Cleaner Production, 167*, 1177–1183. https://doi.org/10.1016/j.jclepro.2017.07.237

Hoogendoorn, B., Guerra, D., & Van Der Zwan, P. (2015). What drives environmental practices of SMEs? *Small Business Economics, 44*(4), 759–781. https://doi.org/10.1007/s11187-014-9618-9

Isenberg, D. J. (2010). How to start an entrepreneurial revolution. *Harvard Business Review, 88*(6), 41–50.

Isenberg, D. J. (2014). What an entrepreneurship ecosystem actually is. *Harvard Business Review.* https://hbr.org/2014/05/what-an-entrepreneurial-ecosystem-actually-is

ISO. (2010). *ISO 26000: 2010—guidance on social responsibility.* https://www.iso.org/obp/ui/#iso:std:iso:26000:ed-1:v1:en

Kotler, P., & Lee, N. (2004). *Corporate social responsibility: Doing the most good for company and your cause.* Wiley

Málovics, G. (2009). *A stakeholder-centred approach to corporate sustainability. [A vállalati fenntarthatóság érintettközpontú vizsgálata].* PhD Dissertation. International PhD Programme in Regional Development. [Doktori értekezés. Pécsi Tudományegyetem Közgazdaságtudományi Kar Regionális Politika és Gazdaságtan Doktori Iskola]. https://ktk.pte.hu/sites/ktk.pte.hu/files/images/kepzes/phd/Malovics_Gyorgy_disszertacio.pdf

Mahmood, A., Naveed, R. T., Ahmad, N., Scholz, M., Khalique, M., & Adnan, M. (2021). Unleashing the barriers to CSR implementation in the SME sector of a developing Economy: A thematic analysis approach. *Sustainability, 13*(22), 12710. https://doi.org/10.3390/su132212710

Malecki, E. J. (2018). Entrepreneurship and Entrepreneurial Ecosystems. Geography Compass, 12, e12359. https://doi.org/10.1111/gec3.12359

Matten, D., & Moon, J. (2008). "Implicit" and "explicit" CSR: A conceptual framework for a comparative understanding of corporate social responsibility. *Academy of Management Review, 33*(2), 404–424. https://doi.org/10.5465/amr.2008.31193458

Maroufkhani, P., Wagner, R., & Ismail, W. K. W. (2018). Entrepreneurial ecosystems: A systematic review. *Journal of Enterprising Communities, 12*(4), 545–564. https://doi.org/10.1108/jec-03-2017-0025

Martins, A., Branco, M. C., Melo, P., & Machado, C. F. (2022). Sustainability in small and medium-sized enterprises: A systematic literature review and future research agenda. *Sustainability, 14*(11), 6493. https://doi.org/10.3390/su14116493

Metzker, Z., & Štreimikis, J. (2020). CSR activities in the Czech SME segment. *International Journal of Entrepreneurial Knowledge, 8*(1), 49–64. https://doi.org/10.37335/ijek.v8i2.101

MPRSZ. (2017). *Research on corporate social responsibility in Hungary. [Kutatás a hazai vállalatok társadalmi felelősségvállalásáról.]* Budapest.

Németh, K., Németh, Sz., Heidrich, B., & Vajdovich, N. (2022). Financial and non-financial goals and performance indicators in the light of a research of family wineries in Hungary. [Pénzügyi és nem pénzügyi célok és teljesítménymutatók hazai családi borászatok felmérése tükrében.] *Space—Economy—Society Journal [Tér Gazdaság Ember], 1*(10), 9–28.

Porter, M. E., & Kramer, M. R. (2002). The competitive advantage of corporate philantropy. *Harvard Business Review,* December.

Ray, R. S., & Sharma, T. (2022). Towards cluster-based sustainability and CSR framework in Indian small and medium enterprises—a case study on garment industry. In *Responsible leadership and sustainable management* (pp. 67–81). https://doi.org/10.1007/978-981-16-7614-7_5

Salvetti, N., & Jeurissen, R. (2022). The role of institutional mechanisms in inducing corporate socially responsible behaviour: A study into the garment sector of Bangladesh. In: J. Talapatra, N. Mitra, & R. Schmidpeter (Eds.), *Emerging economic models for sustainable businesses. Responsible leadership and sustainable management.* Springer, Singapore. https://doi.org/10.1007/978-981-16-7614-7_4

Shalhoob, H., & Hussainey, K. (2022). Environmental, social and governance (ESG) disclosure and the small and medium enterprises (SMEs) sustainability performance. *Sustainability, 15*(1), 200. https://doi.org/10.3390/su15010200

Sharma, T., & Ray, R. S. (2022). Responsible leadership in uncertain times—past discourse and present scenario. In *Responsible leadership and sustainable management* (pp. 1–13). https://doi.org/10.1007/978-981-19-4723-0_1

Simatupang, T. M., Schwab, A., & Lantu, D. C. (2015). Introduction: Building sustainable entrepreneurship ecosystems. *International Journal of Entrepreneurship and Small Business, 26*(4), 389–398. https://doi.org/10.2139/ssrn.3161598

Stam, E. (2017). Measuring entrepreneurial ecosystems. In *International studies in entrepreneurship* (pp. 173–197). https://doi.org/10.1007/978-3-319-63531-6_9

Szennay, Á., Szigeti, C., Beke, J., & Radácsi, L. (2021). Ecological footprint as an indicator of corporate environmental performance—empirical evidence from Hungarian SMEs. *Sustainability, 13*(2), 1000. https://doi.org/10.3390/su13021000

Talat, N., & Bhaduri, S. (2022). Responsible leadership at the time of the pandemic: SMEs in India. In *Responsible leadership for sustainability in uncertain times: Responsible leadership and sustainable management* (pp. 157–170). https://doi.org/10.1007/978-981-19-4723-0_9

Tolstykh, T., Gamidullaeva, L., Shmeleva, N., Wozniak, M., & Vasin, S. (2021). An assessment of regional sustainability via the maturity level of entrepreneurial ecosystems. *Journal of Open Innovation: Technology, Market, and Complexity, 7*, 5. https://doi.org/10.3390/joitmc7010005

United Nations. (2000). *United Nations millenium declaration.* https://www.refworld.org/docid/3b00f4ea3.html

United Nations. (2015). *Transforming our world: The 2030 agenda for sustainable development.* Retrieved June 15, 2021, from https://www.un.org/ga/search/view_doc.asp?symbol=A/RES/70/1&Lang=E; https://sdgs.un.org/goals

Uvarova, I., Mavļutova, I., & Atstāja, D. (2021). Development of the green entrepreneurial mindset through modern entrepreneurship education. *IOP Conference Series, 628*, 012034. https://doi.org/10.1088/1755-1315/628/1/012034

Vogel, D. (2006). *The market for virtue—the potential and limits of corporate social responsibility.* Brookings Institution Press.

Vajdovich, N., Heidrich, B., Németh, S., & Németh, K. (2022). Where do we go from Here? Difficulties in interpreting non-economic goals of family business-the case of the Hungarian wine sector. In *International conference on organizational science development: Society's challenges for organizational opportunities.* https://doi.org/10.18690/um.fov.3.2022.74

Zsuzsanna Győri PhD, Head of the Centre of Excellence for Sustainability Impacts in Business and Society (CESIBUS) and senior research fellow at the Faculty of Finance and Accountancy of Budapest Business University. She teaches courses on Business Ethics, Responsible and Sustainable Company and Entrepreneurship. Her research fields include corporate social responsibility, sustainability in higher education, entrepreneurs with disabilities, as well as values-based business.

Regina Zsuzsánna Reicher PhD, Member of the Centre of Excellence for Sustainability Impacts in Business and Society (CESIBUS) and Associate Professor at the Budapest University of Economics and Business, Faculty of Finance and Accounting. She teaches courses in business economics, operations and inventory management. His research interests include corporate social responsibility in the SME sector, generational change in the labour market, and studying optimal corporate processes.

Anita Kolnhofer-Derecskei PhD, is currently working as an associate professor at the Budapest Business School, Faculty of Finance and Accountancy where she is teaching among others Economics and Research Methodology. She leads research where various generations are studied at the labour market and participates in several research projects including this one (CESIBUS). As an economic psychologist, she has been researching in the fields of behavioural and social economics as well as economic psychology. She has a proven track record of high-profile academic papers using various research methodologies and several publications from interdisciplinary field of psychology and economics.

Chapter 9
Exploring the Effects of ESG Scores and Carbon Emissions on Abnormal Stock Returns: A Two-Step Approach with Random Forest and Panel Regressions

Emre Güven⑩ **and Renee Pesor**⑩

Abstract As sustainable finance becomes more prevalent and climate change concerns more urgent, the role of non-financial information has never been more important. However, identifying the influential indicators remains a formidable challenge. Our research explores the impact of ESG scores and carbon emissions on abnormal stock returns, utilizing a dataset that includes granular Refinitiv ESG scores and CO_2 emission data from 4,513 global publicly listed companies across two decades (2002–2022). We employ a two-step approach that combines machine learning and fixed effects panel regressions. The results show that all ESG scores analyzed in our study, except the Controversies Score, exhibit non-positive impact on abnormal returns. A one-point increase in the main ESG Score is associated with a 0.2% decrease in abnormal returns. Furthermore, all carbon emissions metrics have a non-positive impact on abnormal returns, however, the effect varies considerably depending on the metric used. A 1% increase in annual CO_2 emissions correspond to a 0.027% decrease in abnormal returns. Our results suggest that superior carbon performance might be a more effective factor than higher ESG scores in achieving higher abnormal returns. The implications of our study extend beyond the financial markets, highlighting the importance of carbon emissions within the corporate sustainability initiatives and environmental policy.

Keywords ESG · CO_2 emissions · Abnormal stock returns · Sustainable finance · Random forest

E. Güven (✉) · R. Pesor
Estonian Business School, A. Lauteri 3, 10114 Tallinn, Estonia
e-mail: emre.guven@ebs.ee

© The Author(s), under exclusive license to Springer Nature Singapore Pte Ltd. 2024   185
M. Kooskora and A. Kekkonen (eds.), *Performance Challenges in Organizational Sustainability*, Responsible Leadership and Sustainable Management,
https://doi.org/10.1007/978-981-97-5548-6_9

9.1 Introduction

ESG, which stands for environmental, social, and governance, is a set of criteria used to assess corporate social performance and identify associated costs, risks, and opportunities. Built upon the concepts of socially responsible investing, integrating ESG framework into sustainable business models and investment decisions has become increasingly crucial for companies and investors. The share of the global ESG-oriented assets under management has reached 14.4% of all assets in 2021 and is expected to grow to 21.5% by 2026 (PwC, 2022). By encouraging businesses and managers to adopt more sustainable practices via greater investment in more sustainable companies, ESG is now recognized as a crucial tool for enabling positive societal changes on a global scale (Pástor et al., 2021). In this regard, ESG investing is also aimed at tackling environmental issues including climate change.

Climate change is one of the most challenging global problems today and requires urgent action to mitigate the wide-ranging risks including coastal degradation, biodiversity loss, food and health crises, escalation and amplification of natural disasters, social instability, resource conflicts, and economic deceleration (IPCC, 2014). Scientific evidence indicates that the high concentration of anthropogenically generated greenhouse gases in the atmosphere is the main cause of climate change and therefore emissions must be reduced significantly (IPCC, 2007). The United Nations (UN) urges immediate and concrete actions to reduce global emissions by 45 percent by 2030 and attain a net-zero emissions target by 2050. For this purpose, they also emphasize the importance of integrating the carbon neutrality goals into all economic and fiscal policies and decisions. In addition to the international cooperation to reduce global emissions with treaties such as the Kyoto Protocol or Paris Agreement, a proactive business response to climate change is also crucial for transitioning to a low-carbon economy because a significant portion of greenhouse gas emissions stems from industrial production (Hoffman & Busch, 2008). Businesses not only have a social responsibility for their impact on the environment but also bear potential business risks associated with climate change. The increase in stakeholder awareness of those risks has intensified the demand for companies to disclose comprehensive information on their carbon emissions, as well as corporate policies on the environment and climate change (Eleftheriadis & Anagnostopoulou, 2014). In the past, such disclosures were confined to information mainly from firms in sensitive industries, but with the growing popularity of ESG over the last two decades, now they are also an integral part of the all-encompassing and comprehensive ESG data within the environmental pillar.

However, before financial markets can allocate additional capital to environmentally responsible firms as a means of contributing to climate change-related efforts further, ESG investing must demonstrate an improved risk-return profile for investors. Recent surveys on individual and institutional investors reveal that most investors who utilize ESG data are driven by financial rather than ethical reasons, although a substantial part of ESG investors also tend to be motivated by concerns over climate change-related risks (Amel-Zadeh & Serafeim, 2018; Giglio et al., 2023). Furthermore, most market participants believe that financial markets are undervaluing the long-term risks associated with climate change (Stroebel & Wurgler, 2021). Should investors be convinced about such a mispricing in the market and demonstrate higher demand for firms with perceived lower risk and higher profitability indicated by ESG factors, it can be expected that ESG scores might generate higher abnormal returns (Delmas et al., 2015). On the other hand, even if ESG scores can represent underlying risk factors, stocks with higher ESG scores may still generate lower than expected returns due to their lower risk exposure (Cornell, 2021).

Lastly, the debate persists on whether the ESG score, derived from a diverse range of indicators, can reflect all pertinent risks accurately. Therefore, our goal is to assess if the more specific ESG scores at granular levels, or CO_2 emissions as a rather straightforward measure addressing directly for climate change-related risks can act as more precise and discernible tools to guide investments with higher than expected returns. Given these metrics we propose already represent certain underlying risks, our focus would be solely on their ability to influence abnormal returns.

With this perspective, the purpose of this study is to conduct an analysis of ESG scores and CO_2 emissions and their relationship with abnormal stock returns. Drawing on these considerations, the focus of this research is guided by the following research questions:

1. Do higher ESG scores, including the pillar and category level scores, lead to higher abnormal returns?
2. Does better carbon emission performance lead to higher abnormal returns?
3. Can CO_2 emissions metrics be more effective factors in achieving higher abnormal returns compared to ESG scores?

The formulated research questions are investigated in a two-step approach, which combines non-parametric and parametric analysis methods to separately capture the factors' impact on abnormal returns. Firstly, a random forest model is applied, which is known for its powerful predictive capabilities within the realm of machine learning techniques (e.g., see Jun, 2021), to capture complex and non-linear relationships between diverse input features and stock returns, and the random forest residuals (i.e., the difference between actual and random forest predicted returns, or abnormal returns) are obtained. Secondly, these residuals are applied as the dependent variable in fixed effects panel regressions, where ESG and CO_2 factors are the independent variables. This two-step method enables us to isolate the effect of ESG scores and CO_2 emissions indicators on stock returns from various effects such as systematic risk or expected returns implied by the available financial information of a firm. The use of fixed effects allows us to further control for unobserved factors, thereby increasing the robustness of the approach.

This study contributes to the literature in several ways. Firstly, our two-step approach for computing more precise abnormal returns by using a random forest model and subsequently analyzing them via fixed effects regression offers noteworthy contributions to the existing literature. Secondly, considering the recent debate over whether environmentally conscious investing should pivot from ESG to carbon emissions (e.g., The Economist, 2022), we offer a novel empirical perspective in the context of financial returns. Lastly, our analysis can provide more comprehensive conclusions by employing a moderately large sample over an extensive timeframe and offering a granular assessment down to the ESG category level.

This chapter has the following structure. Section 9.2 reviews relevant theoretical and empirical literature. Section 9.3 describes the data and explains the research methodology applied. Section 9.4 presents and discusses the results. Finally, Sect. 9.5 summarizes our main findings and conclusions.

9.2 Literature Review

To explain their impact on financial performance, literature on ESG and carbon performance mostly overlap in theories which are mainly rooted in earlier research of corporate social responsibility or environmental performance. Within the context of our study, we present the most relevant theories. The stakeholder theory (Freeman, 2010; Jones, 1995) suggests that a firm may achieve higher financial performance through effective management of its stakeholders' expectations. In this regard, a competitive advantage can be achieved by enhancing the social legitimacy of external stakeholders. Given that ESG and carbon emission data are among the most relevant non-financial information (Eccles et al., 2011), firms which integrate ESG or carbon performance into their business strategy may gain higher market value expectations from investors (Gallego-Álvarez et al., 2015; Ioannou & Serafeim, 2019). Furthermore, according to the risk mitigation hypothesis, firms with higher ESG scores or carbon performance can have lower risk exposure, particularly to potential costs such as abatement, litigation, remediation, or reputational costs (Brouwers et al., 2018; Karwowski & Raulinajtys-Grzybek, 2021; Trinks et al., 2020). As a result of reduced risk, these firms have lower volatility of future earnings, lower credit risk, lower cost of debt, and subsequently achieve higher financial performance (Barth et al., 2022; Kleimer & Viehs, 2018). However, while the ESG and CO_2 emissions-related data can be expected to have an effect on corporate financial performance, by following the stakeholder theory, an opposite direction in this relationship can occur as well. For instance, the slack resources theory suggests that firms with already strong financial performance may have greater opportunities to invest to improve ESG or carbon performance, implying that a reciprocal causality may be present with financial performance (Schaltegger & Synnestvedt, 2002). Thus, high corporate social performance could be partly determined by the size of the company, which needs to be controlled for in empirical studies. Moreover, information availability can be considered an important precondition for a positive relationship to emerge between corporate social performance and financial performance (Schuler & Cording, 2006). Accurate disclosure concerning ESG matters, including carbon emissions, may signal investors and other stakeholders about the presence of good management practices in the company. The effectiveness of such signalling can be determined by its observability (Janney & Folta, 2006; Shen, 2006), which implies that a firm needs to report and beforehand measure its impact. While measuring can be costly, Srivastava (2001) argues that this may further increase the credibility of a signal. Thus, ESG and/or emissions-related information may serve as input for the decisions of many stakeholders. These decisions partly determine the financial performance of a company (Schuler & Cording, 2006).

As empirical research in the literature, there is a large volume of published studies investigating ESG scores as a factor that can influence stock returns. Although the earlier studies proposed ESG as a potential factor which can lead to higher abnormal returns (Friede et al., 2015), findings from various recent empirical studies object to any benefit from using ESG information that is not already captured by well-known equity factors (e.g., Kumar, 2019; Naffa & Fain, 2022). Hubel and Scholz (2020) suggest that ESG factors may increase the explanatory power of standard asset pricing models, however, they found no evidence for a systematic return premium or discount through ESG factors. Breedt et al. (2019) find that ESG information fails to achieve higher risk-adjusted returns and claim that ESG cannot be considered as a unique equity factor. In a meta-analysis exploring the relationship between ESG and financial performance by using more than 1000 studies published between 2015 and 2020, Whelan et al. (2021) report that only a third of investor-focused studies report excess returns from ESG investing. On the other hand, they find that the majority of studies find a positive relationship between low-carbon strategies and financial performance.

However, literature on carbon performance, especially about its financial impact, is relatively scarce compared to the literature on ESG. Although many empirical studies suggest a positive relationship between carbon performance and financial performance (e.g., Garvey et al., 2018; Griffin et al., 2017; Trinks et al., 2022), there are also inconclusive or contradicting results (e.g., Brouwers et al., 2018; Delmas et al., 2015; Gallego-Álvarez et al., 2015; Lewandowski, 2017). Therefore, a consensus has yet to be established due to the various inherent limitations present within the literature. Firstly, the strength and significance of empirical results appear to be mainly determined by the choice of metrics employed to measure carbon performance and/or financial performance (Busch & Lewandowski, 2018). Secondly, the findings may not be consistent without an international standard in emission reporting. A large disparity exists among the firms' reporting emissions in different scopes, especially in Scope 3, and this variation in measurement may skew the data with a small number of large emitters and a large number of small emitters (Garvey et al., 2018). Similarly, unreliable carbon emission data that are not verified by independent third parties may also not accurately reflect the relationship with financial performance (Kim et al., 2015). Thirdly, there may be issues of endogeneity, self-selection or sampling bias when using data collected from surveys or voluntary disclosures since firms with better carbon performance may be more likely to contribute to these surveys or voluntarily disclose emission information (Chen &

Gao, 2012; Saka & Oshika, 2014). Lastly, only a small number of studies in the literature utilize extensive worldwide data, while most of them rely on limited samples from particular countries or industries.

It is worth noting the lack of evidence which suggests ESG scores can accurately reflect a firm's carbon performance. Even though carbon emission performance is an intrinsic part of the ESG score within the environmental pillar, its weight, significance, or impact on stock returns may be diluted by a myriad of different ESG factors. In addition, most ESG score raters normalize the scores within each industry, potentially allowing firms from large emitting industries having relatively higher ESG scores. In this context, Boffo et al. (2020) present several important findings. Firstly, in the case of some ESG raters, firms with worse carbon performance receive high environmental pillar scores. Secondly, rather than carbon emission measures, environmental pillar scores are mainly driven by the long-term environmental policies adopted. Lastly, the portfolios with high environmental pillar scores can be exposed to industries with high emissions at the relatively same level or even higher. In another study with a small sample of the largest emitters, Elmalt et al. (2021) report that the correlation between ESG scores and carbon performance is not significant even when controlled for the country and firm-level variation. In addition, they find that improvements in carbon performance do not necessarily result in higher ESG scores for large emitters. These insights from the literature highlight significant challenges within the realm of ESG investing. Investors who are environmentally conscious or intend to hedge climate risks may be misled into thinking that ESG scores, despite their environmental component, can fully address their concerns about climate change and potentially invest in ways that are contrary to their environmentally driven motivations. From a policy-making perspective, further evidence is necessary to ensure that global implementation of ESG investing in its current state can serve as a useful tool in combating climate change.

9.3   Methods

9.3.1   Data

For this study, we obtained annual data from Refinitiv for all global publicly traded companies that had Refinitiv ESG scores, CO_2 equivalent emissions, and relevant market- and accounting-based firm-specific financial information available between 2002 and 2022. We use Refinitiv data as it offers one of the most comprehensive ESG databases dating back to 2002 (Refinitiv, 2022).

Within this research, the term "ESG scores" refers to the ESG combined score, the overall ESG score, the four ESG pillar scores (including the Controversy Score), and the ten ESG category scores (see Table 9.1). Each of these scores ranges from 0 to 100, where higher scores indicate better performance (for instance, a high controversy score indicates lower controversial issues). In addition, all ESG scores determine a

Table 9.1 Structure of Refinitiv's ESG scores

ESG combined (ESGC) score			
ESG score			ESG controversy (C) score
Environmental (E) pillar score	Social (S) pillar score	Governance (G) pillar score	
Resource use score	Workforce score	Management score	
Emissions score	Human rights score	Shareholders score	
Environmental innovation score	Community score	Corporate social responsibility score	
	Product responsibility score		

(*Source* Compiled by authors, based on Refinitiv, 2022)

relative industry-based performance within the peer group. Similar to other sustainability rating agencies, Refinitiv calculates ESG scores at any level by employing separate weight matrices for individual industry groups, based on the categorization provided by "The Refinitiv Business Classification (TRBC) Industry Group", which we also adopt in our study.

For deriving all CO_2 emission-related variables, we obtained the "CO_2 Equivalent Emissions Total" data from Refinitiv, which is described as the total CO_2 (carbon dioxide) and CO_2 equivalent[1] emissions in tonnes. Based on the Greenhouse Gas Protocol definitions, carbon emissions are classified into three categories: Scope 1 (direct) emissions are from sources that are directly owned or controlled by the firm; Scope 2 (indirect) emissions are from purchased electricity; and Scope 3 (other indirect) emissions are from all other indirect sources. This emission data we deploy represents the sum of Scope 1 and Scope 2 emissions. This measure can reflect the most important operational actions by the firm, including investments and innovations that impact GHG emissions (Misani & Pogutz, 2015). Scope 1 and 2 emissions are easier to measure, have stricter disclosure requirements, include more systematic reporting, provide more available and higher quality data, and are known to exhibit minimal variation across different data providers (Bolton & Kacperczyk, 2021; Lewandowski, 2017). Furthermore, consistent with the previous literature (Busch & Lewandowski, 2018), our study utilizes both absolute and relative indicators for carbon performance. As an absolute emissions metric, we use the aforementioned annual CO_2 equivalent emissions in tonnes. As relative emissions metrics, we use the "emissions to size" which is annual CO_2 equivalent emissions in tonnes divided by market capitalization in million US dollars, and "emissions to sales" which is annual CO_2 equivalent emissions in tonnes divided by annual revenues in million US dollars.

In the context of carbon emissions within Refinitiv's (2022) ESG methodology, "emission category score", a subset of the environmental pillar, is calculated by

---

[1] Methane (CH_4), nitrous oxide (N_2O), hydrofluorocarbons (HFCS), perfluorinated compound (PFSC), sulphur hexaflouride (SF_6) and nitrogen trifluoride (NF_3).

combining evaluations across four distinct themes: emissions, waste, biodiversity, and environmental management systems. Furthermore, the "emissions theme score", a subset of the "emission category score", is calculated by aggregating 47 different emissions-related indicators and data points. This includes the "CO_2 Equivalent Emissions Total" data, which we use for capturing emissions in our study. Notably, all sub-scores, indicators, and data points are weighted differently for each industry group. This complex and multidimensional nature of ESG score calculations also suggests a possibility that the correlation between the absolute CO_2 emissions and ESG scores could be insignificant.

All market- and accounting-based firm-specific financial data are in US dollars and represent the latest available information at the end of a given year from the stock markets or financial reports, which have been obtained from Refinitiv. In addition to firm-specific data, we utilize other key financial and macroeconomic indicators. The one-month US Treasury bill yield as a representative measure for the risk-free rate and annual returns of the MSCI World Equity Index to capture global market return are obtained. Additionally, for each country corresponding to a firm's country of risk,[2] the dataset is further complemented by macroeconomic data obtained from the World Bank: the annual gross domestic product (GDP) growth rate, consumer price index (CPI), and unemployment rate. Exhaustive lists for the descriptions of variables can be found in Tables 9.2 and 9.3.

As part of our data preparation procedure, we excluded the upper and lower 0.1% of data concerning the "$CO_2.Equivalent.Emissions.Total$" variable to negate the potentially scarce but significant data errors. Our final sample consists of 4,513 companies and 27,376 company-year observations.

9.3.2   Analysis Methods

The dependent variable in this study is the companies' abnormal return, which is defined as the difference between the actual and expected stock returns. Actual stock returns are calculated with the following formula:

$$Actual\ return_t^i = \left(\frac{P_t^i + D_t^i}{P_{t-1}^i} \right) - 1 \qquad (9.1)$$

---

[2] The company's primary country of risk based on the StarMine Countries of Risk Model. The StarMine Countries of Risk Model uses four sources of data, which are, in order of importance: revenue distribution by geography, the location of a company's headquarters, the country where its primary equity security listing trades, and financial reporting currency. The model provides estimates on the countries to which a company is exposed and estimates a fractional contribution to each. The fraction is a value between 0 and 1, where a higher value indicates the company has higher exposure to the country. The primary country of risk is the country with the largest contribution (from Refinitiv).

Table 9.2 Features used in the random forest model

	Defintion	Unit	Source of data
Cash.Flow	Change in cash flow	US dollars	Refinitiv
CPI	Consumer price index		World Bank
Current.Ratio	Current ratio		Refinitiv
EBITDA.Margin.Percent	EBITDA (earnings before interest, taxes, depreciation, and amortization) margin	Percent	Refinitiv
GDP.Growth	Annual GDP growth rate	Percent	World Bank
Gross.Profit.Margin	Gross profit margin	Percent	Refinitiv
Inventory.Turnover	Inventory turnover ratio		Refinitiv
MSCI.World.Equity.Index.Return	Annual return of MSCI world equity index	Percent	Refinitiv
Net.Income.Before.Taxes.Growth.Percent	Net income before taxes growth rate	Percent	Refinitiv
Net.Profit.Margin	Net profit margin	Percent	Refinitiv
Operating.Profit.Margin.Percent	Operating profit margin	Percent	Refinitiv
Quick.Ratio	Quick ratio		Refinitiv
RF	Risk-free rate	Percent	Refinitiv
ROA.Total.Assets.Percent	Return on assets (ROA)	Percent	Refinitiv
ROE.After.Tax	Return on equity (ROE) after tax	Percent	Refinitiv
Total.Assets.Reported	Total assets	US dollars	Refinitiv
Total.Current.Assets	Total current assets	US dollars	Refinitiv
Total.Current.Liabilities	Total current liabilities	US dollars	Refinitiv
Total.Equity	Total equity	US dollars	Refinitiv
Total.Liabilities	Total liabilities	US dollars	Refinitiv
Total.Revenue	Total revenue	US dollars	Refinitiv
TRBC.Industry.Group.Name	Thomson reuters business classification industry group name		Refinitiv

(continued)

Table 9.2 (continued)

	Defintion	Unit	Source of data
Unemployment.Rate	Unemployment RATE	Percent	World Bank
Working.Capital.Turnover.Ratio.Current	Working capital turnover ratio		Refinitiv

Table 9.3 Independent variables (CO_2 emissions metrics and ESG scores) used in panel regressions

	Definiton	Unit	Source of data
CO_2.Equivalent.Emissions.Total	Total CO_2(carbon dioxide) and CO_2 equivalent emissions	Tonnes	Refinitiv
CO_2.to.Market.Cap	Tonnes of CO_2 and CO_2 equivalent emissions per market capitalization in million dollars	Tonnes per million US dollars	Refinitiv
CO_2.to.Sales	Tonnes of CO_2 and CO_2 equivalent emissions per total annual revenue in million dollars	Tonnes per million US dollars	Refinitiv
ESG.Combined.Score	Refinitiv ESG combined score		Refinitiv
ESG.Score	Refinitiv ESG score		Refinitiv
Environmental.Pillar.Score	Refinitiv ESG environmental pillar score		Refinitiv
Social.Pillar.Score	Refinitiv ESG social pillar score		Refinitiv
Governance.Pillar.Score	Refinitiv ESG governance pillar score		Refinitiv
ESG.Controversies.Score	Refinitiv ESG controversies score		Refinitiv
Resource.Use.Score	Refinitiv ESG resource use score		Refinitiv
Emissions.Score	Refinitiv ESG emissions score		Refinitiv
Environmental.Innovation.Score	Refinitiv ESG environmental innovation score		Refinitiv
Workforce.Score	Refinitiv ESG workforce score		Refinitiv
Human.Rights.Score	Refinitiv ESG human rights score		Refinitiv
Community.Score	Refinitiv ESG community score		Refinitiv
Product.Responsibility.Score	Refinitiv ESG product responsibility score		Refinitiv
Management.Score	Refinitiv ESG management score		Refinitiv
Shareholders.Score	Refinitiv ESG shareholders score		Refinitiv
CSR.Strategy.Score	Refinitiv ESG corporate social responsibility (CSR) Strategy Score		Refinitiv

where $Return_t^i$ is the return of company i at year t, and P_t^i is the last available stock split adjusted closing price in a given year t, while P_{t-1}^i is the price from the previous year, and D_t^i is the dividend per share. The expected returns are estimated by applying a data mining technique in machine learning with the following model:

$$Expected \ return_t^i = f\left(x_t^i\right) \tag{9.2}$$

where the Expected return is the return predicted with a random forest (Breiman, 2001) prediction function $f(x_t^i)$, based on the input features represented by x_t^i. This is implemented in R with the randomForest package. For reducing and assessing the overfitting of the data, when applying random forest, the firms have been randomly divided into 80% as the training and 20% as the test data. The reduction of overfitting is important since the model can become otherwise overly complex and thus may capture too much noise. While the latter could result in effective predictions for the historical data used to create the model, the predictions can be less accurate for novel, unseen data (Dietterich, 1995). This could reduce the generalizability of the results (Delgado & Oyedele, 2021).

Furthermore, the features used in the random forest include mainly various financial metrics, which reflect companies' growth, profitability, efficiency, liquidity, and leverage, as well as national macroeconomic indicators. They have been identified in the machine learning literature as important attributes for predicting stock returns (Toochaei & Moeini, 2023; Zhang et al., 2014). In addition to these factors, we have considered other variables we deem important in predicting expected returns, such as annual return of the MSCI World Equity Index to represent the global market return, or the Thomson Reuters Business Classification Industry Group Name to normalize the industry-specific effects. See Table 9.2 for the full list of features.

Furthermore, for each company-year observation in the data, the predicted returns from the random forest model were subtracted from actual returns. This enabled to obtain residuals or abnormal returns, which represent the unexplained portion in stock returns and can be expressed as:

$$Abnormal.Return_t^i = Actual \ return_t^i - Expected \ return_t^i \tag{9.3}$$

where $Abnormal.Return_t^i$ is the abnormal stock return of company i at year t. There residuals from the random forest models serve as a robust means to account for a multitude of complex and non-linear relationships that may shape stock returns, while not imposing the constraint of model parsimony. However, it is important to note that this predictive modeling approach does not provide beta coefficients, which are typically used to analyze how specific independent variables affect the dependent variable. Thus, the abnormal returns are further applied in fixed effects panel regressions as the dependent variable. The latter is explained with independent variables in the following baseline models:

$$Abnormal.Return_t^i = \sum_{j=1}^{Jk} \left(\beta_{jk} ESG\,Level_{i,t}^{jk} \right) + \alpha_i + \delta_t + \varepsilon_{i,t} \qquad (9.4)$$

where *ESGLevel* denotes four sets of ESG scores on different levels *j*, on the company *i* at year *t*. These levels include $ESGLevel^1 = [ESGC.Score]$, which refers to the combined ESG score and $ESGLevel^2 = [ESG.Score]$, that is the main ESG score unadjusted to ESG controversies. Furthermore, the sub-components of these levels consist of $ESGLevel^3 = [Environmental.Pillar.Score, Social.Pillar.Score, Governance.Pillar.Score, ESG.Controversies.Score]$, which denotes the pillar scores and controversies. Finally, the category scores include $ESGLevel^4 = [Resource.Use.Score, Emissions.Score, Environmental.Innovation.Score, Workforce.Score, Human.Rights.Score, Community.Score, Product.Responsibility.Score, Management.Score, Shareholders.Score, CSR.Strategy.Score]$. The error term is denoted by ε. An alternative model specification includes the following:

$$Abnormal.Return_t^i = \beta_1 EMS_{i,t}' + \beta_2 ENV_{i,t}' + \alpha_i + \delta_t + \varepsilon_{i,t} \qquad (9.5)$$

where $EMS_{i,t} = [Log.CO_2, Log.CO_2.to.Market.Cap, Log.CO_2.to.Sales]$ denotes a vector of carbon emissions metrics which were log-transformed after adding +1. Furthermore, $ENV_{i,t} = [0, ESG.Score, Environmental.Score, Emissions.Score]$ refers to a vector with environment-related ESG score variables. The inclusion of 0 allows for separate regressions for each metric within EMS vector as individual independent variables. The ESG score and CO_2 data are included together in the model as it would allow to isolate each other's effects from their beta coefficients. Lastly, α_i and δ_t refer to firm and year fixed effects, respectively, which have been applied in R with the lfe software package. The use of fixed effects is particularly beneficial when dealing with factors affecting the dependent variable that either remain constant or exhibit gradual changes (Firebaugh et al., 2013). In a meta-analysis, Capon et al. (1990) reported that the factors influencing financial performance exhibit indeed a notable degree of stability over time. Furthermore, according to Coles and Li (2020), approximately 40% of the variance in corporate financial performance can be accounted for by firm-specific fixed effects. Thereby, models that forecast financial performance without considering these effects could be susceptible to omitted variable bias, as stated by Li (2016). Additionally, as argued by Kvande et al. (2019), the inclusion of fixed effects has the potential to substantially reduce the uncertainty associated with causal inferences. Due to the presence of serial correlation and heteroskedasticity, indicated by the Breusch-Godfrey/Wooldridge ($p < 0.01$) and the Breusch-Pagan ($p < 0.01$) tests, respectively, cluster-robust standard errors (SE) at the firm level have been applied in the panel regression, as suggested by Audretsch et al. (2019). We conclude this section by presenting the description of independent variables (Table 9.3), and the descriptive statistics of the independent variables (Table 9.4).

Table 9.4 Descriptive statistics of independent variables (CO_2 emissions metrics and ESG scores)

	Min	Max	Mean	Median	SD
CO_2.Equivalent.Emissions.Total	20.640	230,740,000,000.000	4,717,622.028	307,870.000	16,401,422.510
CO_2.to.Market.Cap	0.001	35,943,359,433.740	720.326	53.752	4,820.513
CO_2.to.Sales	0.001	47,330,373,303.654	559.471	58.690	3,714.032
ESG.Combined.Score	2.325	95.100	55.462	55.954	15.958
ESG.Score	2.325	95.861	58.205	59.145	16.723
Environmental.Pillar.Score	0.000	99.144	56.925	58.850	21.757
Social.Pillar.Score	0.258	98.470	58.780	60.341	20.984
Governance.Pillar.Score	0.408	99.441	58.323	60.351	20.725
ESG.Controversies.Score	0.446	100.000	88.172	100.000	25.265
Resource.Use.Score	0.000	99.915	62.732	66.843	26.025
Emissions.Score	0.000	99.915	64.839	68.269	24.091
Environmental.Innovation.Score	0.000	99.895	35.370	32.534	32.492
Workforce.Score	0.254	99.922	69.569	73.779	22.448
Human.Rights.Score	0.000	99.528	46.111	48.333	33.387
Community.Score	0.000	99.922	61.558	67.081	27.947
Product.Responsibility.Score	0.000	99.917	57.654	63.793	30.109
Management.Score	0.154	99.983	59.206	62.046	26.688
Shareholders.Score	0.051	99.988	55.185	57.151	27.855
CSR.Strategy.Score	0.000	99.977	58.626	62.716	27.772

9.4   Results and Discussion

The random forest model managed to explain 28.19% of the variation in the returns. Figure 9.1 shows that the global market return (*MSCI.World.Equity.Index.Return*) seems to be the most important attribute for predicting returns. Furthermore, based on the training data, this model had a Mean Squared Error (MSE) of 0.154, Root Mean Squared Error (RMSE) of 0.393, and Mean Absolute Error (MAE) of 0.245. The same model produced also relatively small values with testing data (MSE = 0.141, RMSE = 0.375, MAE = 0.238). Such similar values between the training and test data suggest that the obtained model does not seem to suffer from overfitting.

Table 9.5 presents the findings from the panel regressions where the abnormal returns, derived by using residuals of the random forest model, serve as the dependent variable, and ESG scores at each level are applied as independent variables. The beta coefficients seem to indicate that all ESG scores, except the ESG Controversies Score, show a negative impact on abnormal returns; however, these are at varying levels of statistical significance. More specifically, with high statistical significance (p < 0.01), a one-point increase in the ESG Score corresponds on average to a 0.2% decrease in abnormal returns. On the other hand, with the same statistical significance level, a one-point increase in the ESG Controversies Score corresponds to a 0.04% increase in abnormal returns. As expected with these divergent effects, the ESG Combined Score shows a smaller economic and statistical significance, given that it is the combination of the ESG Score and ESG Controversies Score. Furthermore, the Environmental Pillar Score reveals a statistically significant effect (p < 0.05), where a one-point increase indicates a 0.1% decrease in abnormal returns. The Social Pillar Score has the same effect size but at a weaker statistical significance level (p < 0.1). Meanwhile, the Governance Pillar Score shows neither an economic nor a

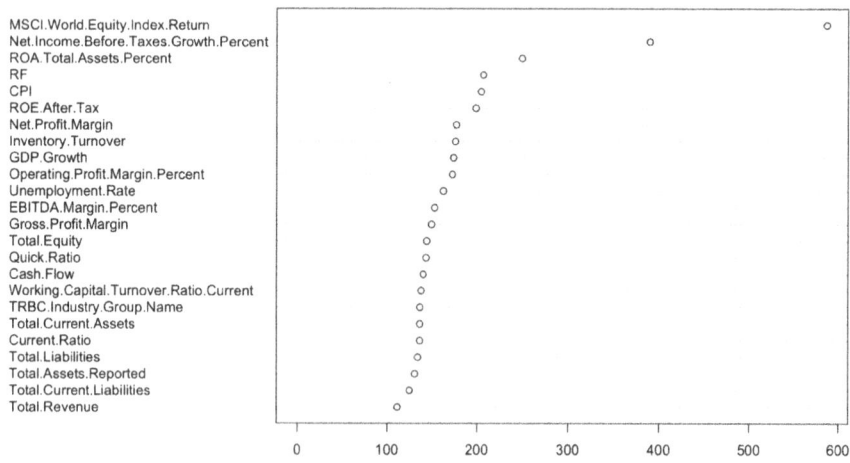

Fig. 9.1 Importance/contribution of random forest features in predicting stock returns

statistically significant effect. Among the ten ESG category scores, only three exhibit a statistically significant ($p < 0.05$) effect, which are all negative but with a relatively smaller economic impact. Specifically, a one-point increase in the Resource Use Score (from the Environmental pillar), Community Score (from the Social pillar), and Shareholders Score (from the Governance pillar) are associated with a marginal reduction in abnormal returns of 0.05%, 0.1%, and 0.03%, respectively.

Although their economic significance may be still open for debate, the observed negative relationships between ESG scores and abnormal returns can be interpreted in several ways. Should investors perceive ESG scores as reliable indicators of underlying risk factors, then they might be willing to accept lower returns as a trade-off for reduced risk (Cornell, 2021). Although less likely, investors' preference for stocks with higher ESG scores may be driven by ethical considerations, leading them to be more tolerant of lower returns. However, our study excludes the potential explanation that underperformance is due to the costs involved in implementing ESG strategies, based on the fact that these costs would already be reflected in the accounting-based information (Delmas et al., 2015), and therefore on the predicted returns. In this regard, our findings do not necessarily contradict previous literature which suggests a positive relationship between corporate social and financial performance (e.g., Busch & Friede, 2018; Friede et al., 2015; Orlitzky et al., 2003; Pesor, 2022; Wang et al., 2015).

Table 9.6 displays the results from panel regressions, where the dependent variable is abnormal returns, involving three distinct CO_2 emissions metrics each used both independently and in combination with three specific ESG scores (from different levels) which incorporate CO_2 emissions in their calculations. Namely, these three CO_2 emissions metrics analyzed are the logarithmic value of absolute CO_2 emissions ($Log.CO_2$), the logarithmic value of CO_2 emissions relative to market capitalization ($Log.CO_2.to.Market.Cap$), and the logarithmic value of CO_2 emissions relative to sales ($Log.CO_2.to.Sales$), while the specific ESG scores considered are the ESG Score, Environmental Pillar Score, and Emission Score. The findings reveal a relationship where higher absolute CO_2 emissions are associated with lower abnormal returns. Even after controlling for the ESG Score, the Environmental Pillar, and the Emissions Score, the direction of this relationship remains unchanged and CO_2 emissions seem to have largely the same effect sizes across different regressions. The statistically significant beta coefficients ($p < 0.01$) indicate that a 1% increase in CO_2 emissions corresponds to a 0.027% lower abnormal returns. Moreover, the emissions-to-size metric seems to have a stronger effect on abnormal returns compared to absolute emissions, as 1% higher CO_2 emissions scaled by size, measured by market capitalization, is associated with 0.125% lower abnormal returns. However, significant findings are not observed in the case of emissions to sales metric. Furthermore, the conclusions about the effect of the three selected ESG scores remain the same in terms of their direction, as reported earlier.

These findings suggest broader implications regarding the role of CO_2 emissions information in financial markets. Firstly, the CO_2 emissions data may be indicative of future risks not yet reflected in accounting performance. The negative relationship between emissions and abnormal returns aligns with the hypothesis that investors

Table 9.5 Panel regression results: ESG Scores

Dependent Variable: Abnormal.Return

	(1)	(2)	(3)	(4)
ESG.Combined.Score	−0.001* (0.0003)			
ESG.Score		−0.002*** (0.0004)		
Environmental.Pillar.Score			−0.001** (0.0003)	
Social.Pillar.Score			−0.001* (0.0003)	
Governance.Pillar.Score			−0.0003 (0.0002)	
ESG.Controversies.Score			0.0004*** (0.0001)	
Resource.Use.Score				−0.0005** (0.0002)
Emissions.Score				−0.0001 (0.0002)
Environmental.Innovation.Score				−0.00002 (0.0001)
Workforce.Score				−0.0002 (0.0002)
Human.Rights.Score				−0.0001 (0.0002)
Community.Score				−0.001** (0.0002)
Product.Responsibility.Score				−0.00002 (0.0002)
Management.Score				−0.0003 (0.0002)
Shareholders.Score				−0.0003** (0.0002)
CSR.Strategy.Score				−0.0001 (0.0002)
FIRM FE	Yes	Yes	Yes	Yes
YEAR FE	Yes	Yes	Yes	Yes
Observations	22,033	22,033	22,033	22,033
R2	0.183	0.183	0.184	0.184
Residual Std. error	0.389	0.389	0.389	0.389

Note * $p < 0.1$; ** $p < 0.05$; *** $p < 0.01$

Table 9.6 Panel regression results: CO_2 emissions metrics and CO_2 emissions-related ESG scores

Dependent Variable: Abnormal.Return

	(1)	(2)	(3)	(4)	(5)	(6)	(7)	(8)	(9)	(10)	(11)	(12)
Log.CO₂	−0.027*** (0.006)	−0.025*** (0.006)	−0.026*** (0.006)	−0.026*** (0.006)								
Log.CO₂.to.Market.Cap					−0.125*** (0.007)	−0.124*** (0.007)	−0.124*** (0.007)	−0.125*** (0.007)				
Log.CO₂.to.Sales									−0.004 (0.006)	−0.003 (0.006)	−0.004 (0.006)	−0.005 (0.006)
ESG.Score		−0.001*** (0.0003)				−0.001*** (0.0004)				−0.002*** (0.0004)		
Environmental.Pillar.Score			−0.001*** (0.0002)				−0.001*** (0.0003)				−0.001*** (0.0003)	
Emissions.Score				−0.001*** (0.0002)				−0.001*** (0.0002)				−0.001*** (0.0002)
FIRM FE	Yes	Yes	Yes	Yes	Yes	Yes	Yes	Yes	Yes	Yes	Yes	Yes
YEAR FE	Yes	Yes	Yes	Yes	Yes	Yes	Yes	Yes	Yes	Yes	Yes	Yes
Observations	22.033	22.033	22.033	22.033	22.033	22.033	22.033	22.033	22.033	22.033	22.033	22.033
R2	0.184	0.184	0.184	0.184	0.212	0.212	0.212	0.212	0.183	0.183	0.183	0.183
Residual Std. Error	0.389	0.389	0.389	0.389	0.382	0.382	0.382	0.382	0.389	0.389	0.389	0.389

Note * $p < 0.1$; ** $p < 0.05$; *** $p < 0.01$

tend to apply a discount to companies exhibiting poor carbon performance, possibly factoring in the higher potential costs and risks associated with climate change. Secondly, the disparity observed in different CO_2 emissions metrics in terms of their relationship with abnormal returns can potentially be attributed to the appropriateness of the specific metric used to discount these risks (Busch & Lewandowski, 2018). Our findings reveal a case for the emissions-to-size metric's potential to be used as a factor to achieve higher abnormal returns while accounting for the climate change-related risks. By normalizing emissions adjusted for the company's size, this metric facilitates a less biassed measure of companies' carbon performance and related risks, allowing for comparative evaluation among their peers. From investors' point of view, it can be an insightful and practical indicator that can directly measure the carbon footprint of their investments or portfolios, essentially functioning as "CO_2 emissions per dollar invested". However, due to its underlying market capitalization variable, the findings are subject to endogeneity and multicollinearity issues, therefore more robust empirical evidences are needed. Meanwhile, a relatively smaller impact size of annual absolute CO_2 emissions on abnormal returns is in line with prior literature (Busch & Lewandowski, 2018). Given its strong correlation with firm size, it can be challenging for investors to assess a firm's carbon performance or related risks by using only the absolute emissions information (Kim et al., 2015). On the other hand, the absence of a substantial effect from emissions to sales metric is consistent with existing research as well, particularly with the robust findings of Bolton and Kacperczyk (2021) indicating this variable may not accurately distinguish the firms that are more exposed to carbon emission risk. A plausible reason for this is the large variations in the underlying revenue variable (Lewandowski, 2017). In addition, the empirical findings from this metric might suffer from endogeneity and multicollinearity issues, however not as much as the emissions-to-size metric.

In summary, our results indicate that all ESG scores, except for the Controversies Score, exhibit a non-positive effect on the abnormal returns. Also, all three carbon emissions metrics we tested demonstrate a non-positive effect. These findings lead to the following conclusions which address our previously stated research questions. Firstly, higher ESG scores do not necessarily lead to higher abnormal returns, in fact, they are more inclined to yield a contrary outcome. The underperformance of stocks with higher ESG scores is likely a result of the investors' trade-off for their lower risks. Secondly, better carbon performance may lead to higher abnormal returns, however, this is contingent on the CO_2 emissions metric chosen. In addition, more robust empirical evidences are necessary. Thirdly, although the effect sizes of ESG scores and CO_2 emissions metrics are not directly comparable due to scale differences, it can be inferred from the contrasting patterns observed in our analysis that CO_2 emissions metrics, compared to ESG scores, could be more effective factors for achieving higher abnormal returns.

It is crucial to address the following potential limitations that provide context for the interpretation of the results presented. Firstly, there can be uncertainty concerning the direction of the relationship between abnormal returns and ESG scores, as well as between abnormal returns and emissions-related data. This issue is more pronounced in the case of the emissions-to-size metric, as the underlying component (market capitalization) can independently be influenced by the changes in abnormal returns. This refers to the endogeneity arising from reverse causality or simultaneity. It can occur when the dependent variable partially influences the independent variable, causing the latter to become related to the error term, as explained by Wooldridge (2002). Furthermore, already financially successful companies might be simply able to afford to sacrifice their resources to implement strategies to improve their ESG or carbon performance. This uncertainty refers to the concept of "slack resources" and the challenge of determining the exact direction of the relationship. Moreover, endogeneity can also arise due to measurement errors and omitted variable bias (Wooldridge, 2002). While the former is often beyond our control and related to data quality, the latter has been mitigated through various techniques. These approaches include the use of non-parametric methods such as random forests to disentangle market-related effects from stock performance, as well as the application of parametric fixed effects panel regression. Nevertheless, it is essential to acknowledge that our study may provide merely an indication of causality and the actual causal relationships could remain a subject of debate.

Additionally, it's worth noting that some effects of certain factors might change and affect findings over time. The relationship between ESG or carbon performance and financial performance may evolve or even disappear as suggested by the efficient market hypothesis, especially when broader market awareness increases. Furthermore, it is important to acknowledge that the generalizability of our findings may be limited to our sample of publicly traded stocks which have ESG and CO_2 emissions data available in the Refinitiv database. This potential selection bias is important to note when applying our results to a broader context. Lastly, variations in methodologies adopted by ESG data providers and potential disagreements in ESG data (as discussed by Berg et al., 2022) introduce another layer of complexity to our study's findings as well. In conclusion, while our study provides valuable insights, it is crucial to remain aware of these limitations and their implications when interpreting the results.

9.5 Conclusion

The main objective of this study is to investigate ESG scores and carbon emissions for their relationship with abnormal stock returns. More specifically, we aim to answer if higher ESG scores or better carbon emissions performance can contribute to greater abnormal returns, and whether CO_2 emissions metrics can be more influential than ESG scores in achieving greater abnormal returns. In addition, we evaluated if abnormal returns can be influenced by granular level ESG scores, including pillar and category scores, and carbon emissions metrics. We utilized a comprehensive annual dataset, spanning from 2002 to 2022 and comprising 4,513 publicly listed companies, which encompasses a variety of metrics, including granular ESG scores down to the category level scores, and CO_2 emissions. Our methodology involves a two-step approach, combining random forest and fixed effects regressions. In the first step, a random forest model is applied to predict stock returns and the residuals are obtained as abnormal returns. This approach allows us to observe the abnormal returns that are isolated from the effects of various factors such as information already reflected on financial reports, industry or country-specific effects, risk-free returns, or global market returns. In the second step, the abnormal returns are used as dependent variables in fixed effect panel regressions which incorporate various ESG scores and CO_2 emission metrics as independent variables.

Our findings can be summarized as follows. Firstly, all ESG scores, except the Controversies Score, have a non-positive relationship with the abnormal returns. A one-point increase in the main ESG score indicates a 0.2% decrease in abnormal returns. This might imply that ESG scores represent underlying risk factors, therefore investors accept lower returns as a trade-off for lower risks, or perceived as such, from companies with higher ESG scores. Also, it should be noted that only a few ESG scores at pillar or category levels have an effect on abnormal returns with statistical and economical significance. Secondly, for all of the three CO_2 emissions metrics used in this analysis, we observe a non-positive relationship with abnormal returns, whereas a 1% increase in absolute CO_2 emissions corresponds to a 0.027% lower abnormal returns. This might suggest that investors discount high emitting companies for their future climate change-related risks. Thirdly, the effect on the abnormal returns varies depending on the CO_2 emissions metric chosen. While the emissions-to-size metric seems to have the largest effect size, emission-to-sales metric shows no significant effect. Lastly, while higher ESG scores might indicate lower risks, they also suggest lower abnormal returns; however, superior carbon performance might imply higher abnormal returns and lower risks of future climate change-related costs. Therefore, even it is not straightforward to compare the effect sizes in different scales, the results hint at the possibility that carbon emissions might be a more appropriate factor to achieve higher abnormal returns than ESG scores.

The findings would offer valuable insights not only for sustainable or environmentally conscious investors or stock markets participants in general but also for managers seeking to understand which ESG or CO_2 emissions-related factors can contribute to shareholder value more. As a suggestion for future research, firstly, different machine learning models can be implemented to potentially improve predictive efficiency. For instance, random forest could be combined with boosting to predict expected market returns more precisely. Secondly, changes in the relationship between ESG score or carbon performance indicators and stock performance over time, together with the impact of events such as environmental regulations might be another interesting research avenue. Lastly, a country-specific study could be especially important as it would allow for a deeper understanding of how local and regional factors can influence the relationships between variables and their effects on financial performance.

References

Amel-Zadeh, A., & Serafeim, G. (2018). Why and how investors use ESG information: Evidence from a global survey. *Financial Analysts Journal, 74*(3), 87–103.

Audretsch, D. B., Hülsbeck, M., & Lehmann, E. E. (2019). Public cluster policy and firm performance: Evaluating spill over effects across industries. *Entrepreneurship and Regional Development, 31*(1–2), 150–165. https://doi.org/10.1080/08985626.2018.1537153

Barth, F., Hübel, B., & Scholz, H. (2022). ESG and corporate credit spreads. *The Journal of Risk Finance, 23*(2), 169–190.

Berg, F., Koelbel, J. F., & Rigobon, R. (2022). Aggregate confusion: The divergence of ESG ratings. *Review of Finance, 26*(6), 1315–1344.

Boffo, R., Marshall, C., & Patalano, R. (2020). *ESG investing: Environmental pillar scoring and reporting.* OECD Paris. https://www.oecd.org/finance/esg-investing-environmental-pillar-scoring-and-reporting.pdf

Bolton, P., & Kacperczyk, M. (2021). Do investors care about carbon risk? *Journal of Financial Economics, 142*(2), 517–549.

Breedt, A., Ciliberti, S., Gualdi, S., & Seager, P. (2019). Is ESG an equity factor or just an investment guide? *The Journal of Investing, 28*, 32–42.

Breiman, L. (2001). Random forests. *Machine Learning, 45*, 5–32.

Brouwers, R., Schoubben, F., & Van Hulle, C. (2018). The influence of carbon cost pass-through on the link between carbon emissions and corporate financial performance in the context of the European union emissions trading scheme. *Business Strategy and the Environment, 27*, 1422–1436.

Busch, T., & Friede, G. (2018). The robustness of the corporate social and financial performance relation: A second-order meta-analysis. *Corporate Social Responsibility and Environmental Management, 25*(4), 583–608. https://doi.org/10.1002/csr.1480

Busch, T., & Lewandowski, S. (2018). Corporate carbon and financial performance: A meta-analysis. *Journal of Industrial Ecology, 22*(4), 745–759.

Capon, N., Farley, J. U., & Hoenig, S. (1990). Determinants of financial performance: A meta-analysis. *Management Science, 36*(10), 1143–1159. https://doi.org/10.1287/mnsc.36.10.1143

Chen, L. H., & Gao, L. S. (2012). The pricing of climate risk. *Journal of Financial and Economic Practice, 12*(2), 115–131.

Coles, J. L., & Li, Z. (2020). Managerial attributes, incentives, and performance. *The Review of Corporate Finance Studies, 9*(2), 256–301.

Cornell, B. (2021). ESG preferences, risk and return. *European Financial Management, 27*(1), 12–19.

Delgado, J. M. D., & Oyedele, L. (2021). Deep learning with small datasets: Using autoencoders to address limited datasets in construction management. *Applied Soft Computing, 112*, 1–17. https://doi.org/10.1016/j.asoc.2021.107836

Delmas, M. A., Nairn-Birch, N., & Lim, J. (2015). Dynamics of environmental and financial performance: The case of greenhouse gas emissions. *Organization & Environment, 28*(4), 374–393.

Dietterich, T. G. (1995). Overfitting and undercomputing in machine learning. *ACM Computing Surveys, 27*(3), 326–327. https://doi.org/10.1145/212094.212114

Eccles, R. G., Serafeim, G., & Krzus, M. P. (2011). Market interest in nonfinancial information. *Journal of Applied Corporate Finance, 23*(4), 113–127.

Eleftheriadis, I. M., & Anagnostopoulou, E. G. (2014). Relationship between corporate climate change disclosures and firm factors. *Business Strategy and the Environment, 24*(8), 780–789.

Elmalt, D., Kirti, M. D., & Igan, D. (2021). *Limits to private climate change mitigation* (No. 16061). International Monetary Fund.

Firebaugh, G., Warner, C., & Massoglia, M. (2013). Fixed effects, random effects, and hybrid models for causal analysis. In S. L. Morgan (Ed.), *Handbook of causal analysis for social research* (pp. 113–132). Springer.

Freeman, R. E. (2010). *Strategic management: A stakeholder approach.* Cambridge University Press.

Friede, G., Busch, T., & Bassen, A. (2015). ESG and financial performance: Aggregated evidence from more than 2000 empirical studies. *Journal of Sustainable Finance & Investment, 5*(4), 210–233.

Gallego-Álvarez, I., Segura, L., & Martínez-Ferrero, J. (2015). Carbon emission reduction: The impact on the financial and operational performance of international companies. *Journal of Cleaner Production, 103,* 149–159.

Garvey, G. T., Iyer, M., & Nash, J. (2018). Carbon footprint and productivity: Does the "E" in ESG capture efficiency as well as the environment? *Journal of Investment Management, 16*(1), 59–69.

Gibson Brandon, R., Krueger, P., & Schmidt, P. S. (2021). ESG rating disagreement and stock returns. *Financial Analysts Journal, 77*(4), 104–127.

Giglio, S., Maggiori, M., Stroebel, J., Tan, Z., Utkus, S. P., & Xu, X. (2023). *Four facts about ESG beliefs and investor portfolios.* NBER Working Paper No. 31114.

Griffin, P. A., Lont, D. H., & Sun, E. Y. (2017). The relevance to investors of greenhouse gas emission disclosures. *Contemporary Accounting Research, 34*(2), 1265–1297.

Hoffmann, V. H., & Busch, T. (2008). Corporate carbon performance indicators. *Journal of Industrial Ecology, 12,* 505–520.

Hübel, B., & Scholz, H. (2020). Integrating sustainability risks in asset management: The role of ESG exposures and ESG ratings. *Journal of Asset Management, 21,* 52–69.

Ioannou, I., & Serafeim, G. (2019). *Corporate sustainability: A strategy?* Harvard Business School Accounting & Management Unit Working Paper No. 19-065.

Janney, J. J., & Folta, T. B. (2006). Moderating effects of investor experience on the signaling value of private equity placements. *Journal of Business Venturing, 21*(1), 27–44.

Jones, T. M. (1995). Instrumental stakeholder theory: A synthesis of ethics and economics. *Academy of Management Review, 20*(2), 404–437.

Jun, M. (2021). A comparison of a gradient boosting decision tree, random forests, and artificial neural networks to model urban land use changes: The case of the Seoul metropolitan area. *International Journal of Geographical Information Science, 35*(11), 2149–2167.

IPCC. (2007). *Climate change 2007: Synthesis report.* Intergovernmental Panel on Climate Change (IPCC).

IPCC. (2014). *Climate change 2014: Synthesis report.* Intergovernmental Panel on Climate Change (IPCC).

Karwowski, M., & Raulinajtys-Grzybek, M. (2021). The application of corporate social responsibility (CSR) actions for mitigation of environmental, social, corporate governance (ESG) and reputational risk in integrated reports. *Corporate Social Responsibility and Environmental Management, 28*(4), 1270–1284.

Kim, Y. B., An, H. T., & Kim, J. D. (2015). The effect of carbon risk on the cost of equity capital. *Journal of Cleaner Production, 93,* 279–287.

Kleimeier, S., & Viehs, M. (2018). *Carbon disclosure, emission levels, and the cost of debt.* https://ssrn.com/abstract=2719665

Kumar, R. (2019). ESG: Alpha or Duty? *The Journal of Index Investing, 9*(4), 58-66.

Kvande, M. N., Bjørklund, O., Lydersen, S., Belsky, J., & Wichstrøm, L. (2019). Effects of special education on academic achievement and task motivation: A propensity-score and fixed-effects approach. *European Journal of Special Needs Education, 34*(4), 409–423.

Lewandowski, S. (2017). Corporate carbon and financial performance: The role of emission reductions. *Business Strategy and the Environment, 26*(8), 1196–1211.

Li, F. (2016). Endogeneity in CEO power: A survey and experiment. *Investment Analysts Journal, 45*(3), 149–162.

Misani, N., & Pogutz, S. (2015). Unraveling the effects of environmental outcomes and processes on financial performance: A non-linear approach. *Ecological Economics, 109,* 150–160.

Naffa, H., & Fain, M. (2022). A factor approach to the performance of ESG leaders and laggards. *Finance Research Letters, 44*, 102073.

Orlitzky, M., Schmidt, F. L., & Rynes, S. L. (2003). Corporate social and financial performance: A meta-analysis. *Organization Studies, 24*(3), 403–441. https://doi.org/10.1177/017084060302 4003910

Pástor, L., Stambaugh, R. F., & Taylor, L. A. (2021). Sustainable investing in equilibrium. *Journal of Financial Economics, 142*, 550–571.

Pesor, R. (2022). *A contingent relationship between corporate social and financial performance: The role of information demand and the signaling environment* [Doctoral thesis, Estonian Business School]. EBS Doctoral Theses. https://ebs.ee/sites/default/files/Doctoral%20Thesis/Pesor%20web.pdf

PwC. (2022). *Asset and wealth management revolution 2022.* https://www.pwc.com/gx/en/financ ial-services/assets/pdf/pwc-awm-revolution-2022.pdf

Refinitiv. (2022). *Environmental, social and governance scores from Refinitiv.* https://www.ref initiv.com/content/dam/marketing/en_us/documents/methodology/refinitiv-esg-scores-method ology.pdf

Saka, C., & Oshika, T. (2014). Disclosure effects, carbon emissions and corporate value. *Sustainability Accounting, Management and Policy Journal, 5*(1), 22–45.

Schaltegger, S., & Synnestvedt, T. (2002). The link between 'green' and economic success: Environmental management as the crucial trigger between environmental and economic performance. *Journal of Environmental Management, 65*(4), 339–346.

Schuler, D. A., & Cording, M. (2006). A corporate social performance-corporate financial performance behavioral model for consumers. *The Academy of Management Review, 31*(3), 540–558.

Shen, J. (2006). *Acquisitions of public versus private firms: Causes and consequences.* INSEAD.

Srivastava, J. (2001). The role of inferences in sequential bargaining with one-sided incomplete information: Some experimental evidence. *Organizational Behavior and Human Decision Processes, 85*(1), 166–187.

Stroebel, J., & Wurgler, J. (2021). What do you think about climate finance? *Journal of Financial Economics, 142*, 487–498.

The Economist. (2022). ESG should be boiled down to one simple measure: Emissions. *The Economist.* https://www.economist.com/leaders/2022/07/21/esg-should-be-boiled-down-to-one-simple-measure-emissions

Toochaei, M. R., & Moeini, F. (2023). Evaluating the performance of ensemble classifiers in stock returns prediction using effective features. *Expert Systems with Applications, 213.*

Trinks, A., Mulder, M., & Scholtens, B. (2020). An efficiency perspective on carbon emissions and financial performance. *Ecological Economics, 175*, 106632.

Trinks, A., Ibikunle, G., Mulder, M. & Scholtens, B. (2022). Carbon intensity and the cost of equity capital. *The Energy Journal, 43*(2).

Wang, Q., Dou, J., & Jia, S. (2015). A meta-analytic review of corporate social responsibility and corporate financial performance: The moderating effect of contextual factors. *Business and Society, 55*(8), 1083–1121. https://doi.org/10.1177/0007650315584317

Whelan, T., Atz, U., Van Holt, T., & Clark, C. (2021). *ESG and financial performance: Uncovering the relationship by aggregating evidence from 1,000 plus studies published between 2015–2020.* NYU STERN Center for sustainable business.

Wooldridge, J. M. (2002). *Econometric analysis of cross section and panel data.* MIT Press.

Zhang, X., Hu, Y., Xie, K., Wang, S., Ngai, E. W. T., & Liu, M. (2014). A causal feature selection algorithm for stock prediction modeling. *Neurocomputing, 142*, 48–59.

Emre Güven is a PhD candidate in Management at Estonian Business School (EBS). He holds degrees of MSc in International Financial Markets (University of Southampton, UK) and BSc in Management (Binghamton University, USA). His current research focuses on ESG, low-carbon economy and sustainable business. His other research interests include financial markets, green finance, and behavioural finance

Renee Pesor is a researcher and a lecturer at Estonian Business School (EBS). He studies sustainability-related topics and teaches subjects concerning economics as well as quantitative research methods. Renee has a PhD in management sciences and is an index evaluator of companies at the Responsible Business Forum Estonia

Chapter 10
Estonian Top-Level Executives' Attitudes Towards Sustainability and Corporate Social Responsibility

Mari Kooskora and **Annika Arras**

Abstract The aim of this study was to identify the attitudes of top-level executives in Estonia towards sustainability. It also explored their perspectives on corporate social responsibility and their adherence to the fundamental principles of sustainable development. Placed within a global context, this study emphasized sustainable development. The analysis in this study drew from academic literature and empirical research conducted by the authors. A web-based survey was administered to top-level executives from some of Estonia's most influential companies. The data reveals that the attitudes of Estonia's most influential top executives closely align with the sustainable development framework, with a primary focus on economic, social, and environmental concerns. However, it was observed that the social and economic dimensions are better balanced than the environmental dimension, which appears to create differences of opinion among top executives. The study did not confirm the perceived equilibrium between the three pillars of sustainable development in Estonia's most influential companies, as per the top executives' perspectives. Nevertheless, there is potential for achieving greater balance between the three pillars of sustainable development, as top executives express a significant commitment to sustainability issues in their companies' future business success, even at the expense of short-term profit margins.

Keywords Sustainable development · Sustainable business model · Estonian top-level executives · Attitudes on corporate social responsibility · Triple bottom line

M. Kooskora (✉)
Estonian Business School, Tallinn, Estonia
e-mail: mari.kooskora@ebs.ee

A. Arras
Miltton New Nordics, Tallinn, Estonia

© The Author(s), under exclusive license to Springer Nature Singapore Pte Ltd. 2024   209
M. Kooskora and A. Kekkonen (eds.), *Performance Challenges in Organizational Sustainability*, Responsible Leadership and Sustainable Management,
https://doi.org/10.1007/978-981-97-5548-6_10

10.1   Introduction

Sustainability is a concept with diverse interpretations both as a term and a field (Kuhlman & Farrington, 2010; Purvis et al., 2019; Sakalasooriya, 2021). It is often associated primarily with environmental and nature conservation issues, categorizing these concerns under the so-called 'green' domain (Zu, 2019). Consequently, sustainability issues often do not reach the top management of companies, unless they are directly involved in businesses impacting the environment (Latapí Agudelo et al., 2019). Sustainability represents an ongoing societal development grounded in balancing current and future needs (Cutter, 2013; Dahlsrud, 2008; WBCSD, 2000). To ensure sustainable development, equilibrium must be established between the social, economic, and environmental domains, requiring consideration across all facets of life (Esop & Kooskora, 2023).

Milton Friedman, a prominent advocate for free-market economies and a respected economist, formulated in the 1970s that the sole social responsibility of businesses is profit maximization, as long as they adhere to agreed-upon rules of the game, specifically respecting free and fair competition without deceit and fraud. Fifty years later, we have reached a global juncture where we must question the relevance of these rules articulated by Friedman in today's context.

In 2015, the United Nations established global Sustainable Development Goals (SDGs) to secure sustainable development by 2030 (UN, 2015). These goals require the commitment of all member states, including Estonia. Businesses are the engines of economic growth in all countries and, simultaneously, the most significant influencers of sustainable development (Accenture, 2020). Today companies originally created with the purpose of profit generation (Friedman, 1970) are focusing on social responsibility, which entails recognizing the impact of their actions on the surrounding environment (Latapí Agudelo et al., 2019). Moreover, the integration of corporate social responsibility (CSR) principles into business operations can be considered as a means by which companies can contribute to sustainable development (Rudnicka, 2016).

The primary objective of the current study is to identify the attitudes of top-ranking executives in Estonia concerning sustainability, with a particular emphasis on their perspectives regarding corporate social responsibility and their adherence to the fundamental tenets of sustainable development. This research is contextualized within the broader scope of global sustainable development. A web-based survey was employed to collect data from senior executives occupying leadership positions in Estonia's most influential companies and to find answers to the following research questions:

1. What are the perceptions and attitudes held by senior-level executives concerning sustainability and corporate social responsibility?
2. To what degree do the perceptions of senior-level executives harmonize with the imperative of achieving equilibrium among the three core dimensions of sustainable development?

However, in academic literature, the definition and interpretation of a sustainable business model vary widely, highlighting the absence of a prevailing approach. Therefore, this study views sustainability primarily as a mindset. It posits that incorporating sustainability themes into a company's strategic framework and processes can transform the business model's context, rather than necessarily altering the fundamental business model itself.

10.2 Defining Sustainable Development

The concept of sustainable development has gained international significance over the past decade, with its roots traceable to the 1987 Brundtland report "Our Common Future" (Jarvie, 2016). This landmark report by the World Commission on Environment and Development marked the first conceptual connection between the environment and development. It emphasized the integration of the three pillars of sustainable development: economic, social, and environmental dimensions (commonly known as the Triple Bottom Line, TBL, Elkington, 1994, 2004). Nevertheless, its implementation was subject to diverse interpretations at the national levels (Khan et al., 2021).

The three pillars (TBL) concept continues to serve as a fundamental framework for understanding sustainable development and is instrumental in defining a sustainable business model (Govidan et al., 2021). Such a model integrates the three pillars, incorporates the interests of diverse stakeholders, including environmental and societal concerns. This integration of sustainability into a company's mission and processes is pivotal in driving competitive advantage through innovation (Bocken et al., 2014). Thus, the cornerstone of sustainable development, corporate social responsibility, and a sustainable business model is the simultaneous consideration of environmental, social, and economic aspects and with this knowledge, it is possible to establish a logical sequence of dependencies that provides a clear explanation of how companies contribute to sustainable development. However, for example Daly (1996) who challenges the conventional notion that growth is always good, believes that there is no balance between these pillars and the environment should be priority.

It is noteworthy that the key factors contributing to an organization's success or failure often emanate from management principles. The success of companies hinges more on their fundamental values than on intricate strategies (Kooskora, 2013). These values are frequently communicated indirectly but manifest distinctly in the conduct of the leadership (Walumba et al., 2008; Ghate & Ralston, 2011). Leadership assumes a pivotal role in cultivating an ethical organizational culture through the ethical behaviour of leaders, the organization's mission, vision, and values (Kooskora, 2006). Furthermore, Melé (2012) underscores the significance of ethical criteria in aspects such as employee recruitment, performance evaluations, continuous monitoring, management decisions guided by ethical values, daily routines, and internal structures and procedures.

10.2.1   Framework of Sustainable Business Model

The foundations of sustainable management are deeply ingrained in the framework of a sustainable business model. Although no singular theory prevails, there exist prevalent concepts surrounding the qualities that effective leaders should embody and how these qualities can contribute to a company's sustainable development (Dreier et al., 2019). However, the ongoing discourse surrounding social responsibility is inherently intertwined with individual traits, attitudes, values, and modes of argumentation. Attitudes regarding social responsibility are significantly shaped by personal characteristics (Kooskora, 2008). The process of personal transformation is gradual and often fraught with uncertainty, displaying resistance to persuasion or argumentation, as proposed by Mudrack (2007). This provokes the persistent query of whether the normative debate concerning the imperative nature of social responsibility will ever attain a conclusive resolution.

However, still to this day, the most prominent division in the realm of sustainable business models and corporate social responsibility revolves around the clash between the proponents of the Friedman school and their counterparts (Meehan et al., 2006), which can be characterized as a profound ideological discord. As affirmed by the study conducted by Mason and Mudrack in 1997, a firm belief in the primacy of business interests reflects a deep-seated respect for organizational authority, particularly among adherents of conventional societal values (Mason & Mudrack, 1997). Supporters of the traditional societal model often attribute social issues to departures from moral norms rather than perceiving them as broader outcomes of political or economic deficiencies (Murray, 1984).

10.2.2   Sustainable Business Leadership

An organization committed to the interests of both society and shareholders necessitates leaders who exemplify their current and future self-image. These leaders must bridge their personal convictions with those who hold different worldviews, speak candidly when obstacles arise, and acknowledge their responsibility in this regard, all while recognizing that there are no definitive answers or formulas (Zu, 2019). It is imperative that leaders consistently align their actions with their words (Gentile, 2001) to build trust (Del Baldo & Baldarelli, 2017) and sustain purpose (DDI, 2018). When leaders' personal values and ethics align with those of the organization, it reduces dissonance and bolsters sustainability performance (Posner & Schmidt, 1993). According to Magni and Pennarola (2015), responsible leadership is grounded in five pillars: (1) consideration of stakeholders and ethical culture; (2) dignity and fairness; (3) setting an example and empowerment; (4) a climate valuing diversity and inclusion; (5) long-term goal-setting. Through this model, a responsible leader can steer the organization towards supporting sustainable development.

Responsible leadership permeates various levels: individual, team, and organizational. Responsible individuals must possess versatile thinking, encompassing ethics (foresight, transparency, perseverance), aesthetics (Melé, 2009; Sansone, 2014), and the decision-making structure of leaders relies on their primary virtues, where determination (courage), prudence (life experience), moderation (self-control), and justice endow dignity to the leader's actions (Bastons, 2007). As per theories of sustainable leadership, leaders play a significant role in fostering social capital (Avery & Bergsteiner, 2011) across all levels, acting as bearers of sustainable values through dynamic, inclusive, and collaborative leadership processes.

However, leadership isn't solely about leading others but leading with others, fostering the dissemination of sustainable values both within and outside the organization (Kooskora, 2013). In the words of De Baldo and Baldarelli (2017), "a sustainable business model originates from a sustainable leadership model, characterized by change-oriented, responsible, ethically moral, and values/virtue-based leadership". While the influence of leaders on the organization has been well-studied, the converse, understanding how working with sustainable values affects personal meaning and job satisfaction, remains less explored. A broader question arises regarding the extent to which sustainable business practices influence an individual's moral behaviour (De Colle & Werhane, 2008).

Furthermore, can a person become more ethical and moral through their work? The debate continues, emphasizing the alignment of values, but explanatory theories remain scarce, particularly with regard to the psychological aspects connecting an individual to an organization's sustainability (Stern, 1992). Nevertheless, leaders who grasp how a company's sustainable activities positively impact employee satisfaction and motivation consciously integrate this into their leadership style (Mengel, 2004).

Drawing from the preceding discussion on sustainable business models and leadership, one can define sustainable leadership as meaning-based leadership. It is evident that sustainability, corporate social responsibility, meaningful work, and stakeholder considerations are intrinsically intertwined (Kooskora & Vilumets, 2021). These substantial concepts are not to be viewed in isolation; meaningful leadership necessitates adherence to the underlying principles of social responsibility and sustainable development, and vice versa (Zu, 2019). Leadership plays an exceptionally vital role in sustainable development (Kooskora, 2013). The impact of leaders on an organization, both internally and externally, is not always overtly expressed but often implicitly manifested in the leader's conduct (Ghate & Ralston, 2011). Therefore, it can be argued that a company's contribution to sustainable development is significantly contingent on the company's leader, their beliefs, attitudes, and value system (Zu, 2019).

10.3   The State of Sustainable Development in Estonia

10.3.1   Studies of Responsible Business Practices of Estonian Companies

In recent years, several significant events have taken place within the European Union aimed at attaining global sustainable development goals and climate objectives (Rogelj et al., 2016; Sachs et al., 2022). Moreover, in the coming decade, a pivotal question arises regarding the attainment of these goals and to what extent Estonian national institutions, politicians, and entrepreneurs are prepared to collaborate and adapt to the new regulations arising from the European Green Deal.

The inception of conscientious responsible business practices in Estonia dates back to 2005 when the Responsible Business Forum (VEF) was established by visionary entrepreneurs. VEF represents an assembly of companies dedicated to fostering an understanding of their collective societal responsibility. By the close of 2020, the network had expanded to 78 members, encompassing businesses of diverse sizes, social enterprises, and three individuals (VEF, 2020). Since 2007, VEF has been annually conducting a comprehensive assessment of corporate responsibility in Estonia, bestowing certificates and labels on responsible companies (VEF Index, 2020). These labels are earned through a meticulous questionnaire that aligns with internationally and nationally recognized foundational documents pertaining to responsible business practices (Kooskora, 2016), including, since 2020, alignment with the Sustainable Development Goals that support sustainable development.

In addition to scholarly research carried out at the Estonian Business School (Kooskora, 2006; 2008a, b; 2015; Kooskora & Cundiff, 2019) and other Estonian research centres, two consulting firms, Miltton and Sustinere, have played pivotal roles in researching and advancing the realm of responsible business practices in Estonia and consistently issuing reports based on various studies. In 2018, the business consultancy firm Miltton conducted a qualitative study on behalf of VEF to evaluate the current state of responsible business practices in Estonia (VEF, 2018). The study's objective was to gather insights and recommendations from top executives across various sectors concerning corporate social responsibility activities, with a focus on understanding leaders' perceptions of the field. At that time the following key findings were revealed (VEF, 2018): Responsible business practices in Estonia lack widespread recognition. These activities often lack meaning and a thorough impact analysis. External pressures, such as foreign owners' will or strong external pressures, frequently drive these actions. Entrepreneurs favour voluntary incorporation of responsible principles within their companies and resist additional government regulations. Presently, there is a lack of expectations for the government to set an example. Initiatives should commence with enhancing awareness in this field.

Sustinere (2019) has analyzed the annual reports of Estonia's 100 most impactful companies since 2018, assessing how thoroughly these companies describe the sustainability of their social and environmental impacts, the principles of responsible leadership, and their broader societal role. A significant conclusion from their 2018 annual report analysis, released in 2019, is that environmental management stands out as the weakest reporting category in the annual reports of Estonia's 100 most influential companies, while personnel and work environment receive the strongest reporting.

Furthermore, Sustinere (2019) urges Estonian companies to recognize their wider societal role and influence, suggesting that they analyze their activities in light of the UN Sustainable Development Goals. Internationally, aligning core activities with these goals is considered one of the most significant trends in sustainability management. Nevertheless, only two of the top 100 influential Estonian companies referenced this alignment in their reports. Another critical recommendation presented by Sustinere (2019) emphasizes the need for improved management of environmental impacts, enhancing Estonia's credibility as an international partner, particularly as environmental and climate concerns take centre stage in the sustainable development of developed nations.

10.3.2   Studies of Societal Expectations on Estonian Companies

As previously discussed in sections on sustainable development and business activities, it is imperative for companies to assess their impact on stakeholders. Consequently, understanding societal expectations, target audiences, and stakeholders' needs is of great importance. Pioneering studies in Estonia, such as Miltton's "Head out of the Sand!" (2018; 2020), aim to provide insights into this realm. These studies seek to identify the most critical expectations, topics, channels for conveying them, and the roles of stakeholders in the context of responsible and socially active corporate activities, as perceived by employees, consumers, and citizens.

In a study published in early March 2020 (Miltton, 2020), it was found that the most significant issue for Estonians, as indicated by 49% of respondents, is the circular economy, waste reduction, and recycling. Moreover, it's worth noting that in the context of the need for a balance between the three pillars of sustainable development, there have been noticeable shifts in Estonian values. Environmental concerns have surged while social concerns have waned, resulting in the emergence of climate change in the top five most important topics for Estonians, standing alongside environmental conservation for the first time. A substantial 58% of respondents expect companies to take concrete actions that demonstrate responsibility. Leaders, entrepreneurs, and top specialists exhibit the strongest support for this view, with 64% of them believing that actions should precede words. Consumers and employees also express distinct preferences; 43% of them find it important that the products or services they purchase have a stance on social issues, and a significant 57% would consider leaving their jobs if their employer or immediate superior expressed unacceptable values or positions, either verbally or through actions (Miltton, 2020).

Another study explored citizens' awareness of the United Nations Sustainable Development Goals, revealing that 82% of Estonians had never heard of them (Miltton, 2019).

10.4 Current Research Among Estonian Top-level Executives

10.4.1 Sample and Research Design

By conducting this study we aim to identify the attitudes of top-ranking executives in Estonia concerning sustainability, with a particular emphasis on their perspectives regarding corporate social responsibility and their adherence to the fundamental tenets of sustainable development. To collect data from senior executives occupying leadership positions in Estonia's most influential companies a web-based survey was employed with a purposefully selected sample. As per Etikan (2016), this approach doesn't rely on sub-theories or limit the number of participants, with the researchers determining who possesses the required knowledge or experience for achieving the research objective.

Our sample comprises representatives of the most influential Estonian companies, specifically top executives of Estonian registered companies with an annual turnover exceeding 30 million euros. Initially, the database included 2484 individuals, and after adjustments, the sample consists of 963 individuals, representing top executives from the most influential companies in Estonia. The gender distribution in the sample is 15% female and 85% male. According to Eurostat (2019) data, in 2019, 63% of top executives in Estonia were male, and 37% were female. A compilation by the "Estonian Business Newspaper" (Äripäev, 2019) overviewing 1500 top executives in Estonia indicated that 12% were female. Additionally, a study by consulting firm Sustinere (2018) analyzing the annual reports of the 100 most influential companies in Estonia highlighted that only 16% of the board members in these companies were female. Thus, the sample is considered representative in terms of gender distribution.

The average age of the sample is 50 years, with a similar age distribution for both males and females. The majority of top executives in the most influential Estonian companies fall within the age range of 40 s and 50 s, whereas only 10% of the sample falls into younger or older age groups. According to statistics presented in Äripäev in 2018, the majority of board members in Estonian companies were between the ages of 35–54 (Alvarez et al., 2018).

The research design and data collection method are tailored to the research questions. The study employs an explanatory mixed-method approach, encompassing quantitative data collection and qualitative methods to derive conclusions (Punch, 2005). Quantitative analysis is used to identify and explain patterns, developing nomological knowledge, while qualitative research aims to comprehend reality by exploring the essence of the phenomenon, revealing hidden aspects (Bhattacherjee,

2012). This study employs a survey format for data collection, distributed to the target group via email, to ensure that the most representative data is obtained.

Tanner (2018) outlines potential errors in survey research, including coverage error (lack of representativeness), sampling error (lack of precision), nonresponse error (due to factors like a fast-paced lifestyle or low motivation), and measurement error (arising from questionnaire design and respondents' desire to present themselves favourably for social acceptance). In this study, the primary risk is low response activity due to the busy lives of the sample participants, focusing only on high-priority issues. Motivating respondents to participate is a crucial consideration in questionnaire design and implementation (Dillmann et al., 2009). Overall, response activity in web surveys is generally low (Sue & Ritter, 2007).

The questionnaire construction employs a combination of closed, multiple-choice questions typically used in quantitative research and open-ended questions that encourage respondents to provide opinions and judgments, typical of qualitative research (Jamshed, 2014). This mixed approach aims to establish a connection between the first and second research questions. Open-ended questions help respondents articulate their attitudes, presenting arguments that can support or challenge responses provided in closed-ended questions. This contextualizes statistical data.

The questionnaire encompasses various scales suited to the purpose of each question and its underlying structure, including binary scales, ordinal scales, rating scales, and composite scales for measuring attitudes (Õunapuu, 2014). The questionnaire is divided into three thematic blocks, which are not explicitly presented to respondents but are located on different pages within the questionnaire.

Block I   Gathers background information about the respondent's company.
Block II   Explores top executives' personal choices related to sustainability in their daily lives, offering insights into their attitudes towards sustainability across various life domains.
Block III Investigates interpretations and attitudes concerning sustainability and corporate social responsibility, including open-ended questions to delve into understanding and attitudes.

10.4.2 Research Process and Data Analysis

To distribute the questionnaire, the authors utilized the data collection and analysis platform SogoSurvey, an ISO 27001 certified company that adheres to GDPR requirements. The research's purpose was introduced and explained and data usage principles were outlined, assuring participants of data anonymization and generalization in the cover letter. Additionally motivation for participation was emphasized to mitigate the risk of low response activity due to participants' busy lives.

Our study employed a multifaceted data analysis approach tailored to the research objectives: First, Descriptive Statistics (Loeb et al., 2017) method was utilized to effectively organize and present the collected data in a clear and concise manner. Second, Inferential Statistics (Costello & Osborne, 2005) was employed to enable comprehensive assessments, draw informed conclusions, and make reliable predictions based on the data. And third, the Qualitative Directed Content Analysis (Saldaña & Omasta, 2016) approach was utilized to delve into the attitudes and opinions articulated in the open-ended responses, offering valuable insights into the participants' perspectives.

However, within this chapter our main focus is on qualitative content analysis, whereas the analysis of the open-ended responses related to sustainable development and corporate social responsibility entails a systematic process of keyword coding to reveal patterns and key themes.

According to Virkus (2016), qualitative content analysis involves grouping text segments with similar meanings, representing both explicitly expressed and implied messages. The open-ended responses were coded into groups of keywords representing different the three dimensions of sustainability: economic, social, and environmental. Additionally, a more general category, including keywords, such as general development, long-term perspective, sustainability, lasting impact, future generations, etc.

10.4.3   Main Findings of the Study

The sample of our study consisted of 963 individuals in management, boards, and ownership roles in Estonian companies with an annual turnover exceeding 30 million euros. The survey was distributed in late 2020, with a response rate of 25.55%. In total, 215 individuals completed the questionnaire fully or partially. Demographically, the sample was predominantly male (85%) with an average age of 50 years. Nearly half of the companies involved were founded in the 1990s (47%), while 29% were established between 2000 and 2010. Notably, 32% of company owners did not originate from Estonia, and 51% of the companies engaged in export activities. Among these, 32% had a larger share of exports compared to domestic market sales.

10.4.3.1   Top Executives' Personal Choices Regarding Sustainability

The questionnaire explored top managers' personal choices and behavioural preferences in various everyday life situations, offering insights into their receptiveness to sustainable development topics. The respondents reported relatively responsible behaviour in terms of environmental responsibility in their daily lives, such as waste sorting (93%) and preferring environmentally friendly bags (90%). However, 96% of respondents used cars for daily commuting, with limited usage of more environmentally friendly options.

Opinions on broader environmental topics, like the feasibility of achieving climate neutrality by 2050, were more diverse, with 42% believing it's achievable, 42% expressing uncertainty due to a lack of knowledge, and 17% deeming it unattainable. Regarding alignment with global climate goals, 39% believed the actions of the

Estonian state and companies in Estonia were in line with these goals, 32% disagreed, and 29% were uncertain. To assess attitudes related to the social dimension of sustainable development, executives were asked if they had engaged in voluntary work not directly linked to their business activities. In response, 69% had done so, indicating a general inclination among leaders to contribute to the benefit of society.

10.4.3.2   Gender Balance in Leadership Positions

When examining gender balance in leadership roles in Estonian companies, respondents were divided; 49% considered there were enough women in key decision-making positions, while 51% believed there weren't. Considering the importance of gender balance in sustainable development (UN, 2015) and the fact that only 16% of leaders in Estonia's top 100 influential companies are women (Sustinere, 2018), this raises questions about the awareness and contributions of top managers in Estonia's influential companies to sustainable development. This topic requires further research, as no definitive answers can be derived from this study.

10.4.4   Interpretation and Attitudes Toward Sustainability and Corporate Social Responsibility

When asked to define sustainability (Jarvie, 2016; Kuhlman & Farrington, 2010) in a general sense (sustainable development) and within their companies (sustainable business model, e.g., Govidan et al., 2021), respondents' 154 open responses predominantly linked sustainability to the environmental dimension, particularly nature conservation and climate concerns (mentioned 91 times). Economic aspects were associated with sustainability by 69 respondents, yet none saw sustainability as purely financial or solely linked to profit expectations. The social dimension was expressed by 67 respondents, often emphasizing human well-being and contributions to communities. In addition, there was a significant number of mentions associated with overall development, both from a company and societal perspective, with recurring keywords like long-term, sustainable, and enduring.

Examples of such responses included: "Sustainability means a balanced development that keeps our planet habitable for future generations" (ID: 215) and "Sustainable business means the voluntary integration of economic, environmental, and social dimensions into company management and activities, taking into account various stakeholders and creating added value for all" (ID: 218). However, while a general understanding of sustainable development aligns with earlier discussed frameworks (see Sect. 10.1), attitudes towards sustainable development show a strong inclination towards the environmental dimension, with economic and social dimensions also present but to a lesser extent.

This can be clearly seen from the following examples: "For me, it means that a person/company has a minimal impact on the surrounding environment or compensates for their actions when necessary" (ID: 7). Furthermore, one of the respondent emphasized the importance of nature conversation by saying: "We need to talk about NATURE CONSERVATION, and everyone needs to contribute, the entire society. Currently, about 59% of this burden is carried by landowners. From the perspective of a company, we need to align with the goals of the Green Deal, which means contributing to NATURE CONSERVATION, even when a company has no direct contact with nature. We all leave an ecological footprint that we need to start compensating for through ecosystem services" (ID: 92).

10.4.4.1 Understanding of Corporate Social Responsibility

Further, the study enabled us to collect 137 open responses regarding the understanding of corporate social responsibility (CSR, e.g., Latapí Agudelo et al., 2019). During the coding process, it became evident that in the first third of the responses, many respondents did not significantly differentiate between sustainability and the principles of corporate responsibility. In some cases, respondents referred to what had been previously expressed about sustainability in their responses. For example the respondents said: "I value responsibility towards the environment and people. In addition to a sustainable mindset, I support activities directed towards the community" (ID: 33) and "Creating value for the environment, communities, and society in an acceptable way" (ID: 106).

However, the coding results revealed a more frequent mention of the economic and social dimensions than was the case with sustainability, primarily in the context of creating employee well-being. In a perfectly balanced manner, both social and environmental dimensions were mentioned 90 times each, while the economic dimension was mentioned 72 times. All three dimensions were mentioned 54 times, which is proportionally higher considering the number of responses and demonstrated a more comprehensive and conscious expression. For example, one of those broader and more comprehensive approaches: "It's necessary to maintain a balance and continually consider all aspects related to the company's operations. Responsibility is a broad concept that touches on business behaviour (business ethics), social behaviour, and the environment. Responsible behaviour also supports profitability in the long term" (ID: 155).

10.4.4.2 Social Dimension of Responsibility

In the realm of the social dimension (Dahlsrud, 2008; WBCSD, 2000), survey respondents often emphasized the significance of employees and their well-being, as exemplified by these responses: "Considering employees' interests, equal pay for similar positions, safety during transportation, team fairness, and reducing our environmental footprint" (ID: 55) and "As a family-friendly employer, being responsible and sustainable involves caring for employees' mental and physical health" (ID: 116). Furthermore, some participants provided specific action plans detailing what they believed companies should undertake in terms of responsibility: "1. Comply with laws, pay taxes properly, and set an example. 2. Preserve nature and our environment. 3. Maintain profitability and create jobs" (ID: 79).

In the context of corporate social responsibility, respondents exhibited a higher degree of detail compared to earlier questions. In several cases a comprehensive and responsible approach that integrates across all facets of business was described: "Responsibility encompasses business ethics, social behaviour, and environmental concerns, while still aiming for profitability in the long term" (ID: 155). Additionally, "Our top daily priorities include climate and energy issues, gender equality, and education. We believe in embedding these principles in our activities because we recognize our impact on society as a financial company" (ID: 126). To conclude, the open responses reflect an alignment between the understanding and attitudes towards corporate social responsibility and the fundamental principles of sustainable development and corporate responsibility. Notably, corporate responsibility exhibits a more balanced emphasis on the three dimensions compared to the broader concept of sustainability.

10.4.4.3   Balancing the Three Pillars of Sustainable Development

Regarding the three fundamental principles of sustainable development (see Elkington, 1994, 2004), two different types of questions were asked. One required respondents to assess their company's impact on economic, social, and environmental dimensions, while the other asked for their position on a statement evaluating the impact of all three dimensions. The responses reveal that top executives place high importance on the economic and social dimensions, but the environmental dimension is perceived as less significant.

To summarize, the importance of these pillars is rated as follows (considered as "very important" or "important" by respondents): 94% for economic, 98% for social, and 87% for environmental. Notably, only 32% considered the environmental dimension as very important, and 13% found it unimportant. When evaluating the impact of all three dimensions collectively, only 19% strongly agreed with the statement, in contrast to 45% who rated each dimension as "very important" separately. This shows that these executives do not view the three fundamental principles of sustainable development as equal.

Moreover, several respondents expressed their doubts and criticism towards Estonian alignment with global climate goals (see Sachs et al., 2022; Rogelj et al., 2016), which can be seen from the following examples: "The goal is achievable, but current actions are not entirely in line with it. We need a more significant and systematic approach" (ID: 78); "There is too much 'greenwashing,' but something has to start somewhere" (ID: 32); "Estonia has chosen the path of trading with statistics, not changing behaviour and attitudes. Thus, the goals won't be achieved in the short or long term" (ID: 15) and even expressing that: "The goal itself is wrong" (ID:

166). Thus the top executives of these Estonian most influential companies have rather diverse opinions in relation to the global climate goals and especially about the alignment of the activities of Estonian state and companies.

10.4.4.4   Awareness of Sustainable Development Goals

Understanding the attitudes of top executives regarding sustainability necessitated assessing their awareness of sustainable development goals (UN, 2015), which are globally recognized. Surprisingly, 55% of these executives were not aware of these goals. This contrasts with a study among Estonian people (Miltton, 2020), which found that 82% had never heard of them, demonstrating a noticeable gap compared to global top executives who exhibited full awareness in the Accenture (2020) survey. However, there were also more knowledgeable responses presented, for example: "In business, one could say that sustainability means being profitably viable in the long term. Achieving this in today's world means considering all 17 of the UN's goals. While they are currently receiving varying degrees of attention, it is certain that ignoring them or consciously evading them will ultimately have a significantly negative impact on a company's fortunes" (ID: 155).

Another question aimed to identify who, in the respondents' opinions, should contribute to sustainable development goals. Individuals were recognized as vital contributors, but only 51% saw companies as significant contributors. This alignment with awareness levels implies that the perceived importance of corporate contributions may be influenced by limited awareness rather than executive attitudes. Furthermore, a resounding 97% of respondents acknowledged the importance of sustainability for their company's future success. Additionally, the majority (80%) accepted a short-term profit reduction to facilitate investments in sustainability.

Additionally, our questionnaire inquired about obstacles to implementing sustainable development strategies. Compared to a global survey (Accenture, 2020), where 26% of corporate executives cited a lack of business profit as an issue, a significant 46% of Estonia's influential corporate executives admitted insufficient knowledge in integrating sustainable development principles into their strategies. Other cited obstacles included state regulations, the complexity of the subject, and challenges in internal buy-in. For example: "State legislative regulations do not allow for sustainable operation to remain competitive" (ID: 15); "This topic is very confusing, correct and incorrect information is available simultaneously. A lot of populism by activists" (ID: 18) and "This path is more complex, requires more in-depth knowledge and constant pushing. The biggest obstacle is selling the idea within the company—it's a long process that only yields results over time" (ID: 69).

10.4.5   Main Conclusions and Balancing the Three Pillars

Overall, top executives of Estonia's most influential companies demonstrate awareness and alignment with sustainable development principles, encompassing economic, social, and environmental aspects (see Elkington, 1994, 2004). Nevertheless, their attitudes show a pronounced focus on the environmental dimension. However, it's crucial to consider that these responses are self-reported and might reflect an idealized perspective rather than actual behaviour. There's evident polarization among executives regarding specific environmental questions, underlining the complexity of achieving environmental goals. In summary, while these executives show strong support for sustainability and recognize the importance of corporate contributions, further investigation is needed to understand their perspectives more comprehensively and bridge the awareness gap related to sustainable development goals.

Furthermore, the assessment of the importance of the three dimensions—economic, social, and environmental—revealed a notable conflict, particularly concerning environmental impact. While environmental issues are seen as significant on a global scale, their importance diminishes when viewed from a local or company-specific perspective. This suggests that executive attitudes are influenced by the prevailing public climate debate (Zu, 2019) but lack understanding when it comes to assessing environmental impacts within their company context. Therefore, it is recommended that influential business leaders in Estonia engage more deeply in evaluating their companies' environmental impact to enhance their awareness in this area.

Regarding the social dimension (Dahlsrud, 2008; WBCSD, 2000), the majority acknowledged its importance. Respondents emphasized community support, well-being, and caring for others. However, concerning gender equality, the respondents' opinions were in strong contradiction with sustainable development goals. Consequently, the vision of sustainability held by Estonia's top executives aligns with the definition of continuous societal development in balance with current and future needs. This understanding is further supported by keywords from open responses, emphasizing development, and long-term sustainability.

The attitudes of Estonia's business leaders towards corporate social responsibility align with their perception of sustainable development, emphasizing the broader impact of companies in Estonia in a global context. All three dimensions—economic, social, and environmental—continue to be in focus and are considered important. However, there's a shift in proportions between the social and environmental dimensions, indicating that some companies may have been more involved in developing their principles of social responsibility, showing a more comprehensive and informed manner of expression.

The understanding of balance among the three pillars of sustainable development can be evaluated as follows: while some respondents view sustainability as three-dimensional, nearly two-thirds express the necessity of two dimensions, and only a few have a one-dimensional perspective. However, room for development remains, as sustainable business models should maintain a balance between all three dimensions, remaining coherent and responsible across all stakeholders.

Whereas a notable shift away from a dominant focus on the economic dimension is observed, demonstrating a transformation in Estonia's business culture towards meaning-based management aligned with sustainable development. Estonia's top business leaders perceive the economic and social dimensions as more balanced than the environmental dimension. While this conclusion is based on attitudes, not concrete actions, it is encouraging that the majority of these leaders consider sustainability-related issues important and are willing to make short-term profit sacrifices for long-term sustainability investments.

Future research could include a deeper analysis of the personalities of Estonia's top business leaders to understand their impact on responsible leadership in companies. Additionally, research should evaluate executive attitudes in comparison to their companies' actual performance in the same areas. Given global sustainability demands, further research is needed on climate and environmental issues in corporate social responsibility. Finally, a follow-up study should focus on gender equality issues in leadership, as this study has generated numerous unanswered questions in this regard.

10.5   Concluding Remarks

The purpose of this study was to identify the attitudes of top executives in influential Estonian companies towards sustainability, corporate social responsibility, and their alignment with the core principles of sustainable development. Based on the collected data, it is evident that these top executives are well-informed and aware of sustainability. Their attitudes closely correspond to the fundamental principles of sustainable development, encompassing economic, social, and environmental dimensions. Furthermore, their views on corporate social responsibility also mirror their understanding of sustainable development, signifying their capacity to recognize the global impact of Estonian companies.

However, it is notable that while they see economic and social dimensions as more balanced, the environmental dimension does not hold the same weight in their perception. This disparity occasionally appeared when answering questions related to sustainability aspects. Questions regarding environmental and gender balance led to polarized responses among these executives. From their attitudes, it is clear that there isn't a well-defined balance among the three pillars of sustainable development, which is essential for sustainable development itself.

Nonetheless, the study implies potential for a greater balance among these pillars. Top executives overwhelmingly agree that sustainability-related issues are vital for their companies' future success, even if it involves a short-term reduction in business profits. Despite the perceived contribution of Estonia's influential companies to sustainable development, this contribution is not always consciously recognized due to limited awareness of sustainable development goals. In some cases, it may be incidental or driven by other motives. Furthermore, sustainability remains an ongoing process of societal development, demanding a balance between present and future needs. Estonia and its entrepreneurs have committed to achieving global sustainable development goals, ensuring sustainability both locally and globally. To meet these objectives, there is a need to further cultivate a more pronounced balance among the three pillars of sustainable development.

References

Accenture & United Nations Global Compact. (2020). *The decade to deliver: A call to business action.* CEO Study on Sustainability 2019.

Alvarez, A., Rõuk, V., Suu, J., & Must, B. (2018). What is the average Estonian manager like? [Milline on Eesti keskmine juht?] *Äripäev, 22*(05). https://www.aripaev.ee/uudised/2018/05/22/milline-on-eesti-keskmine-juht

Äripäev. (2019). Äripäev. 2019. Estonian Economic Lexicon, Top Executives of Estonia 2019 [Eesti Majanduse Leksikon, Eesti Tippjuhid 2019]. As Äripäev.

Avery, G., & Bergsteiner, H. (2011). Sustainable leadership practices for enhancing business resilience and performance. *Strategy & Leadership, 39*(3), 5–15.

Bastons, M. (2007). The role of virtues in the framing of decisions. *Journal of Business Ethics, 78*(3), 389–400.

Bhattacherjee, A. (2012). *Social science research: Principles, methods, and practices.* Textbooks Collection, 3. https://digitalcommons.usf.edu/oa_textbooks/3

Bocken, N. M. P., Short, S. W., Rana, P., & Evans, S. (2014). A literature and practice review to develop sustainable business model archetypes. *Journal of Cleaner Production, 65*, 42–56.

Costello, A. B., & Osborne, J. (2005). Best practices in exploratory factor analysis: Four recommendations for getting the most from your analysis. *Practical Assessment, Research, and Evaluation, 10*(1), 7.

Cutter, S. (2013). Building disaster resilience: Steps toward sustainability. *Challenges in Sustainability, 1*, 72–79.

Dahlsrud, A. (2008). How corporate social responsibility is defined: An analysis of 37 definitions. *Corporate Social Responsibility and Environmental Management, 15*(1), 1–13.

Daly, H. (1996). *Beyond growth: The economics of sustainable development.* Beacon Press.

DDI. (2018). *Global leadership forecast 2018: 25 Research insights to fuel your people strategy.* Retrieved June 28, 2023, from https://www.ddiworld.com/glf2018/purposeful-leadership

De Colle, S., & Werhane, P. H. (2008). Moral motivation across ethical theories: What can we learn for designing corporate ethics programs. *Journal of Business Ethics, 81*(4), 751–764.

Del Baldo, M., & Baldarelli, M.-G. (2017). Renewing and improving the business model toward sustainability in theory and practice. *International Journal of Corporate Social Responsibility, 2*(1), 1–13.

Dillmann, D. A., Smyth, J. D., & Christian, L. M. (2009). *Internet, mail, and mixed-mode surveys: The tailored design method* (3rd ed.). Wiley.

Dreier, L., Nabarro, D., & Nelson, J. (2019). *Systems leadership for sustainable development: Strategies for achieving systemic change.* Harvard Kennedy School.

Elkington, J. (2004). Enter the triple bottom line. In A. A. Henriques & J. Richardson (Eds.), *The triple bottom line: Does it all add up?* (pp. 1–16). Earthscan.

Elkington, J. (1994). Towards the sustainable corporation: Win–Win–Win business strategies for sustainable development. *California Management Review, 36*, 90–100. https://doi.org/10.2307/41165746

Esop, K., & Kooskora, M. (2023). Institutionalizing SDGs and CSR policies in Estonia. In K. Summers (Ed.), *Exploring cities and countries of the world* (vol. 4, pp. 25–53). Nova Science Publishers, Inc. ISBN: 979-8-88697-634-2

Etikan, I. (2016). Comparison of convenience sampling and purposive sampling. *American Journal of Theoretical and Applied Statistics, 5*(1).

Eurostat. (2019). Eurostat 2019. https://ec.europa.eu/eurostat/cache/beta/womenmen_2020/ee_et/bloc-2c.html?lang=et

Friedman, M. (1970). The social responsibility of business is to increase its profits. The *New York Times Magazine.*

Gentile, M. C. (2001). Preparing business leaders to manage social impacts: Lessons from the field. *Journal of Human Values, 7*(2), 107–115.

Ghate, D., & Ralston, R. E. (2011). *Why businessmen need philosophy: The capitalist's guide to the ideas behind Ayn rand's Atlas shrugged.* New American Library (Penguin Group), New York.

Govindan, K., Shaw, M., & Majumdar, A. (2021). Social sustainability tensions in multi-tier supply chain: A systematic literature review toward conceptual framework development. *Journal of Cleaner Production, 279*, 123075. https://doi.org/10.1016/j.jclepro.2020.123075

Jamshed, S. (2014). Qualitative research method-interviewing and observation. *Journal of Basic Clinical Pharmacy, 5*(4), 87–88. https://doi.org/10.4103/0976-0105.141942

Jarvie, M. E. (2016). Brundtland report. *Encyclopedia Britannica.* https://www.britannica.com/topic/Brundtland-Report

Khan, I. S., Ahmad, M. O., & Majava, J. (2021). Industry 4.0 and sustainable development: A systematic mapping of triple bottom line, circular economy, and sustainable business models perspectives. *Journal of Cleaner Production, 297*, 126655. https://doi.org/10.1016/j.jclepro.2021.126655

Kooskora, M. (2006). Perceptions of business purpose and responsibility in the context of radical political and economic development: The case of Estonia. *Business Ethics: A European Review, 15*(2), pp.183–199.

Kooskora, M. (2016). Building the capacity for CSR through supportive initiatives in Estonia. In *Key initiatives in corporate social responsibility* (pp. 243–258). Springer, Cham.

Kooskora, M. (2015). Corporate social responsibility in estonia: moving towards a more strategic approach. In S. O. Idowu, R. Schmidpeter, & M. S. Fifka (Eds.), *Corporate social responsibility in Europe: United in sustainable diversity* (pp. 291–311). Springer.

Kooskora, M. (2013). Change, values, and sustainability networking and researcher bias. *Journal of Management & Change, 31*(1/2), 11–15.

Kooskora, M. (2008a). Corporate governance from the stakeholder perspective, in the context of Estonian business organizations. *Baltic Journal of Management, 2*(3), 193–217.

Kooskora, M. (2008b). *Understanding corporate moral development in the context of rapid and radical changes: The case of Estonia.* Jyväskylä University Printing House.

Kooskora, M., & Cundiff, K. (2019). The development towards corporate sustainability in a transitional economy, case Estonia. *Journal of East European Management Studies*, 203–221. https://doi.org/10.5771/9783845298696-203

Kooskora, M. & Vilumets, Ü. (2021). The Role of Meaningful Work in the Context of Startup Events and Entrepreneurial Activities. In: Mitra, N. & Schmidpeter, R. (Ed.). *Corporate Social Responsibility in Rising Economies.* (31−50). Springer. (CSR, Sustainability, Ethics & Governance). https://doi.org/10.1007/978-3-030-53775-3_3

Kuhlman, T., & Farrington, J. (2010). What is sustainability? *Sustainability, 2*(11), 3436–3448. https://doi.org/10.3390/su2113436

Latapí Agudelo, M. A., Jóhannsdóttir, L., & Davídsdóttir, B. A. (2019). Literature review of the history and evolution of corporate social responsibility. *International Journal of Corporate Social Responsibility, 4*(1).

Loeb, S., Dynarski, S., McFarland, D., Morris, P., Reardon, S., & Reber, S. (2017). *Descriptive analysis in education: A guide for researchers* (NCEE 2017–4023). National Center for Education Evaluation and Regional Assistance.

Magni, M., & Pennarola, F. (2015). *Responsible leadership*. EGEA.

Mason, E. S., & Mudrack, P. E. (1997). Are individuals who agree that corporate social responsibility is a "fundamentally subversive doctrine" inherently unethical? *Applied Psychology: An International Review, 46*(2), 135–152. https://doi.org/10.1111/j.1464-0597.1997.tb01221.x

Meehan, J., Meehan, K., & Richards, A. (2006). Corporate social responsibility: The 3C-SR model. *International Journal of Social Economics, 33*(5/6), 386–389.

Melé, D. (2012). *Management ethics: Placing ethics in the core of good management*. Palgrave Macmillan.

Melé, D. (2009). *Business ethics in action: Seeking human excellence in organizations*. Palgrave Macmillan.

Mengel, T. (2004). From responsibility to values-oriented leadership: Six theses on meaning and personal life and work environments. In *International network on personal meaning*.

Miltton. (2020). *Opinion survey on corporate social activity and social involvement: Get out of the sand! [Ettevõtete Ühiskondliku Aktiivsuse ja Sotsiaalse Kaasamise Arvamusuuring: Pea Liiva Alt Välja!]*. https://miltton.ee/uuringuraport-ettevotetelt-oodatakse-positiivset-muutust-loovaid-juhtimisotsuseid

Miltton. (2019). *Witnessing an ESG revolution—seeking a common language for investors and companies*. https://miltton.ee/esg-revolutsioon-investorid-ja-ettevotted-uhise-keele-otsingul

Miltton. (2018). *Opinion survey on corporate social activity and social involvement: Get out of the sand! [Ettevõtete Ühiskondliku Aktiivsuse ja Sotsiaalse Kaasamise Arvamusuuring: Pea Liiva Alt Välja!]*. https://miltton.ee/pea-liiva-alt-valja-ettevotte-uhiskondliku-aktiivsuse-ja-sotsiaalse-kaasamise-arvamusuuring

Murray, C. A. (1984). *Losing ground: American social policy 1950–1980*. Basic Books.

Õunapuu, L. (2014). *Qualitative and quantitative research method in social sciences [Kvalitatiivne ja Kvantitatiivne Uurimisviis Sotsiaalteadustes]* (p. 211). University of Tartu; 1 e-book [Tartu Ülikool; 1 e-book].

Posner, B. Z., & Schmidt, W. H. (1993). Values congruence and differences between the interplay of personal and organizational value systems. *Journal of Business Ethics, 12*(5), 341–347.

Punch, K. (2005). *Introduction to social research—quantitative & qualitative approaches*. Sage.

Purvis, B., Mao, Y., & Robinson, D. (2019). Three pillars of sustainability: In search of conceptual origins. *Sustainability Science, 14*, 681–695. https://doi.org/10.1007/s11625-018-0627-5

Rogelj, J., Den Elzen, M., Höhne, N., Fransen, T., Fekete, H., Winkler, H., Schaeffer, R., Sha, F., Riahi, K., & Meinshausen, M. (2016). Paris agreement climate proposals need a boost to keep warming well below 2°C. *Nature, 534*(7609), 631–639.

Rudnicka, A. (2016). Understanding sustainable business models. *Journal of Positive Management, 7*(4), 52–60.

Sachs, J. D., Kroll, C., Lafortune, G., Fuller, G., & Woelm, F. (2022). *Sustainable development report 2022*. Cambridge University Press.

Saldaña, J., & Omasta, M. (2016). *Qualitative research: Analyzing life*. Sage Publications.

Sakalasooriya, N. (2021). Conceptual analysis of sustainability and sustainable development. *Open Journal of Social Sciences, 9*, 396–414. https://doi.org/10.4236/jss.2021.93026

Sansone, F. (2014). *Responsible leadership: The 10 rules for being a leader in the knowledge economy. [Leadership Responsabile: Le 10 Regole Per Essere Leader Nell'Economia della Conoscenza]*. F. Angeli.

Stern, P. C. (1992). Psychological Dimensions Of Global Environmental Change. *Annual Review of Psychology, 43*, 269–302.

Sue, V. M., & Ritter, L. A. (2007). *Conducting online surveys*. Sage Publications.

Sustinere. (2019). *Analysis of Estonia's most impactful companies: Open and transparent annual social impact reporting*. Report [Eesti Suurima Mõjuga Ettevõtete Analüüs: Avatud ja Läbipaistev Ühiskondliku Mõju Aastaaruandlus. Raport].

Sustinere. (2018). *Analysis of Estonia's most impactful companies: Open and transparent annual social impact reporting*. Report [Eesti Suurima Mõjuga Ettevõtete Analüüs: Avatud ja Läbipaistev Ühiskondliku Mõju Aastaaruandlus. Raport]

Tanner, K. (2018). Chapter 6—survey designs. In K. Williamson, & G. Johanson (Eds.), *Research methods* (2nd edn, pp. 159–192). Chandos Publishing.

UN (2015). Transforming our world: The 2030 Agenda for Sustainable Development. *United Nations* https://sdgs.un.org/2030agenda

VEF. (2020). *VEF index (Forum of responsible business).* [VEF Indeks (Vastutustundliku Ettevõtluse Foorum). 2020. indeks.csr.ee.] Homepage. Retrieved November 28, 2020

VEF. (2018). *VEF index (Forum of responsible business) [VEF (Vastutustundliku Ettevõtluse Foorum)].* Uuringu Kokkuvõte. http://www.csr.ee/wp-content/uploads/2018/12/VEF-riigik ogus-2018ME.pdf

Virkus, S. (2016). *Qualitative content analysis [Kvalitatiivne Sisuanalüüs].* Tallinn University [Tallinna Ülikool]. Retrieved November 29, 2020, from https://www.tlu.ee/~sirvir/Intervjuu_ vaatlus_ja_sisuanals/kvalitatiivne_sisuanals.html

Walumbwa, F., Avolio, B., Gardner, W., Wernsing, T., & Peterson, S. (2008). *Authentic leadership: Development and validation of a theory-based measure* (vol. 24). Management Department Faculty Publications. https://digitalcommons.unl.edu/managementfacpub/24

WBCSD. (2000). *Corporate social responsibility: Making good business sense.* World Business Council for Sustainable Development.

Zu, L. (2019). Purpose-driven leadership for sustainable business: From the perspective of Taoism. *International Journal of Corporate Social Responsibility, 4*(1), 1–31.

Mari Kooskora, PhD, is an Associate Professor, researcher, trainer, advisor and Head of Centre for Business Ethics at Estonian Business School who has expertise in business ethics, responsible leadership and organisational sustainability for over 20 years in 12 countries. She is the author of research papers published in nationally and internationally recognised journals and has given numerous conference presentations. Her main research interests are ethics and responsibility in business and leadership, sustainability and women in leadership. As a board member of ISBEE (International Society of Business and Economics Ethics) and EUMMAS (European Marketing and Management Association) and previously also Responsible Business Forum Estonia and Transparency International Estonia, member of Business and Professional Women, European Business Ethics Network and several other international and local networks she is actively contributing to the development of more balanced and sustainable business and governance.

Annika Arras, MBA, is a Founder, Partner and CEO at consultancy Miltton New Nordics in Estonia, a subsidiary of Miltton Group, a pan-New-Nordics consultancy. She is an experienced political communication expert, who is interested in purpose driven organisations and sustainable business models. Prior to joining Miltton in 2016 she successfully headed the election campaigns for Estonia's previous Prime Ministers' and Vice-President of European Commission. She has consulted organisations in strategic communication from the Caucasus to the Nordics. In 2016 Annika founded the European Women's Academy of Political Leadership and Campaigning (now rebranded to Alliance of Her) together with ALDE and FNF where she trains and mentors high-level female politicians to become more influential in politics.

She is also a spokesperson on corporate social responsibility, advising companies and business leaders to build sustainable business models and works one-on-one with business leaders to help them to build their leader's image and executive presence. LinkedIn: https://ee.linkedin.com/in/ annika-arras.

Part IV
Case Studies in Organizational Sustainability

Chapter 11
The Fintech Sustainability Model Proposal: A Reflection on the Economic, Social Values, a Double Materiality View

Germán DelValle-Araluce⬤, **Jose Luis Retolaza**⬤, **and Leire San-Jose**⬤

Abstract After a period of fifteen years since Fintech birth, it has come a long way up to now in which almost each point of the financial value chain has been affected by their irruption. At present, what is less understood is which are the elements that can definitively consolidate Fintech as a new, differentiated, and sustainable sector; these elements are connected to value creation. This research aims to identify those elements that contribute to their long-term sustainability. Thus, we will analyze economic and social view of Fintech industry. To respond, we have identified four key aspects: the relevance of business models, trust as powerful mediator, the paradox around sustainability so-called the Fintech Economic Unsustainability Paradox, and social value as a principal element in their social performance. We contribute to the literature by presenting the Fintech Sustainability Model, a new framework that aggregates the above four aspects, which could be the issues that underpin policies towards Fintech long-term sustainability, and allow understanding of the analysis of double materiality, what it entails their competitiveness in comparison to the traditional financial industry.

Keywords Fintech · Sustainability · Economic value · Social value · Trust · Fintech economic unsustainability paradox · Business model · Finance

11.1 Introduction

The Fintech financial industry, such as it is known nowadays as part of the overall financial industry, is only fifteen years old; it was born as a consequence of the conjunction of two central elements: technology, which offered the possibility of

G. DelValle-Araluce · J. L. Retolaza
University of Deusto, Bilbao, Spain

L. San-Jose (✉)
University of the Basque Country UPV/EHU, Bilbao, Spain
e-mail: leire.sanjose@ehu.eus

© The Author(s), under exclusive license to Springer Nature Singapore Pte Ltd. 2024
M. Kooskora and A. Kekkonen (eds.), *Performance Challenges in Organizational Sustainability*, Responsible Leadership and Sustainable Management,
https://doi.org/10.1007/978-981-97-5548-6_11

doing the same things in a different and easier way; and the loss of trust (Cojoianu et al., 2021) in traditional industry after the financial crisis, which provided the opportunity to its birth. Accordingly, the 2008 financial crisis, as an example of a breakdown of trust, became the opportunity for that kind of technological newcomers, which began to erode the more traditional activities conducted by banks. Thus, by the middle of the second decade of the twenty-first century the term "Fintech" became widespread in the market as the union of the prior concepts, "finance" and "technology"; this was reflected in the academic literature, which began to pay increasing attention to Fintech research from 2015 onwards (Sun et al., 2023).

But Fintech could not have disrupted the traditional industry without the breadth of technologies and their deep relationship with more than twenty-five innovations that have subsequently emerged (i.e., crowdfunding, peer-to-peer (P2P) lending, foreign exchange applications, personal financial management, block chain, Initial Coin Offerings—ICOs, cryptocurrencies, smart contracts, robot-advisory, etc.) (Gomber et al., 2018).

So far, by navigating in a protected regulatory environment (Fung et al., 2020; Ozili, 2018), they have disrupted the main pieces of it, i.e., business models, products and services, processes, and functionalities (Gomber et al., 2018; Gozman et al., 2018). In doing that disruption, Fintech have tried to create a barrier to entry by differentiating themselves from traditional ways of doing business in the financial sector; but this has proved to be insufficient, as incumbents have reacted to gain access to innovations (Haddad & Hornuf, 2019; Palmie et al., 2020). And, in addition, performance remains one of the achievements to be fulfilled (Carbo-Valverde et al., 2022); the time needed to reach it represents a disadvantage for Fintech, but an opportunity for incumbents.

In short, if Fintech want to ensure their long-term competitiveness and sustainability, they will probably have to step up their value proposition. Only if they can demonstrate a differentially higher value for society as a whole will they be able to capture an increasing share of the market.

Therefore, considering the significant changes that future may bring in the Fintech industry, the aim of this paper is to identify the elements of so-called Financial Sustainability Model, and then, analyse not only economical business models, but also the potential social benefit or harm in terms of value generation and distribution for society as a whole, compared to traditional financial institutions. For doing that, through the deductive-synthetic methodology, an in-depth literature review identifies the elements which best represent the economic and social values added by Fintech.

11.2 Background

By following the main elements that make up the Fintech ecosystem (Gomber et al., 2018; World Bank and International Monetary Fund, 2018), the literature has built the architecture of this new industry around them. Ten general dimensions can be identified and, on a deeper level, at least twenty-eight sub-dimensions. The latter can be clustered into three high-level categories, which offer a first insight into the degree of development of the Fintech industry so far (Table 11.1). Firstly, aspects related to the early stages of the industry and closer to the world of entrepreneurship, such as technology, innovation, or management (Bollaert et al., 2021; Cojoianu et al., 2021; Chen et al., 2019; Gomber et al., 2018; Gozman et al., 2018; Haddad & Hornuf, 2019; Kolokas et al.; 2022; Lee & Shin, 2018; Palmie et al., 2020). Secondly, there are other sub-dimensions that deepen in the financial structural issues and, therefore, nearer to traditional financial industry (efficiency, risk, and regulatory items) (Arner et al., 2016; Carbo-Valverde et al., 2022; Fung et al., 2020; Li et al., 2020; Moretto et al., 2019; Ozili, 2018; World Bank and International Monetary Fund, 2018). And, finally, a third group of elements, most of them close to the social sphere, which need to be analyzed in greater depth; all of these have to do with value, both economic and social (Arner et al., 2020; Carbo-Valverde et al., 2022; Daud et al., 2022; Haddad & Hornuf, 2019; Lee & Shin, 2018; Moretto et al., 2019; Ozili, 2018; World Bank and International Monetary Fund, 2018).

In this context, sustainability represents one of the youngest topics studied in the literature; thus, within the scope of his study, Ellili (2023) finds that 80% of the research linking the fields of sustainability and Fintech has been published as of 2020. When analyzing the relationship between Fintech and sustainability, some authors connect sustainable development with the UN Sustainable Development Goals (SDGs); to achieve them, credit provision, among others, was identified as one of the key drivers (Arner et al., 2020).

However, others claim that the Fintech business model does not participate in the loan/borrowing intermediation business (Moro-Visconti et al., 2020). Finally, there are those who argue the negative correlation between ease of access to loans and Fintech (Haddad & Hornuf, 2019). This disparity can be understood under the major difference of two financial models, one related to peer-to-peer (P2P lending) in which Fintech only participates as a market connector between lenders and borrowers (Fig. 11.1), and the other in which traditional banking industry participates as a lender itself (Moro-Visconti et al., 2020).

A second line of research refers to the variety of sustainability features provided by Fintech (Chueca & Ferruz, 2021), which represent the building blocks of trust through the creation of social value (McKillop et al., 2020), and through the development of Sustainable Business Models (SBM) by means of digital processes and inclusive value creation (Sannino et al., 2020). Financial inclusion is probably the most relevant of those sustainability elements (Al-Okaily et al., 2021; Arner et al., 2020; Ellili, 2023; Lutfi et al., 2021).

Finally, some other lines have been researched, such as: the positive social impact of blockchain technology (Garg et al., 2021), the positive effect of Fintech technology on both the risk-adjusted return on capital (RAROC) and the amount of loans available for green projects (Mirza et al., 2023), the relationship between the sustainability profile of Fintech and their market value (Merello et al., 2022), and the significant bidirectional causal relationship between Fintech, Cleantech, and Green Economy (Metawa et al., 2022).

Table 11.1 Categories, dimensions, and sub-dimensions of fintech ecosystem

Dimension	Sub-dimension	Impact in literature		
		Fin	Tech	Soc
1 Technology	1.1 Underlying innovations	No influence	High	No influence
	1.2 Processes	No influence	High	No influence
	1.3 Effectiveness	High	High	No influence
2 Innovation	2.1 Business model—loans	Low	Low	Low
	2.2 Business model—rest	High	High	No influence
	2.3 Products and services	High	High	No influence
3 Entrepreneurship	3.1 Finance	High	No influence	No influence
	3.2 Management	High	No influence	No influence
4 Management	4.1 Competitiveness	High	No influence	No influence
	4.2 Opportunity	High	No influence	No influence
5 Finance	5.1 Incomes	Medium	No influence	No influence
	5.2 Efficiency	High	High	No influence
	5.3 Performance	Low	No influence	No influence
6 Risk	6.1 Financial risk	Medium	Medium	Medium
	6.2 Technological risk	No influence	High	High
7 Regulations	7.1 Credit regulations	Medium	No influence	Medium
	7.2 Compliance	Medium	Medium	Medium
8 Sustainability	8.1 Economic sustainability	Low	No influence	Low
	8.2 Social sustainability	Low	No influence	Low
9 Stakeholders	9.1 Shareholders	Medium	Medium	Medium
	9.2 Competitors	High	No influence	High
	9.3 Customers and suppliers	High	No influence	High
	9.4 Employees	No influence	No influence	Medium
	9.5 Institutions	No influence	No influence	Medium
	9.6 Society	No influence	No influence	Low
10 Institutions	10.1 Externalities	No influence	No influence	Low
	10.2 Costs of transaction	No influence	No influence	Low
	10.3 Economies of scale	No influence	No influence	Low

Source Own elaboration

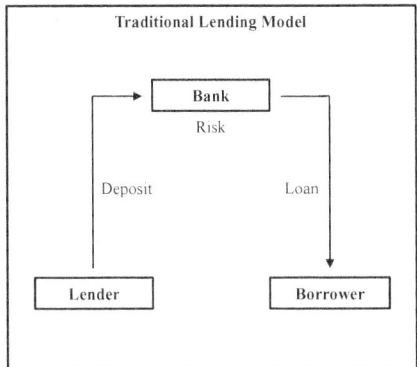 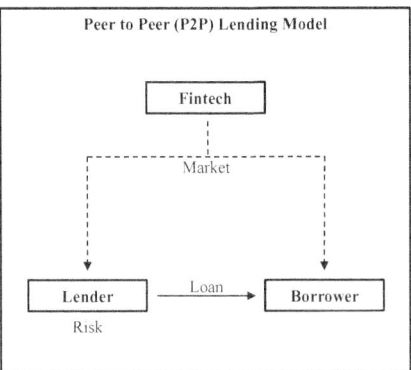

Fig. 11.1 Lending, comparison between traditional and peer to peer models. *Source* Own elaboration

But, despite these lines of research, the literature goes less deeply into the explanation of the features that can guarantee Fintech industry sustainability itself; therefore, it is necessary to understand whether there are elements that can definitively consolidate Fintech as a new differentiated and sustainable sector (Carbo-Valverde et al., 2022). These elements are connected to value creation, understanding it from both an economic and a social perspective.

From the point of economic value, it is not clear whether Fintech will ultimately be able to offer lending broadly, which is the real core of the financial business. This would require two nuclear capabilities, capital and risk management, the essence of the banking business, for which it is necessary to secure data and algorithms. And from the social value perspective, it will be necessary to review the impacts on its social efficiency (San-Jose et al., 2014), since the Fintech model generates both positive and negative externalities (Table 11.2) that modify the costs of transaction (Coase, 2013).

At the moment, the existence of Fintech depends both on two key elements: firstly, its ability to differentiate itself from the traditional financial industry by offering a significantly higher level of services (e.g., instant payments, lower costs, faster credit acquisition, wider access to personal financial management, multi-channel access to services, financial inclusion through the availability of finance to more segments of

Table 11.2 Externalities generated by Fintech industry

Externalities	
Positive	Negative
Customer convenience	Risk management
Financial inclusion	Legal considerations
Economic growth	Financial needs
Environment enhancement	Accounting issues

Source Own elaboration

customers, and so forth) (Gomber et al., 2018), although this may just be a temporary advantage, since the latter can easily adjust to the new landscape (Haddad & Hornuf, 2019; Palmie et al., 2020); and, secondly, the existence of a relaxed regulatory framework, which facilitates their activity in relation to the traditional financial industry (Fung et al., 2020; Ozili, 2018).

11.3 Objectives

The research seeks two main objectives:

1. To identify the elements that contribute to the long-term economic sustainability of Fintech as a differentiated sub-sector within the financial industry, with special attention to the role played by regulation and trust; to meet it, the variables involved in the different business models in relation to their competitiveness and sustainability under alternative regulatory scenarios are explored.
2. On the other hand, the social impact, positive or negative, that the modification in the generation and distribution of value may have on the stakeholders that make up the Fintech social ecosystem is analyzed.

With this proposal, the study of Fintech is approached from the perspective of a double materiality analysis in relation to the financial industry environment and the social reality in which they are embedded, trying to respond simultaneously to the impact of social stakeholders (regulators, competitors, public opinion, etc.) on the Fintech industry, and of the latter on society (competition, transaction costs related to clients, trust, etc.). In other words, the aim would be to simultaneously identify the economic and social value generated by this new sub-sector of the financial industry at the moment and what the displacement of this value might be in the future, if a possible change in the demand for trust were to lead to incremental or disruptive regulatory changes.

That purpose will be reflected on so-called Financial Sustainability Model that we will show in the next section, as a proposal that we have done to integrate both aspects, economic and social aspects that will converge on answering different questions:

- What is the economical business Fintech model that is sustainable on long-term?
- What is the key element that integrate economic and social aspects on Fintech industry?
- What is the contribution of institutions that is necessary for Fintech to be successful?
- What social impact should Fintech have?

11.4   Findings: The Fintech Sustainability Model (FSM)

At the beginning, Fintech industry was mainly seen as a direct competitor of the traditional industry, with basically the same financial business model, but with a big advantage over them: their capacity to offer a high-level customer experience (Gomber et al., 2018). However, in these moments, these advantages are slowly losing their attractiveness and differentiation, as the traditional industry is also developing them; so, the two industries might appear to be in a process of convergence towards the mainstream. In this context, this section reviews the main elements that make up the Fintech industry in comparison with the traditional one.

Fintech sustainability model, like that of the financial sector as a whole, is built on both economic and social value. Economic value represents the necessary condition for sustainability as any unprofitable business is not viable in the long run. Nevertheless, for the time being, the Fintech industry has to demonstrate its profitability (Carbo-Valverde et al., 2022) as a differentiated sub-sector within the overall financial industry. Several elements may explain this (Table 11.3). First, which business models are selected in each case to participate, as they condition the needs to be met by Fintech and, consequently, their cash flows. Second, the costs of running their business, which lead to the necessary capital to be raised; basically, in the early stages, these are concentrated in technology and human capital. Third, the youth of the company and the rate at which new customers are added, what is essential for securing incomes; this is where pricing policy becomes a key issue to address. Fourth, fairly close to the previous one, the background of the management team, as the balance between technological, financial, and managerial competences is useful. Finally, the competence scenario, where incumbents attitude represents the central barrier to overcome, which can be moderated by the intervention of the institutions and their regulations.

Table 11.3 Fintech, economic, and social value elements	*Economic value elements*
	Business Model selected
	Cost of running the business (capital)
	Age of the company
	Background of management team
	Competence scenario
	Social value elements
	Effectiveness in supply of products and services
	Efficiency in processes
	Financial inclusion
	Creation of added value
	Value distribution among stakeholders

Source Own elaboration

Once the economic aspects are secured, the social value represents the glue that can build the long-term sustainability of Fintech, becoming a competitive advantage, differential to that of the traditional industry. World Bank and International Monetary Fund (2018), in its Bali Fintech Agenda, cite some of the key social benefits that the emergence of Fintech can bring. This way, effectiveness in the supply of products and services and efficiency through the optimization of processes are two main elements for building customer confidence, both involve enhancing customer experience, the former by increasing convenience and the latter by reducing transaction costs. These are the foundations on which other social benefits have been built by Fintech over the years, such as financial inclusion (Al-Okaily et al., 2021; Arner et al., 2020; Ellili, 2023; Lutfi et al., 2021), creation of added value, and its distribution among their stakeholders. As a result, both economic and social value, integrated under a unique vision in a double materiality matrix (Fig. 11.2), can provide a global perspective on the market position and competitiveness of the Fintech industry relative to the traditional one.

Within the double materiality matrix, each Fintech is represented by a binomial point (Fintech$_{ij}$), whose horizontal component FT$_i$ is a function of the economic value elements and its vertical component FT$_j$ of the social value elements. Thus, the respective economic and social values of the total Fintech industry estimated from the aggregation of the unitary elements could be compared with their equivalents in the traditional financial industry.

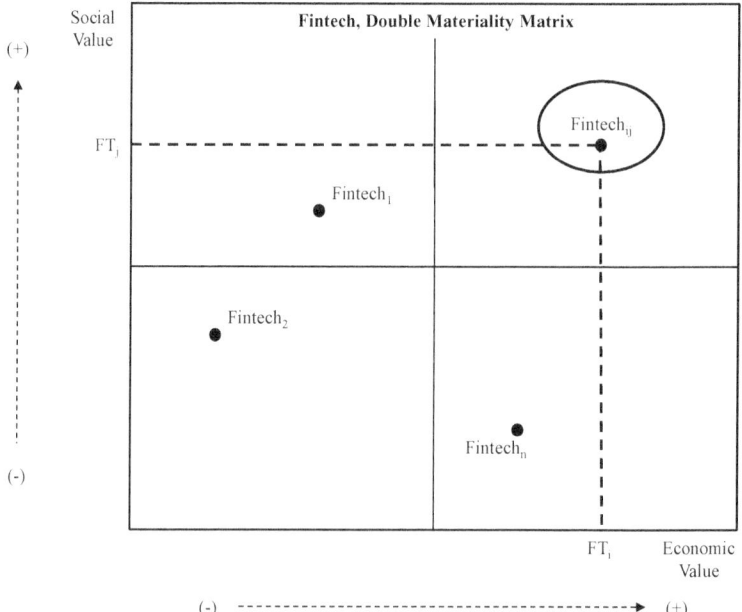

Fig. 11.2 Fintech, double materiality matrix. *Source* Own elaboration

11.4.1 Business Models Typologies

The Fintech revolution is about how traditional financial business models can be disrupted by technology. This is the lever that has powered the birth of more than twenty-five innovations (Gomber et al., 2018), most of them to enhance traditional business models and others to give rise to new ones. Nevertheless, it can be observed that these improvements are not always sufficient, since the feasibility of business models is dependent not only on technology, but also on their own structure and regulations. Hence, there is not a general consensus in the academia on the scope of business models that shape the Fintech industry.

Some business models are quite broadly considered, such as payments, lending, investment management services, financial markets (Chueca & Ferruz, 2021; Gomber et al., 2018; Lee & Shin, 2018; Moro-Visconti et al., 2020; Thakor, 2020), and crowdfunding (Chueca & Ferruz, 2021; Lee & Shin, 2018; Moro-Visconti et al., 2020; Thakor, 2020). However, others are recognized only in some cases, as deposits (Gomber et al., 2018; Thakor, 2020), and insurance services (Lee & Shin, 2018; Moro-Visconti et al., 2020; Thakor, 2020). And, finally, others appear less frequently, as clearing and settlement services (Thakor, 2020), digital currencies (Chueca & Ferruz, 2021; Thakor, 2020), automatic operations and P2P trading (Chueca & Ferruz, 2021; Gomber et al., 2018), and smartphone wallets (Chueca & Ferruz, 2021).

In this context, it is relevant to delimit which of the variety of above business models are to be considered, taking into account two criteria: cash flows, as a standard tool for measuring economic performance; and their relevance, in the sense of their universal acceptance by the global financial industry. Following them, five business models have been shortlisted:

11.4.1.1 Payment Services Business Model

This model (Gomber et al., 2018; Thakor, 2020) represents the first entry point for Fintech into the financial services industry; lower capital requirements, higher technological skills of the newcomers, and lower financial risks, made this world prone to early development. By simplifying processes to deliver excellent service, they meet two simultaneous objectives: the increase of customer experience and the reduction of costs. Three main customer segments can be identified, retail, enterprises, and corporates.

Improvements in credit card functionalities and instant payment technologies are two central innovations for all segments, but mainly for retail customers via mobile phones. In addition, Application Programming Interfaces (API) have become the most widespread technology in the business world, enabling the simplification of many business processes by connecting directly enterprises with their banks, thus facilitating near-instant cash management and consequently improving efficiency. And lastly, functionalities related to cross-border payments have allowed global corporations to settle positions around the world; in this respect, the latest advances in blockchain technology are shaping a much more secure future for transactions.

11.4.1.2 Deposits and Loans Business Model

This business model probably represents the main challenge for Fintech. Along with payments, deposit-taking and lending are the two core activities that have defined financial business since its origin in the early days. The objectives of risk control and financial stability guide the mindset of the regulatory institutions; for this reason, this business is subject to pre-approval by them. Thus, if improvement of the business model were necessary, it would have to be accompanied by changes in regulation. This is a path that the World Bank and International Monetary Fund (2018) are beginning to reflect in their Bali Fintech Agenda, as they consider the promotion of Fintech as a necessary tool to improve global sustainability; but, as of today, it is still a way to go, depending on a thorough prior analysis of the consequences in terms of risk and stability of the financial system.

Meanwhile, this characteristic of Fintech is so significant that there are those who claim, based on the analysis of their balance sheets, income and cash flow statements, that this is the main structural difference between Fintech and traditional financial industries (Moro-Visconti et al., 2020). Indeed, "the Fintech are technically not involved in the leading themselves" (Lee & Shin, 2018, p. 39), and, as a consequence, makes the decline of traditional financial industry's share of the deposit and lending business unlikely (Thakor, 2020). In this way, there are proposals to move along the lines of transforming the basis of the credit business from collateral property rights to a new system of cash flows founded on big data (Arner et al., 2020). As a consequence, this maybe the largest source of cash flow generation outside the Fintech sphere today, which could call into question its long-term economic sustainability; but, on the favourable side, this also implies that firms will not have to comply with capital requirements, thus softening costs.

In addition, the deposit side of this business model requires one of the most difficult intangible resources for Fintech to satisfy that is trust (Teece, 2014); despite the confidence they convey upfront, the time when customers put their money in other hands represents the highest level of trust they can offer. As a result, at present, operational accounts are basically only widely delivered as a means of facilitating the operation of payment services rather than as a deposit in their own right; and this is because of their proximity to the technological innovations that have been developed to improve them, mainly through digital channels.

And on the lending side, Fintech restrictions have given rise to the birth of a new financial service, P2P loan platforms (Gomber et al., 2018), which are substitutes but not part of the core business and, therefore, with a different level of cash flow generation. In this P2P model, the Fintech firm does not commit its balance sheet to the granting of the loan, but rather intermediates in the relationship between lender and borrower, as a third party in the transaction. Consequently, there is no risk to be covered by Fintech. Similarly, the segment to be served is narrower than in the traditional industry, typically reduced to customers with shorter-term financing needs.

In the end, the deposit and loan business model probably represents the main unresolved element of the fintech industry at the moment, all the more so as lending is at the very heart of the UN SDGs (Arner et al., 2020). But its resolution would imply the development of new ways of risk assessment.

11.4.1.3 Investment Management Business Model

The emergence of big data has changed the investment management value proposition scenario; technologies such as robo-advisory (Gomber et al., 2018) make it possible to centralize the Know Your Client (KYC) decisions and offer an individualized respond to client's portfolio needs, taking into account their financial behaviour and risk appetite. This innovation facilitates the offering of advanced investment services to ever-wider client segments, meeting multiple objectives: (i) the improvement of customer satisfaction and, consequently, loyalty; (ii) the advancement of financial inclusion, by incorporating new customers; (iii) the boosting of Fintech revenues; and (iv) the reduction of costs. On the other side, risks have to do with data confidentiality and the necessity of fraud avoidance.

Investment in markets has seen the appearance of technological innovations that have brought real-time trading closer, with instant brokerage services, or the emergence of cryptocurrencies and their connected innovations (e.g., digital wallets); all of which have opened up new lines of revenue and customer satisfaction. But, again, these are not risk-free innovations, what reinforces the need for control.

11.4.1.4 Financial Markets Business Model

Innovations in financial markets (Gomber et al., 2018) bring some services that could change the shape of this business model; thus, new self-executing smart contracts may reduce the costs of human mistakes by applying contractual conditions when triggers are activated; in contrast, new risks of misprogramming are emerging. In addition, some other innovations, such as cryptocurrency Initial Coin Offerings (ICOs), blockchain-based settlements, cross-border custody services, or risk and regulation management technologies are ready to change the near future of financial markets, both by adding new revenue streams and by increasing customer satisfaction.

11.4.1.5 Insurance Services Business Model

The model that has been the most recently impacted by innovations is the insurance services one. The use of bigdata may conform new ways of efficiency by applying personal conditions to each customer on the basis of their particular background; this would benefit both the customer and the firm. Nonetheless, relevant risks emerge from data management that need to be secured.

11.4.2   Trust as a Mediator of Economic and Social Values

On the path to building sustainability, Trust (McKillop et al., 2020; Merello et al., 2022; Sannino et al., 2020) represents a significant mediator of Economic and Social Values. This is the central element that explains the arise of Fintech as a new industry (Cojoianu et al., 2021) and may become the differential that allows for its long-term consolidation. But trust-building is a slow process. Even in the hardest times of financial crisis, the lack of confidence in the traditional industry did not suddenly lead customers to Fintech in multitudes; by the contrary, at the beginning, only some segments of customers, mainly young and tech-savvy ones, stood out from the traditional companies as early adopters of Fintech; and it is not coincidence that the first services provided were those related to payments, where excellence in service did not require large risk assumptions by them. It was only when this stage was consolidated that an increasing number of customers from all segments started to switch to the new entrants; this was the time for credit provision, where P2P model (Lee & Shin, 2018) began to spread among customers. Nonetheless, the authentic benchmark of trust does not really occur until customers accept the risk of making deposits at the Fintech companies with their own money; but as it will see below, that is what it is all about at the moment.

All in all, trust becomes a key element in the construction of Fintech sustainability; the other has to do with the moderation of institutions, which could play a critical role in the future evolution of this industry.

11.4.3   Institutions and the Fintech Economic
Unsustainability Paradox (FEU Paradox)

The Fintech financial industry has founded its quick development by navigating a protected regulatory environment (Fung et al., 2020; Ozili, 2018). This framework is directly linked to the role that institutions play in the banking industry, which could not be understood without the set of regulations, norms, and conventions that governs their conduct.

Throughout these first decades of the century, Institutional Theory has converged with Entrepreneurship Theory (and, therefore, with Fintech, as a part of it). Thus, Scott's (2008) first definition of the three pillars (cultural-cognitive, normative, and regulative elements) of Institutional Theory, was accepted as a standard theoretical framework in entrepreneurial research (Su et al., 2017). It was followed by (i) the definition of legitimacy as a key resource and entrepreneurship as an institution builder (Bruton et al., 2010), (ii) the coining of social entrepreneurship (Stephan et al., 2015) and the factors that promote it (government, post-materialism, and cooperative cultural norms), (iii) the identification of a research gap in industrial level (e.g., Fintech) (Su et al., 2017), and (iv) the final finding of the positive impact of institutions on both economic and social performance (Ferreira et al., 2023).

In this context a paradox arises in the financial industry, given that it is a particularly regulated sector, within which Fintech are an exception (Fung et al., 2020; Ozili, 2018). On the one hand, if they continue to enjoy the beneficial exception, they will find it difficult to access the core of the financial business model, i.e., lending. But on the other hand, if the exception disappears, they will need access to critical resources that are hard to come by: capital (funding), and data and algorithms for risk (knowledge). In conclusion, in both cases cash flows are not sufficiently ensured, making it difficult to guarantee its long-term economic value and, consequently, sustainability. As a result, Proposition 1 summarizes this paradox in its statement, bringing a new contribution to the literature.

Proposition 1. The Fintech Economic Unsustainability Paradox (FEU Paradox)

> The establishment of beneficial contextual regulatory environments that seek to protect the consolidation of the Fintech industry may result in the paradox of preventing its long-term sustainability.

There are some external indicators that point in this direction; e.g., the growing number of Fintech that are concentrating their activity towards business to business (B2B) model, by focusing on offering services to the main financial companies, overcoming the business to consumer (B2C) model, which was the first trend in the early years of Fintech disruption. This kind of activities allows them to avoid the high costs of raising new capital, since their needs are significantly lower than those of undertaking financial positions on their balance sheets. As a consequence, there are signs that Fintech industry could be forking in two main streams, the initial one offering B2C services and the more recent B2B (Bittini et al., 2022).

Institutions have much to say in building the future of this industry; as a major player in the Fintech ecosystem, they moderate both the relationships between the main business models identified and Economic Sustainability, and between social benefits and Social Sustainability.

11.4.4   Social Benefits, Key Elements in Fintech Competitiveness

The above considerations highlight the fact that the Fintech industry is evolving towards new paths of addressing its sustainability. In this context, the current global trend in the improvement of social value provides areas of opportunity. Thus, there are two features that will condition the consolidation of Fintech as a new differentiated and sustainable industry in the long run without the risk of being reabsorbed by the traditional financial industry. On the favourable side, confidence in Fintech as a powerful resource. Thus, Cojoianu et al. (2021) find explanations for the emergence of the Fintech industry both in the erosion of trust in the incumbent financial sector and in the importance of contextual social norms. However, on the opposite side, its weakness in creating economic value is also noted, as the previous FEU Paradox concludes. In this framework, it is argued that the long-term sustainability of Fintech depends on its capability to create differential social value. Thus, a new contribution to the literature refers to the ability of Fintech to increase their social value contribution, and consequently their trust, as Proposition 2 states.

Proposition 2. Trust and Social Value, Two Key Elements of Fintech Competitiveness

In a context of lack of confidence in the traditional financial industry, Fintech have the opportunity to develop a sustainable competitive advantage by exploiting their trust resources and differential capabilities to create significantly greater social value than incumbents.

Trust building has been evolving throughout the life of Fintech industry since its emergence. In the early stages, it was more of a reaction against the traditional financial industry due to the 2008 global financial crisis (Cojoianu et al., 2021) than confidence on the new actors themselves (see Vasquez & San-Jose, 2022) about the trust need of Fintech based on reputation, risk, price, and regulation).

With the aim to increase the confidence, highlighting the social benefits is useful; thus, two main social benefits are expected from the Fintech proposal. On the one hand, the increase of customer convenience; one cannot understand the quick advance of Fintech in the early years after the financial crisis without first displaying the importance of the *customer centric* culture which began to be widely spread in those days. As proposed by Fintech, the customer became the centre of the financial relationship, and any aspect that might prevent this vision was a point for improvement; hence, technology turned out the tool that could fulfil the experience of clients. And, on the other hand, the reduction of costs of transaction (Coase, 2013); again, technology was revealed as a solution, since it could do the same things at a significantly lower cost, allowing the reduction, or even elimination, of many costs that had been heretofore supported by customers. An important means to achieve these reductions had to do with the multi-channel possibilities offered by technology, enabling the replacement of traditional bank branches by new digital channels which were cheaper and more attractive to customers, especially but not only young people.

As a consequence of these two important advantages, the level of service perceived by customers grew exponentially, breaking down one of the main barriers to entry that the traditional financial industry had been building up by investing heavily over many years. This was the turning point that triggered the reaction of traditional incumbents (Haddad & Hornuf, 2019; Palmie et al., 2020); from that moment on, the race to satisfy customer trust by increasing their experience became a principal objective, not only for the Fintech industry but also for the traditional one. This might be understood as the main change in the culture of the financial sector resulting from the previous global financial crisis; but, at the same time, it was the point at which Fintech could begin to lose their incipient competitive advantage.

Historically, one of the primary functions of the financial industry has been the financing of economic growth; as a result, it is widely acknowledged as a major social benefit. However, if Fintech firms cannot access to provide it because of the current regulatory framework, they will not be able to finance either economic growth or another important sequence of SDGs goals, among which environment is listed as one important social benefit.

11.4.5   The Fintech Sustainability Model (FSM)

As seen, several structural differences can be found between traditional and Fintech industries. In order to explore them further, a new framework has been developed by the authors, the Fintech Sustainability Model (FSM) (see Fig. 11.3). It offers a way to identify the main elements involved in the long-term sustainable growth of the Fintech industry and therefore its theoretical future, either as a stand-alone industry within the financial landscape or as part of its value chain. This FSM framework is constituted by the four elements explained up to this point.

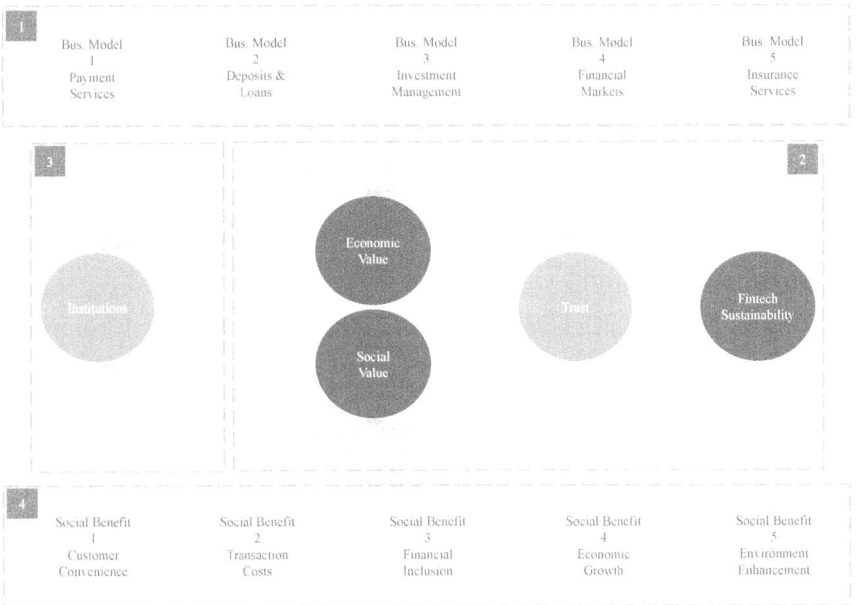

Fig. 11.3 The Fintech sustainability model (FSM). *Source* Own elaboration

11.5   Contributions

This study approaches a novel avenue for understanding the Fintech industry; thus, unlike previous research, where the focus was mainly on the benefits they bring to stakeholders and the means by which they do so, this one aims to understand which are the elements that may ensure its own long-term sustainability as a differentiated sub-sector within the overall financial industry. Understanding this issue is of major importance, since if the sector sustainability failed, relevant consequences in terms of value creation and its distribution among stakeholders could arise. In this context, the research contributes to the expansion of literature in a threefold aspect.

Firstly, by proposing a new FEU Paradox, which raises the difficulty of forecasting the economic evolution of Fintech, neither in the current relaxed regulatory framework they enjoy, nor in the general financial regulatory one; and this is due to the uncertain ability of Fintech to access all the business models offered by the financial industry, particularly the deposit/loan one, a real core of the business. The implications of this paradox are crucial, as its strict application could lead to the disappearance of the sub-sector as an independent industry in the long-term or its conversion into a niche within the overall value chain, thus losing their opportunity to offer financial universal business.

Secondly, in exploring the differential social value contribution that Fintech could offer, a new line of opportunity is opened up. To the extent that social value is a source of trust generation, in conjunction with economic value it could become a sufficient condition for the consolidation of Fintech. This means that the contribution of social value becomes a strategic objective in itself for the future of the sub-sector, beyond a simple secondary indicator, given that it may represent the differential element of competitiveness compared to the traditional financial industry.

And finally, as the search for the elements that ensure the sustainability of Fintech is deepening, a new conceptual framework comes to light. This one, entitled The Fintech Sustainability Model—FSM, is set out as the main contribution of this research. In it, four elements that facilitate the achievement of sustainable growth as the ultimate goal of Fintech are identified.

The general implications of this new model are quite remarkable; thus, FSM offers a roadmap for institutions in establishing the future regulatory framework, for entrepreneurs, providing them with basic guidelines that can support the success of their project, for consumers, who can assess and compare the different value propositions of each firm, and for investors, as a useful tool in their decision making.

All in all, this research offers a new perspective of Fintech industry; it comes to fill a gap in the literature concerning the future of an industry that has seen a rapid evolution in fifteen years from the exploitation of a historic opportunity, resulting from the conjunction of the financial crisis and the consequent loss of customer confidence in traditional institutions, the succession of technological innovations that have emerged in this short period of time, and the placing of the customer at the centre of the business. But this is a sector that is currently at a crossroads; once the incumbents are incorporating the new ways of doing business of Fintech, the space for the latter is shrinking and increasingly contingent on the decisions taken by the institutions regarding the future regulatory framework. In this context, FSM provides a useful framework for shaping the course of the industry in the near future.

11.6 Conclusions

Fintech have come a long way since their birth after 2008 crisis as a new sub-sector within the financial industry; to date, they have affected almost every point in the value chain, with a particular positive impact on customer convenience. Nonetheless, it is unclear whether they will be able to consolidate as a differentiated sector in the long run or will eventually be reabsorbed into the mainstream industry. Understanding this issue is of major importance, since if the latter happened, relevant consequences could arise in terms of value creation and its distribution among stakeholders. Thus, considering the significant changes that future may bring in the Fintech industry, this research seeks to identify sustainable business models over time, as well as to analyze the potential social benefit or harm in terms of value generation and distribution for society as a whole, compared to traditional financial institutions.

The study is approached from the perspective of a double materiality analysis in relation to the financial industry environment and the social reality in which they are embedded, trying to respond simultaneously to the impact of social stakeholders (regulators, competitors, public opinion, etc.) on the Fintech industry, and of the latter on society (competition, transaction costs related to clients, trust, etc.). In other words, the aim would be to simultaneously identify the economic and social value generated by this new sub-sector of the financial industry at the moment and what the displacement of this value might be in the future, if a possible change in the demand for trust were to lead to incremental or disruptive regulatory changes.

In line with the objectives, the study identifies the four elements that might ensure the long-term sustainability of Fintech (a core business with double materiality, a combination of Economic and Social Value benefits); Business Models, one of the main elements that have been disrupted by the Fintech innovations; Trust, which mediates the relationships of the latter; Institutions, the key that addresses the sector sustainability as a whole; and Social Benefits, as the opportunity for Fintech to consolidate their model. They are gathered under a new framework, the FSM, a useful tool for decision making and for shaping the course of the industry in the near future.

Some relevant lines of future research remain open: a confirmatory study of the principal outcomes found in this analysis; the paper of institutions in changing, or not, the current regulatory framework; the role played by each of the different stakeholders; a more in-depth study of the ways in which trust may conform the basis of sustainability; the function of loans in the construction of social benefits; the variables that define the double materiality matrix; or the impact of transaction costs on the efficiency compared between the two sub-sectors, traditional and Fintech.

References

Al-Okaily, M., Al Natour, A. R., Shishan, F., Al-Dmour, A., Alghazzawi, R., & Alsharairi, M. (2021). Sustainable Fintech innovation orientation: A moderated model. *Sustainability, 13*(24), 13591. https://doi.org/10.3390/su132413591

Arner, D. W., Barberis, J., & Buckley, R. P. (2016). Fintech, RegTech, and the reconceptualization of financial regulation. *Northwester Journal of International Law & Business, 37*(3), 371–415.

Arner, D. W., Buckley, R. P., Zetzsche, D. A., & Veidt, R. (2020). Sustainability, Fintech and financial inclusion. *European Business Organization Law Review, 21*(1), 7–35. https://doi.org/10.1007/s40804-020-00183-y

Bittini, J. S., Rambaud, S. C., López, J., & Moro-Visconti, R. (2022). Business models and sustainability plans in the Fintech, InsurTech, and PropTech industry: Evidence from Spain. *Sustainability, 14*(19), 12088. https://doi.org/10.3390/su141912088

Bollaert, H., Lopez-de-Silanes, F., & Schwienbacher, A. (2021). Fintech and access to finance. *Journal of Corporate Finance, 68*(June), 101941. https://doi.org/10.1016/j.jcorpfin.2021.101941

Bruton, G. D., Ahlstrom, D., & Li, H. (2010). Institutional theory and entrepreneurship: Where are we now and where do we need to move in the future? *Entrepreneurship Theory and Practice, 34*(3), 421–440. https://doi.org/10.1111/j.1540-6520.2010.00390.x

Carbo-Valverde, S., Cuadros-Solas, P. J., & Rodriguez-Fernandez, F. (2022). Entrepreneurial, institutional and financial strategies for Fintech profitability. *Financial Innovation, 8*(15), 2–36. https://doi.org/10.1186/s40854-021-00325-2

Chen, M. A., Wu, Q., & Yang, B. (2019). How valuable is Fintech innovation? *Review of Financial Studies, 32*(5), 2062–2106. https://doi.org/10.1093/rfs/hhy130

Chueca Vergara, C., & Ferruz Agudo, L. (2021). Fintech and sustainability: Do they affect each other? *Sustainability, 13*(13), 7012. https://doi.org/10.3390/su13137012

Coase, R. H. (2013). The problem of social cost. *The Journal of Law and Economics, 56*(4), 837–877.

Cojoianu, T. F., Clark, G. L., Hoepner, A. G. F., Pazitka, V., & Wojcik, D. (2021). Fin vs. tech: Are trust and knowledge creation key ingredients in Fintech start-up emergence and financing? *Small Business Economics, 57*(4), 1715–1731. https://doi.org/10.1007/s11187-020-00367-3

Daud, S. N. M., Ahmad, A. H., Khalid, A., & Azman-Saini, W. N. W. (2022). Fintech and financial stability: Threat or opportunity? *Finance Research Letters, 47*, 102667. https://doi.org/10.1016/j.frl.2021.102667

Ellili, N. O. D. (2023). Is there any association between Fintech and sustainability? Evidence from bibliometric review and content analysis. *Journal of Financial Services Marketing* (forthcoming). https://doi.org/10.1057/s41264-022-00205-5,10.1057/s41264-022-00200-w

Ferreira, J. J., Fernandes, C. I., Veiga, P. M., & Gerschewski, S. (2023). Interlinking institutions, entrepreneurship and economic performance. *International Journal of Entrepreneurial Behaviour & Research, Forthcoming.* https://doi.org/10.1108/IJEBR-07-2022-0640

Fung, D. W. H., Lee, W. Y., Yeh, J. J. H., & Yuen, F. L. (2020). Friend or foe: The divergent effects of Fintech on financial stability. *Emerging Markets Review, 45*, 100727. https://doi.org/10.1016/j.ememar.2020.100727

Garg, P., Gupta, B., Chauhan, A. K., Sivarajah, U., Gupta, S., & Modgil, S. (2021). Measuring the perceived benefits of implementing blockchain technology in the banking sector. *Technological Forecasting and Social Change, 163*, 120407. https://doi.org/10.1016/j.techfore.2020.120407

Gomber, P., Kauffman, R. J., Parker, C., & Weber, B. W. (2018). On the Fintech revolution: Interpreting the forces of innovation, disruption, and transformation in financial services. *Journal of Management Information Systems, 35*(1), 220–265. https://doi.org/10.1080/07421222.2018.1440766

Gozman, D., Liebenau, J., & Mangan, J. (2018). The innovation mechanisms of Fintech start-ups: Insights from SWIFT's innotribe competition. *Journal of Management Information Systems, 35*(1), 145–179. https://doi.org/10.1080/07421222.2018.1440768

Haddad, C., & Hornuf, L. (2019). The emergence of the global Fintech market: Economic and technological determinants. *Small Business Economics, 53*(1), 81–105. https://doi.org/10.1007/s11187-018-9991-x

Kolokas, D., Vanacker, T., Veredas, D., & Zahra, S. A. (2022). Venture capital, credit, and fintech start-up formation: A cross-country study. *Entrepreneurship Theory and Practice, 46*(5), 1198–1230. https://doi.org/10.1177/1042258720972652

Lee, I., & Shin, Y. J. (2018). Fintech: Ecosystem, business models, investment decisions, and challenges. *Business Horizons, 61*(1), 35–46. https://doi.org/10.1016/j.bushor.2017.09.003

Li, J., Li, J., Zhu, X., Yao, Y., & Casu, B. (2020). Risk spillovers between Fintech and traditional financial institutions: Evidence from the U.S. *International Review of Financial Analysis, 71*, 101544. https://doi.org/10.1016/j.irfa.2020.101544

Lutfi, A., Al-Okaily, M., Alshirah, M. H., Alshira'h, A. F., Abutaber, T. A., & Almarashdah, M. A. (2021). Digital financial inclusion sustainability in Jordanian context. *Sustainability, 13*(11), 6312. https://doi.org/10.3390/su13116312

McKillop, D., French, D., Quinn, B., Sobiech, A. L., & Wilson, J. O. S. (2020). Cooperative financial institutions: A review of the literature. *International Review of Financial Analysis, 71*, 101520. https://doi.org/10.1016/j.irfa.2020.101520

Merello, P., Barbera, A., & De la Poza, E. (2022). Is the sustainability profile of Fintech companies a key driver of their value? *Technological Forecasting and Social Change, 174*(January), 121290. https://doi.org/10.1016/j.techfore.2021.121290

Metawa, N., Dogan, E., & Taskin, D. (2022). Analysing the nexus of green economy, clean and financial technology. *Economic Analysis and Policy, 76*(December), 385–396. https://doi.org/10.1016/j.eap.2022.08.023

Mirza, N., Umar, M., Afzal, A., & Firdousi, S. F. (2023). The role of Fintech in promoting green finance, and profitability: Evidence from the banking sector in the euro zone. *Economic Analysis and Policy, 78*(June), 33–40. https://doi.org/10.1016/j.eap.2023.02.001

Moretto, A., Grassi, L., Caniato, F., Giorgino, M., & Ronchi, S. (2019). Supply chain finance: From traditional to supply chain credit rating. *Journal of Purchasing and Supply Management, 25*(2), 197–217. https://doi.org/10.1016/j.pursup.2018.06.004

Moro-Visconti, R., Cruz Rambaud, S., & Lopez Pascual, J. (2020). Sustainability in Fintechs: An explanation through business model scalability and market valuation. *Sustainability, 12*(24), 10316. https://doi.org/10.3390/su122410316

Ozili, P. K. (2018). Impact of digital finance on financial inclusion and stability. *Borsa Istanbul Review, 18*(4), 329–340. https://doi.org/10.1016/j.bir.2017.12.003

Palmie, M., Wincent, J., Parida, V., & Caglar, U. (2020). The evolution of the financial technology ecosystem: An introduction and agenda for future research on disruptive innovations in ecosystems. *Technological Forecasting and Social Change, 151*(February), 119779. https://doi.org/10.1016/j.techfore.2019.119779

Sannino, G., Di Carlo, F., & Lucchese, M. (2020). CEO characteristics and sustainability business model in financial technologies firms: Primary evidence from the utilization of innovative platforms. *Management Decision, 58*(8), 1779–1799. https://doi.org/10.1108/MD-10-2019-1360

San-Jose, L., Luis Retolaza, J., & Torres Prunonosa, J. (2014). Efficiency in Spanish banking: A multistakeholder approach analysis. *Journal of International Financial Markets Institutions & Money, 32*(September), 240–255. https://doi.org/10.1016/j.intfin.2014.06.005

Scott, W. R. (2008). *Institutions and organizations: Ideas and interests*. Sage.

Stephan, U., Uhlaner, L. M., & Stride, C. (2015). Institutions and social entrepreneurship: The role of institutional voids, institutional support, and institutional configurations. *Journal of International Business Studies, 46*(3), 308–331. https://doi.org/10.1057/jibs.2014.38

Su, J., Zhai, Q., & Karlsson, T. (2017). Beyond red tape and fools: Institutional theory in entrepreneurship research, 1992–2014. *Entrepreneurship Theory and Practice, 41*(4), 505–531. https://doi.org/10.1111/etap.12218

Sun, Y., Li, S., & Wang, R. (2023). Fintech: From budding to explosion, an overview of the current state of research. *Review of Managerial Science, 17*(April), 715–755. https://doi.org/10.1007/s11846-021-00513-5

Teece, D. J. (2014). The foundations of enterprise performance: Dynamic and ordinary capabilities in an (economic) theory of firms. *Academy of Management Perspectives, 28*(4), 328–352. https://doi.org/10.5465/amp.2013.0116

Thakor, A. V. (2020). Fintech and banking: What do we know? *Journal of Financial Intermediation, 41*(January), 100833. https://doi.org/10.1016/j.jfi.2019.100833

Vasquez, O., & San-Jose, L. (2022). Ethics in Fintech through users' confidence: Determinants that affect trust. *Ramon Llull Journal of Applied Ethics*, 1(13), 1–51. https://doi.org/10.34810/rljaev1n13Id398681

World Bank and the International Monetary Fund. (2018). *The Bali Fintech agenda*. Chapeau paper.

Germán DelValle-Araluce is expert in banking; after thirty-five years as professional at BBVA, a leading European bank, he is currently researching the relationship between traditional financial industry and fintechs as a PhD student at Deusto Business School. From his executive positions in retail banking related to resources, commercial and small company businesses, and as member of the boards of directors of Norpension, entity which manages Basque pension plans, and BBVA Depositary Bank, he has contributed to the processes that have shaped the current state of the art of the industry, particularly after the global financial crisis: recovery of customer confidence, technological implications, industry concentration, and regulatory framework. Currently, he contributes to social value building as a member of both The Club of Rome and SECOT, the former a worldwide volunteer organization focused on facing society and planet emergencies, and the latter a member of the CESES confederation, with over 25,000 senior volunteers in the EU.

Jose Luis Retolaza is an Associate Professor at Deusto Business School and Director of AURKILAN Institute for Business Ethics Research in Bilbao (Spain); also, he is a Visiting Scholar at Darden Business School in United States during the second term of 2015. Jose Luis is the Scientific Director of Global Economic Accounting (GEAccounting) company wich aim is to monetize the social value of organizations (social accounting) and integrate in the strategy of companies (https://www.geaccounting.org/). The current research focuses on Stakeholder Theory, Social Value and Social Efficiency in the financial entities. He is a member of ECRI (Ethics in Finance & Social Value) research group and HUME. He is author of several publications in scientific journals national and international, and he has participated in numerous national and international conferences. He acts as reviewer member of ranked journals (Business & Society, CIRIEC, INNOVAR, Society for Business Ethics or Contemporary Economics).

Leire San-Jose is currently Full Professor at the University of the Basque Country (UPV/EHU) in Bilbao (Spain). She is the leader of ECRI, a research group on Ethics in Finance and Social Value (https://www.ehu.eus/en/web/ecri). Previously, she was a Visiting Research Fellow at Huddersfield Business School (UK) (2009–2022), as well as a visiting professor at Loyola University Chicago and at Darden Business School. Her most important publications are about ethics in finance, social value, impact, social efficiency and stakeholder theory. She has published in impact journals such as Journal of Business Ethics, Sustainability, European Management Journal, Corporate Social Responsibility and Environmental Management and CIRIEC. She organized EBEN-Spain conference in 2010 and ISBEE in 2022 held in Bilbao.

Chapter 12
The Role of Socially Responsible Human Resource Management in Employee Voice Enhancement and Diminishing Silence: Bibliometric Analysis and Systematic Literature Review

Laima Jeseviciute-Ufartiene● and **Hava Yasin**●

Abstract The globe faces human capital deterioration, climate change, poverty, and inequality. The principal vision of the United Nations (UN) is to transform the world through sustainable development. Human capital is one of the significant affectees and the most essential component of the sustainable development goals (SDGs) of the organization of economic cooperation and development. Human capital management concerning corporate social responsibility (CSR) covers the social aspects of sustainability. The focus of this study is to explore and review the role of socially responsible human resource management (SRHRM) for employee well-being, specifically in the context of employee voice enhancement strategies and catering to employee silence. The research trends regarding focus on employee voice in the area of SRHRM are determined through bibliometric analysis, applying R-Tool, and systematic literature review using PRISMA methodology. The research results indicate how the emergence of sustainable human resource management (HRM) has enhanced the well-being of employees in the context of encouraging the voice of the employee, who is the most important internal stakeholder of organizations. It also entails providing productive employment opportunities and investment and development of Human capital. Findings fill the research gaps, identifying where HRM practitioners, policymakers, and researchers need to focus in the future. Additionally, this study sheds light on the methodologies and theories used to explain the employee voice phenomenon in previous studies.

Keywords Employee voice · Employee silence · Responsible HRM · Social responsibility · Sustainability

L. Jeseviciute-Ufartiene · H. Yasin (✉)
Vilnius Gediminas Technical University, Vilnius, Lithuania
e-mail: hava.yasin@vilniustech.lt

L. Jeseviciute-Ufartiene
e-mail: Laima.jeseviciute-ufartiene@vilniustech.lt

12.1 Introduction

Global instability is worsened by COVID-19 and Russia's invasion of Ukraine (OECD, 2022). Those events transformed business operations across the globe, and now economies are facing many challenges in finding ways to cope with the challenges. Organizations are also figuring out how to adapt to the numerous changes and challenges both crises provide as economies worldwide struggle to respond to the twin crises of a worldwide pandemic and climate change (Paulet et al., 2021). The globe faces human capital deterioration, climate change, poverty, and inequality. Nevertheless, to protect the environment and the lives of humans, natural assets and civilization must operate sensibly and sustainably (Obaideen et al., 2022). The major vision of the United Nations (UN) is to transform the world through sustainable development. To effectively accomplish the main goal of sustainability, the United Nations established an action plan that included a set of 17 Sustainable Development Goals (SDGs) that must be fulfilled by 2030 (United Nations, n.d).

According to The United Nations' 2030 Agenda for Sustainable Development, which has 17 SDGs and 169 targets, the EU is committed to contributing actively to maximizing progress towards the SDGs (The EU Budget, 2023). Businesses are thus urged to be sustainable, which entails considering stakeholder requirements and contributing to the development of a more resilient society (Ozeliene, 2018, as cited in Skačkauskienė, 2022). The EU made considerable strides over the last five years to guarantee decent work and economic expansion—sustainable development goal # 8 (SDG-8) (Eurostat, 2023). SDG goal # 8 involves ensuring the right, promote, and secure environment for employees. Moreover, it also entails providing productive employment opportunities and investment and development of Human capital.

Human capital is one of the major affecters of these serious underlying tensions. Hence, the sustainability of human capital has been one of the important components of the sustainable development goals (SDGs) of the organization of economic cooperation and development (OECD, 2022). Such a strategy pushes organizations to widen their focus beyond only economic objectives and goals and incorporate environmental and social aspects as well (Paulet et al., 2021).

Responding to the present situation, an increasing number of industries and organizations declare that they are dedicated to sustainability, an interdisciplinary notion that includes ecological, social, and financial challenges, including both internal and external aspects. (Sánchez-Hernández et al., 2016). Although sustainable management entails the use of internal as well as external policies that help foster a more sustainable future, the majority of sustainable strategies and initiatives are solely directed at external target groups (Sánchez-Hernández et al., 2021). Nevertheless, a prevalent assumption in academics is that sustainable development can only be realized by balancing focus across three related elements that are social, organizational in nature, and the person in question (Sánchez-Hernández et al., 2021).

A rising topic referred to as sustainable HRM offers a means for HRM to aid an organization's transition to a wider focus and longer-term perspective (Kramar, 2021). Hence sustainable HRM is a way ahead of traditional HRM that majorly focuses on the financial goals of the organization whereas sustainable HRM emphasizes both economic objectives as well as social and environmental objectives.

12.2   Objectives

The major focus of this study is to explore and review the role of SRHRM for employee well-being specifically in the context of employee voice enhancement strategies and catering to employee silence. In particular, investigation of SRHRM's role in enhancing employee well-being in the context of employees' voice (EV) and employees' silence (ES). This is closely related to sustainable development goals (SDG)—8 (decent work and economic growth) and SDG—16.6 as well which refers to the right of freedom of expression and assurance that decision-making is receptive, across the board, interactive, and representative on every level (United Nations, 2023). In addition to a systematic review of the role of SRHRM for ES and EV, this study will also highlight the theories and methodologies that have been adopted to study this stream of research.

12.3   Research Background

There is a widely recognized area of study that is corporate social responsibility (CSR) (Aguinis & Glavas, 2012) that covers the social aspects of sustainability. CSR is defined as "context-specific organizational actions and policies that take into account stakeholders' expectations and the triple bottom line of economic, social, and environmental performance" (Aguinis, 2011 as cited in Paulet et al., 2021). CSR aimed at employees evolved from the term SRHRM to encompass CSR guidelines and procedures focused on stakeholders of the company (Chen et al., 2023).

However, many organizations have faced significant obstacles when it comes to the strategic development of CSR priorities and their integration into routine managerial procedures (Omidi & Dal Zotto, 2022). Organizations emphasized the importance of HRM as a response to this challenge (Jamali et al., 2014). To incorporate CSR, HRM must create policies and procedures that promote organizational CSR strategy and help businesses achieve their triple bottom-line goals (Podgorodnichenko et al., 2022). One of the primary duties that an organization must carry out is to consider its employees as one of its key stakeholders, expressing its relationship with them in more ways than just allocating resources to achieve maximum performance (Lu et al., 2019). In a bilateral interaction, the European Commission also emphasized the importance of employees being informed and consulted, as well as participating more actively in all aspects of the company (Bastian & Poussing, 2023). They further argued that therefore, although employees have generally been the favoured counterparts of businesses, the implementation of CSR should likewise prioritize employees (Bastian & Poussing, 2023).

A socially responsible HR management (SRHRM) strategy may therefore be implemented by the organization in response to worker interests (Santana et al., 2020). SRHRM can be explained as "encompasses those policies and practices that contribute to improving the work and quality of life of employees, following the principles of CSR" (López-Fernández et al., 2018). Evaluating the impacts of such corporate social responsibility (CSR) procedures on employees covered the major part of the research that examines the connection between CSR and HRM (Santana et al., 2020).

Rayner and Morgan (2017) illustrated that to date, debates on sustainable HRM have mainly neglected the significance of the employee as a stakeholder to adopt a more macro-level perspective. Moreover, Paulet et al. (2021) argued that an important element, employee voice is largely missing in the sustainable HRM debate. They further asserted that the creation of employee voice tools is essential to the execution and upkeep of sustainable HRM. Furthermore, Omidi and Dal Zotto (2022) pointed out that the employee who is the most important internal stakeholder is largely ignored in CSR literature. Podgorodnichenko et al. (2022) placed a major emphasis on employee involvement to achieve CSR goals because it constitutes one of the key outputs of a well-built sustainable HRM framework, which leads to other significant organizational and individual-level results.

The absence of employee voice can do more than harm that can be imagined for organizations. For instance, corporate scandals like the "death cabinet" at IKEA frequently occur, which not only harms the firm and society greatly but also casts doubt on the organization's corporate ethics and creates a crisis of trust in society (Zhao et al., 2023). Thus, employee silence is harmful in several ways it creates hurdles in developing meaningful CSR-related strategies in the organizations, and hinders organizational output and prestige. Such lack of timely employee voice about problems in routine matters at organizations like IKEA (harmful cabinet issue), Volkswagen (emissions scandal), and General Motors (ignition avoidance) have put many organizations' financial stability, reputation, reliability, and security of people and society at stake.

As literature shows SRHRM literature has focused on employees majorly but employee voice is still lacking in sustainable HRM literature. The present study is an effort to show the holistic picture of what role SRHRM has played in employee voice enhancement or in tackling employee silence during the last ten years. Considering employee voice's vital role in incorporating CSR strategies into business models and in timely pointing out problems in ongoing routine matters of organizations, it is indispensable to shed light on what has already been done in this domain and to know what more needs to be done. Holland et al. (2019) also have highlighted that over the next few years, advances in employee voice in Europe will be something to keep a careful eye on. Therefore, the bibliometric analysis is conducted to determine the research trends in the SRHRM domain in the context of employee voice and a systematic literature review is developed to know what role socially responsible HRM has played in the enhancement of employee voice and to combat or manage employee silence.

12.4   Methodology

The research trends regarding focus on employee voice in the area of socially responsible human resource management combine two research methods:

(1) a systematic literature review (SLR) as a qualitative approach to determine the role of employee-focused CSR/SRHRM practices in enhancing voice and diminishing silence. The preferred reporting item for systematic reviews and meta-analysis (PRISMA) methodology approach was followed for the systematic review of studies as these guidelines have been extensively approved and adopted, and it was aimed to assist authors in preparing transparent explanations of their examinations (Trifu et al., 2022) (Fig. 12.1).

(2) a bibliometric analysis as a quantitative approach, applying R-Tool. R-Tool is used to construct and visualize bibliometric structures (Aria & Cuccurullo, 2017). The recent R-package is widely used in science and provides the most flexible environment for an open-source route to participation (Rodríguez-Soler et al., 2020). This method is used to analyze selected research by the PRISMA method objectively and reliably mapping information about the source, authors, and papers. This three-level analysis (Table 12.1) provides knowledge about the prevalence and relevance of the topic, main themes and tendencies in time, and collaboration of the authors and among countries on the topic.

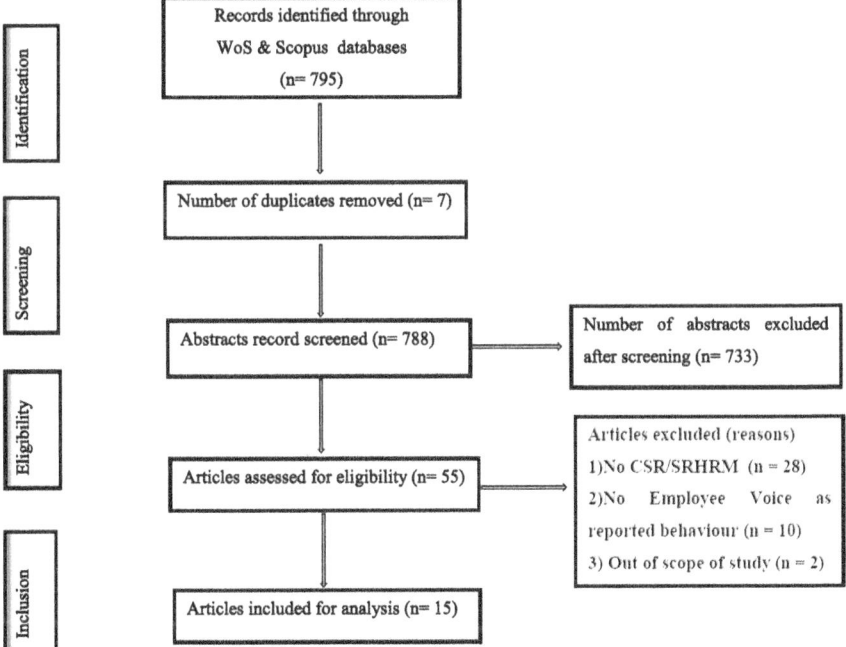

Fig. 12.1 PRISMA-based article selection (own compiled)

Table 12.1 Specifications of bibliometrics analyses (own compiled applying Aria and Cuccurullo (2017))

Level of analysis	Metrics	Unit of analysis	Bibliometric technique	Structural technique	Structure
Source	Source dynamics	Journal	Co-citation	Network	Conceptual
Authors	Authors' productivity, countries	Authors countries	Co-citation and collaboration	Network	Intellectual and social
Documents	Most frequent topics, keywords	Titles Keywords Abstracts	Collaboration co-words	Network thematic mapping	Intellectual conceptual

12.4.1 Inclusion and Exclusion Criteria Using PRISMA

At first, protocols were decided to conduct SLR for instance selection of databases for article search, duration of previous literature, inclusion and exclusion criteria were decided, etc. The major goal of the study was to conduct an SLR to know the impact of SRHRM on employee voice and silence. Articles were searched through Scopus and Web of Science (WoS) databases on the 6th of October, 2023. The combination of keywords that were used to search for articles at both of the databases (Scopus and Web of Science) were "ALL = ("Sustainability") OR ALL = ("Socially responsible human resource management") OR ALL = ("SRHRM") AND ALL = ("Employee voice") OR ALL = ("Employee silence")". Categories of fields that were selected for article search were Management, Business, and Industrial Relations Labor for both Web of Science and Business Management and Accounting and Social Sciences for the Scopus database. Moreover, only peer-reviewed articles were searched. English language was selected for both of the databases to search for relevant studies and articles published in the last decade (2013–2023) were considered. 407 articles from Scopus and 388 articles from WoS were found respectively (Fig. 12.1).

After the first automatic compilation on WoS and Scopus databases and the removal of duplicates (Fig. 12.1), the authors made the screening of titles and abstracts. In terms of exclusion criteria, all of those items were removed from consideration where voice or silence and CSR or SRHRM practices were not discussed. 55 full articles were read, assessed, and reasonably excluded (Fig. 12.1), and for final systematic review and bibliometrics analysis 15 articles have been selected.

Separate lists of WoS and Scopus lists were compiled for the application of data in a bibliometrics data frame as it is a technical requirement. The comparison of two databases was not the aim of this research, thus, the authors combined manually data using Scopus style as a main framework. The final analysis included 15 articles and the range of the year was from 2017 to 2023.

12.5   The Main Findings and Discussion

A full read of finally selected articles was analyzed by applying quantitative and qualitative approaches. In these sections, results are presented starting with bibliometrics analyses and finalizing with a systematic literature review. The first part of the analysis is dedicated to describing the prevalence of CSR and SRHRM regarding employees' voice or silence; to show the tendencies of research on the topics and relations among scientists around the world. The second part is deepening knowledge of CSR and SRHRM regarding employees' voice or silence, enclosing the research gaps, and determining demand for future research.

12.5.1   Findings and Discussion of Bibliometrics Analysis

Prepared bibliometrics analysis had an intention to perceive trends of topics and sources for CSR and SRHRM regarding employees' voice or silence analysis. Thus, only related to this topic articles were analyzed using bibliometrics tools. The main information about the analyzed documents is presented in Table 12.2. Specifically on the topic compiled documents formed a short list of relevant articles. Thus, only one period of time from 2017 to 2023 was used for data analysis. Among 15 analyzed documents we compiled relations among 38 scientists and 1207 their cited documents. Titles, keywords, and abstracts were analyzed by applying word and concept analysis.

12.5.1.1   Analysis of Sources

Analyzing the relevance of CSR and SRHRM regarding employees' voice or silence the most relevant source is "Journal of Business Ethics" because it had a 3 H impact size and 80 local citations in comparison with other journals (Fig. 12.2).

In Table 12.3 it could be seen the source dynamics. The amount of articles on the analyzed topic has been growing over the last two years in different journals 20.09 percent (Table 12.2). The most cited journal "Journal of Business Ethics" started to publish articles on the topic since 2020, while the "International Journal of Business Excellence" was publishing yearly the articles on analyzed topics since 2019. It shows that the topic is becoming more relevant than it was previously, bearing in mind that from 2013 to 2016 none of the topically relevant articles were identified at all.

Analyzing the co-citation network of sources (Fig. 12.3) three clusters identified with the most frequently published articles on SCR and SRHRM:

(1)   The first one related to psychological and sociological studies: "Journal of Business Ethics" and "Journal of Applied Psychology";

Table 12.2 Main bibliometrics information about analyzed documents (own using Biblioshiny)

Description	Results		
Main information about data			
Timespan	2017:2023		
Sources (Journals, Books, etc.)	13		
Documents	15	Article	14
		Book chapter	1
Annual growth rate, %	20,09		
Document average age	2,53		
Average citations per doc	16,13		
References	1207		
Document contents			
Keywords plus (ID)	46		
Author's keywords (DE)	72		
Authors	38		
Authors of single-authored docs	2		
Single-authored documents	3		
Co-Authors per document	2,93		
International co-authorships, %	26,67		

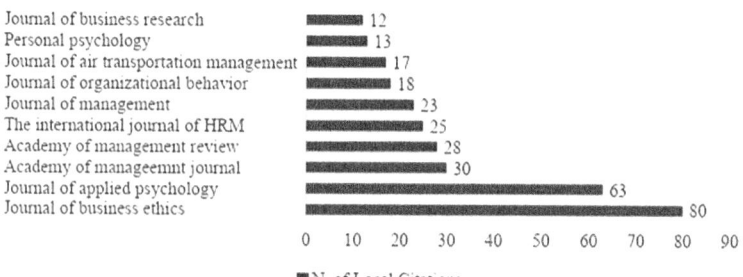

Fig. 12.2 Local citation index of analyzed TOP 10 sources (own compiled using Biblioshiny)

(2) The second one related to management studies: "Journal of Management" and "Academy of Management Review";

(3) The third one related to human resource management: "Journal of Organizational Behaviour" and "The International Journal of Human Resource Management".

We would like to note that relations among all three clusters exist. The journals of each cluster have citations among the other two clusters. Closer and bigger circles of sources in the figure indicate the closer relation and higher citation. Thus, in the analysis mentioned journals are the most relevant for the analyzed topic.

Table 12.3 DynamicsTOP 10 sources publishing articles on the relevant topic (compiled using Biblioshiny)

Year	2017	2018	2019	2020	2021	2022	2023
Journal of business ethics	0	0	0	1	1	1	3
Contemporary studies in economic and financial analysis	0	0	0	0	0	1	1
Corporate social responsibility and environmental management	0	0	0	0	0	1	1
Ethics and behaviour	0	0	0	0	0	0	1
Frontiers in psychology	0	0	0	0	1	1	1
International journal of business excellence	0	0	1	1	1	1	1
International journal of business innovation and research	0	1	1	1	1	1	1
International journal of business science and applied management	0	0	0	0	1	1	1
International journal of human resource management	0	1	1	1	1	1	1
Journal of air transport management	1	1	1	1	1	1	1
Management decision	0	1	1	1	1	1	1
Social responsibility journal	0	0	0	1	1	1	1
Tourism management	0	0	0	0	0	1	1

Fig. 12.3 Co-citation network of sources (compiled using Biblioshiny)

12.5.1.2   Analysis of Authors

The scientific production of authors indicates low scientific productivity and a low level of H index (Table 12.2). It could be treated as a limitation of scientific experience in the scientific work. On the other hand, it could be understood as the development of a newly relevant topic. The last idea is validated as relevant after applying

Table 12.4 Authors' production, H index, and local citations (own compiled using Biblioshiny)

Authors	Published articles	Articles Fractionalized	H index	Author	Local citations
Ghani B	2	0,38	2	Chen Q	1
Memon KR	2	0,38	2	Chen S	1
Rao MK	2	0,67	1	Cheng H	1
Vihari NS	2	0,67	1	Cheng J	1
Atay E	1	0,50	1	Ghani B	1
Azim MT	1	0,13	1	Khalid S	1
Byon KK	1	0,25	1	Lai J	1
Castillo D	1	0,13	1	Liao Z	1
Chen Q	1	0,33	1	López-Fernández AM	1
Chen S	1	0,25	1	Memon KR	1
Cheng H	1	0,25	1	Ooi SK	1
Cheng J	1	0,33	1	Tian C	1

Fig. 12.4 Corresponding clusters of authors among countries (compiled using Biblioshiny)

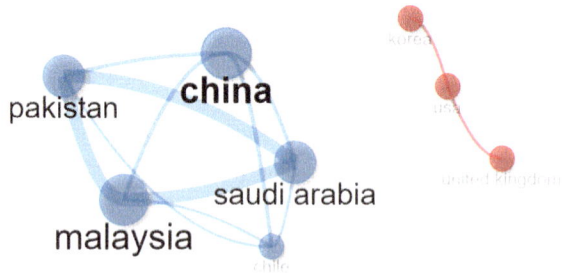

thematic analysis of abstract information in the analysis of documents (Fig. 12.7 and Table 12.4).

Analysis of authors corresponding among countries indicates that authors from USA, China, UK, Pakistan, Australia, India, Korea, Italy, Indonesia, Turkey, Canada, and the Netherlands are less corresponding internationally for scientific research than such countries as Portugal, Sweden, Denmark, Finland, Spain, New Zealand or Malaysia. Still, the authors from the USA, China, and the UK are the most corresponding scientists locally and internationally. The main two clusters of authors among countries were identified (Fig. 12.4).

12.5.1.3   Analysis of Documents

Documents analysis includes a compilation of information from titles, keywords, and abstracts. Analysis of titles indicates five clusters (Fig. 12.5). There are four

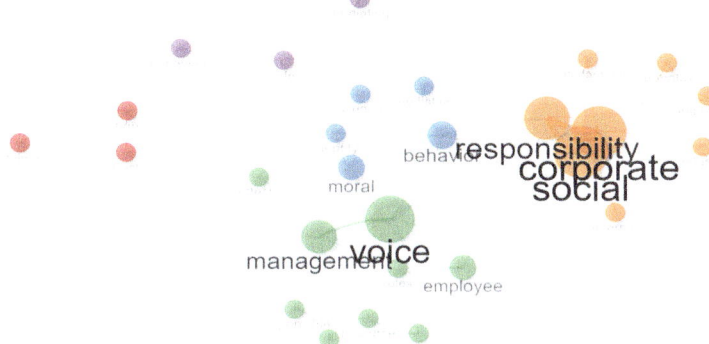

Fig. 12.5 Co-occurrence network analysis of titles (compiled using Biblioshiny)

interrelated clusters from titles. The biggest two clusters of the titles are corporate social responsibility and employee voice management. The less interrelated cluster of titles is moral behaviour but still, it is connected with the biggest two clusters of the titles.

The least interrelated cluster of titles is HRM sustainable trust. This cluster is related just to employees' voice management. The fifth cluster is the mediating behaviour role and this cluster of titles is not related to any other indicated cluster of the titles.

Analysis of the authors' keywords (Fig. 12.6) indicates that the most relevant keywords of analyzed topics are voice behaviour, moral identity, corporate social irresponsibility, social exchange theory, organizational identification, and trust in management.

This analysis of keywords indicates the most frequently used concepts. It does not show which concept would be the most developed and relevant currently. Thus, trend topics (Table 12.5) and thematic mapping (Fig. 12.7) of information from abstracts were analyzed.

The trend topic such as "corporate" and "social" for scientific analysis has been repeatedly analyzed in scientific documents from 2019 to 2020 year. "Voice" and "responsibility" were the same frequently applied in research, but the most recent topic is related to "employee", "voice" and "management" (Table 12.5). This information is deeply classified by applying a thematic map compiled from abstracts (Fig. 12.7). It endeavours that "employees corporate responsibility" is the most relevant and developed topic. At the same time "study voice social" topic is still on the square of the relevant and developed density. The least relevant and developed topics that could be indicated as declining topics are "engagement climate increase" and "safety economic multiple".

Bibliographic analysis has shown that CSR/SRHRM analysis involving employee voice or silence is a relevant research topic in nowadays scientific research. The discussed trends indicate that there has been a greater interest in this topic since

Fig. 12.6 Word cloud of authors' keywords (compiled using Biblioshiny)

Table 12.5 Trend topics (own compiled using Biblioshiny)

Trend topic item	Frequency	Year_q1	Year_med	Year_q3
Corporate	9	2019	2020	2021
Social	9	2019	2020	2021
Responsibility	7	2018	2020	2021
Voice	7	2018	2021	2022
Employee	5	2022	2022	2023
Management	5	2019	2022	2022

2017 because until then relevant publications including CSR/SRHRM analysis with employees' voice/silence were not identified in the WoS or Scopus databases. The source analysis enclosed that research is mostly published in several niche journals concerning ethics or psychology. Thus, greater interest in organization management and business management is required. At the same time, it should be noted that sustainability issues are arising everywhere in the world. Thus, the expansion of collaboration among authors should become a purpose-solving CSR/SRHRM challenge regarding employees' voice or silence management in organizations.

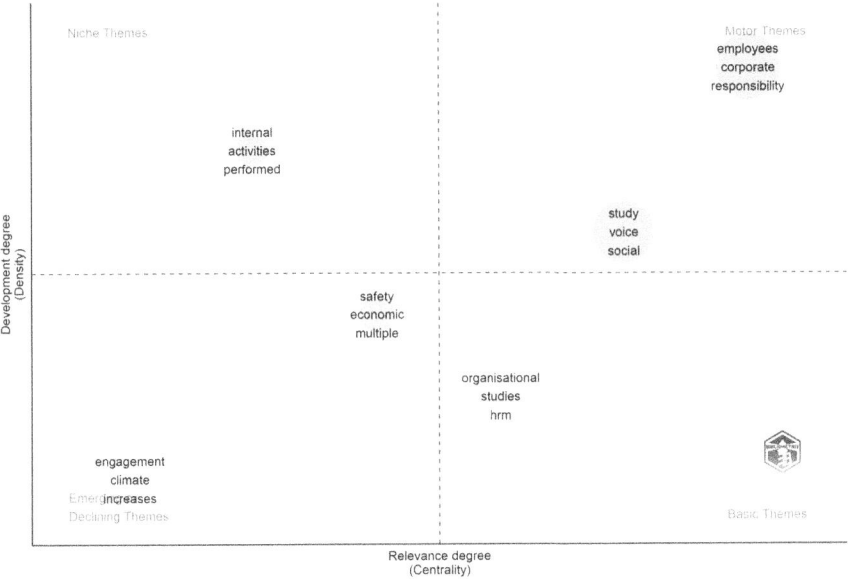

Fig. 12.7 Thematic map compiled from abstracts (compiled using Biblioshiny)

12.6   Findings and Discussion of Systematic Literature Review

This section explains the role of CSR/SRHRM practices in improving employee voice and managing silence.

12.6.1   Role of CSR/SRHRM Practices to Enhance Employee Voice and Manage Silence

Chen et al. (2023) examined that the CSR aimed at employees, moderated the intervening association among leader unethical pro-organizational leadership behaviour (UPB) and subordinate silence through moral ownership, making this association weaker for subordinates who sense a higher (vs. lower) amount of CSR focused to employees. These findings shed light on the importance of moderation impact of CSR practices (a crucial element of SRHRM) aimed at employees, and improve our complex knowledge about the conditions whereby the detrimental effects of leader UPB could be minimized (Chen et al., 2023).

It was also revealed that CSR practices not only enhanced the voice behaviour of employees but also impacted the negative employee voice. Memon et al., (2021) studied the impact of internal CSR (taking care of employees' well-being) and external CSR (organization participation in social causes) on prohibitive voice behaviours (PVB)—opposing organizational policies and practices out loud. They investigated that internal CSR-related activities impacted PVB negatively through job satisfaction and external CSR-related activities also impacted PVB negatively through partial mediation of job satisfaction. Hence these findings highlighted that CSR practices not only support enhancing employee voice but also are equally beneficial to controlling negative voices of employees (PVB).

While exploring the role of CSR and CS irresponsibility on employee voice, Jang et al. (2022) discovered that CSR plays a significant role in enhancing two elements of employee voice online employee review (OER) volume (volume of employee voice online) and online employee review (OER) valence (employee job satisfaction review online). Jang et al. (2022) further investigated the joint effect of CSR and CSI on employee voice and explored that the favourable effect of CSR on employee voice behaviour is moderated by CSI, which increases its positive influence on OER volume while decreasing the impact on OER valence. These findings shed light on the fact that organizations' CSR (CSI) practices can create positive (negative) firms' ethical environments subsequently it can impact employee voice behaviour in a good or bad way on OER valence (Jang et al., 2022).

Liao et al. (2022) described that socially responsible human resource management (SRHRM) is positively associated with ethical voice (EV) via ethical self-efficacy. Additionally, findings also indicated that organizational identification moderated the intervening effect of ethical self-efficacy on the association between SRHRM and EV. It appeared that the intervening impact is far stronger when employees have a greater sense of organizational identification. Moreover, Prince et al. (2022) found that sustainable human resource (HRM) management positively impacted employee well-being via sequential mediation of trust in management and employee voice behaviour. These findings highlighted the fact that as a result of sustainable HRM management's trust in employees enhanced motivated employees to raise their voice and all these aspects positively impacted employee well-being in the organization.

The reviewed studies presented the CSR/SRHRM practices as a strong antecedent of employee voice. Memon et al. (2021) investigated that CSR practices (internal and external) impacted the promotive voice of employees positively via organizational trust and psychological empowerment. These results exhibit that the presence of CSR practices in organizations enhanced organizational trust of employees through the presence of organizational justice in the organizations and that ultimately helped employees to be psychologically empowered and subsequently promotive voice of employees developed (Memon et al., 2021). Furthermore, Wang et al., (2019) explored that CSR is positively and significantly associated with promotive voice and prohibitive voice employee behaviour.

Moreover, they found that other-focused climates (organizational climates that value employees) intervened in the associations between CSR and two types of voice promotive and prohibitive. Hence, it appeared that CSR practices can enhance promotive and prohibitive voices by advancing the other-focused climate in the organization. Furthermore, results highlighted that a self-focused climate (organizational climate where everyone thinks about only their interest) intervened in the connection between CSR and two forms of voice behaviours—promotive and prohibitive. These findings underlined the importance of CSR policies and shed light on how CSR practices can motivate workers to raise their voices (promotive and prohibitive) by curbing a self-focused climate.

According to Vihari et al. (2018), employee voice which is an outcome of participative management plays a key role as a mediator between sustainable human resource management (SHRM)and organizational flexibility. SHRM emphasizes participative management, which gives employees a sense of respect and empowerment (Shen & Zhu, 2011 as cited in Vihari et al., 2018). These purported elements motivate employee to voice their ideas on any impending and present company processes and positively impact employee voice (Vihari et al., 2018). Ilkhanizadeh and Karatepe (2017) found that CSR practices positively correlated to voice behaviour and career satisfaction of employees directly as well as via (mediating effect of) work engagement. They also illustrated that flight attendants reciprocated CSR practices positively by engaging in voice behaviour making valuable suggestions for improvements and developing positive behaviour at work on the part of employees was also reported.

Hu and Jiang (2016) illustrated that the idea of employee-oriented human resource management (EOHRM) emerged from corporate social responsibility and human resource management literature. They found that the voice behaviour of employees was positive in the presence of EOHRM through the mediating effect of trust in management that employees have on them. Furthermore, it was discovered that moral identity, through management trust, moderated the indirect impact of EOHRM on voice behaviour as well. These findings underline the significance of EOHRM initiatives in encouraging employee voice and in enhancing employees' trust in management as well. López-Fernández (2019) also found that organizations that participate in CSR are regarded to have a significant effect on organizational performance when there is a greater management of collaborator voice.

Zhao et al. (2022) explored that SRHRM positively affected autonomous motivation (individual behaviour based on self-will) and controlled motivation (an individual who is internally or externally driven to act) resulting impacted moral voice. Additionally, findings also revealed that when employee values align with the values of the organization, SRHRM significantly stimulates employees' motivation for moral voice. This finding is a guide for managers in the recruitment phase to consider those applicants whose values synchronize with the company's values (Zhao et al., 2022).

Along with the positive aspects of CSR, literature highlighted the negative side of CSR initiatives as well. Launching effective corporate social responsibility (CSR) practices requires managing employees' mistrust of CSR and raising their awareness of it (Kim et al., 2018). Employees being internal stakeholders have more information about CSR policies and past examples of CSR practices that drive them to be sceptical about the genuineness of CSR practices (McShane & Cunningham, 2012). In line with this scepticism of employees, Kim et al., (2018) found that persuasion knowledge (the uncertainty felt by employees) of CSR practices is negatively related to voice behaviour. This might indicate that if employees perceive that CSR strategies are fulfilling self-centred objectives, then they are not convinced to voice their opinions for CSR policy acceptance.

Additionally, voice behaviour was found positive in the presence of promotion focus (employees' willingness to grow and achievements) of employees. Another worth-noted finding is promotion focus positively moderated the relationship between persuasion knowledge and employee voice. Hence results indicated that those employees who believe in promotion focus are highly likely to take risks to alter the current situation and will speak up about CSR practices even though they are suspicious about CSR initiatives.

Moreover, Atay and Terpstra-Tong (2019) investigated the highest-fatality mine accident in Turkey in the context of corporate social irresponsibility. They found that upper management's avarice and lack of morality are the major reasons that they disregarded employee welfare and safety procedures. Moreover, unethical human resource policies enhanced the vulnerability of mining employees because of poor employee voice culture. The effect of CSR in managing silence was also revealed through systematic literature. Yan et al. (2022) illustrated that for those employees who perceive a greater degree of CSR, the intervening impact of felt obligation towards the organization was greater on the negative association among moral identity and silent behaviour. Hence, it appeared that CSR practices significantly supported diminishing silence behaviours.

While reviewing the systematic review it appeared that mediating variables are playing a significant role in the positive association between SRHRM/CSR practices and employee voice (Fig. 12.8).

Findings revealed that much work has been done on exploring mediators that helped make significant connections between SRHRM/CSR practices and employee voice such as work engagement, job satisfaction, other-focused climate, trust in management, organizational trust of employees, psychological empowerment, autonomous motivation, and controlled motivation. As compared to mediating variables there is less work on moderating variables is found. Future research work in this domain will bring more insight into this sphere of research.

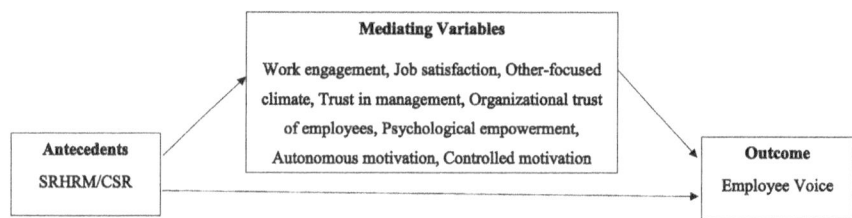

Fig. 12.8 Detail of mediating variables that positively connected SRHRM/CSR to employee voice in reviewed studies (own compiled)

12.6.2   Theories/Theoretical Models Used in the CSR/ SRHRM and Voice/Silence Literature

This section identifies the renowned theories that are majorly utilized in the CSR-Voice/Silence literature. Social exchange theory was mostly adopted to study CSR and voice behaviour connection (Ilkhanizadeh & Karatepe, 2017; Hu & Jiang, 2016; Memon et al., 2021). This theory argues that employees value resources along with support more highly if offered at the company's discretion as compared to as part of legal requirements (Newman et al., 2015 as cited in Hu & Jiang, 2016).

Ethical climate theory has also been used in this stream of literature. An ethical climate is yielded when employees believe that "certain forms of ethical reasoning or behaviour are expected standards or norms for decision-making within the firm" (Martin & Cullen, 2006, p. 177). Based on ethical climate theory and voice behaviour as theoretical grounds, it is proposed that ethical CSR/CSI affects the ethical environment of the organizations and ultimately affects employee voice behaviours (Jang et al., 2022). Moreover, social cognitive theory is used in the literature to understand the positive effect the CSR aimed at employees (Chen et al., 2023). This theory exerts that how people view the context of an organization impacts how they make sense of and learn to know their professional environment, impacting their job-related perceptions and actions.

To study voice behaviours concerning CSR, social influence theory has been used. According to the social influence theory, individuals within a social system have the power to affect one another's views and behaviours (Rice et al., 1990 as cited in Kim et al., 2018). Furthermore, self-verification theory has been adopted in the literature to investigate the effect of moral identity on employee silence (Yan et al., 2022). This theory exerts that individuals have a desire, to look for reinforcement and confirmation of their pre-existing self-perception, regardless of how it is negative (Swann, 1983, 2011 as cited in Yan et al., 2022).

In the academic literature, self-determination theory is used to understand the connection between SRHRM and employee moral voice (Zhao et al., 2022). According to self-determination theory, the external environment in which individuals live may stimulate as well as sustain their work-related motivation and hence affect how they act (Deci & Ryan, 2008).

12.6.2.1   Methodologies Used in Reviewed Studies

While studying the effect of CSR/SRHRM practices on the voice and silence behaviour of employees, we found out that most of the studies were quantitative (Table 12.6).

Out of 15 reviewed studies, 13 were quantitative. Out of those 13 quantitative studies 11 studies adopted survey methodology, one study used a three-wave survey methodology to collect data and the remaining one study collected secondary data. There was only one qualitative study that followed interview methodology and the

Table 12.6 Methodologies employed in peer-reviewed articles (own compiled)	Methodology	No. of studies
	Survey	11
	Three-wave survey	1
	Case study	1
	Interviews	1
	Secondary data	1

last reviewed article was the case study. These findings highlighted the fact that most of the empirical studies are quantitative. To explore the role of SRHRM in employee voice and silence more qualitative studies are required. A review of the literature has also shown that there is the least work is done regarding the role of SRHRM in diminishing employee silence. Hence, in-depth examination of this phenomenon will help to sustain human voice in an organizational context which is an important aspect of the well-being of employees.

12.6.2.2 Discussion on SRHRM Measurement and Its KPIs Relating to Employees' Voice or Silence

Systematic or bibliometrics data analyses did not reveal key performance indicators (KPIs) for measuring SRHRM relating to employees' voice or silence. Estimation and determination of KPIs are essential to understand practical implications and SRHRM implementation in an organization. Thus, an additional literature review for KPIs in databases was realized. It can be stated that the KPIs of SRHRM are related to measuring employees' health and well-being, and organizational strategies need to incorporate the social, economic, and ecological dimensions as three pillars of sustainability. In line with SRHRM and its Sustainable Development Goals, measuring health and well-being (HWB) is a critical challenge for businesses of all sizes and a fundamental component of social sustainability (Dolcini et al., 2023). The well-being and satisfaction of the employees are at the forefront of debate due to enhanced stress, the transformation of work-setting, and lockdown regulations as a result of the pandemic COVID-19 (Al-Jubari et al., 2022). In light of the available literature and organizational policies Dolcini et al. (2023) identified appropriate key performance indicators which have an impact on the performance of the organizations in the context of HWB. Moreover, they found that a set of metrics employed to evaluate and reflect HWB effectiveness tends to be limited to health problems, indicators of employee well-being were lacking in the KPI disclosure statements of European companies and were limited to for instance, employer satisfaction index, and employer attractiveness. Additionally, studies also discussed employee well-being-related KPIs for instance employee satisfaction (Gebhardt et al., 2022) under the umbrella of social indicators not separately.

Furthermore, Hristov and Chirico (2019) examined the literature and found KPIs connected to sustainability elements and pointed out that scholars have emphasized

Fig. 12.9   KPIs investigated by Hristov and Chirico (2019) and Dolcini et al. (2023)

the basic function of social metrics to measure the performance of social merits. They identified social measures linked to employee well-being as a consequence of systematic analysis. Those indicators are: average time spent on discretionary activities, rate of promotion, equal opportunities, occupational health and safety metrics, work performance metrics, and employee satisfaction indicators (Fig. 12.9).

Employee voice is one of the important aspects of employee well-being. King et al. (2021) identified that the majority of the organizations they studied had procedures in place that enabled employees to bring forward proposals for improvements in the organization. They further elaborated that it was worth noting that, although many organizations strove to increase communication (typically a single direction, with a few interactive communications), they placed far less emphasis on the second aspect of the term, impacting decisions in the workplace.

Few studies shed light on the KPIs to measure voice engagement in organizations for instance Neri et al. (2021) developed a checklist of KPIs to measure organizational sustainability, and one of the KPIs covering the social dimensions, employee satisfaction, includes employee involvement as a performance indicator. Furthermore, while identifying KPIs in the context of HWB Dolcini et al. (2023) identified opinion survey on satisfaction (participation) as a key performance indicator. They also discovered that "Workers' participation-consultation and communication on OHS (occupational health and safety)" was used as one of the KPIs in the sphere of Occupational health and safety in the Global Reporting Initiatives (GRI) standards.

These KPIs can be employed by the public and private sectors in order to evaluate their organizational performance in the domain of employee well-being which is one of the key areas of social sustainability. Furthermore, Dolcini et al. (2023)

demonstrated that significantly more work is required to construct KPIs for employee well-being. Moreover, it also appeared that even though formal and informal voice channels have been deployed in a number of public and private organizations, very few KPIs to measure employee voice were found. In other words, employee voice has not been thoroughly incorporated in the KPI disclosure statements of organizations.

In the future, more work is needed to build KPIs related to employee well-being overall and specifically in the context of employee voice. The most ignored phenomenon is employee silence, no proper strategies have been formulated to combat, control, and manage employee silence hence no KPIs exist related to this issue. It was also found that most organizations encourage one-way communication while fruitful output and valuable decisions require two-way communication. Organizations need to provide communication channels that should facilitate two-way communication.

In order to remain sustainable and attain SDG goals, organizations need employee involvement. The employees who deal with the actual situation related to business matters, sometimes have valuable suggestions and can point out flaws far better than top or middle management. At the same time organizations are also struggling with sustainability-related issues and in order to face this challenge employees' voluntary efforts are required as well. This is not possible without employees' discretionary involvement. To make it happen rigorous work is required to enhance voice and mitigate silence-related strategies. Hence, human resource professionals, policymakers, and strategists must acknowledge these gaps and work in this area.

12.7 Conclusion

Sustainability of the planet is an emerging and much-needed concept of the twenty-first century and human capital is one of the major aspects of sustainability elements. In an organizational context, employees hold a prime place being the main source of competitive advantage. Moreover, the United Nations' SDGs emphasize well-being and freedom of expression (SDG #8 & 16.6 respectively) of human capital that bound organizations to look for ways to improve employee well-being. As a result, now organizations are formulating sustainable practices (CSR/SRHRM) to ensure the betterment of employees. Hence the present study highlighted the impact of CSR/SRHRM practices on employee voice enhancement and in diminishing silence through bibliographic analysis and systematic literature review.

A bibliographic analysis has revealed that the examination of CSR and SRHRM in the context of employee communication and participation is an important and emerging area of inquiry in contemporary scientific research. There was a notable absence of relevant publications within the databases of Web of Science (WoS) or Scopus. Thus, there is a pressing need for an expanded interest in this subject within the fields of organizational management and business management. Simultaneously, it is essential to recognize that sustainability concerns have gained global significance, necessitating greater collaboration among researchers to address the challenges associated with CSR and SRHRM concerning the management of employee communication and participation within organizations.

A systematic literature review of studies highlighted the positive role of CSR/SRHRM practices in enhancing employee voice. Moreover, results also revealed that CSR not only impacted positively to enhance voice behaviour but also played the role of controlling negative voices and emerged as the strong antecedent of employee voice. The analysis also shed light on role of mediators that positively connected CSR to employee voice as compare to moderators. Additionally, a small number of studies highlighted the negative impact of CSR practices on employee voice as well. Employees being internal stakeholders have inside information if they perceive that the organization formulates self-centred CSR policies it negatively affects voice behaviour.

Previous findings showed the relationship of SRHRM and employee ethical voice via ethical self-efficacy and it is suggested that future studies should look at more fundamental mechanisms from different angles. Future research might additionally examine the association between internal corporate social responsibility and employee voice not solely between types of firms as well as among industries to see if there are any differences. It would also be useful to investigate how employees perceive internal corporate social responsibility. Furthermore, future studies may investigate whether employee-oriented HRM practices have a distinct impact on promotive voice and prohibitive voice behaviours or not.

Investigation highlighted that in the future there are several crucial variables like job embeddedness, psychological contract, or customer orientation that need to be investigated to determine their roles as mediating variables in the relationship between corporate social responsibility and employee voice and career satisfaction. Moreover, it is also revealed that the relationship between CSR/CSI (corporate social irresponsibility) and employee voice was analyzed before the COVID-19 pandemic in the T & H (tourism & hospitality) industry. However, the association between these during the period of COVID-19 is still unclear, and that requires further investigation.

Limitations and future recommendations

The systematic analysis identified the number of underexplored areas. Reviewed studies highlighted the fact that employee-focused CSR/SRHRM practices are studied mostly as the antecedent of employee voice, in the future moderating and mediating the role of employee-focused CSR/SRHRM practices may be investigated as well. Furthermore, most of the academic literature is related to CSR-employee voice, and only very few studies investigated the role of CSR in managing silence. This is a large gap in the academic literature that needs to be filled.

Additionally, the negative side of employee-focused CSR/SRHRM practices is less explored. Investigation of negative exploration of CS irresponsibility will help to take those measures that are impeding making CSR practices fruitful. As far as limitations are concerned present study explored two databases (Scopus and Web of Science), the study of more databases will provide more insights into this sphere of research. Furthermore, the current study incorporated only peer-reviewed articles, investigation of books and conferences will help to explore more avenues in this domain of research.

References

Aguinis, H., & Glavas, A. (2012). What we know and don't know about corporate social responsibility: A review and research agenda. *Journal of Management, 38*(4), 932–968.

Al-Jubari, I., Mosbah, A., & Salem, S. F. (2022). Employee well-being during COVID-19 pandemic: The role of adaptability, work-family conflict, and organizational response. *SAGE Open, 12*(3), 215824402210961. https://doi.org/10.1177/21582440221096142

Aria, M., & Cuccurullo, C. (2017). Bibliometrix: An R-tool for comprehensive science mapping analysis. *Journal of Informetrics, 11*(4), 959–975.

Atay, E., & Terpstra-Tong, J. L. Y. (2019). The determinants of corporate social irresponsibility: A case study of the Soma mine accident in Turkey. *Social Responsibility Journal, 16*(8), 1433–1452.

Bastian, F., & Poussing, N. (2023). Analyzing the employee/employer relationships in the corporate social responsibility context: An empirical investigation of SMEs. *Corporate Social Responsibility and Environmental Management, 30*(4), 2011–2020.

Chen, S., Tian, C., Cheng, H., & Lai, J. (2023). The effect of leader unethical pro-organizational behaviour on subordinate silence: The mediating role of moral ownership. *Ethics & Behavior*, 1–15.

Deci, E. L., & Ryan, R. M. (2008). Facilitating optimal motivation and psychological well-being across life's domains. *Canadian Psychology/psychologie Canadienne, 49*(1), 14.

Dolcini, M., Brambilla, A., Gola, M., & Capolongo, S. (2023). Health and well-being key performance indicators in corporate sustainability disclosure. A review of sustainability reports from a sample of major European companies. *Acta Biomed, 94*, 1–13. https://doi.org/10.23750/abm.v94iS3.14334

Eurostat. (2023). *How has the EU progressed towards the SDGs?* Eurostat. Retrieved May 24, 2023, from https://ec.europa.eu/eurostat/web/products-eurostat-news/w/wdn-20230524-1

European Commission. (2023). *The EU budget and the sustainable development goals.* Retrieved August 6, 2023, from https://commission.europa.eu/strategy-and-policy/eu-budget/performance-and-reporting/horizontal-priorities/eu-budget-and-sustainable-development-goals_en

Gebhardt, M., Thun, T. W., Seefloth, M., & Zülch, H. (2022). Managing sustainability—does the integration of environmental, social and governance key performance indicators in the internal management systems contribute to companies' environmental, social and governance performance? *Business Strategy and the Environment, 32*(4), 2175–2192. https://doi.org/10.1002/bse.3242

Holland, P. J., Teicher, J., & Donaghey, J. (2019). *Employee voice at work.* Springer.

Hristov, I., & Chirico, A. (2019). The role of sustainability key performance indicators (KPIs) in implementing sustainable strategies. *Sustainability, 11*(20), 5742. https://doi.org/10.3390/su11205742

Hu, X., & Jiang, Z. (2016). Employee-oriented HRM and voice behavior: A moderated mediation model of Moral Identity and trust in management. *The International Journal of Human Resource Management, 29*(5), 746–771. https://doi.org/10.1080/09585192.2016.1255986

Ilkhanizadeh, S., & Karatepe, O. M. (2017). An examination of the consequences of corporate social responsibility in the airline industry: Work engagement, career satisfaction, and voice behavior. *Journal of Air Transport Management, 59*, 8–17. https://doi.org/10.1016/j.jairtraman.2016.11.002

Jamali, D. R., El Dirani, A. M., & Harwood, I. A. (2014). Exploring human resource management roles in corporate social responsibility: The csr-hrm co-creation model. *Business Ethics: A European Review, 24*(2), 125–143. https://doi.org/10.1111/beer.12085

Jang, S., Kim, B., & Lee, S. (2022). Impact of corporate social (ir) responsibility on volume and valence of online employee reviews: Evidence from the tourism and hospitality industry. *Tourism Management, 91*, 104501.

Kim, K., Byon, K. K., Song, H., & Kim, K. (2018). Internal contributions to initiating corporate social responsibility in sport organizations. *Management Decision, 56*(8), 1804–1817.

King, D., Shipton, H., Smith, S., Rendall, J., & Renkema, M. (2021). *Talking about voice: Insights from case studies.* Chartered Institute of Personnel and Development.

Kramar, R. (2021). Workplace performance: A sustainable approach. *Asia Pacific Journal of Human Resources, 59*(4), 567–581.

López-Fernández, A. M. (2019). Internal corporate social responsibility and leadership effects on voice management and organisational performance: Analysis of collaborator perceptions across organisations in Mexico. *International Journal of Business Excellence, 19*(2), 151–167.

López-Fernández, M., Romero-Fernández, P. M., & Aust, I. (2018). Socially responsible human resource management and employee perception: The influence of manager and line managers. *Sustainability, 10*(12), 4614.

Liao, Z., Cheng, J., & Chen, Q. (2022). Socially responsible human resource management and employee ethical voice: Roles of employee ethical self-efficacy and organizational identification. *Corporate Social Responsibility and Environmental Management, 29*(4), 820–829.

Lu, X., Zhu, W., & Tsai, F. S. (2019). Social responsibility toward the employees and career development sustainability during manufacturing transformation in China. *Sustainability, 11*(17), 4778.

Martin, K. D., & Cullen, J. B. (2006). Continuities and extensions of ethical climate theory: A meta-analytic review. *Journal of Business Ethics, 69*, 175–194.

McShane, L., & Cunningham, P. (2012). To thine own self be true? Employees' judgments of the authenticity of their organization's corporate social responsibility program. *Journal of Business Ethics, 108*, 81–100.

Memon, K. R., Zada, M., Ghani, B., Ullah, R., Azim, M. T., Mubarik, M. S., Vega-Muñoz, A., & Castillo, D. (2021). Linking corporate social responsibility to workplace deviant behaviors: Mediating role of job satisfaction. *Frontiers in Psychology, 12*. https://doi.org/10.3389/fpsyg.2021.803481

Neri, A., Cagno, E., Lepri, M., & Trianni, A. (2021). A triple bottom line balanced set of key performance indicators to measure the sustainability performance of industrial supply chains. *Sustainable Production and Consumption, 26*, 648–691. https://doi.org/10.1016/j.spc.2020.12.018

Obaideen, K., Abdelkareem, M. A., Wilberforce, T., Elsaid, K., Sayed, E. T., Maghrabie, H. M., & Olabi, A. G. (2022). Biogas role in achievement of the sustainable development goals: Evaluation, challenges, and guidelines. *Journal of the Taiwan Institute of Chemical Engineers, 131*, 104207. https://doi.org/10.1016/j.jtice.2022.104207

Omidi, A., & Dal Zotto, C. (2022). Socially responsible human resource management: A systematic literature review and research agenda. *Sustainability, 14*(4), 2116. https://doi.org/10.3390/su14042116

OECD. (2022). *Global outlook on financing for sustainable development 2023: No sustainability without equity.* OECD Publishing, Paris. Retrieved October 15, 2023, from https://www.oecd.org/finance/global-outlook-on-financing-for-sustainable-development-2023-fcbe6ce9-en.htm

Paulet, R., Holland, P., & Bratton, A. (2021). Employee voice: The missing factor in sustainable HRM? *Sustainability, 13*(17), 9732.

Podgorodnichenko, N., Edgar, F., & Akmal, A. (2022). An integrative literature review of the CSR-HRM nexus: Learning from research-practice gaps. *Human Resource Management Review, 32*(3), 100839.

Prince, R., Vihari, N. S., & Rao, M. K. (2022). Examining the effects of sustainable HRM on work wellbeing: The role of voice behaviour and trust in management. In *Managing risk and decision making in times of economic distress, Part B* (pp. 159–171). Emerald Publishing Limited.

Rayner, J., & Morgan, D. (2017). An empirical study of 'green'workplace behaviours: Ability, motivation and opportunity. *Asia Pacific Journal of Human Resources, 56*(1), 56–78.

Rodríguez-Soler, R., Uribe-Toril, J., & Valenciano, J. D. P. (2020). Worldwide trends in the scientific production on rural depopulation, a bibliometric analysis using bibliometrix R-tool. *Land Use Policy, 97*, 1–20.

Santana, M., Morales-Sánchez, R., & Pasamar, S. (2020). Mapping the link between corporate social responsibility (CSR) and human resource management (HRM): How is this relationship measured? *Sustainability, 12*(4), 1678.

Skačkauskienė, I. (2022). Research on management theory: A development review and bibliometric analysis. *Problems and Perspectives in Management, 20*(2), 335–347.

Sánchez-Hernández, M. I., Vázquez-Burguete, J. L., García-Miguélez, M. P., & Lanero-Carrizo, A. (2021). Internal corporate social responsibility for sustainability. *Sustainability, 13*(14), 7920.

Sánchez-Hernández, M. I., Gallardo-Vázquez, D., Barcik, A., & Dziwiński, P. (2016). The effect of the internal side of social responsibility on firm competitive success in the business services industry. *Sustainability, 8*(2), 179.

Trifu, A., Smîdu, E., Badea, D. O., Bulboacă, E., & Haralambie, V. (2022). Applying the PRISMA method for obtaining systematic reviews of occupational safety issues in literature search. *MATEC Web of Conferences, 354*, 00052. https://doi.org/10.1051/matecconf/202235400052

United Nations. (n.d.). *Transforming our world: The 2030 agenda for sustainable development, department of economic and social affairs.* United Nations. Retrieved October 12, 2023, from https://sdgs.un.org/2030agenda

United Nations. (2023). *Peace, justice and strong institutions—united nations sustainable development.* United Nations. https://www.un.org/sustainabledevelopment/peace-justice/

Vihari, N. S., Jada, U., & Rao, M. K. (2018). Empirical linkage between sustainable HRM and organisational flexibility: A sem-based approach. *International Journal of Business Innovation and Research, 17*(1), 65. https://doi.org/10.1504/ijbir.2018.10015133

Wang, J., Zhang, Z., & Jia, M. (2019). Echoes of corporate social responsibility: How and when does CSR influence employees' promotive and prohibitive voices? *Journal of Business Ethics, 167*(2), 253–269. https://doi.org/10.1007/s10551-019-04151-6

Yan, A., Guo, H., Zhou, Z. E., Xie, J., & Ma, H. (2022). How moral identity inhibits employee silence behavior: The roles of felt obligation and corporate social responsibility perception. *Journal of Business Ethics, 187*(2), 405–420. https://doi.org/10.1007/s10551-022-05263-2

Zhao, H., Chen, Y., & Liu, W. (2022). Socially responsible human resource management and employee moral voice: Based on the self-determination theory. *Journal of Business Ethics, 183*(3), 929–946. https://doi.org/10.1007/s10551-022-05082-5

Laima Jeseviciute-Ufartiene, PhD, is a professor of management department in the faculty of Business Administration at Vilnius Gediminas Technical University and associate professor of business department at Kaunas university of applied sciences. She defended PhD thesis in 2010 in the management science field. Since then, she has published more than 50 articles in different types of journals. Her scientific interests include such research objects as organization development and management while analysing its leaders, employees and consumers, their perception on sustainability of environment and its management. Jeseviciute-Ufartiene has led and still is leading has been or still is a scientific member of several national and international scientific projects funded by different parties such as European Union, Ministry of Health of the Republic of Lithuania, and Research Council of Lithuania. L. Jeseviciute-Ufartiene has multiple experience participating in Erasmus+ excgange programs and NordPlus Sprint programs mentoring and leading students of internastional teams.

Hava Yasin is an accomplished scholar in Management Sciences, currently pursuing her Ph.D. at Vilnius Gediminas Technical University, Lithuania. A native of Pakistan, Yasin began her academic journey with a Bachelor's degree from Pakistan. She further expanded her academic horizon by obtaining a Master's in Business Administration with a specialization in Human Resource Management from Tallinn University of Technology, Estonia, in 2019. With over seven years of professional experience as Assistant Director in Management and Administration, Yasin's research interests predominantly lie in Organizational Behavior and Human Resource Management